# The KING JAMES BIBLE WORD BOOK

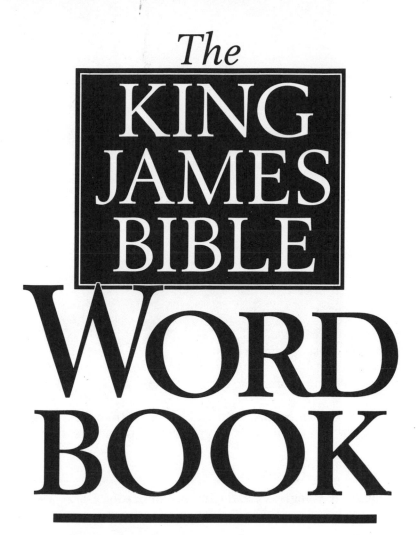

A contemporary dictionary of curious and archaic words found in the King James Version of the Bible

by

RONALD BRIDGES and LUTHER A. WEIGLE

THOMAS NELSON PUBLISHERS
Nashville • Atlanta • London • Vancouver

**Library of Congress Cataloging-in-Publication Data**

Bridges, Ronald F.
   [Bible word book]
   The King James Bible word book / by Ronald Bridges and Luther A. Weigle.
     p.  cm.
   Originally published: The Bible word book. 1960.
   Includes bibliographical references and index.
   ISBN 0-7852-8093-6
   1. Bible. English—Glossaries, vocabularies, etc.  2. Bible.
English—Versions—Authorized.  3. English language—Etymology.
I. Weigle, Luther Allan, 1880–1976.  II. Title.
BS440.B66  1994
220.5'2033—dc20                                                94–15181
                                                       CIP

Printed in the United States of America
1 2 3 4 5 6 7 8 — 00 99 98 97 96 95 94

# PUBLISHER'S PREFACE

Despite the availability of many new translations and paraphrases of God's word, the venerable King James Version still posts more sales each year than any other. Wholly apart from its achievement as an accurate translation accessible to the ordinary people of its day, the King James (or Authorized) Version lives as a specimen of the English language unsurpassed in its grace and beauty. But even as time and history refuse to stand still, so also the living English language refuses to freeze in time. Words and expressions once common become fully obsolete, or they take on new meanings, meanings at times opposite to those of an earlier time. Especially in such cases, the casual reader of today may read a word from the sixteenth century but give to it a twentieth-century meaning and think nothing of doing so. The reader's current meaning may still make sense within the sentence, but it will not be the sense intended by the sixteenth-century writer. To the extent this is so, communication breaks down, and what the writer wished to say is, in part or whole, lost.

Readers of the King James Version want to understand it accurately and fully. And because English has changed a great deal in the last nearly four centuries, they need an authoritative guide that will help them make proper sense of the words and phrases that are rarely or never used by speakers of English today, as well as alert them to expressions whose common meanings today differ from those of the past.

To meet this need, Thomas Nelson is pleased to release again the only volume that provides such information for all users and lovers of the King James Bible: *The King James Bible Word Book*. Released originally in 1960 as *The Bible Word Book,* this volume serves as a dictionary dedicated specifically to the King James Version. Its 827 articles on the King James words and phrases most affected by changes in English offer casual readers and students, ministers and scholars unique and valuable information not available in any other volume. The Publisher releases this authoritative classic with the hope that those who use the cherished King James Version will, with the help of *The King James Bible Word Book,* find it to be more inspiring and understandable than ever.

# AUTHORS' PREFACE

This book is concerned with words used in the King James Version of the Bible which have become obsolete or archaic, or have changed in meaning or acquired new meanings, so that they no longer convey to the reader the sense which the King James translators intended them to express. Most of these words were accurate translations in 1611, but they have become ambiguous or misleading.

The language of the King James Version of the Bible was sixteenth-century English, for it was a revision of English versions that went back to Wyclif in the late fourteenth century and to Tyndale and his successors from 1525 on. And it was sixteenth-century English at its best—"the noblest monument of English prose." There is general agreement with the verdict of its revisers in 1881, who expressed admiration for "its simplicity, its dignity, its power, its happy turns of expression . . . the music of its cadences and the felicities of its rhythm."

Yet the development of Biblical studies, the discovery of ancient manuscripts, and the new knowledge of Bible lands and languages afforded by archaeology have made its revision desirable; and the changes in English usage have made it necessary. The Revised Version was published in 1881–1885, the American Standard Version in 1901, and the Revised Standard Version in 1946–1952. These revisions were authorized by the Convocation of the Province of Canterbury, Church of England, in 1870, or by the International Council of Religious Education, representing the Protestant churches of the United States and Canada, in 1937.

The present volume owes its title to *The Bible Word-Book,* by William Aldis Wright, the second edition of which, revised and enlarged, was published in England in 1884, succeeding a first edition prepared with the help of the Reverend J. Eastwood, published in 1866. Wright has articles on 2,316 archaic words and phrases in the Authorised Version of the Bible and the Book of Common Prayer. He gives for each a brief definition and statement of etymological derivation, then quotes examples of its use in English literature, chiefly of the sixteenth century. For these illustrations, his book is of lasting value.

Today the situation is different. Three revisions of the King James Version have been published, and there have been notable new translations of the Bible into modern speech. The thirteen-volume *Oxford English Dictionary* affords a wealth of illustration for the varied senses of English usage. The etymology of the English words is indicated in all of the larger dictionaries.

The new *Word Book* herewith presented bears little resemblance, therefore, to the work of seventy-five years ago. It is intended for the general public and is meant to be read as well as to be used for reference. Its purpose is (1) to explain what the King James translators meant when they used a word or phrase which is now obsolete or archaic, and (2) to state what word or phrase is used to replace it in the revised versions or modern translations. Illustrations from general literature are cited only where they seem to be helpful; and these are usually taken from Shakespeare, Ben Jonson, or Milton, on the assumption that their works will be readily available to the reader.

There are articles on 827 words and phrases in this book. These are drawn from the language of the Old and New Testaments. The book does not include articles on the language of the Apocrypha, the Book of Common Prayer, or the Preface to the King James Version entitled "The Translators to the Reader." It does not include articles on proper names or on the names of animals, trees, jewels, and the like, which are properly subjects for a Bible dictionary. There are no articles on quaint forms of spelling in the original 1611 edition of the King James Version, which later editions have changed or eliminated.

Quotations from the King James Version are not labeled as such. Quotations from other versions are labeled, unless the context makes that unnecessary. Naturally, comparisons are most often between the King James Version and the Revised Standard Version, since this is the latest revision and the one which has dealt most clearly with the problem of archaic language. Other modern translations are cited where these are helpful, but in general the discussion remains within the basic structure of the Tyndale-King James tradition.

The comprehensive Index on pages 393–422 lists more than eighteen hundred additional words. These are words that do not appear in the King James Version but are used by the revised versions or other modern translations instead of the archaic terms which have become misleading. The Index will guide the reader to the pages in this volume on which each of these new Bible words appears or is discussed.

# Bibliography and Abbreviations

*The Bible Word-Book* by William Aldis Wright was published by The MacMillan Company, London, 1884.

The translations of the Bible referred to in the present book are those by John Wyclif and his associates, made between 1380 and 1400; William Tyndale, 1525–1535; Miles Coverdale, 1535; "Thomas Matthew," a pseudonym of John Rogers, 1537; Richard Taverner, 1539; the Great Bible, 1539; the Geneva Bible, 1560; the Bishops' Bible, 1568, revised 1572; the Rheims New Testament, 1582; the Douay Bible, 1609; the King James Version (KJ), 1611; the Revised Version (RV), 1881–1885; the American Standard Version (ASV), 1901; the Revised Standard Version (RSV), 1946–1952.

Translations of the New Testament into modern speech are *The Twentieth Century New Testament,* 1898–1904, and individual translations by R. F. Weymouth, 1903; James Moffatt, 1913; Edgar J. Goodspeed, 1923; William G. Ballantine, 1923; Charles B. Williams, 1949; J. B. Phillips, 1947–1958. New translations of the Gospels are by Charles C. Torrey, 1933, revised 1947; and E. V. Rieu, 1952. Translations of the Bible into modern speech are by James Moffatt, finally revised in 1935; by J. M. P. Smith and associates for the Old Testament, with Goodspeed's New Testament, in *An American Translation,* 1931; by S. H. Hooke in *The Basic Bible,* 1949; by Ronald Knox, 1944–1954; and by the Confraternity of Christian Doctrine, 1948–1959.

The reference work to which this book owes most is the *Oxford English Dictionary* (OED); next to it, *Webster's New International Dictionary, Second Edition.* There are excellent articles on words in the four-volume Hastings' *Dictionary of the Bible.* The volumes of *The Interpreter's Bible* are of great value for comparison of KJ and RSV. The Hebrew lexicon referred to in this book is by Brown, Driver, and Briggs (BDB), published by the Clarendon Press in 1907, corrected impression 1952. The Greek lexicons are by J. H. Thayer, 1885, fourth edition, reprinted 1953; and by W. F. Arndt and F. W. Gingrich, 1957.

Valuable concordances are by John Bartlett for the works of Shakespeare, by James Strong and by Robert Young for the King James Version of the Bible, by M. C. Hazard for the American Standard Version of the Bible, and *Nelson's Complete Concordance of the Revised Standard Version Bible.*

This bibliographical note does not attempt to list the sources consulted in the preparation of this book. Some of them are indicated in the text; to name them all would extend this note unduly.

# THE
# KING JAMES
# BIBLE WORD BOOK

**A, AN.** The most familiar of the archaic uses of "a" or "an" that occur in KJ is "an hungred," which appears in Matthew 4.2; 12.1, 3; 25.35, 37, 42, 44; Mark 2.25; Luke 6.3. This expression, in each of these cases, comes from Tyndale. In Mark 11.12 the same Greek verb was translated "he hungred" by Tyndale and "he was hungry" by KJ. The "an" is a prefix probably meant to have intensive force, but there is no correspondingly intensive expression in the Greek.

The use of "a" as a "worn-down proclitic form of preposition" (OED) with a verbal noun, to denote a process or continued action, occurs in Luke 8.42, "she lay a dying"; Luke 9.42, "as he was yet a coming"; John 21.3, "I go a fishing"; Hebrews 11.21, "when he was a dying"; 1 Peter 3.20, "while the ark was a preparing." These expressions also come from Tyndale, with various changes in spelling, of course. Tyndale's rendering of Peter's word to his fellow disciples was "I goo a fysshynge."

The phrase "in building" occurs in 1 Kings 6.7; Ezra 5.16; John 2.20 in the passive sense of "being built"; and it occurs in the active sense in 1 Kings 6.12, 38; Ezra 4.4. The "worn-down" form of this phrase, "a building," appeared in the 1611 edition of KJ, 2 Chronicles 16.6, "the timber thereof, wherewith Baasha was a building." It so remained until 1769, when Dr. Blayney deleted the "a." In 1873, Dr. Scrivener, editor of the Cambridge Paragraph Bible, restored the "a"; but subsequent publishers of KJ have not followed his example.

Other prepositional uses of "a" are in 2 Chronicles 2.18, "set the people a work," and 1 Corinthians 9.7, "Who goeth a warfare any time at his own charges?" RSV reads "make the people work" and "Who serves as a soldier at his own expense?" Other adjectival uses are 2 Corinthians 10.6, "having in a readiness to revenge" (RSV "being ready to punish"), and Luke 9.28, "about an eight days" (RSV "about eight days").

A glimpse of the English language in the making is afforded by comparison of Acts 13.36, "David . . . fell on sleep," and 7.60, "he fell asleep." The Greek verb is identical in these two cases; the difference in rendering goes back to Coverdale and the Great Bible, which had "fell on slepe" and "fell a slepe." Compare also "await" and "in wait" (Acts 9.24; 20.19). In the parable of the Last Judgment, Matthew 25.31–46, Tyndale and Geneva had "thursted" (vs. 35, 42) and "a thurst" (vs. 37, 44); KJ has "thirsty" (vs. 35, 37, 42) and "athirst" (vs. 44).

**ABHOR** once had the relatively quiet meanings which it derived from the Latin *abhorreo*, to shrink from, to be averse to, to differ from, to be inconsistent with. We must so understand the dictum of

1

Spinoza or Samuel Johnson that "nature abhors a vacuum," or the line in the *Te Deum*, "Thou didst not abhor the Virgin's womb." But these meanings are now obsolete, and the word has become fraught with emotion. It means to hate vehemently, to abominate, to regard with loathing or disgust.

The King James Version employs "abhor" 43 times, to represent 14 different Hebrew or Greek words; RSV retains it in more than half these cases. In Exodus 5.21 "made our savour to be abhorred" is changed to "made us offensive"; and in 2 Samuel 16.21 "abhorred of thy father" is changed to "odious to your father." The statement, in connection with the sin of the sons of Eli, that "men abhorred the offering of the LORD" does not refer to a general public consequence of their misdeeds, but simply describes the sin of these two men. RSV reads, "the men treated the offering of the LORD with contempt" (1 Samuel 2.17). "I despise myself" is a better rendering than "I abhor *myself*" (Job 42.6), and "rejected Israel" than "abhorred Israel" (Psalm 78.59). ". . . abhorred his sanctuary" is "disowned his sanctuary" (Lamentations 2.7), and "made thy beauty to be abhorred" is "prostituted your beauty" (Ezekiel 16.25). In Isaiah 66.24 "an abhorring" means a thing that is abhorred: "they shall be an abhorrence to all flesh."

In two passages KJ has construed the Hebrew wrongly. ". . . blesseth the covetous, *whom* the LORD abhorreth" (Psalm 10.3) is correctly translated, "the man greedy for gain curses and renounces the LORD." The LORD's word to Ahaz (Isaiah 7.16), "the land that thou abhorrest shall be forsaken of both her kings," means "the land before whose two kings you are in dread will be deserted."

**ABIDE.** The original meaning is to wait, stay, remain; and that meaning prevails today. But other uses of the word in early English have faded or dropped into provincialisms. RSV renders Numbers 31.23 "everything that can stand the fire" instead of "abide the fire." And it replaces "abide" with "endure" in the cry of the prophets: "Who can endure the day of his coming?" "Who can endure the heat of his anger?" (Malachi 3.2; Nahum 1.6; see also Joel 2.11 and Jeremiah 10.10).

The OED recognizes the intensive use of "abide" in the negative which other dictionaries ignore or define weakly as "tolerate." A woman who says "I can't abide onions" is putting more into it than inability to tolerate. There is a shudder of aversion. She is one with Coverdale who in 1535 rendered Job 19.17, "Myne owne wyfe maye not abyde my breth." KJ puts this very vaguely, "My breath is strange to my wife." RSV makes better sense with "I am repulsive to my wife," taking the Hebrew to mean "spirit" rather than "breath."

Tyndale's rendering of John 8.43, "ye cannot abyde the hearynge of my wordes," was abandoned by KJ for "ye cannot hear my word"; but the sense of the passage is restored by RSV, "you cannot bear to hear my word."

The brother-word "bide" is not used in the modern Bible but Tyndale used it in Mark 10.7, "And for this thingis sake shall a man leve father and mother and byde by his wyfe." KJ reads "cleave to his wife" and RSV, more clearly, "be joined to his wife." "Bide" is in common use in Britain, especially in the North, and is borrowed in America in such terms as Bide-a-wee. "To bide by an agreement" and "to bide one's time" are good plain American as they were good English from King Alfred to Shakespeare.

In addition to the Hebrew word for stay or remain, 13 other Hebrew words are occasionally translated "abide" in KJ. Their primary meanings are such as: go in, sojourn, whirl, encamp, bear, spend the night, stand still, stand up, sit, dwell, cleave to, and even be. The 12 Greek words translated "abide" in the New Testament are not so scattered in meaning. An interesting passage is Acts 20.23, where Tyndale had Paul say concerning his journey to Jerusalem that "bondes and trouble abyde me." KJ kept "abide me," but added a note *"Or,* wait for me." RV and ASV deleted this note; but RSV has adopted it for the text, "imprisonment and afflictions await me."

The translation of Ecclesiastes 8.15, "for that shall abide with him of his labour the days of his life," is misleading, for it seems to say that food, drink, and mirth are the only abiding results of labor. But the writer is referring to them as its cheering accompaniment—"for this will go with him in his toil through the days of life which God gives him under the sun."

The RSV retains "abide" in a few passages in the Old Testament, especially in poetry such as Psalms 49.12, "Man cannot abide in his pomp," or 91.1, "who abides in the shadow of the Almighty." In the New Testament it is retained in passages of high spiritual significance—John 5.38, the 15th chapter of John, 1 Corinthians 13.13, 1 Peter 1.23, and throughout 1 John and 2 John.

**ABROAD.** This is a spacious word, popular with Elizabethan writers. Shakespeare uses it frequently in all senses including the modern sense of in foreign lands. More commonly he uses it for broadly, widely, at large, or for outside the house, in the streets, away from home. KJ uses it in the older senses only. Sometimes the old meaning is clear enough from the context but sometimes it is not, especially with literal-minded readers. For example, Jeremiah 6.11 reads "I am full of the fury of the LORD; I am weary with holding in: I will pour it out upon the children abroad." The revised versions have "the children in the street."

The word "abroad" simply means "outside" in the sanitary provisions of Deuteronomy 23.10, 12, 13 and the rules governing loans (24.11). The marriages "abroad" of the thirty daughters and the thirty sons of one of the ancient judges of Israel were merely marriages "outside his clan" (Judges 12.9).

"Come abroad" stands for the Hebrew word which means "be made known" (Esther 1.17) and for the Greek phrase which means "come to light" (Mark 4.22; Luke 8.17). "His name was spread abroad" is more literally translated "his name had become known" (Mark 6.14).

**ACCEPT.** In Biblical usage the word "accept" implies approval and pleasure in receiving. Exceptions are "the owner shall accept the oath" (Exodus 22.11) and "refusing to accept release" (Hebrews 11.35). The passage which KJ renders "accept of the punishment of their iniquity" (Leviticus 26.41, 43) is better translated "make amends for their iniquity."

The expression "accept the person" is a translation of the Hebrew "lift up the face" of another person. In various contexts it means to show favor, be gracious to, grant a request, or show partiality. When David is represented as saying to Abigail "I have accepted thy person," it means "I have granted your petition" (1 Samuel 25.35). "God accepteth no man's person" means "God shows no partiality" (Galatians 2.6). A similar KJ phrase is "God is no respecter of persons" (Acts 10.34), which is also translated in RSV "God shows no partiality." (See PERSON)

**ACCEPTABLE,** according to OED, means "capable, worthy, or likely to be accepted or gladly received; hence, pleasing, agreeable, gratifying, or welcome." KJ uses the word in this sense, with all its implication that what is acceptable is "well pleasing." RSV preserves this tradition, as unaware as the dictionary is that the current use of the word in ratings of merchandise and personnel may indicate less than the best—the minimum instead of the maximum in favor. In a few cases RSV makes more explicit the implication of pleasure or favor. It uses "pleasing words" (Ecclesiastes 12.10), "a time of favor" and "the year of the LORD's favor" (Isaiah 49.8; 61.2). Asher is blessed as "the favorite of his brothers" (Deuteronomy 33.24), and Mordecai is "popular with the multitude of his brethren" (Esther 10.3).

Two New Testament texts, in which the word "accepted" is replaced by a clearer translation of the Greek, are "So whether we are at home or away, we make it our aim to please him" (2 Corinthians 5.9), and "to the praise of his glorious grace which he freely bestowed on us in the Beloved" (Ephesians 1.6).

**ACQUAINT** is used (Job 22.21) in the obsolete sense of familiarize, accustom, habituate. "Acquaint now thyself with him, and be at peace" means "Agree with God, and be at peace." In itself, that is good counsel; but in the context of Eliphaz' groundless accusations of Job (22.5–11) it suggests that he surrender his integrity. The whole chapter should be read, with detailed comparison of KJ and RSV.

In Ecclesiastes 2.3 "yet acquainting mine heart with wisdom" is rendered by RSV "my mind still guiding me with wisdom."

**ADDICTED** was employed in a good sense in the sixteenth and seventeenth centuries, but now is generally used of bad habits. The KJ rendering, "they have addicted themselves to the ministry of the saints," has been changed in RSV to read, "they have devoted themselves to the service of the saints" (1 Corinthians 16.15). Shakespeare uses "addict," "addicted," or "addiction" five times, always of trivial or less desirable habits.

> "But, if't be he I mean, he's very wild;
> Addicted so and so."
> *Hamlet,* II, 1, 19

**ADMIRE, ADMIRATION** were used in the seventeenth century simply to denote wonder or astonishment, without any implication of praise or approval. Thomas Fuller, the church historian, writing in 1639, said of Mohammedanism that it was "admirable how that senseless religion should gain so much ground on Christianity"—by which he meant that this fact was amazing. He elsewhere told of Cardinal Pole delivering "a dry sermon . . . many much admiring the jejuneness of his discourse"—that is, they were astonished at its emptiness. In Milton's *Paradise Lost,* Satan was confronted at the gates of Hell by a monster Shape, and "the undaunted Fiend what this might be admired"—that is, Satan wondered what this might be (Book II, line 677).

In Shakespeare's *Hamlet* (I, 2, 192) when Horatio tells Hamlet that he had seen the ghost of "the king your father," Hamlet responds with a startled exclamation of surprise, to which Horatio answers:

"Season your admiration for awhile
With an attent ear, till I may deliver,
Upon the witness of these gentlemen,
This marvel to you."

This evidence is enough to show that when the writer of Revelation 17.6, as reported in KJ, expressed "great admiration" for the woman arrayed in scarlet, "drunken with the blood of the saints, and with the blood of the martyrs of Jesus," he meant simply to declare his wonder and astonishment at her. ASV translates the statement: "when I saw her, I wondered with a great wonder." RSV has: "When I saw her I marveled greatly."

The other occurrences are 2 Thessalonians 1.10, "to be admired" (RSV "to be marveled at"); and Jude 16, "having men's persons in admiration because of advantage" (RSV "flattering people to gain advantage").

**ADVENTURE,** as a verb, means "venture" in Deuteronomy 28.56, "venture to set the sole of her foot upon the ground"; and in Acts 19.31, where Paul's friends at Ephesus "begged him not to venture into the theater." Jotham's statement, "my father fought for you, and adventured his life far, and delivered you out of the hand of Midian," reads in RSV, "my father fought for you, and risked his life, and rescued you from the hand of Midian" (Judges 9.17).

**ADVERTISE** appears twice in KJ, Numbers 24.14 and Ruth 4.4. Its meaning is simply to tell or inform without any of its twentieth-century connotations of wide public notice. When Balaam said, "I will advertise thee what this people shall do to thy people," he meant "I will let you know. . . ." The statement of Boaz to the kinsman of Ruth, "I thought to advertise thee," was not a threat; what he said was simply, "I thought I would tell you of it." Shakespeare uses "advertise" and "advertisement" a dozen times in this sense.

"I have advertised him by secret means
That if about this hour he make this way
Under the color of his usual game,
He shall here find his friends with horse and men
To set him free from his captivity."
*King Henry VI, Part III,* IV, 5, 9–13

**ADVICE, ADVISE.** "Take advice" is used by KJ in the obsolete sense of deliberate, consult, take counsel (Judges 19.30; 2 Chronicles 25.17). When the prophet Gad, in the name of the LORD, offered to David his choice of three punishments—seven years of famine, three months of flight before his enemies, or three days of pestilence—his final word was "Now advise, and see what answer I shall return to him that sent me" (2 Samuel 24.13). The account in 1 Chronicles 21.12 has "Now advise thyself . . ." In both accounts the verb "advise" is used in the obsolete sense of consider and decide. The Hebrew verbs are different; RSV uses "consider" in 2 Samuel and "decide" in 1 Chronicles.

In the story of Nabal, Abigail, and David, the word "advice" is a mistranslation of the Hebrew word *ta'am,* which means discretion or discernment (1 Samuel 25.33). David recognizes in Abigail's plea the restraining voice of the LORD, and replies: "Blessed be the LORD, the God of Israel, who sent you this day to meet me! Blessed be your discretion, and blessed be you, who have kept me this day from bloodguilt." The revised versions agree in the translation "discretion" here.

**ADVISEMENT.** The Chronicler, in the midst of the chapter where he describes the growing strength of David's army, inserts a parenthetical disclaimer that David ever fought on the side of the Philistines against Saul (1 Chronicles 12.19). This verse is confusedly translated in KJ. RSV reads, "Some of the men of Manasseh deserted to David when he came with the Philistines for the battle against Saul. (Yet he did not help them, for the rulers of the Philistines took counsel and sent him away, saying, 'At peril to our heads he will desert to his master Saul')." The phrase "upon advisement" in the KJ rendering means that they consulted and took counsel together, as a result of which they reached the decision to send him away. This is an obsolete meaning of the word "advisement." In current language, to have something "under advisement" usually implies more leisurely consideration than the rulers of the Philistines could give in David's case.

**AFFECT.** The original meaning of the verb "affect" was aim at, aspire to, try to obtain or do. Shakespeare uses it frequently in this sense. "There is a lady in Verona here whom I affect" (*Two Gentlemen of Verona,* III, 1, 81). OED notes that as late as 1776, Thomas Jefferson wrote in his memoirs, "He has affected to render the military independent of, and superior to, the civil power."

This meaning is now obsolete. The modern reader is familiar with "affect" in the sense of make a display of liking, as in affecting a new fashion; this meaning sometimes connotes the pretense of liking a thing or a person. The word is so used three times in Galatians 4.17–18: "They zealously affect you *but* not well; yea, they would exclude you, that ye might affect them. But *it is* good to be zealously affected always in *a* good *thing,* and not only when I am present with you." RSV reads, "They make much of you, but for no good purpose; they want to shut you out, that you may make much of them. For a good purpose it is always good to be made much of, and not only when I am present with you."

In Acts 14.2 "made their minds evil affected against the brethren" is more simply translated, "poisoned their minds against the brethren."

**AFFECTION** is a good word today, connoting feelings that are pure and decent and high-minded. But the word was once applied to any mental state, and it is sometimes used in KJ for those that are low. "Vile affections" (Romans 1.26) is in RSV "dishonorable passions." "Inordinate affection" (Colossians 3.5) is "passion." "Affections and lusts" (Galatians 5.24) is "passions and desires."

On the other hand *"Be* kindly affectioned one to another with brotherly love" (Romans 12.10) remains little changed—RSV has "love one another with brotherly affection." With reference to Titus, "his inward affection is more abundant toward you" (2 Corinthians 7.15) is reworded, "his heart goes out all the more to you." "Affectionately desirous" remains unchanged in 1 Thessalonians 2.8.

David's statement, "because I have set my affection to the house of my God" (1 Chronicles 29.3) means "because of my devotion to the house of my God."

**AFFINITY** appears in the Bible only in the primary sense derived from the Latin *affinitas,* relationship by marriage, especially that between a father and a son-in-law. "Solomon made affinity with Pharaoh king of Egypt" (1 Kings 3.1) means "Solomon made a marriage alliance with Pharaoh king of Egypt." So also "Jehoshaphat . . . joined affinity with Ahab" (2 Chronicles 18.1) means "Jehoshaphat . . . made a marriage alliance with Ahab." It is an unwelcome duty to report that even OED slipped here and listed this text as an example of affinity by inclination or attraction rather than as the marriage alliance that it was. In the prayer of Ezra, "Should we again break thy commandments, and join in affinity with the people of these abominations?" (9.14) means "shall we break thy commandments again and intermarry with the peoples who practice these abominations?"

**AFORE** appears 7 times in KJ, always in the sense of prior time, while "before" appears in this same sense more than 150 times. The *Concordance to Shakespeare* indicates a similar preference for the modern form. RSV does not use "afore," which survives chiefly in the word "aforesaid" and the expression "malice aforethought."

**AFOREHAND** appears once: "she is come aforehand to anoint my body to the burying" (Mark 14.8). The "is come" is not justified by the Greek, and is eliminated by the revised versions. RSV has "she has anointed my body beforehand for burying." KJ uses "beforehand" 5 times.

**AFORETIME** means formerly, previously, or of old. It appears 7 times in KJ, and "beforetime" 11 times. RSV retains "beforetime" once (Isaiah 41.26). The only passage to awaken questions is Job 17.6, where "aforetime I was as a tabret" is an error. The Hebrew phrase which means "before" in the sense of "in the presence of" was taken by the KJ translators to mean "before" in the sense of "formerly," and they mistook the word for the act of spitting, *topheth*, to be a form of *toph*, which means tabret, timbrel, or tambourine. RV resorted to an interpretation: "I am become an open abhorring." ASV went to the other extreme: "they spit in my face." RSV translates the verse:

> "He has made me a byword of the peoples,
> and I am one before whom men spit."

**AFTER,** denoting time, place, or order, is as easily understood in the Bible as in the language of today. But KJ frequently uses "after" in the archaic sense of according to, like, or as. In these cases it usually represents the Hebrew preposition $k$ or the Greek preposition *kata*. In Genesis 1 and 6–8 "after his (their) kind(s)" means "according to its (their) kind(s)." RSV retains the KJ rendering, however, in 1.26, "in our image, after our likeness," and in 5.3, "in his own likeness, after his image," because the Hebrew thus changes the order and wording of the phrases.

Of the many Old Testament examples, the following may be cited, giving the rendering of KJ followed by that of RSV: Exodus 21.9, "after the manner of daughters" ("as with a daughter"); Exodus 28.15, "after the work of the ephod" ("like the work of the ephod"); Exodus 30.13, "after the shekel" ("according to the shekel"); Exodus 34.27, "after the tenor of these words" ("in accordance with these words"); Numbers 4.2, "after their families" ("by their families"); 2 Kings 8.2, "after the saying" ("according to the word"); 2 Chronicles 10.14, "after the advice" ("according to the counsel"); Isaiah 44.13, "maketh it after the figure of a man" ("shapes it into the figure of a man"). In the last of these citations especially, the entire verse should be read in the two versions.

Examples from Shakespeare are "frame the business after your own wisdom," *King Lear*, I, 2, 107; and the Queen's word to Imogen:

> "No, be assured you shall not find me, daughter,
> After the slander of most stepmothers,
> Evil-eyed unto you . . ."
> *Cymbeline*, I, 1, 70–72

Among New Testament examples: Luke 2.27, "after the custom of the law" ("according to the custom of the law"); Acts 15.1, "after the manner of Moses" ("according to the custom of Moses"); Acts 26.5, "after the most straitest sect" ("according to the strictest party"); Romans 8.4, "after the flesh" ("according to the flesh"); Titus 1.1. "the truth which is after godliness" ("the truth which accords with godliness").

In some situations this older use of "after" survives in the language of today. We still name a son after his father, or name a building after the person for whom we wish it to be a memorial. Examples of RSV's retention of the idiom in such contexts are Genesis 4.17; Deuteronomy 3.14; 2 Samuel 18.18; Luke 1.59. It also retains "after the pattern" (Exodus 25.40), "a man after my heart" (Acts 13.22), and "after the order of Melchizedek" (Psalm 110.4; Hebrews 5.6; 7.17). Note, however, that the more exact translation of Hebrews 7.15–16 replaces three after's by other prepositions.

Occasionally, the adverb "after" is awkwardly used in KJ. Examples are: Genesis 33.7, "and after came Joseph near and Rachel" ("and last Joseph and Rachel drew near"); 1 Kings 17.13, "and after make for thee" ("and afterward make for yourself"); Ezekiel 41.5, "After he measured" ("Then he measured"); Acts 3.24, "those that follow after" ("those who came afterwards").

**AGAINST** means opposite, confronting. It is generally understandable as used in KJ, but occasionally is ambiguous or has an obsolete sense. "Take all the heads of the people, and hang them up before the LORD against the sun" (Numbers 25.4) means "Take

all the chiefs of the people, and hang them in the sun before the LORD."
The instruction to Aaron, "When thou lightest the lamps, the seven
lamps shall give light over against the candlestick" (Numbers 8.2) is
more accurately translated, "When you set up the lamps, the seven
lamps shall give light in front of the lampstand." As Abigail rode on
her mission of good will, David and his men came down, not "against
her," but "toward her" (1 Samuel 25.20). "Opposite" is a clearer translation than "against" in Deuteronomy 34.6, 2 Samuel 16.13, 1 Kings
20.29, and Esther 5.1. In Mark's account of the crucifixion of Jesus,
"the centurion, which stood over against him" means "the centurion,
who stood facing him" (15.39). In the account of Paul's voyage to
Rome, "against Cnidus" and "against Salmone" mean "off Cnidus"
and "off Salmone" (Acts 27.7).

The KJ rendering of Romans 2.5, "But after thy hardness and impenitent heart treasurest up unto thyself wrath against the day of wrath
and revelation of the righteous judgment of God" is reworded by RSV,
"But by your hard and impenitent heart you are storing up wrath for
yourself on the day of wrath when God's righteous judgment will be
revealed."

A curious use of "against" in a sense relating to time or preparation occurs in Genesis 43.25, "against Joseph came" (RSV "for
Joseph's coming"); Exodus 7.15, "against he come" (RSV "for him");
and 2 Kings 16.11, "against king Ahaz came" (RSV "before King
Ahaz arrived"). Shakespeare used "against" in this sense:
>"I'll charm his eyes against she do appear."
>*A Midsummer Night's Dream*, III, 2, 99.

**AGONE.** An old form of the past participle of the verb "go," similar
to the Anglo-Saxon *agan*. It was contracted to "ago" as
early as 1300, and from Caxton on this has been the ordinary form in
printed prose; but "agone" has remained as an archaic and poetic
variant. It is used once in KJ—"three days agone I fell sick" (1 Samuel
30.13). The same book, 9.20, has "three days ago." It looks as
though the choice of "agone" was for euphony, because of the succeeding vowel "I." The revisers in 1881–1901 took no account of this,
rendering the clause, "three days ago I fell sick." RSV preserves
euphony by changing the order of the words—"I fell sick three days
ago."

**AGREE** is coupled with "to," in obsolete usage, three times. "Thou
art a Galilean, and thy speech agreeth *thereto*" (Mark 14.70)
is Tyndale's rendering, kept by subsequent versions made from the

Greek. But the translations from the Latin Vulgate, Wyclif, and Rheims do not have the last clause. The revised versions omit it, for it is not present in the ancient Greek manuscripts which were not available to Tyndale and the KJ translators. "And to him they agreed" is reworded in RSV "So they took his advice" (Acts 5.40); "to this agree the words of the prophets" reads more naturally "with this the words of the prophets agree" (Acts 15.15).

**AHA** is an interjection expressing joy, satisfaction, or triumph. This may be innocent, as in Isaiah 44.16, "he roasts meat and is satisfied; also he warms himself and says, 'Aha, I am warm, I have seen the fire!' " Or it may be satisfaction over the misfortune of an enemy or rival, as in the psalmist's prayer that his enemies may not rejoice over him and say to themselves, "Aha, we have our heart's desire!" (Psalm 35.21, 25). So also in Psalms 40.15; 70.3; Ezekiel 25.3; 26.2; 36.2.

The Hebrew interjection thus translated is *he'aḥ*, which in one passage KJ represents by "Ha, ha." This passage (Job 39.24–25) is about the war horse: "He swalloweth the ground with fierceness and rage: neither believeth he that *it is* the sound of the trumpet. He saith among the trumpets, Ha, ha; and he smelleth the battle afar off, the thunder of the captains, and the shouting." RSV has:

"With fierceness and rage he swallows the ground;
he cannot stand still at the sound of the trumpet.
When the trumpet sounds, he says 'Aha!'
He smells the battle from afar,
the thunder of the captains, and the shouting."

When the revisers in 1885 changed the "Ha, ha" in this passage to "Aha!" they were criticized for giving the horse a human cry. But "Ha, ha" is also human, and expresses laughter. The older translations were even more "human." Coverdale, the Great Bible, and the Bishops' Bible had the horse saying "tush." The Geneva Bible was the first to use "Ha, ha," which KJ adopted. The Douay Bible simply used the Latin "Vah."

In Mark's account of the crucifixion of Jesus (15.29–30), RSV reads, "And those who passed by derided him, wagging their heads, and saying, 'Aha! You who would destroy the temple and build it in three days, save yourself, and come down from the cross!' " The Greek interjection here is *oua*, which the Latin represents by *vah*. The Geneva Bible translated it by "Hey," KJ by "Ah," the revised versions of 1881 and 1901 by "Ha!"

**ALARM.** "God himself *is* with us for *our* captain, and his priests
with sounding trumpets to cry alarm against you" (2
Chronicles 13.12) reads in RSV, "God is with us at our head, and
his priests with their battle trumpets to sound the call to battle against
you." The word "alarm" came from the Italian *all' arme,* "To arms!"
The Mosaic law with respect to the trumpets is given in Numbers
10.1–10, and verse 9 enjoins their use in war. Shakespeare used the
word "alarm" in this sense, and often spelled it "alarum."

"Sound, sound alarum! we will rush on them."
*King Henry VI, Part I*, I, 2, 18
"Now, when the angry trumpet sounds alarum
And dead men's cries do fill the empty air."
*King Henry VI, Part II*, V, 2, 3–4

**ALBEIT.** An old word, made by combining "all" with the subjunctive
mood of the verb "be" and a following subject "it." The
meaning, if written out in full, is "although it be that." It has precarious standing in KJ, where it appears twice. In Ezekiel 13.7 the
word of the LORD condemns the lying prophets who "say, The LORD
saith *it;* albeit I have not spoken." Here the Hebrew has the simple
connective which is usually translated "and." Some modern translations use "and," some "when," some "although."

Asking Philemon to receive Onesimus, not just as a returned slave
but as a Christian brother, Paul goes on to write: "If he has wronged
you at all, or owes you anything, charge that to my account. I, Paul,
write this with my own hand, I will repay it—to say nothing of your
owing me even your own self" (vs. 18–19 RSV). The last clause reads
in KJ, "albeit I do not say to thee how thou owest unto me even thine
own self besides." The "albeit" is an awkward rendering which appeared in the Geneva Bible and was accepted by the KJ translators.
Tyndale had "So that I do not saye to thee . . ." Rheims had "I will
repay it: not to say to thee that thou owest me thine owne self also."
This is a clause expressing purpose, introduced in the Greek by *hina*
and in the Latin by *ut,* which may not be properly translated by a
concessive "albeit" or "although."

**ALIKE.** The emphasis of "alike," as used in the Bible, is not so much
upon identical form or structure as upon some point of
similarity. "Whether they both *shall be* alike good," Ecclesiastes 11.6,
is better translated "whether both alike will be good." The question is not whether their goodness will be in all respects iden-

tical, but whether both, the one as well as the other, will be good.

The basic idea of the Hebrew word which usually underlies KJ "alike" is "together," and KJ so translates it more than a hundred times. It is the word used "when the morning stars sang together" (Job 38.7). So "they lie down alike in the dust" (Job 21.26) and "all *things come alike* to all" (Ecclesiastes 9.2) imply nothing more than the common fate of mortal human beings.

The KJ rendering of Psalm 33.15, "He fashioneth their hearts alike," is ambiguous; and the Hebrew is better represented by the revised versions, ". . . the hearts of them all." In Psalm 139.12, "the darkness and the light *are* both alike *to thee*," there is no Hebrew for "both alike to thee"; the clause says simply "darkness is as light."

**ALL.** In Hebrews 7.7, "without all contradiction the less is blessed of the better," the word "all" is used in the sense of "any"; and the meaning is more clearly expressed by RSV, "It is beyond dispute that the inferior is blessed by the superior." In Deuteronomy 22.3, "with all lost thing of thy brother's" means "with any lost thing . . ."

The word "all" is ambiguous in Peter's statements, "we have forsaken all" (Matthew 19.27) and "we have left all" (Mark 10.28; Luke 18.28), for it may refer to persons or things or both. But KJ has here introduced a difference in the verbs which the Greek does not have, and has ignored a difference in their objects which the Greek has. An exact translation gives "left everything" in Matthew and Mark and "left our homes" in Luke.

The intensive expression "all manner of" is frequently used by KJ where the Hebrew or the Greek simply has the word for "all." For example, 1 Peter 1.15, "in all manner of conversation" means "in all your conduct."

Occasionally KJ introduces ambiguity by the position it gives to the word "all." It represents Jesus as saying when he offered the cup to his disciples at the Last Supper, "Drink ye all of it" (Matthew 26.27). But in the Greek of which this is supposed to be a translation, the word for "all" is in the nominative case. It modifies the subject of the verb, not its object. Jesus did not tell his disciples to drink all of the contents of the cup; he invited all of them to drink. This was correctly expressed in some of the earlier English translations. Tyndale had "Drink of it every one." The Geneva Bible had "Drink ye every one of it." RSV reads "Drink of it, all of you."

In James 3.2 KJ reads "For in many things we offend all." That seems to mean that we are offensive to everybody. But here again the

Greek word for "all" is in the nominative case; it is not the object of the verb, but modifies the subject. And here again the earlier English translations had been correct. The KJ translators fell into ambiguity by copying the rendering of the Rhemish Version. RSV reads "For we all make many mistakes."

**ALLEGE.** To "allege" now means merely to assert, but in the sixteenth century it meant to adduce evidence, hence to cite or quote authorities. That is what it means in Acts 17.2–3, where we are told by KJ that for three weeks Paul "reasoned with them out of the scriptures, opening and alleging, that Christ must needs have suffered, and risen again from the dead." Yet Webster cites this text as evidence that "allege" means "to assert without proof, but with the implication of readiness or ability to prove." Does the editor imagine that Paul spent three weeks brandishing the Scriptures, implying that he could prove what he was asserting, but failing actually to cite or quote any evidence? That so excellent a dictionary could go so far astray is just an additional bit of evidence that the archaic language of KJ easily misleads the reader. RSV translates the passage: "They came to Thessalonica, where there was a synagogue of the Jews. And Paul went in, as was his custom, and for three weeks he argued with them from the scriptures, explaining and proving that it was necessary for the Christ to suffer and to rise from the dead, and saying, 'This Jesus, whom I proclaim to you, is the Christ.' "

**ALLIED** may mean connected by kinship or marriage, or joined by a league or formal treaty. KJ states that Eliashib, the high priest in the time of Nehemiah, *"was* allied unto Tobiah," the Ammonite who did all that he could to hinder Nehemiah's work (Nehemiah 13.4). This probably refers to some connection by marriage. Both Tobiah and his son had married women of Judah (6.17–19), and Eliashib's grandson had married the daughter of Sanballat, Tobiah's associate. Yet just how Eliashib and Tobiah were connected, and to what extent they were allied, are nowhere stated. The Hebrew simply means "near to," in the sense of a close personal relationship. RSV preserves the ambiguity by the rendering, "was connected with Tobiah."

**ALLOW** is used five times in KJ. In each case it has the sense of praise, approve, or accept—the common meaning of "allow" in the sixteenth and seventeenth centuries, derived from the Latin *allaudare,* to praise. Jesus' accusation of the lawyers (Luke 11.48), "ye allow the deeds of your fathers," does not imply that they had any power to permit or prohibit what their fathers did. That was history, past and done. What he said was, "you approve the deeds of your fathers." The Greek word means literally "join in thinking well of." The revised versions use the word "consent"—"you consent to the deeds of your fathers."

When the KJ translators used the word "allow" in Paul's vivid description of the predicament of the sinner (Romans 7.15)—"that which I do I allow not: for what I would, that do I not; but what I hate, that do I"—they used it in the sense of approve. Their rendering would be expressed today in the words, "I do not approve what I am doing." But in this case they mistranslated the Greek verb, which means know or understand. What Paul said was, "I do not understand what I am doing." RSV translates: "I do not understand my own actions. For I do not do what I want, but I do the very thing I hate."

Paul's statement in 1 Thessalonians 2.4 does not mean merely that God permitted him to be entrusted with the preaching of the gospel, but that God approved him for this mission. RSV uses the word "approve" in Romans 14.22 also, and the word "accept" in Acts 24.15.

**ALL TO.** The King James Version records that when Abimelech approached the door of the tower of Thebez, to set it afire, "a certain woman cast a piece of a millstone upon Abimelech's head, and all to brake his skull" (Judges 9.53). The modern reader, unless he is acquainted with Old and Middle English, is not sure what the last clause means. Does it state the woman's purpose or tell the result of her action? If the result, what was it? Does "all to brake" mean "almost broke" or "quite broke"?

A literal translation of the Hebrew is "crushed his skull," and that is what the KJ translators meant by their expression.

The prefix "to-," like the German "zer-" and the Latin and English "dis-," expressed separation, and "to-break" meant break asunder or in pieces. This prefix came also to be used with verbs containing no idea of separation, and with these verbs it simply emphasized or intensified their meaning—for example "to-establish" meant establish perfectly or entirely. The word "all" was often used with the prefix "to-," as adding further emphasis or intensity. In time "all to" and "all-to" began to be regarded as adverbs meaning completely or entirely.

Coverdale's rendering of Proverbs 6.15 was "Sudenly shal he be al tobroken, and not be healed." The KJ translators did not retain the "all to" expression in this verse, which they rendered: "suddenly shall he be broken without remedy." RSV has "in a moment he will be broken beyond healing."

Milton wrote of Wisdom that her wings "were altoruffled, and sometimes impaired" (*Comus*, 380). In Bunyan's *Pilgrim's Progress*, Christina tells the Interpreter about the efforts of Mrs. Timorous to persuade her not to undertake the journey, and says, "She all-to-be-fooled me." The expression so appears in the Oxford Edition. It was too much for the editor of an edition published by the American Tract Society about a hundred years ago, who changed it to read, "She also befooled me."

There are excellent treatments of this now obsolete usage in OED, under *All*, C, 14 and 15; *To-*, prefix²; and *To-break*.

**ALWAY** is a space term, "all the way," which has from the first been applied to time, meaning "all the time." It was once supposed to express continuous duration while ALWAYS stood for consistent, regular recurrence, meaning "every time." If this distinction ever existed, it began very early to be ignored and has long been lost. "Alway" is now archaic and poetic; "always" is the prose word which carries both meanings.

"Alway" appears 23 times in KJ, and "always" 62 times. Attempts have been made to show that the KJ translators observed a distinction, writing "Lo, I am with you alway" (Matthew 28.20) and "I make mention of you always in my prayers" (Romans 1.9). But in most cases no such distinction can be discerned. KJ has "set upon the table shrewbread before me alway" (Exodus 25.30) and "cause the lamp to burn always" (27.20). It has "The Cretians *are* alway liars" (Titus 1.12) and "I foresaw the Lord always before my face" (Acts 2.25). RSV follows modern usage, and has abandoned "alway." Shakespeare did not use "alway."

**AMAZE, AMAZEMENT.** These were once stronger words than they are now. To amaze was to stun or stupefy, as by a blow on the head, or to overcome with fear, to terrify. In accounts of old battles many a warrior fell to the ground "amazed." He was not astonished; he was knocked cold. Isaak Walton's *The Compleat Angler* (1653) warns that "the sight of any shadow amazes the fish."

The four Hebrew verbs which KJ represents by "amazed" mean to be dismayed, terrified, dumbfounded, appalled. RSV uses these stronger terms in the Old Testament. Examples are: "Now are the chiefs of Edom dismayed" (Exodus 15.15); "the men of Benjamin were dismayed, for they saw that disaster was close upon them" (Judges 20.41); "they will look aghast at one another" (Isaiah 13.8); "I will make many peoples appalled at you" (Ezekiel 32.10).

The Greek terms used in the New Testament are not so heavy, and "amazed," "amazement," "astonished," "astonishment," "astounded" are used in all modern translations. There are two outstanding passages where these words are insufficient. The statement that Jesus in Gethsemane "began to be sore amazed, and to be very heavy" means that he "began to be greatly distressed and troubled" (Mark 14.33). Peter's counsel to the women to be "not afraid with any amazement" means to "let nothing terrify you" (1 Peter 3.6).

**AMBASSAGE** is an old form for "embassy" which appears in Luke 14.32. The same Greek word is used in Luke 19.14, where KJ translates it by "message." RSV uses "embassy" in both contexts.

**AMERCE** is an old Latin-French form which adds the idea of mulcting to that of a simple fine, having the victim *à merci*, at one's mercy. OED defines it as "to punish by an arbitrary fine." It is just the right word for the angry Prince in *Romeo and Juliet* (III, 1, 195):
"But I'll amerce you with so strong a fine
That you shall all repent the loss of mine."
It is not the right word, however, in the one passage where it occurs in KJ, "they shall amerce him in an hundred *shekels* of silver" (Deuteronomy 22.19). There is nothing arbitrary here; this is part of the Deuteronomic code of law, which prescribes the exact amount of the fine to be imposed under certain conditions. ASV and RSV translate "they shall fine him a hundred shekels of silver."

**AMIABLE** means lovable, lovely. In the sixteenth and seventeenth centuries it was applied to things as well as to persons. "They keep their churches so cleanly and amiable" is a quotation from Howell (1644) cited by OED. This echoes the one appearance of the word in KJ: "How amiable *are* thy tabernacles, O LORD of hosts!" (Psalm 84.1). The Rheims New Testament had "whatsoever holy, whatsoever amiable" in Philippians 4.8, where KJ has "whatsoever things *are* pure, whatsoever things *are* lovely."

"Amiable" is now used only of persons or their words or actions.

And it refers not so much to loveliness as to an even-tempered friendliness that awakens friendliness in return. Modern English translations of Psalm 84.1 are: "How lovely is thy (your) dwelling place" (Smith, Confraternity, RSV); "How dear thy dwelling is" (Moffatt); "How I love thy dwelling place" (Knox).

**ANCIENT** is used in the Old Testament, as in literature generally, to refer to times long past and to the persons who lived in those times. But it is also used to refer to the older persons of any time. The revised versions of the Bible retain the word "ancient" in the first of these senses—for example, "ancient mountains" (Deuteronomy 33.15), "ancient times" (Isaiah 46.10), "ancient kings" (Isaiah 19.11), "an ancient nation" (Jeremiah 5.15), "the ancient landmark" (Proverbs 22.28), "the proverb of the ancients" (1 Samuel 24.13).

When used in the second sense, "ancient" stands for quite different Hebrew words, which mean old, older, or aged. The "ancient men" of Ezra 3.12 were "old men" who had seen the first house of God and wept with joy at the laying of the foundation for the second. "The child shall behave himself proudly against the ancient" (Isaiah 3.5) is now rendered, "The youth will be insolent to the elder." "I understand more than the ancients" (Psalm 119.100) means "I understand more than the aged."

Job's statement, "With the ancient *is* wisdom" (12.12), means "Wisdom is with the aged." In this case the Hebrew word is *yashish*, a word which is used four times in the book of Job and nowhere else in the Scriptures. KJ translates it in the other three cases as "aged men" (15.10), "the aged" (29.8), and "very old" (32.6).

In the book of the Apocrypha entitled "The History of Susanna" KJ introduces "two of the ancients of the people," and refers to them as "ancient judges," in verse 5. But in verse 8 and thereafter they are "the two elders" or "the elders." The same Greek word, *presbuteros,* is used in verses 5 and 8 and all the other cases in the book of Susanna.

"Ancient of days" appears in the vision of Daniel 7, first as an anthropomorphic description (vs. 9), and then as a title (vs. 13, 22), of God. This translation of the Aramaic phrase came from the Geneva Bible, was adopted by the KJ translators, and has entered into English literature and hymnology. Notable hymns are Charles Wesley's "Come, Thou Almighty King," where God is addressed as "Ancient of Days" in the last line of the first stanza; William Cullen Byrant's "Ancient of days, except thou deign"; and Bishop William C. Doane's "Ancient of Days, who sittest throned in glory." RSV retains "Ancient of Days," not only because of its place in English usage, but because it is consonant with other Old Testament passages, such as Job 36.26; Psalms 90 and 102.24–27; Isaiah 41.4. In God the two meanings of the word "ancient" coincide. Among other modern translations, Moffatt has "primeval Being," Smith "Venerable One," and Knox "crowned with age."

**AND, AND IF.** "And" is so constantly used as a coordinate conjunction that its use as a conditional conjunction may easily be forgotten or overlooked. When so used "and" means "if"; it is sometimes strengthened by adding "if," so that "and if" constitutes a repetitious, double-barreled introduction to the supposition or condition. OED gives examples from Shakespeare of the use of both "and" and "and if" in the sense of "if":

"And you will not, sir, I'll take my heels."
*Comedy of Errors*, I, 2, 94
"A sheep doth very often stray,
And if the shepherd be awhile away.
*Two Gentlemen of Verona*, I, 1, 75

In the 1525 edition of Tyndale's New Testament, the last sentence of Matthew 19.17 reads, "But and thou wilt enter into life, keep the commandments." In the revised edition of 1534, Tyndale changed this to "But if thou wilt. . . ." In the 1525 edition Matthew 6.14–15 read: "For and if ye shall forgive other men their trespasses, your father in heaven shall also forgive you. But and ye will not forgive men their trespasses, no more shall your father forgive your trespasses." This rendering was retained in 1534, except that "your heavenly father" was substituted for "your father in heaven."

The expression "But and if" is used by KJ in five passages: "But and if that evil servant shall say in his heart" (Matthew 24.48); "But and if that servant say in his heart" (Luke 12.45); "But and if we say" (Luke 20.6); "But and if thou marry" (1 Corinthians 7.28); "But and if ye suffer" (1 Peter 3.14). In the first four of these cases, the "But and if" comes from Tyndale; in 1 Peter 3.14 it comes from the Rheims New Testament and the Latin Vulgate, which here mistranslated the Greek. ASV and RSV translate the Greek literally, using "But if" (*ean de*) in the first four cases, and "But even if" (*all' ei kai*) in 1 Peter 3.14.

The conditional "and" may be used with a concessive force, meaning "even if" or "though." Tyndale has an excellent example: "that they might touch, and it were but the edge of his vesture" (Mark 6.56). The "and it were but" was retained by subsequent sixteenth-century versions until the Rheims New Testament, which was simply "but." KJ has "if it were but," and RSV "that they might touch even the fringe of his garment." The Greek word is *k'an*, which means "even if." In Acts 5.15 the English versions from Tyndale on translate *k'an* by some form of "at least." RSV has "that as Peter came by at least his shadow might fall on some of them."

The conditional "and" may appear as "an." Some of the examples cited in OED are:

> "There, an 't shall please you."
> *Love's Labour's Lost,* V, 2, 584
> "If an she be a rebel."
> Fielding, *Tom Jones,* II, 2, 154
> "But an if this will not do."
> Coleridge, *Sibylline Leaves,* 273

In KJ, however, it is consistently spelled "and."

**ANGLE,** as noun, is used in KJ in its original sense of a fishhook. "All they that cast angle into the brooks" means "all who cast hook in the Nile" (RSV Isaiah 19.8). "They take up all of them with the angle" is in RSV, "He brings all of them up with a hook" (Habakkuk 1.15). The Hebrew word for "angle" is the one which KJ translates "hook" in Job 41.1, "Canst thou draw out leviathan with an hook?" The English word "angle" came to be used for the rod and line as well, and was in this sense used by Shakespeare in Cleopatra's speech:

> "Give me mine angle; we'll to the river: there,
> My music playing far off, I will betray
> Tawny-finn'd fishes; my bended hook shall pierce
> Their slimy jaws; and, as I draw them up,
> I'll think them every one an Antony,
> And say 'Ah, ha! you're caught.' "
> *Antony and Cleopatra,* II, 5, 10–15

**ANON.** "Immediately" and "straightway" are two words much used in the New Testament, which leave one in no doubt as to their meaning. But unfortunately the Greek words which mean immediately and straightway have also been translated in KJ by the terms "anon," "by and by," and "presently," all of which once meant immediately but now mean soon or after a while. When Jesus entered Peter's house in Capernaum, they told him immediately that Peter's mother-in-law was ill (Mark 1.30); but the modern reader gets the impression that they did some visiting first, for it is said that "anon" they told him of her.

In Matthew's account of the parable of the Sower, Jesus' statement concerning the hearer who is like stony ground (13.20–21) reads in KJ: "But he that received the seed into stony places, the same is he that heareth the word, and anon with joy receiveth it; Yet hath he not root in himself, but dureth for a while: for when tribulation or persecution ariseth because of the word, by and by he is offended." The Greek adverb in each of these verses is *euthus,* which means immediately. The same adverb appears in the corresponding verses of Mark's account, 4.16–17, where KJ translates it in both cases by "immediately." The use of "anon" and "by and by" in Matthew goes back to Tyndale's translation, which was retained by subsequent versions.

Tyndale also affords an early example of the loose use of "anon" which gradually changed its meaning from immediately to soon or after a while. It is in Revelation 11.14, which he translated: "The seconde woo is past, and beholde the thyrd woo wyll come anon." Here the Greek adverb is *tachu,* which means quickly; and here KJ did not follow Tyndale, but used "quickly."

"Anon" was a favorite word with Shakespeare. In the drinking scene at the Boar's Head tavern, *King Henry IV, Part I,* II, 4, he uses it 16 times for the response of a servant to a call for immediate attention.

**ANOTHER** may mean an additional one of the same sort or one that is different. Two notable examples of the use of "another" in these distinct senses are 2 Corinthians 11.4 and Galatians 1.6–7. These passages read: "For if he that cometh preacheth another Jesus, whom we have not preached, or *if* ye receive another spirit, which ye have not received, or another gospel, which ye have not accepted, ye might well bear with *him.*" "I marvel that ye are so soon removed from him that called you into the grace of Christ unto another gospel: Which is not another; but there be some that trouble you, and would pervert the gospel of Christ."

The RSV translation of these passages is: "For if some one comes and preaches another Jesus than the one we preached, or if you receive a different spirit from the one you received, or if you accept a different gospel from the one you accepted, you submit to it readily enough." "I am astonished that you are so quickly deserting him who called you in the grace of Christ and turning to a different gospel—not that there is another gospel, but there are some who trouble you and want to pervert the gospel of Christ." This translation expresses a distinction that is clearly present in the Greek text, using "another" where the Greek has *allos,* and "different" where the Greek has *"heteros."*

Examples of the use of "another" in contexts which modern English expresses differently are: "divided them into the midst, and laid each piece one against another" (RSV "cut them in two, and laid each half over against the other," Genesis 15.10); "from the roof of *one* little chamber to the roof of another" (RSV "from the back of the one side room to the back of the other," Ezekiel 40.13); "every one helped to destroy another" (RSV "they all helped to destroy one another," 2 Chronicles 20.23), "eat every one the flesh of another" (RSV "devour the flesh of one another," Zechariah 11.9).

**ANY,** with reference to persons, may be singular or plural; it may mean any one or any persons. The context makes clear that "any of this way" is plural in Acts 9.2. "When ye stand praying, forgive, if he have ought against any" is not as clear; the Greek is singular, and RSV renders it "if you have anything against any one" (Mark 11.25). "Neither was there any among them that lacked" is confusing; the revised versions of 1881–1901 better it by a change of order, "neither was there among them any that lacked"; RSV has "There was not a needy person among them" (Acts 4.34). "Lest any should say that I had baptized in mine own name" (1 Corinthians 1.15) leaves the number of "any" indeterminate. The Greek has the singular indefinite pronoun; relying upon the text of the ancient manuscripts, RSV translates the verse, "lest any one should say that you were baptized in my name."

"If any of you do err from the truth" seems to the reader of today to refer to a group rather than to one individual (James 5.19). Yet the word "any" is singular, "do err" is singular in the little-used subjunctive mood, and the clause goes on with the words "and one convert him." The entire passage, James 5.13–20, affords an interesting comparison of the English of the two versions. Verses 19–20 read in RSV: "My brethren, if any one among you wanders from the truth and some one brings him back, let him know that whoever brings back a sinner from the error of his way will save his soul from death and will cover a multitude of sins."

**ANY THING** is used as an adverb in Judges 11.25, "And now *art thou any thing better than Balak?*" which means "Now

are you any better than Balak?" In Numbers 17.13, "Whosoever cometh any thing near unto the tabernacle of the LORD shall die" is more
clearly expressed by a literal translation of the repetition which is in
the Hebrew: "Every one who comes near, who comes near to the tabernacle of the LORD, shall die." Paul's statement before Festus (Acts
25.8), "Neither against the law of the Jews, neither against the temple,
nor yet against Caesar, have I offended any thing at all," is truer to the
Greek, and gains clarity and strength, by deleting "any thing." RSV
has "Neither against the law of the Jews, nor against the temple, nor
against Caesar have I offended at all."

**ANSWER.** The expression "answered and said" or "answered, saying" appears frequently in the Bible. OED says that it is
archaic, and that it is "a Hellenism of the New Testament"; but it was
a common Hebrew phrase, which passed into the Greek of the New
Testament by way of the Septuagint. RSV usually replaces it by "answered," though it retains the phrase in a few passages, such as in
Numbers 22.18; 1 Samuel 4.17; 1 Kings 3.27.

Both in the Hebrew and in the Greek the word for "answered"
may be used in cases where no prior question or charge or remark is
recorded. In these cases the "answer" is not to anything that has been
said, but is called forth by some factor or circumstance in the situation. Examples are the accounts of the five spies inciting their fellow
tribesmen to rob Micah (Judges 18.14), Jesus cursing the barren fig
tree (Mark 11.14), the angel at the empty tomb (Matthew 28.5),
Peter addressing the people (Acts 3.12), Peter's question to Sapphira
(Acts 5.8), the elder's question in Revelation 7.13. RSV usually eliminates "answered" in such cases. It retains "answering said to him,"
however, in Luke 7.40, where Jesus speaks in response to Simon's
unspoken thought.

In 2 Kings 1.1 the word "answered" is based upon an error in the
copying of one consonant in the Hebrew text. RSV corrects this in the
light of the Greek Septuagint, and reads "went up" as in verses 9 and
13. The three captains whom the king sent to Elijah followed the same
initial procedure; each, with his men, "went up" to the man of God
as he sat on the top of a hill.

**APOTHECARY** means one who prepares and sells drugs for medici-
nal purposes. It is not a correct translation of the
Hebrew, however; and the revised versions replace it by "perfumer"
in each of the six cases where it appears in KJ. With reference to the
funeral of King Asa, RSV reads, "They laid him on a bier which

had been filled with various kinds of spices prepared by the perfumer's art; and they made a very great fire in his honor" (2 Chronicles 16.14). The dry observation of Ecclesiastes 10.1—"Dead flies cause the ointment of the apothecary to send forth a stinking savour: *so doth* a little folly him that is in reputation for wisdom *and* honour"— is translated in RSV:

"Dead flies make the perfumer's ointment give off an evil odor; so a little folly outweighs wisdom and honor."

The other passages are Exodus 30.25, 35; 37.29; Nehemiah 3.8.

**APPARENTLY** and **EVIDENTLY** were originally strong words referring to sight. They meant visibly, manifestly, clearly, plainly, distinctly. But usage has weakened both words, so that "apparently" may now mean seemingly, and "evidently" is more often used in cases of inference than with respect to matters of sight.

In Shakespeare's *Comedy of Errors* (IV, 1, 78) Angelo angrily orders:

"arrest him, officer.
I would not spare my brother in this case,
If he should scorn me so apparently."

Hobbes, in *Government and Society* (1651) refers to "the prophets, who saw not God apparently like unto Moses."

But the statement that God "apparently" spoke to Moses (Numbers 12.8) means to most people today that He only seemed to do so. RSV translates the verse, "With him I speak mouth to mouth, clearly, and not in dark speech; and he beholds the form of the LORD."

The statement about Cornelius, "He saw in a vision evidently about the ninth hour of the day an angel of God coming in" (Acts 10.3), is rephrased by RSV to read, "About the ninth hour of the day he saw clearly in a vision an angel of God coming in."

In Galatians 3.1, "before whose eyes Jesus Christ hath been evidently set forth, crucified among you" is now reworded, "before whose eyes Jesus Christ was publicly portrayed as crucified."

**APPOINT** is used in KJ as translation for 30 different Hebrew words and 12 different Greek verbs. It is used in RSV almost twice as often, though for a less wide range of Hebrew and Greek terms. Jacob is asked to "name" his wages (RSV Genesis 30.28), and Solomon asks Hiram to "set" the wages to be paid to his men (RSV 1 Kings 5.6). David's servants declare that they are ready to do whatever he "decides"; and the LORD had "ordained to defeat the good counsel of Ahithophel" (2 Samuel 15.15; 17.14). "To appoint unto them that mourn in Zion" means "to grant to those who mourn in Zion" (Isaiah 61.3).

The six hundred Danites, "appointed with weapons of war," were "armed with weapons of war" (Judges 18.11, 16). "Thou hast given us like sheep *appointed* for meat" means "Thou hast made us like sheep for slaughter" (Psalm 44.11). "Appointed to death" is "doomed to die" (Psalm 102.20) or "sentenced to death" (1 Corinthians 4.9). "God hath not appointed us to wrath" is "God has not destined us for wrath" (1 Thessalonians 5.9). "Appoint *him* his portion with the hypocrites" means "put him with the hypocrites" (Matthew 24.51; compare Luke 12.46).

The phrase "appointed time" appears in many passages. It is an erroneous translation in Job 7.1; 14.14 for the Hebrew word which means "warfare" and is so translated in Isaiah 40.2. The RSV of the verses in Job is:

> "Has not man a hard service upon earth,
>     and are not his days like the days of a hireling?"
> "If a man die, shall he live again?
>     All the days of my service I would wait,
>     till my release should come."

**APPOINTMENT.** "That which they have need of, . . . according to the appointment of the priests which *are* at Jerusalem" is more clearly translated, "Whatever is needed . . . , as the priests at Jerusalem require" (Ezra 6.9). "At the appointment of Aaron and his sons" is "at the command of Aaron and his sons" (Numbers 4.27). "By the appointment of Absalom" is "by the command of Absalom" (2 Samuel 13.32).

It is true, however, that Job's three friends "made an appointment together" to come to condole with him and comfort him (Job 2.11). The Hebrew verb here used is translated "let us meet together" in two passages in Nehemiah (6.2, 10). It occurs also in Amos 3.3, where KJ's translation is so ambiguous as to be misleading: "Can two walk together, except they be agreed?" This text has been twisted by well-meaning exhorters into a plea for harmony, and used by bigots to justify the exclusion of dissenters. But the question is simply, "Do two walk together, unless they have made an appointment?"

**APPREHEND** is used in its present sense, to arrest a person in the name of the law, in Acts 12.4, where it is recorded that Herod apprehended (seized) Peter and put him in prison, and in 2 Corinthians 11.32, where Paul writes of the attempt of the governor of Damascus to apprehend (seize) him.

It is used in the obsolete sense, to take possession of, in Philippians 3.12, 13, where it translates the Greek verb which means to obtain, take possession of, make one's own. This is the verb used in 1 Corinthians 9.24 for receiving the prize in a race—"So run, that ye may obtain." The full context, Philippians 3.4–14, should be read. Verse 12 reads in RSV: "Not that I have already obtained this or am already perfect; but I press on to make it my own, because Christ Jesus has made me his own."

**ARK.** The constant use of this word to denote the ark built by Noah (*tebah*) and the ark of the covenant (*'aron*) which was the symbol of the presence of the LORD, tends to make the reader forget that "ark" is a common English noun meaning a chest, box, or coffer. The ark was a household fixture in English homes for centuries, and its manufacture provides the family name Arkwright. The bread-ark and meal-ark used by Shakespeare's mother's family can be seen at the old Arden farm in Warwickshire.

The Hebrew *'aron* is translated "chest" in 2 Kings 12.9, 10 and 2 Chronicles 24.8, 10, 11; and is the word for the "coffin" in which the body of Joseph was placed when he died (Genesis 50.26). The Hebrew *tebah* denotes also the "ark of bulrushes" for the baby Moses. Because of its size and materials RSV translates: "when she could hide him no longer she took for him a basket made of bulrushes, and daubed it with bitumen and pitch; and she put the child in it and placed it among the reeds at the river's brink" (Exodus 2.3).

**ARMHOLE** originally meant armpit and is used in that now obsolete sense in Jeremiah 38.12. RSV translates, "Put the rags and clothes between your armpits and the ropes." The Hebrew word here translated "armpits" means joints of the arms, and may be applied to elbows or wrists. In Ezekiel 13.18 the rendering "sew pillows to all armholes" is misleading. RSV translates "sew magic bands upon all wrists." The entire passage, 13.17–23, should be read in RSV to get the meaning of the oracle. (See KERCHIEF, PILLOW)

**ARTILLERY** is a word that was in use long before there were cannons or howitzers. It was applied to any implements of war. OED cites a sixteenth-century diarist as listing under artillery "drumes, flutes, trumpetes . . ." And it quotes from Samuel Williams' *History of Vermont* (1794): "A club made of hard wood, a stake hardened in the fire, a lance armed with a flint or a bone, a bow and an arrow constituted the whole artillery of an Indian war."

When Jonathan went to the field where David was hiding, and shot three arrows for his little lad to gather, he "gave his artillery unto his lad, and said unto him, Go, carry *them* to the city" (1 Samuel 20.40). The use of "artillery" here was an innovation of KJ, for Tyndale and Coverdale had "weapons," Geneva had "bowe and arrowes," and the Bishops' Bible had "instruments." The revised versions have returned to the natural rendering of Tyndale and Coverdale. RSV reads: "Jonathan gave his weapons to his lad, and said to him, 'Go and carry them to the city.'"

**AS.** In Matthew 12.13, for "like as the other" the revised versions have "like the other." So too "like as a fire" means "like fire" (Jeremiah 23.29); "like as a lion" is "like a lion" (Psalm 17.12); "like as a woman with child" is "like a woman with child" (Isaiah 26.17); "like as all the nations" is "like all the nations" (Deuteronomy 17.14). In 17 other cases, RSV replaces "like as" with "as" or "just as," and follows the rule that "as" may be used to introduce a clause but "like" may not.

In prepositional phrases RSV replaces "as" with "like" where that is the meaning. "Ye shall be as gods" is more accurately translated "you will be like God" (Genesis 3.5). "They sank as a stone" is "they went down like a stone" (Exodus 15.5). It was not "as lightning" but "like lightning" that our Lord saw Satan fall from heaven (Luke 10.18). Other examples are: "like a child" (Luke 18.17); "like sheep" (Matthew 9.36); "like locusts" (Judges 6.5); "like a mantle" (Hebrews 1.12).

The expression "as it were" means simply "like" (Luke 22.44; Revelation 8.10). "A certain vessel descending unto him, as it had been a great sheet" is "something descending, like a great sheet" (Acts 10.11). When the council that condemned Stephen "saw his face as it had been the face of an angel," it means that they "saw that his face was like the face of an angel" (Acts 6.15).

The word "as," in the KJ use of "as it were" and "as it had been," has the sense of "as if" or "as though"—an archaic use which is described in the OED article on *As*, B, 1b and 9. An example from Shakespeare is *King Henry VI, Part II*, I, 1, 103, where the Duke of Gloucester protests against

"Defacing monuments of conquer'd France,
Undoing all, as all had never been!"
Other examples in KJ are Revelation 5.6; 13.3; 15.2.

**AS CONCERNING** is an awkward phrase for "with regard to." In
Leviticus 4.26 appears "an atonement for him as
concerning his sin," in 5.6, "an atonement for him concerning his sin,"
and in 5.10, "an atonement for him for his sin." The Hebrew is the
same in these three cases. RSV uses "atonement for him for his sin."
"Of whom as concerning the flesh Christ *came*" is rendered by RSV,
"of their race, according to the flesh, is the Christ" (Romans 9.5).
Paul's statement to the Philippians (4.15), "no church communicated
with me as concerning giving and receiving, but ye only" means "no
church entered into partnership with me in giving and receiving except
you only."

Other examples of the use of "as concerning" are in Acts 13.34;
28.22; Romans 11.28; 1 Corinthians 8.4; 2 Corinthians 11.21.

**ASSAY,** as verb, occurs six times in the sense of attempt or venture.
RSV replaces it by "attempted" in Deuteronomy 4.34; Acts
9.26; 16.7; Hebrews 11.29. When the youth David volunteered to fight
with Goliath, King Saul gave him a helmet of bronze, a coat of mail,
and a sword. "And David girded his sword upon his armour, and he
assayed to go; for he had not proved *it*." RSV translates the verse:
"And David girded his sword over his armor, and he tried in vain to
go, for he was not used to them" (1 Samuel 17.39). Eliphaz begins
his attempt to comfort Job by inquiring, "*If* we assay to commune
with thee, wilt thou be grieved?" RSV has "If one ventures a word
with you, will you be offended?" (Job 4.2).

RSV uses the words "assay" and "assayer" in Jeremiah 6.27, where
the figure is drawn from the assaying of metals. KJ's rendering—"I
have set thee *for* a tower *and* a fortress among my people"—is due to
confusion between the Hebrew word *baḥon*, which means assayer,
and a similar Hebrew word which means tower. The entire strophe
reads in RSV:

"I have made you an assayer and tester among my people,
that you may know and assay their ways,
They are all stubbornly rebellious,
going about with slanders;
they are bronze and iron,
all of them act corruptly.

The bellows blow fiercely,
    the lead is consumed by the fire;
in vain the refining goes on,
    for the wicked are not removed.
Refuse silver they are called,
    for the LORD has rejected them."

**ASSWAGE** is the old spelling of "assuage." It appears once as an intransitive verb, in the obsolete sense of grow less, abate, subside (Genesis 8.1). In place of "the waters asswaged," RSV reads "the waters subsided." For the same Hebrew verb it has "the anger of the king abated" (Esther 7.10; compare 2.1). "Assuage" is retained as a transitive verb in Job 16.5–6: "the solace of my lips would assuage your pain." *"There is* no healing of thy bruise" (Nahum 3.19) now reads "There is no assuaging your hurt."

**ASTONIED, ASTONISHED, ASTONISHMENT** are derived from the obsolete verb "astone," which appeared also as "astun" and "astony." It meant to stun, strike senseless; or to overwhelm with amazement, to astound. "Astonied" occurs in KJ 10 times, "astonished" 34 times, and "astonishment" 21 times. These are not used in the obsolete sense of being knocked unconscious, but they have heavier connotations, especially in the Old Testament, than "astonish" now has.

In place of "astonied," RSV uses "appalled" (Ezra 9.3, 4; Job 17.8; 18.20), "confused" (Jeremiah 14.9), "perplexed" (Daniel 5.9), "dismayed" (4.19). "That they may . . . be astonied one with another" (Ezekiel 4.17) means "that they may . . . look at one another in dismay." Only in Daniel 3.24 and Isaiah 52.14 is "astonied" replaced by "astonished."

In Jeremiah, "astonished" is replaced by "appalled" (2.12; 50.13) and "horrified" (18.6; 19.8; 49.17). "The priests shall be astonished, and the prophets shall wonder" (4.9) means "the priests shall be appalled and the prophets astounded."

The prophecy of the fate of Babylon, "Babylon shall become heaps, a dwellingplace for dragons, an astonishment, and a hissing, without an inhabitant" (Jeremiah 51.37), is translated by RSV, "Babylon shall become a heap of ruins, the haunt of jackals, a horror and a hissing, without inhabitant." See also verse 41. In similar contexts, "astonishment" is replaced by "horror" (Deuteronomy 28.37; Jeremiah 25.9; 42.18; 44.12; Ezekiel 5.15). "The cup of astonishment" (Ezekiel

23.33) is "a cup of horror"; and "the wine of astonishment" (Psalm 60.3) is "wine that made us reel." The prophecy concerning Jerusalem, "they shall drink water by measure, and with astonishment," means "they shall drink water by measure and in dismay" (Ezekiel 4.16; compare 12.19).

"Astonishment of heart" (Deuteronomy 28.28) means "confusion of mind." The prophecy in Zechariah 12.4, "I will smite every horse with astonishment," means "I will strike every horse with panic."

**AS YET** means hitherto or up to this time, and according to OED implies the expectation or possibility of coming change. It is used correctly in KJ Exodus 9.17, John 20.9, and 2 Corinthians 1.23. But in Jeremiah 31.23 it is a mistranslation of the Hebrew word which in the context means "yet again" or "once more"—the word which KJ itself had translated "again" in verse 4, and "yet" in verse 5, of that chapter.

**AT.** Obsolete uses of the preposition "at" appear in Exodus 19.15, "come not at *your* wives," and Numbers 6.6, "he shall come at no dead body," where the revised versions use "near." In Numbers 30.4, 7 "hold his peace at her" means "say nothing to her." "David enquired at the LORD" means ". . . of the LORD" (1 Samuel 30.8). When King Nebuchadnezzar demanded that his magicians tell him what the dream was which he had forgotten, they protested that only the gods could do that, and that no king had "asked such things at any magician" (Daniel 2.10). When the plotters against Daniel were themselves cast into the den of lions, "the lions had the mastery of them, and brake all their bones in pieces or ever they came at the bottom of the den." RSV has ". . . before they reached the bottom of the den" (6.24).

Shakespeare's *The Winter's Tale* was played at the Globe Theatre on May 15, 1611, which was the year in which the King James Version was published. It contains the lines:

> "Madam, he hath not slept to-night; commanded
> None should come at him." (II, 3, 31)

**ATTENDANCE** originally meant attention. To "give attendance" to something was to give attention to it, to apply one's mind or effort to it. KJ uses the word twice in this obsolete sense. When Paul directs Timothy to "give attendance to reading, to exhortation, to doctrine," it is not simply to be present at the services of the church, but to be responsible for them. RSV translates: "Till I come, attend to the public reading of scripture, to preaching, to teaching" (I Timothy 4.13). The Letter to the Hebrews, affirming that the priesthood of our Lord is superior to the priesthood of Aaron and his descendants, states that he "pertaineth to another tribe, of which no man gave attendance at the altar." RSV has that he "belonged to another tribe, from which no one has ever served at the altar" (Hebrews 7.13).

The word "attendance" is retained in the account of the visit of the queen of Sheba to King Solomon—for "the attendance of his ministers" RSV has "the attendance of his servants" (1 Kings 10.5); 2 Chronicles 9.4). In Esther 7.9 "And Harbonah, one of the chamberlains, said before the king" is better translated, "Then said Harbona, one of the eunuchs in attendance on the king."

**ATTENT** is an older word, derived from the Latin *attentus,* that means the same as "attentive," derived from the French *attentif.* "Attent" is used by KJ in King Solomon's prayer of dedication and the LORD's reply (2 Chronicles 6.40; 7.15); but "attentive" is used in Nehemiah's prayer (1.6, 11) and in Psalm 130.2.

When the chief priests and their friends sought to destroy Jesus, they did not find anything they could do, "for all the people were very attentive to hear him." This translation does not convey the vividness of the Greek, which means "for all the people hung upon his words" (Luke 19.48).

The adverb "attentively" is used when Elihu, seeking to impress Job with the wondrous works of God, describes a thunderstorm (KJ Job 37.1–5). But the exhortation to "hear attentively" is strangely inept in a passage which has the heavens crashing in one's ears. There is no Hebrew word for "attentively"; it is simply the translators' attempt to express the intensive force of the repetition of the verb. The revised versions of 1885–1901 sought to do this by repeating the verb in English—"Hear, oh, hear the noise of his voice." But that does not fit the context any better. RSV gives up the attempt to intensify the verb "hear" and seeks to express the intensity of the storm. It reads: "At this also my heart trembles,
    and leaps out of its place.
Hearken to the thunder of his voice
    and the rumbling that comes from his mouth
Under the whole heaven he lets it go,
    and his lightning to the corners of the earth.

After it his voice roars;
>  he thunders with his majestic voice
>  and he does not restrain the lightnings when his voice is heard.
>  God thunders wondrously with his voice;
>  he does great things which we cannot comprehend."

**AT THE LENGTH** is simply an obsolete form of the phrase "at length," which means finally or in the end. It is used in KJ just once, Proverbs 29.21, as translation for the Hebrew word which denotes the end or ultimate issue of a course of action. RSV translates the verse:
>  "He who pampers his servant from childhood
>  will in the end find him his heir."

**AUDIENCE** is used 12 times in KJ and never means the persons who hear, but the act or state of hearing. RSV substitutes "hearing" 8 times—"in the hearing of the Hittites" (Genesis 23.10, 13, 16); "in the hearing of the people" (Exodus 24.7; Nehemiah 13.1; Luke 7.1; 20.45); "in the hearing of our God" (1 Chronicles 28.8). Abigail's prayer to David to let her "speak in thine audience" was to "speak in your ears" (1 Samuel 25.24). For "give audience" RSV uses "listen" (Acts 13.16; 15.12; 22.22). An example from Shakespeare: "Let me have audience for a word or two" (*As You Like It*, V, 4, 157).

**AVOID** is used once as an intransitive verb, in the sense of go away, withdraw. When Saul cast a javelin at David, thinking to pin him to the wall, "David avoided out of his presence twice" (1 Samuel 18.11). This use of the word "avoid," which is now obsolete, was common in the sixteenth century. Coverdale translated Matthew 16.23, "Auoyde fro me, Sathan." To avoid from a horse meant to dismount. OED quotes from Holinshed's *Scottish Chronicle,* "Quicklie avoiding from his horse." The colloquial phrase "clear out" is really old and correct English for "avoid," that is, make an empty place, a void. In 1 Samuel 18.11, RSV compacts the verb and the preposition and translates, "David evaded him twice."

**AWAY WITH** in Isaiah 1.13 means put up with, tolerate, endure. RSV translates the verse:
>  "Bring no more vain offerings;
>  incense is an abomination to me.

New moon and sabbath and the calling of assemblies—
I cannot endure iniquity and solemn assembly."

This was a well-established idiom in the sixteenth and seventeenth centuries and is not obsolete, though no longer in common use. Tyndale's translation of Matthew 19.11 was "all men can not awaye with that sayinge," but he ended the following verse with "He that can take it, let him take it." The Greek has the same verb for "can not awaye with" and "take it." OED quotes from a sermon of Bishop Sanderson (1621): "He being the Father of lyes . . . cannot away with the Truth." In Shakespeare's *King Henry IV, Part II*, III, 2, 213, Justice Shallow says of Jane Nightwork, "She never could away with me," and Falstaff answers, "Never, never; she would always say she could not abide Master Shallow."

**BACKBITE, BACKBITING, BACKBITER** occur four times in KJ.
*"He that* backbiteth not with his tongue" (Psalm 15.3) is changed by RSV to "who does not slander with his tongue," for the Hebrew verb *ragal* means to go about slandering, and is translated "slander" by KJ in 2 Samuel 19.27, where Mephibosheth complains that his servant Ziba had deceived him and openly lied about him (16.1–4). But RSV retains "a backbiting tongue" in Proverbs 25.23, because here the Hebrew literally means "a tongue of secrecy," and secrecy—"behind one's back"—is the distinctive element in the sort of slander which is also backbiting. In 2 Corinthians 12.20 and Romans 1.30 the Greek words mean "slander" and "slanderers."

**BACKSLIDING** is used 13 times in Jeremiah and 3 times in Hosea as a term for Israel's turning away from God. RSV uses "faithless" or "faithlessness" in 10 of these passages, and "apostasy" in 2. It retains "our backslidings are many" (Jeremiah 14.7), and changes "slidden back by a perpetual backsliding" to "turned away in perpetual backsliding" (8.5). "My people are bent to backsliding from me" is rendered "My people are bent on turning away from me" (Hosea 11.7). In Isaiah 57.17 a consistent translation of the Hebrew changes "he went on frowardly" to "he went on backsliding." But in Hosea 4.16 a quite different Hebrew word is used, which means "stubborn." This verse reads in KJ: "For Israel slideth back as a backsliding heifer: now the LORD will feed them as a lamb in a large place." RSV has:

"Like a stubborn heifer,
    Israel is stubborn;
can the L ORD now feed them
    like a lamb in a broad pasture?"

**BAKEMEATS.** The chief baker, in his dream, was carrying on his head three cake baskets, in the uppermost of which were "all manner of bakemeats for Pharaoh" (Genesis 40.17). Literally translated, the Hebrew means "all sorts of food made by a baker." The word "bakemeat" became obsolete after the sixteenth century, though "sweetmeat" has survived. Shakespeare used "baked meats" in the same sense.

"Look to the baked meats, good Angelica:
    Spare not for cost."
*Romeo and Juliet,* IV, 4, 5
"Thrift, thrift, Horatio! the funeral baked meats
Did coldly furnish forth the marriage tables."
*Hamlet,* I, 2, 180–181

**BAND,** in the sense of that by which a person or thing is bound, occurs 27 times in KJ. It is retained by RSV in Daniel 4.15, 23 and in Hosea 11.4. Elsewhere the various Hebrew and Greek terms so represented are translated by "bonds" (Judges 15.14; Job 39.5; Psalms 2.3; 107.14; Isaiah 28.22; 52.2; 58.6; Jeremiah 2.20; Luke 8.29), "cords" (Job 38.31; Psalm 119.61; Ezekiel 3.25; 4.8), "fetters" (Ecclesiastes 7.26; Acts 16.26), "binding" (Exodus 39.23), "bars" (Leviticus 26.13; Ezekiel 34.27), "ropes" (Job 39.10; Acts 27.40), "ligaments" (Colossians 2.19).

"The bands of the wicked have robbed me" (Psalm 119.61) is an ambiguous rendering which KJ took from the Geneva Bible. In the form of "The congregations of the wicked have robbed me" this had appeared in Coverdale and the Great Bible. Coverdale had gotten the idea from Luther's German Bible. The Bishops' Bible forsook this, and gave a sound translation of the Hebrew; but the second edition of the Bishops' Bible and the King James Version reinstated the erroneous rendering. The Hebrew, the Greek Septuagint, and the Latin Vulgate justify the translation by RSV:

"Though the cords of the wicked ensnare me,
    I do not forget thy law."
"For *there are* no bands in their death" is an opaque utterance which

KJ picked up from the Geneva Bible (Psalm 73.4). Other sixteenth-century versions had "they are in no peril of death"—a rendering which Coverdale had gotten from Luther. Modern scholars generally accept an emendation of the Hebrew text suggested by Ewald, which warrants the translation, "For they have no pangs."

The prophet's symbolic staffs, "Beauty" and "Bands" (Zechariah 11.7–14), were given names which are more intelligibly translated into English by "Grace" and "Union."

**BANQUET.** Whether the word "banquet" means a feast of food and drink or simply a drinking bout is not always easy to determine. The Hebrew word *"mishteh"* means both or either. It occurs in Esther 20 times, and is translated "banquet" 10 times and "feast" or "feasting" 10 times. Four times the Hebrew word for "wine" is added; so KJ has "banquet of wine" and RSV "as they were drinking wine." RSV uses "dinner" for Queen Esther's invitation to the king and Haman. It uses "banquet" rather than "supper" for Herod's birthday party (Mark 6.21) and in Luke 14.12, 16, 17, 24.

"The banquet of them that stretched themselves shall be removed" (Amos 6.7) seems to mean little more than that the feast will come to an end and the plates and glasses removed. RSV translates, "the revelry of those who stretch themselves shall pass away" (read the whole of 6.1–7 in RSV, and the trenchant exegesis by Dean Fosbroke in *The Interpreter's Bible,* vol. 6, pp. 822–825).

In the chapter concerning Leviathan, "Shall the companions make a banquet of him?" (Job 41.6) is a mistranslation due to confusion of similar Hebrew verbs. RSV translates "Will traders bargain over him?"

In 1 Peter 4.3 "walked in . . . banquetings" means "living in . . . carousing." The entire verse should be compared in KJ and RSV.

**BARBARIAN, BARBAROUS.** In its original meaning the term *barbaros* was applied to all non-Greek-speaking peoples, who were regarded as foreigners. In time it acquired the additional meaning of rude or uncivilized, and began to be more widely used. It was applied by Romans to non-Romans. In 2 Maccabees it is applied by Jews to the Greeks, and is also used in the sense of savage as an adjective describing a beast.

In the New Testament *barbaros* is used only in its original sense. RSV retains "barbarians" in Romans 1.14 and Colossians 3.11, but without the capital B which KJ uses. In Acts 28.2, 4 RSV uses "natives," and in 1 Corinthians 14.11 "foreigner," as better suited to the context in each case.

**BASE,** as an adjective, is used by KJ in the archaic sense of low in rank or position, lowly, humble. "The basest of men" (Daniel 4.17) does not mean the most worthless or most wicked of men, but "the lowliest of men" (RSV). "The basest of the kingdoms" (Ezekiel 29.15) means "the most lowly of the kingdoms." When Paul refers to himself in 2 Corinthians 10.1 as "who in presence *am* base among you, but being absent am bold toward you," the meaning is "I who am humble when face to face with you, but bold to you when I am away!" Compare also the renderings of KJ and RSV for 1 Corinthians 1.26–29.

The "certain lewd fellows of the baser sort" who raised an uproar in Thessalonica (Acts 17.5) were "some wicked fellows of the rabble" (RSV). The word which KJ represents by "lewd" is the common Greek word for "wicked," and it gives to the phrase its moral connotations. The word represented by "the baser sort" simply means the crowd in the market place. C. B. Williams translates the phrase "some wicked loafers about the public square."

**BE.** The King James Version frequently uses "be" with a plural subject in the first or third person, where modern usage would say "are." An interesting passage is Genesis 42.31–32, "We *are* true *men;* we are no spies: We *be* twelve brethren." Other examples are: Delilah's cry to Samson, "The Philistines *be* upon thee" (Judges 16.9, 12, 14, 20); Elisha's assurance to his servant, "They that *be* with us *are* more than they that *be* with them" (2 Kings 6.16); and Zechariah's question to the angel, "What *be* these? And he answered me, These *are* the horns . . ." (Zechariah 1.19). In these cases the revised versions use "are" instead of "be."

The KJ translators have "thy sins be forgiven thee" in Matthew 9.2 and "thy sins are forgiven thee" in Luke 5.20, though the Greek text which they used is the same in the two cases. In Jeremiah 17.5, 7 KJ has "Cursed *be*" and "Blessed *is*" for parallel constructions.

In many cases the word "be" as used in KJ is the subjunctive mood of the verb. Many of these are retained by the revised versions, in expressions such as "Blessed be the Lord!" In accordance with modern usage, however, the subjunctive form of verbs is less often used than in the seventeenth century. In Genesis 27.21, for example, the blind Isaac's word to Jacob, "Come near, I pray thee, that I may feel thee, my son, whether thou *be* my very son Esau or not," is expressed by RSV, "Come near, that I may feel you, my son, to know whether you are really my son Esau or not."

**BEAST.** The word "animal" does not appear in KJ, which uses "beast" as a general term for living creatures other than man. "Cattle" is used as a collective name for all live animals held as property or reared for some use. The word "reptile" does not appear, for it was a relatively new word, just beginning to be current in 1611; KJ used the older term "creeping thing." "Fowl" is used twice as often as "bird," and for the same Hebrew and Greek words. Here again, "fowl" was the old generic term for feathered vertebrates, which had begun to be displaced by "bird."

The RSV uses the word "animal" where it is appropriate. It uses "reptile" in the New Testament, but retains "creeping things" in the Old Testament. It uses the phrase "birds of the air" rather than "fowls of the air," and substitutes "bird" for "fowl" as a generic term for the feathered tribes. It retains "cattle" as a collective term for livestock held as property, not restricting it to bovine animals.

What is perhaps the most astonishing error in KJ is its indiscriminate use of the word "beast" in the book of Revelation. John's vision of heaven showed to him, around the throne of God, twenty-four elders and four living creatures who worship him and sing his glory. The Greek word for "living creature" is *zōon;* it is used 20 times to refer to these heavenly beings (chapters 4, 5, 6, 7, 14, 15, 19). Later, he saw a beast rising out of the sea and another which rose out of the earth, and was told of the beast that ascends from the bottomless pit. These beasts are the enemies of God and the objects of his wrath. The Greek word that refers to them is *thērion,* which means "wild beast" (used 27 times in chapters 11, 13, 14, 15, 16, 17, 19, 20).

Yet KJ uses the word "beast" as a translation both for *zōon* and *thērion,* thus failing to make the distinction which the Greek makes between the choir of heaven and the minions of hell. The KJ translators were not the first to make this error; it appears in all the prior translations from Wyclif to Rheims. But it is strange that they did not correct it. The Latin Vulgate makes the distinction, using *animal* for the heavenly beings and *bestia* for the infernal beasts. The KJ translators themselves, moreover, used "living creatures" for the Hebrew term of similar import in chapters 1, 3, and 10 of Ezekiel.

**BECAUSE.** This was originally a phrase, "by (bi, bie, be) cause," often followed by of, why, or that. "Because of" is in common use today. "Because that" occurs in Genesis 2.3, Numbers 11.20, and 20 other passages, but in RSV is replaced by "because."

From the fifteenth to the seventeenth century, "because" was used not only to express a cause or reason, but also to express a purpose. The following quotations from Tyndale illustrate the variety of seventeenth-century usage:

Luke 1.7: "They had no chylde, because that Elizabeth was barren."

Luke 13.14: "the ruler of the sinagoge answered with indignacion (be cause that Iesus had healed on the sabath daye)."

Matthew 12.10: "they axed him sayinge: ys it lawfull to heale apon the saboth dayes? because they might accuse him."

Matthew 20.31: "the people rebuked them, be cause they shulde holde their peace."

John 16.1: "these thinges have I sayde unto you, because ye shuld not be offended."

In the first two of these passages "because that" and "be cause that" translate the Greek *hoti,* which means "because"; in the last three passages "because" and "be cause" represent the Greek *hina,* which means "in order that." KJ changed Tyndale's wording in two of these last three passages, but kept it, to the confusion of the reader, in Matthew 20.31. The revised versions change to modern usage in all cases where "because" was used in the sense of "in order that."

"For because" is an archaic and redundant expression which simply means "because." It is used in KJ Genesis 22.16 and Judges 6.22.

**BENEVOLENCE.** The expression "due benevolence" (1 Corinthians 7.3) comes from Tyndale, who had: "Let the man geve unto the wyfe due benevolence. Lykwyse also the wyfe unto the man." "Benevolence" is here used in the sense of affection or good will toward a particular person. But the ancient Greek manuscripts read simply: "Let the husband give to his wife her due, and likewise the wife to her husband." The Greek word is *opheilē,* which is translated as "debt" in Matthew 18.32 and "due" in Romans 13.7. Paul here uses it for the mutual obligations of husband and wife. Some copyist of the Greek text must have felt that it was not explicit enough, and inserted the Greek word *eunoia,* good will; this addition was picked up by other copyists and appears in most of the late medieval manuscripts. It has been eliminated from modern editions of the Greek text, and from modern translations generally, as early as those by John Wesley and Alexander Campbell.

**BESOM** is an old word for a broom. It occurs once in KJ, where the LORD says of Babylon, "I will sweep it with the besom of destruction" (Isaiah 14.23). Literally translated, the Hebrew means "I will sweep it with the sweeper of destruction." Shakespeare used "besom" just once, in the angry speech of the rebel Jack Cade to Lord Say: "I am the besom that must sweep the court clean of such filth as thou art" (*King Henry VI, Part II*, IV, 7, 34).

**BESTEAD** originally meant placed or situated, but came to be used only in cases of difficulty, disadvantage, hostility, ill fortune, and the like—so acquired such meanings as beset or hard pressed. In its one appearance in the Bible, Isaiah 8.21, "hardly bestead" represents a Hebrew verb which means "hard pressed." ASV translated it by "sore distressed." RSV translates the verse: "They will pass through the land, greatly distressed and hungry; and when they are hungry, they will be enraged and will curse their king and their God, and turn their faces upward."

The word is used in KJ fashion by Shakespeare in *King Henry VI, Part II*, II, 3, 56:

"I never saw a fellow worst bested,
Or more afraid to fight, than is the appellant."

**BESTOW** is used for a variety of meanings in KJ, and stands for six different Hebrew verbs and five Greek verbs. The fourteen hundred chariots and twelve thousand horsemen that King Solomon "bestowed in the cities" were "stationed" there (1 Kings 10.26; 2 Chronicles 9.25). When Gehazi took the gifts from Naaman and "bestowed *them* in the house" the Hebrew means simply that he "put them in the house" (2 Kings 5.24). The rich fool who worried over where to "bestow" his crops was not thinking of giving them away; he meant to keep them, and his problem was where to "stow" or "store" them (Luke 12.17–18). "Thou shalt bestow that money for whatsoever thy soul lusteth after" means "you shall spend the money for whatever you desire" (Deuteronomy 14.26). The word "bestow" is applied by KJ to the payment of workmen (2 Kings 12.15); to the use for the Baals of things dedicated to the LORD (2 Chronicles 24.7); and to Ezra's authorization to provide what is required for the house of God (Ezra 7.20).

In three passages, KJ uses "bestow labour" for the Greek word which it elsewhere translates by "labour" or "toil." These passages are John 4.38, Romans 16.6, and Galatians 4.11; their wording comes from Tyndale. An error in the Greek text of Romans 16.6 has been corrected on the authority of the ancient manuscripts, so that instead of "who bestowed much labour on us" the RSV reads "who has worked hard among you."

**BETHINK THEMSELVES** occurs in 1 Kings 8.47 (= 2 Chronicles 6.37), "if they shall bethink themselves . . . , and repent, and make supplication unto thee . . . , saying, We have sinned. . . ." The phrase is used here in a sense equivalent to "when he came to himself" in the parable of the Prodigal Son (Luke 15.17). RSV translates the Hebrew more literally: "if they lay it to heart . . . , and repent, and make supplication to thee . . . , saying, 'We have sinned. . . .'" Other occurrences of the same Hebrew idiom are Deuteronomy 4.39; 30.1; Isaiah 44.19; 46.8; Lamentations 3.21.

**BETIMES** means early, soon, in good time. It was a common word in Elizabethan English. Shakespeare used it frequently, as in *Macbeth*, IV, 3, 162:

> "Good God, betimes remove
> The means that makes us strangers!"

In *Hamlet*, IV, 5, 49, Ophelia says:

> "To-morrow is Saint Valentine's day,
> All in the morning betime,
> And I a maid at your window,
> To be your Valentine."

"Betimes" is a correct translation of the Hebrew in only one of the five passages where it occurs in KJ. That is Genesis 26.31, where RSV has "In the morning they rose early." In 2 Chronicles 36.15 "The LORD God of their fathers sent to them by his messengers, rising up betimes, and sending" is better translated, "The LORD, the God of their fathers, sent persistently to them by his messengers." "He that spareth his rod hateth his son: but he that loveth him chasteneth him betimes" (Proverbs 13.24) does not convey the meaning of the Hebrew as well as RSV:

> "He who spares the rod hates his son,
> but he who loves him is diligent to discipline him."

In Job 8.5 and 24.5 the words "seek" and "seeking" carry the full meaning without the addition of "betimes."

**BEWRAY** is an old word for reveal or disclose. It had almost the same range of meanings as "betray," except that it lacked the connotation of treachery or disloyalty that "betray" almost always has. Shakespeare used "betray" 67 times and "bewray" 10 times. KJ uses "betray" 42 times and "bewray" 4 times. "Betray" is the word for the act of Judas; and "thy speech bewrayeth thee" describes Peter's unintentional disclosure of his identity (Matthew 26.73).

But the distinction between the two words has not been maintained in English usage. "Bewray" has fallen into disuse, and "betray" is used for reveal or disclose as well as for acts of treachery or disloyalty. As early as 1588, Shakespeare wrote, "I do betray myselfe with blushing" (*Love's Labour's Lost*, I, 2, 138). In 1711, Addison wrote, "If he coughs, or betrays any Infirmity of Old Age" (Spectator No. 6. See OED, *Betray*, 6 and 7).

The result is that "bewray" does not appear in RSV. It has "discloses nothing" (Proverbs 29.24), "betray not the fugitive" (Isaiah 16.3), and "your accent betrays you" (Matthew 26.73).

Proverbs 27.16 is an obscure text, but it is clear that *"which be-wrayeth itself"* is a mistaken rendering. RSV takes verses 15 and 16 together, and translates:

> "A continual dripping on a rainy day
> and a contentious woman are alike;
> to restrain her is to restrain the wind
> or to grasp oil in his right hand."

**BLAIN.** An old word for a blister or large pustule, which is best known in the compound "chilblain." It appears in the account of the plagues of Egypt, "a boil breaking forth *with* blains upon man, and upon beast" (Exodus 9.9, 10). RSV translates "boils breaking out in sores on man and beast."

Wyclif's first translation of Job 2.7 was "He smot Job with the werste stinkende bleyne from the sole of the fot unto the nol." RSV has "afflicted Job with loathsome sores from the sole of his foot to the crown of his head."

**BLASTED, BLASTING.** In Pharaoh's dream, he beheld seven thin ears of corn, "blasted with the east wind" (Genesis 41.6, 23, 27). Isaiah refers to "the grass on the house tops, blasted before it be grown up" (2 Kings 19.26; Isaiah 37.27). In these passages RSV uses "blighted" instead of "blasted." It also uses "blight" instead of "blasting" in passages that connect it with mildew and pestilence as scourges of the land and people (1 Kings 8.37; 2 Chronicles 6.28; Amos 4.9; Haggai 2.17). The word "blight" did not enter the language until the seventeenth century, and was probably not available to the KJ translators; but it has displaced "blast" as a term for plant diseases of atmospheric or unknown origin.

**BLOW UP.** "Blow up the trumpet" (Psalm 81.3) means simply "Blow the trumpet." There is no difference in the Hebrew wording between this verse and other verses about trumpet-blowing in which the word "up" has not been inserted. This expression is the one holdover in KJ of the older usage of a redundant "up" or "out" with "blow." Coverdale had "They blewe out the trompettes" in 1 Maccabees 3.54, but KJ did not retain the "out." "Blow up" today usually means "inflate" or "explode."

**BODY OF HEAVEN.** When Moses, Aaron, Nadab, Abihu, and 70 of the elders of Israel saw the God of Israel, *"there was* under his feet as it were a paved work of a sapphire stone, and as it were the body of heaven in *his* clearness (Exodus 24.10). RSV translates this: "there was under his feet as it were a pavement of sapphire stone, like the very heaven for clearness." Smith and Confraternity have "as clear as the sky itself"; Moffatt "clear as the sky itself."

**BOLLED.** As a result of the hail which the LORD rained upon the land of Egypt, the flax and the barley were ruined, "for the barley *was* in the ear, and the flax *was* bolled" (Exodus 9.31). Tyndale added to his translation a marginal note to the effect that "boulled," as he spelled the word, meant "swollen, i.e. grown into buds." The Hebrew word means bud; ASV translates "the flax was in bloom," and RSV "the flax was in bud."

**BOOK.** The word "book" was formerly applied to any written document of legal significance, and some traces of this usage remain in the Bible. At Mark 10.4, Wyclif's version of 1382 had "a libel, that is, a litil boke of forsakyng," which was condensed in the 1388 revision to "a libel of forsakyng"; Tyndale and his successors had "a testimoniall of devorsement"; Rheims took "a bill of divorce" and KJ "a bill of divorcement"; RSV has "a certificate of divorce." In Isaiah 50.1, where Wyclif had "boc of forsakyng," KJ has "bill of divorcement."

Numbers 5.23 reads in RSV, "the priest shall write these curses in a book, and wash them off into the water of bitterness." Wyclif's first version had "in a libel," and the second "in a litil book"; Tyndale and Coverdale used "bill"; and in the Geneva Bible and thereafter it is "book." In *The Interpreter's Bible* (vol. 2, p. 169) John Marsh remarks that the word "may mean anything useful for writing on, and here may well indicate a stone, from which ink could be easily washed off." Note that the purpose is not to blot out the curses, as KJ says, but to wash them off into the water, which acquires and conveys their potency.

"The book of the purchase" (Jeremiah 32.12) is "the deed of the purchase," and is so translated by the revised versions.

"Let him that is my contrary party, sue me with a lybell," was Coverdale's translation of the last clause of Job 31.35. In time this got toned down to KJ's "my desire *is . . . that* mine adversary had written a book." RSV translates the verse:

"Oh, that I had one to hear me!
    (Here is my signature! let the Almighty answer me!)
    Oh, that I had the indictment written by my adversary!"

The word "libel," which originally had the same meaning as "book," does not appear in KJ.

**BOOTIES** is the plural, now obsolete, of "booty." It appears once in KJ: "Shall they not rise up suddenly that shall bite thee, and awake that shall vex thee, and thou shalt be for booties unto them" (Habakkuk 2.7). RSV reads:

"Will not your debtors suddenly arise,
    and those awake who will make you tremble?
    Then you will be booty for them."

The word "booties" occurs once in Shakespeare, *The Winter's Tale,* IV, 4, 863, where the rogue Autolycus says, "If I had a mind to be honest, I see Fortune would not suffer me: she drops booties in my mouth."

**BOSS.** In the one passage where the word appears (Job 15.25–26), a boss is the convex projection in the center of the face of a shield. The KJ rendering of this passage is: "For he stretcheth out his hand against God, and strengtheneth himself against the Almighty. He runneth upon him, *even* on *his* neck, upon the thick bosses of his bucklers." The "he" which is the subject of these sentences is "the wicked man" of verse 20, who is here represented as running upon

God, even on God's neck, upon the thick bosses of God's bucklers. But this is a strangely inept rendering, quite unjustified by the Hebrew and contrary to the prior sixteenth-century English versions. ASV translates verse 26:

"He runneth upon him with a *stiff* neck,
With the thick bosses of his bucklers."

RSV translates the two verses as one sentence:

"Because he has stretched forth his hand against God,
and bids defiance to the Almighty,
running stubbornly against him
with a thick-bossed shield."

**BOTCH.** An obsolete word for boils or sores. As "the botch of Egypt" it appears in the curse pronounced by Moses upon Israel if it should forsake the LORD (Deuteronomy 28.27, 35). From Wyclif and Tyndale through the sixteenth-century translations to the King James Version, this expression persisted as though "the botch of Egypt" were a distinct and especially fearsome disease. But the Hebrew word represented by "botch" simply means a boil or boils, and is so translated by KJ in every other occurrence. "The botch of Egypt" was the plague of boils referred to in Exodus 9.9–11. The Hebrew word also appears in Leviticus 13.18, 19, 20, 23; in the account of Hezekiah's illness, 2 Kings 20.7 (= Isaiah 38.21); and in Job 2.7.

**BOW,** as verb, occurs often in KJ and is usually clear. "A bowing wall" (Psalm 62.3) is corrected by the revised versions to read, "a leaning wall." "They have set their eyes bowing down to the earth" (Psalm 17.11) is a mistranslation for "they set their eyes to cast me to the ground." In prayer to God, the expression "bow down thine ear" is used in Psalms 31.2 and 86.1 for the Hebrew idiom which KJ correctly translates "incline thine ear" in Psalms 17.6; 71.2; 88.2; 102.2; Daniel 9.18. Hezekiah's prayer (2 Kings 19.16) has "bow down thine ear," but the same prayer in the parallel account (Isaiah 37.17) is translated "incline thine ear." For this Hebrew idiom KJ uses "incline (one's) ear" 22 times and "bow down (bow) thine ear" 5 times.

**BOWELS.** The word "bowels" is used 28 times in the Old Testament. It is used literally in Numbers 5.22; 2 Samuel 20.10; 2 Chronicles 21.15, 18, 19; Psalms 22.14; 109.18. It is used for the stomach in Job 20.14 and Ezekiel 3.3; 7.19. It denotes the womb in

Genesis 25.23; Psalm 71.6; Isaiah 49.1. It denotes the male organs of procreation in Genesis 15.4; 2 Samuel 7.12; 16.11; 2 Chronicles 32.21; Isaiah 48.19. "He that shall come forth out of thine own bowels" is an unnecessary and misleading circumlocution for "your own son."

In 10 cases the word "bowels" is used to denote feelings or emotions. Jeremiah's cry, "My bowels, my bowels!" means "My anguish, my anguish!" (Jeremiah 4.19). Job's plaint, "My bowels boiled," means "My heart is in turmoil" (Job 30.27). "My bowels are troubled" (Lamentations 1.20; 2.11) is better translated "my soul is in tumult."

The rendering of Song of Solomon 5.4, "my bowels were moved for him," is changed by ASV to "my heart was moved for him." RSV, relying upon a slightly different Hebrew text, reads "my heart was thrilled within me."

"The sounding of thy bowels" is a strange expression concerning God (Isaiah 63.15); it means "the yearning of thy heart." This entire verse is recast and more correctly stated in the revised versions. See also Isaiah 16.11.

It is said of Joseph (Genesis 43.30) that "his bowels did yearn upon his brother," which means "his heart yearned for his brother." Similar expressions are found in 1 Kings 3.26 and Jeremiah 31.20.

When Judas fell headlong, his body burst open and "all his bowels gushed out" (Acts 1.18). This is the only New Testament passage which uses the word "bowels" in its literal physical meaning. In eight other cases it is used by KJ in the sense of affection or compassion.

The Greek word which KJ translates by "bowels" does not refer to the intestines specifically but to the "inward parts" or internal organs generally. Like the Greek word for "heart," this word was also used for the feelings and affections. It is translated "inward affection" by KJ in 2 Corinthians 7.15.

In the English language of 1611 both "bowels" and "heart" had this double reference to physical organs and to the emotions of which these organs were supposed to be the seat. Today only "heart" retains the double reference.

When Paul wrote, "Ye are not straitened in us, but ye are straitened in your own bowels" (2 Corinthians 6.12), he meant "You are not restricted by us, but you are restricted in your own affections." When he tells the Philippians (1.8) that he longs for them "in the bowels of Jesus Christ," it means "with the affection of Christ Jesus." Again, in Philippians 2.1 "bowels" means "affection."

In Colossians 3.12 "bowels of mercies" is now translated "compassion"; and "shutteth up his bowels *of compassion* from him" (1 John 3.17) is "closes his heart against him." The short letter of Paul to Philemon comes alive with the substitution of "heart" for "bowels" in verses 7, 12, and 20.

The Greek verb derived from the noun which KJ translates "bowels" is used 12 times in the New Testament, and is always translated by KJ as "have compassion" or "moved with compassion."

**BRAVERY,** in its one occurrence, refers to feminine finery (Isaiah 3.18–23). Shakespeare uses the word once in this sense, and, like Isaiah, lists some of the items.

> "and now, my honey love,
> Will we return unto thy father's house,
> And revel it as bravely as the best,
> With silken coats and caps and golden rings,
> With ruffs and cuffs and fardingales and things;
> With scarfs and fans and double change of bravery,
> With amber bracelets, beads and all this knavery."
> *The Taming of the Shrew,* IV, 3, 52–58.

**BREACH** occurs only as a noun in KJ, usually meaning a break, a broken place, an injury. The word is retained by RSV where it refers to breaches in fortifications or city walls (1 Kings 11.27; Nehemiah 4.7; 6.1; Psalm 60.2; Isaiah 22.9; Ezekiel 26.10; Amos 9.11). The idioms "stood in the breach" (Psalm 106.23) and "the repairer of the breach" (Isaiah 58.12) are also retained. But "to repair the breaches of the house of the LORD" is simply phrased "to repair the house of the LORD" (2 Kings 12.5, 6, 7, 8, 12; 22.5).

The expression "a breach in the tribes of Israel" (Judges 21.15) is kept, but "bindeth up the breach of his people" (Isaiah 30.26) is reworded "binds up the hurt of his people." The KJ rendering of Proverbs 15.4, "A wholesome tongue *is* a tree of life: but perverseness therein *is* a breach in the spirit," has been revised to read:

> "A gentle tongue is a tree of life,
>     but perverseness in it breaks the spirit."

Tyndale's translation of Leviticus 24.20 was, "broke for broke, eye for eye and toth for toth: euen as he hath maymed a man, so shall he be maymed again." In a marginal note he gave "breach" and "fracture" as alternate readings for "broke." The Geneva Bible changed to "breach for breach," and was followed by the Bishops'

Bible and KJ. RSV returns to the other word in Tyndale's margin, and reads: "fracture for fracture, eye for eye, tooth for tooth; as he has disfigured a man, he shall be disfigured."

"Breaches" is an erroneous translation for a Hebrew word which means "landing places" (Judges 5.17). Again, "with breaches" is an erroneous translation for "into fragments" (Amos 6.11).

The only context in which "breach" causes serious confusion is Numbers 14.34, where the LORD sentences the Israelites to forty years in the wilderness, and says, "ye shall know my breach of promise." This phrase has become common for a kind of lawsuit and leaves the modern reader with the uncomfortable inference that the LORD has not only broken his promise to the Israelites but is admitting it in a flint-hearted judgment. But there is no warrant in the Hebrew for the phrase "my breach of promise." The word thus rendered means "my opposition." Tyndale's translation was, "ye shall fele my vengeaunce." The Great Bible had "ye shall know my displeasure." The Geneva Bible introduced the idea of "breach of promise," and was followed by the Bishops' Bible and KJ. Modern translations reject this. RSV returns to the rendering of the Great Bible, "you shall know my displeasure." Moffatt reads "That will teach you what it is to have me against you"; Confraternity has "Thus you will realize what it means to oppose me."

**BREAK UP.** An expression which occurs nine times, to represent seven different Hebrew or Greek verbs. "Break up your fallow ground" (Jeremiah 4.3; Hosea 10.12) remains current English; as does "when the meeting of the synagogue broke up" (Acts 13.43). But elsewhere the expression is used in an obsolete sense for which we now say "break in," "break into" or "break through." KJ itself uses "break through" in Matthew 6.19–20 and Luke 12.39 as translation for the same Greek verb which it renders "broken up" in Matthew 24.43.

The rendering of Job 38.10, "And brake up for it my decreed *place*" is a literalism which confuses the reader of the great chapters that have been called the most exalted poetry in the Bible. No other English translation has this awkward rendering. Those in the Tyndale-Coverdale line used "gave it my commandment." RV and ASV have "marked out for it my bound"; and RSV reads "prescribed bounds for it."

**BRIGANDINE.** A coat of cloth or leather with rings or little plates sewed on to make it a lightweight coat of mail. It was worn by "brigands," who were light-armed foot soldiers, equipped for duty as scouts or skirmishers. This meaning of "brigand" is now obsolete; a brigand today is a bandit, and brigandines have long since passed into history. A "brigantine" was originally a light skirmishing ship, for which "brig" was simply a colloquial abbreviation.

The revised versions use "coat of mail" in Jeremiah 46.4 and 51.3, the only occurrences of "brigandine." The Geneva Bible had called Goliath's coat of mail a "brigandine" (1 Samuel 17.5), but its weight of five thousand shekels made the term inappropriate.

**BRIM** is used in its present sense in 1 Kings 7.23, 24, 26; 2 Chronicles 4.2, 5; John 2.7. But "the brim of the water" (Joshua 3.15) is archaic. In Old English "brim" was a poetical word for the sea or flood, then came to be used for the edge of the water or for its surface. In Joshua 3.15 the Hebrew word represented by "brim" means edge or border. RSV translates: "When those who bore the ark had come to the Jordan, and the feet of the priests bearing the ark were dipped in the brink of the water (the Jordan overflows all its banks throughout the time of harvest), the waters coming down from above stood and rose up in a heap far off, at Adam, the city that is beside Zarethan, and those flowing down toward the sea of the Arabah, the Salt Sea, were wholly cut off; and the people passed over opposite Jericho."

**BRUIT** means a report noised abroad, a rumor, tidings. "All that hear the bruit of thee shall clap the hands over thee," says Nahum in prophecy against Nineveh (RSV "All who hear the news of you clap their hands over you," Nahum 3.19). Jeremiah 10.22, addressed to Judah, reads: "Behold, the noise of the bruit is come, and a great commotion out of the north country, to make the cities of Judah desolate, *and* a den of dragons." RSV has:

"Hark, a rumor! Behold, it comes!—
a great commotion out of the north country
to make the cities of Judah a desolation,
a lair of jackals."

Shakespeare used "bruit" both as noun and as verb. Examples are:
"The bruit thereof will bring you many friends."
*King Henry VI, Part III,* IV, 7, 64
"I find thou art no less than fame hath bruited."
*King Henry VI, Part I,* II, 3, 68
"By this great clatter, one of greatest note
Seems bruited."
*Macbeth,* V, 7, 22

**BUCKLER.** A small, round shield with a knob or "boss" in the center, carried or strapped to the arm for use in hand-to-hand fighting. The dictionary's statement that the Hebrew word *magen* denotes a buckler, and *tsinnah* a large shield covering the whole body, seems to be ignored by KJ, which uses the terms indiscriminately. It translates *magen* as "shield" 47 times and "buckler" only 8 times; and it renders *tsinnah* by "shield" 10 times, "buckler" 5 times, and "target" 5 times. The RSV uses "shield" as a general term, and retains "buckler" only where both words are used or where the Hebrew has that specific meaning. The "thousand bucklers" hanging on the tower of David (Song of Solomon 4.4) are retained, but "lift up the buckler against thee" (Ezekiel 26.8) is replaced by "raise a roof of shields against you." In the great song of faith, Psalm 91, the one who trusts in God is given assurance that "his faithfulness is a shield and buckler" (vs. 4).

**BULLOCK,** as used in KJ, means a young bull. The term is now limited to bulls that have been castrated. Since the animals offered for sacrifice were required to be "without blemish," the word "bullock" is no longer applicable (Leviticus 1.3, 10). RSV uses "bull" or "young bull."

**BUNCH.** An obsolete term for the hump on the back of a camel or of a deformed person. "They will carry . . . their treasures upon the bunches of camels" (Isaiah 30.6) means "they carry . . . their treasures on the humps of camels." In Shakespeare's *King Richard III,* the humpbacked Richard is called "that poisonous bunch-back'd toad" (I, 3, 246) and "that foul bunch-back'd toad" (IV, 4, 81).

**BURDEN.** The Hebrew verb *nasa'* means to lift, carry, take. The related noun *massa'* means a burden that is carried, but also means an oracle, the message of a prophet who lifts up his voice in formal and solemn utterance of the word or vision which has come to him. KJ uses "burden" for both these senses of *massa';* RSV uses "oracle" where that is the meaning (2 Kings 9.25; Isaiah 13.1, etc.; Ezekiel 12.10; Nahum 1.1; Habakkuk 1.1; Zechariah 9.1; 12.1; Malachi 1.1).

In Jeremiah 23.33–40 there is vivid, pointed wordplay upon the double meaning of *massa',* which is expressed by using "burden" in the same double meaning.

**BURN.** A reviewer of RSV wrote: "I had always thought Paul's 'It is better to marry than burn' meant 'burn in hellfire,' but RSV makes it 'aflame with passion,' which is unambiguous if banal."

The text in question is 1 Corinthians 7.9, which reads in KJ, "If they cannot contain, let them marry: for it is better to marry than to burn." The word "burn" here translates a Greek passive infinitive which since the days of the poet Anacreon had been used in the sense of to be inflamed or on fire with emotion, usually with lust or anger. The translation of the RSV—"If they cannot exercise self-control, they should marry. For it is better to marry than to be aflame with passion"—is justified by all lexicons of the Greek language, and adopted in some form by all modern translations. The comment is worth adding that the word "better" does not mean that marriage is the less of two evils; it expresses Paul's judgment that to marry is not a sin (vs. 28 and 36), while Jesus taught that to burn with lustful desire is sinful (Matthew 5.28).

The same Greek word is used in 2 Corinthians 11.29, where KJ has, "Who is weak, and I am not weak? who is offended, and I burn not?" The word "offended" is here used in an obsolete sense which misleads the modern reader. RSV translates the second half of the verse: "Who is made to fall, and I am not indignant?" Goodspeed's translation has "fired with indignation"; Knox's translation "ablaze with indignation."

This word is used three times in 2 Maccabees (4.38; 10.35; 14.45) with its reference to anger made explicit.

**BURSTING.** The word "burst" is used nine times in KJ and is retained by the revised versions in every case. But in Isaiah 30.14 "bursting" is used for a Hebrew noun derived from the verb which means to beat, break into pieces, or crush. Here "in the bursting" means in the breakage; the word "burst" simply means break, as it does in Shakespeare's *The Taming of the Shrew* (Induction, 1, 8): "You will not pay for the glasses you have burst?"

The difficulty in this verse is more serious, however, than the translators' use of a now obsolete meaning. They mistook the Hebrew noun, which denotes not the process of breaking but its results. Instead of "in the bursting of it" the Hebrew means "among its fragments." The older versions had dealt with this correctly. The Vulgate has "de fragmentis eius." The Septuagint, as translated by Thomson, reads "the fragments of which are so small that there cannot be found among them . . ." Martin Luther's translation into German had *von seinen Stücken.* The less accurate English rendering goes back to the Great Bible, from which it passed to the Bishop's Bible and to KJ. The entire verse reads, in the RSV:

> "and its breaking is like that of a potter's vessel
> which is smashed so ruthlessly
> that among its fragments not a sherd is found
> with which to take fire from the hearth,
> or to dip up water out of the cistern."

**BUSINESS** is used in the Old Testament in the same senses for which we would naturally use it today. In the New Testament, however, it is used five times, in each case to represent a different Greek term; and in none of these cases is it retained by RSV.

Jesus' answer to his parents' anxiety (Luke 2.49), "Wist ye not that I must be about my Father's business?" is now translated, "Did you not know that I must be in my Father's house?" The Greek means literally "in the (things) of my Father," an expression used repeatedly in the Greek papyri for "in the house of . . ." This translation was adopted by the Revised Version of 1881, and by almost all subsequent translations of the New Testament. It is the meaning of the Greek idiom, and it fits the context better than the old rendering.

In 1 Thessalonians 4.11 "do your own business" is now rendered "mind your own affairs"; and in Romans 16.2 "assist her in whatsoever business she hath need of you" is now rendered "help her in whatever she may require from you"—an attempt in each case to reproduce the very general and comprehensive character of the expressions used in the Greek. On the other hand, a specific Greek term is used in Acts 6.3, and "appoint over this business" is now replaced by "appoint to this duty."

In his biography of Charles W. Eliot, President of Harvard University, 1869–1909 (Boston: Houghton-Mifflin, 1930) Henry James states that "the Puritan believed, as in a cardinal tenet, that it was consonant with the divine order that he should pursue his own private gain and 'be not slothful in business.'" But the word "business" in this text (Romans 12.11) is used in the sense of "diligence."

The list of meanings which the word "business" had up to the seventeenth century, but which then became obsolete, is long. It includes diligence, activity, briskness, officiousness, eagerness, earnestness, importunity, anxiety, solicitude, care, attention, trouble, difficulty, commotion (OED). Tyndale's translation of Galatians 6.17 was "From hence forth, let no man put me to busynes," and this was retained by Coverdale, the Great Bible, and the Geneva Bible. The same versions had "When Pilate sawe . . . that more busines was made" (Matthew 27.24).

The Greek word in Romans 12.11 is *spoudē,* which means haste, zeal, or earnestness. RSV translates the clause: "Never flag in zeal."

**BUT.** Wyclif often used "but" in the sense of unless. Examples are:

Matthew 5.20: "I seie to you that but your riytfulnesse be more plenteuous, thanne of scribis . . . ye schulen not entre in. . . ."

John 3.2: "no man mai do these signes that thou doist, but god be with hym."

John 3.3: "truli truli I seie to thee, but a man be born again, he mai not se the kyngdom of god."

John 12.24: "truli truly I seie to you. But a corne of whete fall into the erthe and be deed: it dwelleth aloone. . . ."

This use of "but" was beginning to be archaic when Tyndale made his translation, and he substituted for it "except," which remains the usage of KJ in these and similar cases. The RSV uses "unless."

KJ retains this archaic use of "but," however, in Amos 3.7: "Surely the Lord God will do nothing, but he revealeth his secret unto his servants the prophets." This is naturally taken by the reader to be two statements of fact, adversative to one another. He will understand it to mean that instead of doing anything God reveals something. Yet the word "but" here means "unless." ASV has "except he reveal." The RSV rendering is "Surely the Lord God does nothing, without revealing his secret to his servants the prophets."

**BY.** Paul's statement in 1 Corinthians 4.4, "I know nothing by myself," means "I know nothing against myself." This is an obsolete use of "by" which occurs in Shakespeare's *All's Well That Ends Well* (V, 3, 237): "By him and by this woman here what know you?" In Foxe's *Book of Martyrs,* an inquisitor accuses Elizabeth Young, "Thou hast spoken evil words by the queen"; and she answers, "No man living upon earth can prove any such things by me."

The preposition "by" is used in the sense of "during" or "for" as part of the phrase "by the space of"—"this continued by the space of two years" (Acts 19.10). See also Acts 7.42, 13.21, 20.31. It is one of the odd facts about the KJ New Testament that when it uses the word "space" it usually refers to a period of time. (See SPACE)

"By" is so commonly used in forms of swearing or adjuration (see

Matthew 26.63) that this seems to the reader to be its function in
2 Thessalonians 2.1: "Now we beseech you, brethren, by the coming
of our Lord Jesus Christ . . ." But it is here used as a translation for
the Greek word which means "concerning." The RSV reads: "Now
concerning the coming of our Lord Jesus Christ and our assembling
to meet him, we beg you, brethren, not to be quickly shaken in mind
or excited . . ." "Every man is brutish by *his* knowledge" (Jeremiah
51.17) represents Hebrew which KJ translates "Every man is brutish
in *his* knowledge" in Jeremiah 10.14. Neither of these renderings is
accepted by the revised versions or modern translations, however. RSV
reads in both cases, "Every man is stupid and without knowledge."

KJ occasionally uses "by" to translate the Greek preposition which
means "because of" or "for the sake of." In John 6.57, "by the Father"
and "by me" mean "because of the Father" and "because of me." "By
your tradition" (Matthew 15.3, 6) is "for the sake of your tradition."
"For the earth which drinketh in the rain that cometh oft upon it,
and bringeth forth herbs meet for them by whom it is dressed, receiveth blessing from God" (Hebrews 6.7) is more accurately translated, "For land which has drunk the rain that often falls upon it,
and brings forth vegetation useful to those for whose sake it is cultivated, receives a blessing from God."

**BY AND BY** is an adverbial phrase which in the fifteenth and sixteenth centuries meant immediately. Like "anon" and
"presently" it gradually lost this sense and came to mean soon, after
a while, or at some indefinite time in the future.

In Mark's account of the beheading of John the Baptist, KJ has an
odd contrast between the haste of Salome's coming before the king,
the immediacy of the king's answering command to the executioner,
and the leisurely tone of Salome's request that the head of John the
Baptist be given her "by and by" (6.25, 27). But this contrast is not in
the Greek. The adverb for Salome's coming in (vs. 25) and that for
the king's command (vs. 27) are the same—*euthus,* which means
immediately. But the adverb which Salome uses is even stronger—
*exautēs,* which means at once, instantly, at this very hour.

In the parable of the Sower (Matthew 13.21), Jesus said of the
hearer who is like stony ground that when persecution comes he immediately falls away; but KJ has "by and by he is offended." In Luke
17.7, KJ attaches the adverb wrongly. It reads: "Which of you, having a servant plowing or feeding cattle, will say unto him by and
by, when he is come from the field, Go and sit down to meat?" But

the adverb belongs to the last clause. RSV translates: "Will any one of you, who has a servant plowing or keeping sheep, say to him when he has come in from the field, 'Come at once and sit down at table'?"

That even an excellent modern dictionary can be misled by the archaic language of KJ is shown by the fact that the 1913 edition of the *Standard Dictionary*, defining "by and by" as "the hereafter," supported this definition by citing Luke 21.9, where KJ reads "the end *is* not by and by." But "by and by" is here an adverbial phrase which translates the Greek adverb *eutheōs*. RSV reads "the end will not be at once."

**BY COURSE** means "in turn" (1 Corinthians 14.27). The KJ rendering of this verse is, "If any man speak in an *unknown* tongue, *let it be* by two, or at the most *by* three, and *that* by course; and let one interpret." RSV reads, "If any speak in a tongue, let there be only two or at most three, and each in turn; and let one interpret."

**CABIN.** When Jeremiah was put in prison by the princes of Judah, according to KJ, he "was entered into the dungeon, and into the cabins" (Jeremiah 37.16). RSV translates "had come to the dungeon cells." The word "cabin" has always meant what it does now, but in the fourteenth to sixteenth centuries it was used also in the sense of "cell." Shakespeare made a verb of it in *Macbeth*, III, 4, 24: "But now I am cabin'd, cribb'd, confin'd, bound in To saucy doubts and fears." In 1616 *The Country Farm* described bees as "busie making combes, and building of little Cabbins."

**CANDLE, CANDLESTICK.** The "candlestick" which Moses was commanded to make for the tabernacle weighed about 108 pounds. It was of pure gold, hammered, with a base and shaft and six branches (Exodus 25.31–40). It had no candles. "Thou shalt make the seven lamps thereof," verse 37 says. Again and again, in the books of Exodus and Numbers, reference is made to the candlestick of pure gold, with its seven lamps, its vessels, and the oil for the light. But candles are never mentioned. This "candlestick" was a massive, beautifully wrought stand for seven lamps. And the various other candlesticks in KJ were also lampstands—including the seven which stood for the seven churches to which John was commissioned to write (Revelation 1.10–20).

The words which are used in the Hebrew Old Testament and in the

Greek New Testament mean "lamp" and "lampstand," and are so rendered by the revised versions. The introduction of "candle" and "candlestick" was a bit of modernization which reflects British ways of life in the fifteenth and sixteenth centuries.

Two well-known texts from Proverbs, as translated in RSV, are:

"The spirit of man is the lamp of the LORD,
    searching all his innermost parts." (20.27)
"The evil man has no future;
    the lamp of the wicked will be put out." (24.20)

**CANKER** in 2 Timothy 2.17 means gangrene, translating the Greek word from which the Latin *gangrena* and the English "gangrene" are derived. RSV translates the passage: "Avoid such godless chatter, for it will lead people into more and more ungodliness, and their talk will eat its way like gangrene."

**CANKERED** in James 5.3 is used in the obsolete sense of rusted. It translates a Greek verb which means to become rusty, tarnished, corroded. The revised versions agree in substituting "rusted" for "cankered." RSV reads: "Your gold and silver have rusted, and their rust will be evidence against you and will eat your flesh like fire. You have laid up treasure for the last days."

Shakespeare used "canker'd" in this sense in *King Henry IV, Part II*, IV, 5, 72:

"For this they have engrossed and piled up
The canker'd heaps of strange-achieved gold."

**CANKERWORM** means a caterpillar or an insect larva that destroys the buds and leaves of plants. It occurs as rendering for the Hebrew word *yeleq* in Joel 1.4; 2.25 and Nahum 3.15, 16. KJ has "caterpiller" for *yeleq* in Psalm 105.34 and Jeremiah 51.14, 27. In all these cases the reference is to locusts, and RSV so translates. In Joel, where four stages of the development of the locust are distinguished, RSV uses "hopping locust" and "hopper" for *yeleq*. In Jeremiah 51.27, for "rough caterpillers" it has "bristling locusts." (See PALMERWORM)

**CAPTIVITY** is used in KJ, not only to mean a state of imprisonment, subjection, or exile, but also to denote the people who are thus restrained. In this second sense, which is now obsolete, "the captivity" is a collective noun which means "the captives." "They carried away captive the whole captivity" (Amos 1.6) means "they carried into exile a whole people"; and "they delivered up the whole captivity to Edom" (Amos 1.9) means "they delivered up a whole people to Edom."

"I will bring again the captivity of my people of Israel" (Amos 9.14–15) does not mean that God will subject Israel again to captivity, but that he will bring back his captive people and "plant them upon their land." So also Jeremiah 30.3, 18; 33.11. The Hebrew idiom in these verses is used more than 30 times in the Old Testament, and is applied even to Job, who had not been in captivity or exile—"the LORD turned the captivity of Job" (42.10). In agreement with many modern scholars, RSV translates this idiom, "restore the fortunes of." It reads: "the LORD restored the fortunes of Job"; "I will restore the fortunes of my people"; "I will restore the fortunes of the tents of Jacob"; "I will restore the fortunes of the land as at first." Amos 9.14–15 reads:

"I will restore the fortunes of my people Israel,
    and they shall rebuild the ruined cities and inhabit them;
they shall plant vineyards and drink their wine,
    and they shall make gardens and eat their fruit.
I will plant them upon their land,
    and they shall never again be plucked up
    out of the land which I have given them."

"Arise, Barak, and lead thy captivity captive" simply means, "Arise, Barak, lead away your captives" (Judges 5.12). The Hebrew has here the repetition involved in a cognate accusative, the literal rendering of which would be "lead captive your captives." The same construction appears in Psalm 68.18, and in the quotation of this verse in Ephesians 4.8. RSV translates the latter, "When he ascended on high he led a host of captives, and he gave gifts to men." Professor Ernest F. Scott, in his volume of *The Moffatt Commentary*, page 207 writes: "The reference to 'taking captivity captive' (a Hebrew idiom for leading away one's prisoners) takes on a special significance in Paul's allegory. He understands it, apparently, of that spoiling of principalities and powers of which he spoke in Col. 2.15. By his death Christ conquered all that host of spirits which had conspired against him, and he is pictured as leading them captive in his train when he ascended."

**CARE, CAREFUL, CAREFULNESS.** These words may easily be misunderstood, for they appear in KJ not only in the sense of due concern, regard, or oversight, but also in the sense of anxiety or undue solicitude. When Jesus gently reproved Martha for being "careful . . . about many things," it was for being "anxious" (Luke 10.41). "Be careful for nothing" means "Have no anxiety about anything" (Philippians 4.6). "I would have you without carefulness" means "I want you to be free from anxieties" (1 Corinthians 7.32). But Paul was not free from anxiety himself; when he writes of "that which cometh upon me daily, the care of all the churches" (2 Corinthians 11.28), it means "the daily pressure upon me of my anxiety for all the churches." In all these cases we are dealing with the Greek words for anxiety or being anxious. In 1 Peter 5.7, "Casting all your care upon him; for he careth for you," the Greek words for "care" and "careth" are quite different. RSV translates "Cast all your anxieties on him, for he cares about you."

"Carefulness" is used in 2 Corinthians 7.11 to translate the Greek *spoudē*, which means haste, diligence, zeal. RSV here uses "earnestness"—"For see what earnestness this godly grief has produced in you!"

**CARRIAGE,** as used in the Bible, denotes what is carried, rather than the act of carrying or a vehicle by which persons or things are carried.

"After those days we took up our carriages and went up to Jerusalem" (Acts 21.15). Archbishop Trench, writing in 1859, quoted this text and went on to say: "A critic of the early part of this century makes himself merry with these words, and their inaccurate rendering of the original: 'It is not probable that the Cilician tent-maker was either so rich or so lazy.' And a more modern objector to the truthfulness of the Acts asks, 'How could they have taken up their carriages, when there was no road for wheels, nothing but a mountain track, between Caesarea and Jerusalem?' But 'carriage' is a constant word in the English of the sixteenth and seventeenth century for baggage, being that which men carry, and not, as now, that which carries them."

The use of the word "carriages" in this verse is peculiar to KJ. The Great Bible and the Bishops' Bible had "took up our burdens"; the Geneva Bible "trussed up our fardels"; the revised versions of 1881–1901 read "took up our baggage." All of these renderings are over-translations, for the Greek word means simply to get ready or prepare for. Tyndale's translation was "After those days we made ourselves ready, and went up to Jerusalem." RSV agrees with Tyndale, but omits the "ourselves"; it reads, "After these days we made ready and went up to Jerusalem."

When the six hundred Danites who despoiled the house of Micah departed, they "put the little ones and the cattle and the carriage before them" (Judges 18.21). The Hebrew word represented by "carriage" means abundance or riches; the revised versions here translate it by "goods." "David left his carriage in the hand of the keeper of the carriage" (1 Samuel 17.22) means "David left the things in charge of the keeper of the baggage."

"Laid up his carriages" (Isaiah 10.28) means "stores his baggage." "Your carriages *were* heavy loaden; *they are* a burden to the weary *beast*" (Isaiah 46.1) is more accurately translated, "these things you carry are loaded as burdens on weary beasts."

**CASTAWAY.** The noun "a castaway" is used in 1 Corinthians 9.27 as translation for the Greek adjective *adokimos*, which means rejected or unfit—the adjective applied to metals or coins that failed to meet the test. It is a misleading translation because "a castaway" suggests a shipwrecked mariner. In spite of the reference to boxing in verse 26, the dominant metaphor in verses 24 to 27 is that of a race. The word translated "preach" also means proclaim. Paul is saying that he does not want to be rejected or disqualified for the race to which he has exhorted others.

**CAST DOWN** appears in Daniel's description of his vision: "I beheld till the thrones were cast down, and the Ancient of days did sit" (Daniel 7.9). It is a mistaken translation of the Aramaic, however. Coverdale, Matthew, and the Great Bible had "till the seates were prepared." The Geneva Bible and the Bishops' Bible had "till the thrones were set up." The Greek Septuagint and the Latin Vulgate have verbs which mean "were placed." Martin Luther had *bis dass Stühle gesetzt wurden.* KJ stands alone in the rendering "cast down," and the revised versions agree in "were placed." RSV translates verses 9 and 10: "As I looked,

thrones were placed
and one that was ancient of days took his seat;
his raiment was white as snow,
and the hair of his head like pure wool;
his throne was fiery flames,
its wheels were burning fire.
A stream of fire issued
and came forth from before him;
a thousand thousands served him,
and ten thousand times ten thousand stood before him."

**CAST IN HIS TEETH.** In Matthew 27.44 KJ reads: "The thieves also, which were crucified with him, cast the same in his teeth." In Mark 15.32 it has for the same Greek verb and pronoun, "reviled him." The discrepancy goes back to Tyndale, who used "cast in his teeth" in Matthew, and "checked him" in Mark.

The Greek verb is *oneidizō,* which means to revile, reproach, or upbraid. Tyndale used "revile" in Matthew 5.11—"when men revile you"—and "upbraid" in Matthew 11.20—"upbraid the cities"—and at these points his translation has been retained in all subsequent versions.

He was not so fortunate in his rendering of James 1.5: "If any of you lack wisdom, let him ask of God which giveth to all men indifferently, and casteth no man in the teeth: and it shall be given him." Or in his rendering of Mark 16.14: "After that he appeared unto the eleven as they sat at meat, and cast in their teeth their unbelief and hardness of heart, because they believed not them which had seen him after his resurrection."

These texts in Tyndale are the earliest to be cited in OED as examples of a "cast in the teeth" idiom. The form used in James, to cast *a person* in the teeth, is marked as obsolete, with no example cited later than 1642. The form used in Matthew and Mark, to cast *something* in the teeth of a person, is still current English.

Tyndale's use of this idiom in Matthew 27.44, Mark 16.14, and James 1.5 was retained by the Great Bible, the Geneva Bible, and the Bishops' Bible. KJ dropped it for "upbraid" in Mark and James, but kept it in Matthew. The revised versions have dropped it completely; RSV reads "The robbers who were crucified with him also reviled him in the same way."

**CERTAINTY** is used three times in the obsolete sense of the truth, the actual facts, the real circumstances. "That thou mightest know the certainty of those things, wherein thou hast been instructed" (Luke 1.4) means "that you may know the truth concerning the things of which you have been informed." "When he could not know the certainty for the tumult" (Acts 21.34) means "as he could not learn the facts because of the uproar." "Because he would have known the certainty wherefore he was accused of the Jews" (22.30) means "desiring to know the real reason why the Jews accused him."

Shakespeare used "certainty" in this sense in *Hamlet,* IV, 5, 140: "If you desire to know the certainty Of your dear father's death." Laertes did not doubt that his father was dead, but he did not know the facts concerning his death.

A cumbrous rendering is Proverbs 22.21: "That I might make thee know the certainty of the words of truth; that thou mightest answer the words of truth to them that send unto thee." RSV translates:
"to show you what is right and true,
   that you may give a true answer to those who sent you."

**CERTIFY** means to assure, to attest, to declare by a formal or legal certificate. It is too weighty and formal a term to serve as translation for the Hebrew words in the few passages where it appears in KJ Old Testament. "Esther certified the king *thereof*" stands for Hebrew which means simply "Esther told the king" (Esther 2:22). So too in 2 Samuel 15.28 and Ezra 4.14, 16; 5.10; 7.24, "inform," "notify," "make known" are sufficient translations of the Hebrew verbs. In Galatians 1.11 the Greek verb means to make known, to reveal, without any implication of formal attestation.

**CHAFED** occurs in Hushai's counsel to Absalom, 2 Samuel 17.8: "thou knowest thy father and his men, and they *be* mighty men, and they *be* chafed in their minds, as a bear robbed of her whelps in the field." This is as good an example as any of language which some people relish as being quaintly pleasing. To think of a she-bear, robbed of her cubs—or whelps, which is quainter—as being "chafed" over it, is amusing and not particularly misleading. The question is whether this incidental pleasure in style is valid. Does it strengthen or weaken the essential message? The answer of scholars is unanimous: such vagaries, however pleasant, are not harmless; they distract the reader and diminish the force of the text. In 2 Samuel 17.8 the Hebrew word is *mar*, which means "bitter." To chafe means originally to heat, surviving only in our "chafing dish." It early developed the abstract meaning of heating the mind or soul, hence to enrage. Then by a dwindling process it comes to suggest fretting, and much later the modern "irritation by rubbing." "Hot and bothered" would do very well as a slang rendering of "chafed." RSV reads, "You know that your father and his men are mighty men, and that they are enraged, like a bear robbed of her cubs in the field."

**CHALLENGE.** Overworked today, this word occurs only once in KJ: "any manner of lost thing, which *another* challengeth to be his" (Exodus 22.9). The revised versions translate the Hebrew literally. ASV has "any manner of lost thing, whereof one saith, This is it." RSV has "any kind of lost thing, of which one says, 'This is it.' "

"Challenge" was used here in the now obsolete sense of claim, assert one's title or right to something. Shakespeare has it thus in *King Richard II*, II, 3, 134: "I am a subject, and I challenge law." OED quotes Sir Thomas Herbert: "I challenge no thankes for what I publish" (1634). Especially clear is its quotation from Smollett: "An injured friend!—who challenges the name? If you, what Title justifies the claim?" (1746).

**CHAMBERING.** An obsolete word, dating from Tyndale, for sexual excesses. It appears in Romans 13.13: "Let us walk honestly, as in the day; not in rioting and drunkenness, not in chambering and wantonness, not in strife and envying." The Greek word here is a euphemism for sexual indulgence: it appears in the plural and is linked with the Greek word for licentious behavior, also in the plural. RSV translates the verse: "let us conduct ourselves becomingly as in the day, not in reveling and drunkenness, not in debauchery and licentiousness, not in quarreling and jealousy." (See LASCIVIOUSNESS)

**CHAMPAIGN.** An old French word for open level country, a plain. It appears only in Deuteronomy 11.30, where it was spelled "champion" in the 1611 edition. It serves as translation for the Hebrew *arabah*, which KJ uses as a proper name in Joshua 18.18, and elsewhere translates as "desert," "plain," or "wilderness." The revised versions use "Arabah" as a proper name for the depression which includes the Jordan valley, the Dead Sea, and the land leading southward from the Dead Sea to the Gulf of Aqaba. The Dead Sea is referred to as "the sea of the Arabah" in Deuteronomy 3.17; 4.49; Joshua 3.16; 12.3; 2 Kings 14.25, where KJ calls it "the sea of the plain."

**CHANGEABLE.** The "changeable suits of apparel" included in Isaiah's list of feminine finery (Isaiah 3.22) were outer garments for festal occasions, "changeable" in the sense that they would be worn or taken off and laid away as the occasion required. It is not to be understood that they were made of changeable silk or other fabrics that would show different colors under different aspects. RSV calls them "festal robes." The same Hebrew word is used in Zechariah's vision of the high priest being accused by Satan before the angel of the LORD (Zechariah 3.4). It is there contrasted with "filthy garments" and is translated "change of raiment" by KJ and "rich apparel" by RSV.

The "changes of raiment" which Joseph gave to his brothers were festal garments (Genesis 45.22). So likewise were the "thirty change of garments" which Samson wagered (Judges 14.12, 13, 19), and the garments which Naaman brought as a royal gift from the king of Syria to the king of Israel (2 Kings 5.5, 22, 23). Note, in the KJ account of Samson, that the singular form "change" is used as plural.

**CHAPITER** is an architectural term which appears 28 times in KJ. It means the capital or head of a column or pillar, and OED states that it is still an occasional equivalent of "capital." ASV, RSV, and most modern translations use "capital" in its place. The word occurs most often in 1 Kings 7.16–42.

**CHAPMEN.** The King James Version uses this word once (2 Chronicles 9.14), in a passage which states that "the weight of gold that came to Solomon in one year was six hundred and threescore and six talents of gold; Beside *that which* chapmen and merchants brought. . . ." In the parallel passage (1 Kings 10.15) the Hebrew expression for "chapmen" is translated "merchantmen." Literally, it means "men who go about seeking." The revised versions use "traders" in both passages. These men were the traveling buyers and sellers, the explorers and adventurers, of Solomon's far-flung commercial interests. "Chapmen" was not a good translation even in 1611, for the word had begun to lose its original significance as merchant, trader, or dealer, and to be used for itinerant hawkers and peddlers. A "chapbook" was a small pamphlet of popular tales, ballads, tracts, etc., as hawked about by chapmen. The cheap repute of chapmen is reflected in Shakespeare's lines:

"Not utter'd by base sale of chapmen's tongues."
*Love's Labour's Lost*, II, 1, 16
"Fair Diomed, you do as chapmen do,
Dispraise the thing that you desire to buy."
*Troilus and Cressida*, IV, 1, 75

**CHAPT.** "The ground is chapt" is a vivid detail of Jeremiah's picture of the drought in Judah (Jeremiah 14.4). It is peculiar to KJ, for the translations from Coverdale to the Bishops' Bible had "dryed up," the Geneva Bible had "destroyed," and the revised versions of

1885–1901 used "cracked." None of these expressions reproduce the Hebrew, which here employs its own figure of speech, and says "the ground is dismayed." RSV accepts this wording, and to that extent blurs the picture.

**CHARGE,** whether as noun or verb, is used by KJ in senses that are still current or readily understood. There is an archaic flavor to "at his own charges" (1 Corinthians 9.7) and "be at charges with them" (Acts 21.24); RSV has "at his own expense" and "pay their expenses." The Hebrew verb which means to cause (one) to take an oath is rendered "charge with an oath" in Numbers 5.21 and 1 Samuel 14.28; RSV changes the first of these passages to "make the woman take the oath," but retains the second. The same verb is rendered simply "charge" in the Song of Solomon 2.7; 3.5; 5.8, 9; 8.4, and is translated "adjure" by the revised versions. "Let not the church be charged" is more accurately translated "let the church not be burdened" (1 Timothy 5.16). "These things give in charge" means "Command this" (1 Timothy 5.7).

Stephen's dying prayer, "Lord, lay not this sin to their charge" is clear English (Acts 7.60), but RSV has rejected this idiom for a more literal rendering, "Lord, do not hold this sin against them." Compare Acts 23.29, "charged with nothing deserving death"; Romans 8.33, "Who shall bring any charge against God's elect?" and 2 Timothy 4.16, "May it not be charged against them!" In two other cases more is involved than a choice of English idiom; the revised versions give a more accurate rendering of the Hebrew in Deuteronomy 21.8 and Psalm 35.11. With the second of these texts compare Exodus 23.1. The KJ version of Psalm 35.11 is: "False witnesses did rise up; they laid to my charge *things* that I knew not." RSV reads:

"Malicious witnesses rise up;
they ask me of things that I know not."

In 1 Kings 11.28 it is said that Solomon made the young man Jeroboam "ruler over all the charge of the house of Joseph." But the Hebrew represented by "made him ruler" means "gave him charge" and the word represented by "charge" means "forced labor." RSV reads: "The man Jeroboam was very able, and when Solomon saw that the young man was industrious he gave him charge over all the forced labor of the house of Joseph."

**CHARGEABLE** means "burdensome" in KJ, and refers to persons rather than to commodities or accusations. King David refused Absalom's invitation to his sheepshearing "lest we be chargeable

unto thee" (2 Samuel 13.25); RSV "lest we be burdensome to you."
The governors before Nehemiah "were chargeable unto the people,"
which means that they "laid heavy burdens upon the people" (Nehemiah 5.15). Paul reminds the Thessalonians that he worked night
and day, that he "might not be chargeable" to any of them (1 Thessalonians 2.9; 2 Thessalonians 3.8); RSV "might not burden any of
you." "I was chargeable to no man" (2 Corinthians 11.9) means "I
did not burden any one"; the same verb is translated "be burdensome"
by KJ itself in 12.13, 14.

**CHARGER.** An old term, derived from the French, for a platter large
enough to be loaded with roast meat to be carved and
served. The daughter of Herodias, prompted by her mother, asked
Herod to give her the head of John the Baptist on such a platter (Matthew 14.8, 11; Mark 6.25, 28). The "twelve chargers of silver" which
headed the offerings of the twelve tribes of Israel for the dedication
of the altar (Numbers 7) were "twelve silver plates," each silver plate
weighing a hundred and thirty shekels. The "thirty chargers of gold"
at the head of the list of the vessels which Cyrus king of Persia restored
to the house of the LORD in Jerusalem, were "a thousand basins of
gold" (Ezra 1.9–11).

**CHECK.** The noun "check" is used once (Job 20.3), in the obsolete
sense of reproof, censure, or rebuke. In place of "the check
of my reproach," ASV has "the reproof which putteth me to shame,"
and RSV has "censure which insults me." Coverdale in the *Paraphrase
of Erasmus upon the Newe Testament*, Romans 12.17, has: "Yf any
man perhappes offende you, gyue not checke for checke, ne one wrong
for an other." In Shakespeare's *King Lear*, I, 3, 20, Goneril says
concerning her father,

> "Old fools are babes again; and must be used
> With checks as flatteries."

**CHIDE** appears seven times in KJ. It means rebuke, and is retained
by RSV only once—"He will not always chide, nor will he
keep his anger for ever" (Psalm 103.9). In the other passages, it has
the obsolete sense of contend, wrangle, or scold, with loud and angry
words. For the past tense, KJ employs "chode" twice and "did chide"
twice. RSV has "Jacob . . . upbraided Laban" (Genesis 31.36) and
"they upbraided him violently" (Judges 8.1); "the people contended
with Moses" (Numbers 20.3). In the account of the incident at Meribah
which became a tradition often mentioned among the Hebrew people,

RSV has "the people found fault with Moses" and "faultfinding" (Exodus 17.2, 7).

**CHIEFEST.** The Oxford English Dictionary quotes Samuel Johnson's definition of "chief" as "of the first order," and states that in this use it had the comparative "chiefer" and the superlative "chiefest." The superlative is used eight times in KJ, representing seven different Hebrew and Greek terms. Doeg, "the chiefest of the herdmen that *belonged* to Saul," was "the chief of Saul's herdsmen" (1 Samuel 21.7). The sin of the sons of Eli, "to make yourselves fat with the chiefest of all the offerings of Israel my people," is more clearly described by RSV, "fattening yourselves upon the choicest parts of every offering of my people Israel" (1 Samuel 2.29). Samuel placed Saul "at the head of those who had been invited" (1 Samuel 9.22). Hezekiah was buried "in the ascent of the tombs of the sons of David" (2 Chronicles 32.33). The young woman in the Song of Solomon declares that her beloved is "distinguished among ten thousand"—the Hebrew word means that he is as conspicuous as a banner (5.10). In Mark 10.44 the Greek means "whoever would be first among you."

Paul's claim to be "not a whit behind the very chiefest apostles" (2 Corinthians 11.5; 12.11) must be understood in the light of the context. The KJ translation of 11.2–6 is misleading at several points, and these verses should be read in RSV to be understood. The Greek word represented by "very chiefest" is a compound which means literally "super-exceedingly"—it is an adverb used as an adjective. The KJ rendering assumes that Paul is referring to the original apostles, Jesus' own companions; RSV accepts the view of those modern scholars who hold that he is referring to his opponents in Corinth. RSV translates "I think that I am not in the least inferior to these superlative apostles."

**CHOLER.** An old word for anger which Shakespeare often used. It appears in Daniel 8.7, "he was moved with choler," and 11.11, "the king of the south shall be moved with choler." RSV has "was enraged" and "moved with anger." Derived from the Greek *cholos* or *cholē*, which meant both bile and bitter anger, "choler" has the same double meaning. It was one of the "four humors" of the body, according to early physiology, the other three being *sanguis*, *melancolia*, and *phlegma*. The relative balance of these "cardinal humors," which were bodily fluids, was believed to determine a person's temperament and disposition.

**CHURCH** translates the Greek word *ekklēsia*, which is used in the
Septuagint of the Old Testament for the congregation of
the Israelites, and in the New Testament for the congregation of Christian believers. It applies to a local congregation or to the church universal, the body of Christ, to which all who have faith in him belong. The word is not used in the Bible as a name for the building in which believers gather for worship. Paul's advice to some to "keep silence in the church" refers not to a building but to an assembly of Christians for prayer and edification (1 Corinthians 14.26–35). "The church in the wilderness" (Acts 7.38) is better translated "the congregation in the wilderness." The Greek word which KJ renders by "robbers of churches" means either "temple robbers" or "sacrilegious" (Acts 19.37).

**CHURL, CHURLISH.** The adjective "churlish" fits Nabal perfectly
(1 Samuel 25.3), as the translation of a Hebrew adjective which means hard, severe, stubborn, rough, rude. For the corresponding Greek adjective the expression "a hard man" is equally appropriate in the parable of the Talents (Matthew 25.24). But Nabal was more than hard; he was mean, niggardly, bad-tempered, drunken, and a fool—churlish is an apt understatement concerning him.

The noun "churl" is not appropriate in the one passage where it appears, Isaiah 32.5–7. The Hebrew word which it is there intended to represent means one who is crafty, wily, deceitful, knavish. Instead of "The vile person shall be no more called liberal, nor the churl said *to be* bountiful," RSV translates "The fool will no more be called noble, nor the knave said to be honorable." Instead of "the instruments . . . of the churl," RSV has "the knaveries of the knave," reproducing the wordplay of the Hebrew, where *kelai* means knave and *keli* means instrument, implement, or weapon.

**CIEL, CIELING** are obsolete spellings of CEIL, CEILING. "Cieled"
is used four times in the obsolete sense of having walls lined or paneled with wood. In the description of Solomon's temple, it is said that "the greater house he cieled with fir tree" (2 Chronicles 3.5). The Hebrew verb which is represented here by "cieled" means to cover or overlay, and is translated by "overlaid" in the second clause of this verse and also in verses 7, 8, and 9. RSV translates verse 5, "The nave he lined with cypress, and covered it with fine gold. . . ."

The temple in Ezekiel's vision, "cieled with wood round about" (Ezekiel 41.16), was "paneled with wood round about." The word of the LORD by Haggai the prophet (Haggai 1.4) is translated by RSV: "Is it a time for you yourselves to dwell in your paneled houses, while this house lies in ruins?" Compare KJ and RSV renderings of Jeremiah 22.13–14.

"Ceiling" occurs in its modern sense (1 Kings 6.15). For "walls of the cieling" RSV accepts the rendering of the Greek Septuagint, "rafters of the ceiling."

**CLEAN,** as an adverb, means entirely, quite, completely. In Joshua 3.17; 4.1, 11 it is used for the Hebrew verb which means "finish"; "were clean passed over Jordan" is more literally translated "had finished passing over the Jordan." In three passages, Zechariah 11.17, Joel 1.7, and Isaiah 24.19, "clean" is used to express the emphasis or intensity of meaning which the Hebrew conveys by repeating the verb, using both the absolute infinitive and a finite form. (See GENERALLY and SURELY for an explanation of this Hebrew idiom.) "His arm shall be clean dried up" is more accurately translated, "Let his arm be wholly withered!" "Hath made it clean bare" means "has stripped off their bark." "The earth is clean dissolved" represents Hebrew which is better translated, "the earth is rent asunder."

"Is his mercy clean gone for ever? doth *his* promise fail for evermore?" (Psalm 77.8) is strong, effective English, but presents problems to the translator who may wish to retain it. "Is clean gone" does not represent an intensive Hebrew idiom in this case, but simply the verb which means "has ceased." "Mercy" represents the Hebrew word that is more accurately translated by "steadfast love." "Fail" is an ambiguous rendering for the verb that means "come to an end." RSV translates:

"Has his steadfast love for ever ceased?
Are his promises at an end for all time?"

In 2 Peter 2.18 "those that were clean escaped from them who live in error" is reworded by RSV, "men who have barely escaped from those who live in error." Like the other revised versions, RSV is based here upon the ancient manuscripts which contain the Greek adverb for "barely" instead of that for "clean."

**CLIFT** is an earlier form of "cleft." It occurs twice in KJ: "I will put thee in a clift of the rock" (Exodus 33.22), and "in the valleys under the clifts of the rocks" (Isaiah 57.5). The revised versions use "cleft" and "clefts." OED gives evidence that in the sixteenth to eighteenth centuries these words were confused with "cliff," but that confusion is not apparent in KJ. "The cliff of Ziz" means "the ascent of Ziz" (2 Chronicles 20.16), and "the cliffs of the valleys" means "the gullies of the torrents" (Job 30.6). Shakespeare uses "cleft" only as the past tense or participle of the verb "cleave"; he uses "cliff" in its normal sense, and "clift" not at all.

**CLOSE.** "The strangers shall fade away, and be afraid out of their close places" is reworded in RSV: "Foreigners lost heart, and came trembling out of their fastnesses" (Psalm 18.45 = 2 Samuel 22.46). In Micah 7.17 the Hebrew word for "close places" is translated "holes" by KJ and "strongholds" by RSV. The revised versions of 1885–1901 used "close places" in all three passages; it would have been better if RSV had used "strongholds" in all. Micah 7.17 is rendered in KJ: "They shall lick the dust like a serpent, they shall move out of their holes like worms of the earth: they shall be afraid of the LORD our God, and shall fear because of thee." In RSV it reads:

> "they shall lick the dust like a serpent,
>     like the crawling things of the earth;
> they shall come trembling out of their strongholds,
>     they shall turn in dread to the LORD our God,
>     and they shall fear because of thee."

"They kept *it* close, and told no man in those days any of those things which they had seen" means "they kept silence . . ." (Luke 9.36). In the preface to the King James Version, entitled "The Translators to the Reader," they put the question: "How shall they understand that which is kept close in an unknown tongue?"

**CLOSET** is used three times in KJ and means a private room. The Hebrew word in Joel 2.16, "and the bride out of her closet," is translated "chamber" by KJ in Psalm 19.5, "a bridegroom coming out of his chamber." To the reader of today, with a pinched idea of a closet, this discrimination between bridegroom and bride seems hardly fair. RSV remedies that, and translates the Hebrew consistently, by using "chamber" in each case.

The Greek word for which KJ has "closet" in Matthew 6.6 and Luke 12.3 means private room, inner room, or storeroom. It occurs also at Matthew 24.26 and Luke 12.24, where KJ translates it "the secret chambers" and "storehouse."

"Closet" is an ambiguous and misleading word in Matthew 6.6—"enter into thy closet, and when thou hast shut the door, pray to thy Father which is in secret." The sixteenth-century translations, from

Tyndale to the first edition of the Bishops' Bible, had "enter into thy chamber." The unknown editor of the second edition of the Bishops' Bible was responsible for "closet," which the KJ translators accepted. RSV reads: "But when you pray, go into your room and shut the door and pray to your Father who is in secret; and your Father who sees in secret will reward you."

**CLOTHED UPON.** "To be clothed upon" is an awkward literalism for the Greek verb which means to put on a garment over other garments, 2 Corinthians 5.2, 4. Wyclif used "clothed above," and Rheims "overclothed." Tyndale used "clothed with" in verse 2 and "clothed upon" in verse 4; and was followed by the other sixteenth-century versions. RSV has "to put on" in verse 2, and "be further clothed" in verse 4. What Paul desires, says Floyd Filson in *The Interpreter's Bible* (vol. 10, p. 327), is "to put the new garment on over the old, i.e., to receive the promised spiritual body without having to take off the old physical body by death. He wants the end of the age to come before he dies; then he will be transformed without having to die."

**CLOUT** is an old word for a rag, a piece of cloth that has been torn off or is put to humble uses. Such words as breechclout and dishclout are not yet obsolete, but have been almost displaced by breechcloth and dishcloth. In Jeremiah 38.11, not "under the treasury" but in "a wardrobe of the storehouse," Ebed-melech the Ethiopian found "old cast clouts and rotten rags" which he lowered to Jeremiah in the dungeon. The revised versions of 1885–1901 call these "rags and worn-out garments"; RSV "old rags and worn-out clothes." In *King John,* III, 4, 58 Shakespeare has "a babe of clouts," which means a rag doll.

**CLOUTED** means patched. The inhabitants of Gibeon, pretending to have come from a far country, went to Joshua with "old shoes and clouted upon their feet, and old garments upon them" (Joshua 9.5). RSV has "with worn-out, patched sandals on their feet, and worn-out clothes." The rebel Jack Cade, in Shakespeare's *King Henry VI, Part II,* IV, 2, 192 exhorts his followers:

> "And you that love the commons, follow me.
> Now show yourselves men: 'tis for liberty.
> We will not leave one lord, one gentleman:
> Spare none but such as go in clouted shoon."

**COAST.** In his essay "On a Fresh Revision of the New Testament," Bishop Lightfoot, referring to the archaic terms in the language of KJ, wrote: "Among these misleading archaisms the word 'coast' for 'border' or 'region' is perhaps the most frequent. It would be unreasonable to expect the English reader to understand that when St. Paul 'passes through the upper coasts' on his way to Ephesus (Acts 19.1) he does in fact traverse the high land which lies in the interior of Asia Minor. Again, in the Gospels, when he reads of our Lord visiting 'the coasts of Tyre and Sidon' (Matthew 15.21; Mark 7.31) he naturally thinks of the sea-board, knowing these to be maritime cities, whereas the word in one passage stands for 'parts,' and in the other for 'borders,' and the circumstances suggest rather the eastern than the western frontier of the region. And perhaps also his notions of the geography of Palestine may be utterly confused by reading that Capernaum is situated 'upon the sea-coast' (Matthew 4.13)."

The revised versions replace the words "coast" and "coasts," in their obsolete senses, with the terms appropriate to the context, such as border, boundary, country, territory, area, region, land. "Coast" is retained only when the reference is to the land bordering on the sea.

**COCKATRICE** is the word which KJ uses in Isaiah 11.8; 14.29; 59.5 and Jeremiah 8.17 for the Hebrew *tsepha* or *tsiphoni,* a venomous serpent. RV changed this to "basilisk." In Proverbs 23.32 KJ uses "adder" as the English translation for *tsiphoni*—"At the last it biteth like a serpent, and stingeth like an adder." ASV and RSV use "adder" in all five passages.

"The sense-history of this word is exceedingly curious," says OED, and summarizes it in a full column of fine print which is an amazing account of the vagaries of human credulity. It finally defines "cockatrice" as "a serpent, identified with the *basilisk,* fabulously said to kill by its mere glance, and to be hatched from a cock's egg." In heraldry it was figured as "a hybrid monster with the head, wings, and feet of a cock, terminating in a serpent with a barbed tail." Shakespeare refers to "cockatrice" or "basilisk" a dozen times. Tarquin delivers his threat to Lucrece "with a cockatrice' dead-killing eye" (*Rape of Lucrece,* 540).

Wyclif, translating from the Latin Vulgate, used "cockatrice" in the Isaiah texts and in Psalm 91.13. Coverdale, following Martin Luther's *Basilisken,* used "cockatrice" in the Isaiah texts and Jeremiah 8.17. The Geneva Bible was the only sixteenth-century version to use "cockatrice" in Proverbs 23.32 as well—"In the end thereof it wil bite like a serpent and hurt like a cockatrise." The Great Bible and the Bishops' Bible used "adder" in Isaiah 14.29; but KJ reverted to the practice of Coverdale. Neither "cockatrice" nor "basilisk" really has any place in a translation of the Hebrew text of the Bible, for the notions associated with these words were of Latin origin and medieval growth.

**COLLECTION** is, in one specific meaning, "the action of collecting money for a religious or charitable purpose, or to defray expenses, especially at a religious or public meeting; also concretely the money so collected" (OED). In common usage it is too slight a term for the two contexts in which it appears in KJ. In 2 Chronicles 24.6, 9 it stands for "the tax that Moses the servant of God laid upon Israel in the wilderness" (Exodus 30.11–16). In 1 Corinthians 16.1–2 "collection" and "gatherings" stand for the singular and plural of the same Greek word, and refer to the "contribution for the poor among the saints at Jerusalem," the relief fund to which Paul gave much attention in A.D. 53–56. Chapters 8 and 9 of 2 Corinthians, when freed from the archaisms of the old translation, stand forth as a striking, cogent appeal to givers who are in danger of delaying, or even of failing, to fulfil their pledges. In Romans 15.25–28 Paul writes that he is going to Jerusalem with this aid before he can turn westward toward Rome and Spain.

**COLLEGE.** Huldah the prophetess "dwelt in Jerusalem in the college" (2 Kings 22.14; 2 Chronicles 34.22). But "college" is an erroneous translation of the Hebrew *mishneh*, which means the second quarter or district. This word occurs also in Zephaniah 1.10, where KJ translates it "the second." The rendering "college" came from the Geneva Bible, and is ultimately traceable to confusion of *mishneh* with the post-Biblical word *mishnah,* the collection of binding precepts that is the basis of the Talmud and embodies the oral law of Judaism. The revised versions have gotten rid of "the college" and translate *mishneh* "the second quarter."

In justice to the KJ translators of 1611 it should be stated that while they took "in the colledge" for the text, they added a marginal note, "Or, in the schoole, or in the second part."

**COLLOPS** are slices of meat, rashers of bacon, or thick folds of fat upon the body. "Maketh collops of fat on *his* flanks" (Job 15.27) is a vivid translation of Hebrew for which ASV and RSV have "gathered fat upon his loins." (See FLANKS)

**COME BY.** When Paul's ship was caught and driven by a tempestuous northeaster, "we had much work to come by the boat" (Acts 27.16). That seems to mean that the boat had broken loose and was adrift. The Greek, however, means simply that it was hard to control the boat and make it secure. RV and ASV have "we were able, with difficulty, to secure the boat"; RSV "we managed with difficulty to secure the boat."

**COMFORT** comes from the Latin *conforto,* which means to strengthen. Though it was sometimes applied to things or animals, the primary reference of the word is to the strengthening of human beings in body and spirit. Hence the verb "comfort" has various meanings: strengthen, encourage, support, aid, refresh, relieve, soothe, console, make comfortable. The first six of these meanings are now obsolete, except for legal usage and such phrases as "give aid and comfort to the enemy."

Early usage is seen in these examples from Wyclif:

Isaiah 41.7: "he coumfortide hym with nailes."

Psalm 147.13: "he coumfortede the lockis of thi gatis."

Luke 1.80: "the child wexed, and was counfortid in spirit."

Philippians 4.13: "I may alle thingis in him that comfortith me."

In these passages Tyndale and Coverdale used "fastened," "strengthened," "waxed strong," "strengtheneth," and were followed by KJ.

As verb and noun, the word "comfort" is used more than a hundred times in KJ. It is retained by RSV where the meaning is to console or relieve from distress; but it is replaced in the many cases where the meaning is to strengthen, refresh, encourage, exhort, or cheer. Examples are: "by the encouragement of the scriptures" (Romans 15.4); "all may learn and all be encouraged" (1 Corinthians 14.31); "encourage the fainthearted" (1 Thessalonians 5.14); "that their hearts may be encouraged" (Colossians 2.2); "that we may be mutually encouraged" (Romans 1.12); "any incentive of love" (Philippians 2.1); "that I may be cheered" (Philippians 2.19); "heed my appeal" (2 Corinthians 13.11).

**COMFORTABLE.** "Comfortable words" (Zechariah 1.13) are "comforting words." In 2 Samuel 14.17, however, "the word . . . shall now be comfortable" is used to represent a quite different Hebrew expression, which is better translated, "the word . . . will set me at rest."

In the Order for Holy Communion, "the most comfortable Sacrament of the Body and Blood of Christ" and "what comfortable words our Saviour Christ saith," the word "comfortable" is used in the sense of strengthening and inspiring. Though the note of consolation is present, it is not primary. The same is to be said of the words of invitation, "take this holy Sacrament to your comfort." And it should be unnecessary to say that nothing of ease or complacency is here implied.

**COMFORTABLY** is used five times in KJ, always with the verb "speak." It stands for a Hebrew phrase which means "to the heart." RSV lets the English be determined by the context and uses "kindly" (2 Samuel 19.7); "encouragingly" (2 Chronicles 30.22 and 32.6); and "tenderly" (Isaiah 40.2; Hosea 2.14).

**COMFORTER** is a title of the Holy Spirit, translating the Greek term *paraklētos,* used four times in Jesus' parting talk with his disciples, John 14.16, 26; 15.26; 16.7. Jerome left it untranslated in the Latin Vulgate, and the word has passed into the English language as "Paraclete." Wyclif translated it as "coumfortour," however, and Tyndale as "comforter." It was capitalized in the Geneva Bible and KJ.

The Greek word *paraklētos* is translated "advocate" in 1 John 2.1, where it is applied to Jesus Christ himself. It means one who is called; Bishop Samuel Hinds wrote that the call may be "for any purpose of need, whether to strengthen, to console, to guide, to instruct, to plead and intercede for, or otherwise to aid." As applied to the Holy Spirit, RSV translates it "Counselor."

**COMFORTLESS.** A rendering of John 14.18, "I will not leave you comfortless," which goes back to the beginning of the fifteenth century. The Greek word for "comfortless" is *orphanos,* and a literal translation would be "I will not leave you orphans." The meaning is not unconsoled or without comforts, but bereft and destitute. The revised versions use "desolate."

**COMMUNE.** As applied to the interchange of thoughts and attitudes in conversation, the verb "commune" was a colorless term in the sixteenth century. But it now implies an interchange which has a measure of intimacy and a high level of artistic or spiritual content. We would no longer use the word "commune" to describe ordinary conversation or talk that is low or quarrelsome or malicious. The result of this change in English usage is that RSV retains the word in only 2 of the 28 instances of its use by KJ.

For example, where the Psalmist says of the wicked: "They encourage themselves *in* an evil matter; they commune of laying snares privily" (64.5), the present version reads:

"They hold fast to their evil purpose;
they talk of laying snares secretly."

When the scribes and Pharisees were angered by Jesus' attitude toward the sabbath (Luke 6.11), it is stated that "they were filled with madness, and communed with one another what they might do to Jesus." RSV has changed this to read, "they were filled with fury and discussed with one another what they might do to Jesus."

The account in KJ of Judas' bargain to betray Jesus reads (Luke 22.3–6): "Then entered Satan into Judas surnamed Iscariot, being of the number of the twelve. And he went his way, and communed with the chief priests and captains, how he might betray him unto them. And they were glad, and covenanted to give him money. And he promised, and sought opportunity to betray him unto them in the absence of the multitude." It is curious to note the high terms in which this treasonable transaction is described—Judas "communed" with the priests, they "covenanted" with him, he "promised" them. These are words of honor; they do not fit the scene. RSV is more faithful to the Greek, and better describes the situation, by using more objective terms—Judas "conferred" with the priests, they "engaged" to give him money, and he "agreed."

The two passages where the present version retains the word "commune" are Psalms 4.4 and 77.6, both of which are concerned with meditation.

**COMMUNICATE, COMMUNICATION.** KJ uses the verb "communicate" six times and the noun "communication" seven times; but in each case the RSV has chosen another word as a more accurate translation. To say that Paul "communicated" to the heads of the church in Jerusalem the gospel which he was preaching among the Gentiles (Galatians 2.2), fails to describe the situation, for the Greek says that he "laid it before them" with a view to coming to an agreement concerning the most far-reaching question of principle and policy that the church ever faced. In all other cases where it is used in KJ, the verb "communicate" has the sense of "share." It refers, not to words, but to fellowship and generous action.

"To do good and to communicate forget not" (Hebrews 13.16) means "Do not neglect to do good and to share what you have." Paul's injunction to the Galatians (6.6), "Let him that is taught in the word communicate unto him that teacheth in all good things," means "Let him who is taught the word share all good things with him who teaches." When Paul wrote to the Philippians (4.14) "Ye have well done, that ye did communicate with my affliction," he did not refer to letters of sympathy, but to gifts of material aid, as the succeeding verses make perfectly clear. This verse is now translated, "It was kind of you to share my trouble."

In one case the use of the word "communication" is misleading. It is the often-quoted text in 1 Corinthians 15.33, "Evil communications corrupt good manners." That was a copybook maxim in my public-school days which I am sure I copied a thousand times, and I thought that "evil communications" meant profane or obscene language. But the Greek word used here is more comprehensive; it refers to the whole body of social influences, the companionships and associations, in which oral conversation and written communications play only a part. And what is at stake is more than good manners, it is moral character. The Greek word is the one from which the English word "ethics" is derived. The present translation is, "Bad company ruins good morals."

**COMPACTED** means "knit together," in the one passage where it appears (Ephesians 4.15–16). RSV translates these verses: "Speaking the truth in love, we are to grow up in every way into him who is the head, into Christ, from whom the whole body, joined and knit together by every joint with which it is supplied, when each part is working properly, makes bodily growth and upbuilds itself in love."

**COMPEL** is wrongly used twice in KJ. King Saul's servants did not "compel," but "urged" him to eat (1 Samuel 28.23). KJ itself translates the same Hebrew word by "urge" in 2 Kings 5.23 and "press" in 2 Samuel 13.25, 27. Paul, before his conversion, did not "compel" the early Christians to blaspheme; he "tried to make" them do so (Acts 26.11).

**COMPREHEND** comes from a Latin verb which means to seize or grasp. The primary reference of the Latin *comprehendere* was to the physical laying hold of something; but it readily acquired a secondary meaning, and was applied to the intellectual grasp or understanding of a matter. In the sixteenth century the English word "comprehend" was employed in both the physical and the intellectual senses, as was also the related word "apprehend." Today the physical sense of "comprehend" is obsolete, while "apprehend" retains both senses.

For this reason the translation of John 1.5 in KJ has now become misleading: "The light shineth in darkness; and the darkness comprehended it not." That seems to the reader of today to be a statement concerning the stupidity of those who were in the dark, and their lack of understanding. The translation by ASV is better—"the darkness apprehended it not"—but it is still open to the same misunderstanding.

The best translation is that which was given in the marginal note of ASV, and has now been adopted by RSV: "the darkness has not overcome it." The opening sentences of John's Gospel concerning the Word in whom is life and who is the light of men do not close with the anticlimactic idea that it is all very puzzling, but with the triumphant assertion that the light dispels the darkness, and that the darkness cannot overcome the light. Here is the present rendering of the first five verses of the Gospel of John:

"In the beginning was the Word, and the Word was with God, and the Word was God. He was in the beginning with God; all things were made through him, and without him was not anything made that was made. In him was life, and the life was the light of men. The light shines in the darkness, and the darkness has not overcome it."

Other modern translations have "did not master it" (Moffatt); "has never put it out" (Goodspeed, Phillips); "has never overpowered it" (Weymouth, Twentieth Century, Williams); "overcame it not" (Torrey); "did not conquer it" (Rieu).

**CONCEIT** is used by KJ in the sense of conception, imagination. The expression "wise in his own conceit" occurs five times in Proverbs. In four of these cases, however, the Hebrew word means "eyes," and RSV translates literally, "wise in his own eyes" (26.5, 12, 16; 28.11). The other case is 18.11, where KJ has "The rich man's wealth *is* his strong city, and as an high wall in his own conceit." Here the Hebrew word is different, and of less certain meaning. It may mean "imagination"; or it may mean "cover," derived from the verb in Exodus 33.22, "I will cover thee with my hand while I pass by." RSV accepts the latter view, and follows the Greek and Latin versions and Martin Luther's German translation:

"A rich man's wealth is his strong city,
        and like a high wall protecting him."

The expression "wise in your own conceits" is retained by RSV in Romans 11.25. In Job 37.24, where KJ asserts that the Almighty "respecteth not any *that are* wise of heart," RSV has "he does not regard any who are wise in their own conceit." It puts the injunctions of Romans 12.16 in direct terms: "Do not be haughty, but associate with the lowly; never be conceited."

"Conceit" in the sense of an overweening opinion of oneself is used by RSV in the letters of the New Testament. It replaces "swellings" (2 Corinthians 12.20) and "vainglory" (Philippians 2.3). "Puffed up with conceit" and "swollen with conceit" replace "lifted up with pride," "proud," and "highminded" in 1 Timothy 3.6; 6.4, and 2 Timothy 3.4.

**CONCISION** means "cutting to pieces." It is used once (Philippians 3.2) as a contemptuous term for those advocates of Jewish circumcision who would require Gentile Christians to submit to it. This is one of the rare cases where a play on words can be reproduced in different languages. The Latin has *circumcisio—concisio;* Greek, *peritomē—katatomē;* English, circumcision—concision. Modern translators have felt it less desirable to maintain the play on words than to make the meaning clear. Instead of "beware of the concision," RSV therefore reads, "look out for those who mutilate the flesh." It goes on in verse 3, "For we are the true circumcision, who worship God in spirit, and glory in Christ Jesus, and put no confidence in the flesh."

**CONCLUDE** occurs twice in the sense of shut up, restrict, confine. This meaning of the word is now obsolete except in legal language. The passages are Romans 11.32: "For God hath concluded them all in unbelief, that he might have mercy upon all," and Galatians 3.22: "But the scripture hath concluded all under sin, that the promise by faith of Jesus Christ might be given to them that believe." RSV translates: "For God has consigned all men to disobedience, that he may have mercy upon all," and "But the scripture consigned all things to sin, that what was promised to faith in Jesus Christ might be given to those who believe."

In two other passages "conclude" refers to the maintenance of an opinion or the coming to a decision. "Therefore we conclude that a man is justified by faith without the deeds of the law" is more accurately translated, "For we hold that a man is justified by faith apart from works of law" (Romans 3.28). In Acts 21.25, "we have written and concluded" is better expressed, "we have sent a letter with our judgment."

**CONCUPISCENCE** means eager, passionate desire, especially sexual lust. The Latin *concupiscentia* was one of a list of 99 Latin words and phrases from the Vulgate which Bishop Gardiner presented to the Convocation of 1542, insisting that, "for the sake of their germane and native meaning and for the majesty of the matter in them contained," these words should be retained in any translation of the Scriptures or be rendered into English with the least possible change. In the New Testament the Vulgate had used *desiderium* 24 times and *concupiscentia* 14 times as translation for the Greek noun *epithumia*. (See LUST)

Tyndale, translating from the Greek, used "concupiscence" 4 times; the Rheims New Testament, translating from the Vulgate, used "concupiscence" 15 times, including one passage where it has "in concupiscences" for the Vulgate *in desideriis*.

The King James translators followed Tyndale, except in James 1.14, where they replaced his "concupiscence" with "lust." In the 3 texts where they retained "concupiscence," the revised versions have replaced it with "covetousness" (Romans 7.8), "desire" (Colossians 3.5), "lust" (1 Thessalonians 4.5).

**CONDESCEND.** The Oxford English Dictionary defines condescend as "to stoop from one's position of dignity or pride," and quotes Samuel Johnson's definition: "to depart from the privileges of superiority by a voluntary submission; to sink willingly to equal terms with inferiors." Yet there is always something snobbish or patronizing about the word "condescend." The person who condescends never forgets his "superiority" and usually succeeds in reminding others of it.

The word appears just once in the English translation of the Bible, and is there so inappropriate that OED adds a parenthetical note to its quotation of the passage: "The meaning of the translators in 1611 is not clear." The verse is Romans 12.16: "Mind not high things, but condescend to men of low estate." It is translated in RSV, "do not be haughty, but associate with the lowly."

The Greek adjective here is the one which Jesus applied to himself —"I am meek and lowly in heart" (Matthew 11.29). It is the word used in James 4.6—"God opposes the proud; but gives grace to the humble." Its verb appears in "Whoever humbles himself like this child, he is the greatest in the kingdom of heaven" (Matthew 18.4); "he humbled himself and became obedient unto death" (Philippians 2.8). Its noun appears as "humility" (Acts 20.19) or "lowliness" (Ephesians 4.2).

As for the Greek verb which in Romans 12.16 is translated "condescend," there is not the least element of condescension in its meaning, which is, when applied to persons, "associate with," and when applied to circumstances, "adapt oneself to." We can acquit Paul of the charge that he advised Christians to act condescendingly to "men of low estate."

**CONFECTION, CONFECTIONARY** are words which now refer to candy and sweetmeats, things good to eat because of their sugar. As used in KJ, they refer to compounds of spices, things good to smell, whether for perfume or for incense. "Confection" occurs in the instructions given to Moses for the making of the holy incense—"Thou shalt make it a perfume, a confection after the art of the apothecary" (Exodus 30.35). RSV has "make an incense blended as by the perfumer." This was to be used only in the worship of the LORD. "Confectionary" occurs in 1 Samuel 8.13, where the prophet Samuel warns the people who were asking for a king: "he will take your daughters *to be* confectionaries, and *to be* cooks, and *to be* bakers." RSV has, "He will take your daughters to be perfumers and cooks and bakers."

**CONFIDENCES** is ambiguous in Jeremiah 2.37, "the LORD hath rejected thy confidences." It may be taken to mean that Israel had confided in the LORD and had been rejected. But the fact is that Israel was putting its confidence in others, and the prophet is saying that the LORD has rejected these others. RSV translates:

> "for the LORD has rejected those in whom you trust,
>     and you will not prosper by them."

**CONFOUND.** The characteristic use of this word is in the passive voice—"to be confounded"—and in the Old Testament as translation for Hebrew words which mean "to be put to shame." Exceptions to this use are Genesis 11.7, 9, where "confuse their language" is the proper translation; and Jeremiah 1.17, where the Hebrew term means "dismay."

In the New Testament "confound" appears in two passages as translation for the Greek verb which means "to put to shame," 1 Corinthians 1.27, 1 Peter 2.6. It is used twice to translate the verb which means "confuse." In the account of Pentecost, Acts 2.6, the successive versions from Wyclif to Rheims had "were astonied," and KJ changed this to "were confounded." RSV uses "were bewildered." The statement that Paul "confounded the Jews who lived in Damascus by proving that Jesus was the Christ" (Acts 9.22) goes back to Wyclif and appears, with minor variations in wording and spelling, in all the English versions up to and including RSV. KJ substituted "proving" for "affirming," and the revised versions have retained it.

**CONFUSION** is used in the New Testament in its present sense. The city of Ephesus was "filled with confusion" (Acts 19.29). Paul writes to the Corinthians that "God is not a God of confusion but of peace" (1 Corinthians 14.33).

In the KJ Old Testament, "confusion" is used to translate Hebrew words which mean shame, dishonor, and disgrace. Examples are: "confusion of face" (Ezra 9.7); RSV "utter shame." "My confusion" (Psalm 44.15); RSV "my disgrace." "The city of confusion" (Isaiah 24.10); RSV "the city of chaos." "*Their* everlasting confusion" (Jeremiah 20.11); RSV "their eternal dishonor."

**CONSENT** was a more enthusiastic word in the sixteenth and seventeenth centuries than it is now. It then meant to agree together, to be of the same mind, to think and feel alike. It now usually means to accede to or acquiesce in what another proposes or desires. The outstanding example of KJ's use of "consent" in an obsolete sense is Psalm 50.18: "When thou sawest a thief, then thou consentedst with him." The Hebrew verb means be pleased with, take pleasure in. RSV translates "If you see a thief, you are a friend of his." Psalm 83.5, "they have consulted together with one consent," is translated by RSV "they conspire with one accord." "The fear of the LORD fell on the people, and they came out with one consent" (1 Samuel 11.7) is changed by the revised versions to read ". . . as one man," which is a literal translation of the Hebrew.

When Stephen was stoned to death, the "witnesses," who were also the prosecutors and the executioners, laid their clothes at the feet of a young man named Saul, "and Saul was consenting to his death" (Acts 8.1). Years later, when Paul recounted this in the face of the mob at Jerusalem, he said, "I also was standing by and approving, and keeping the garments of those who killed him" (Acts 22.20 RSV). The Greek verb in both passages means "join in thinking well of"; the phrase "to his death" is part of the ancient text in 8.1, but not in 22.20.

**CONSIST** occurs only twice in KJ. It is easily understood in Luke 12.15, "a man's life does not consist in the abundance of his possessions" (RSV). But the meaning is not so clear in Colossians 1.17, "he is before all things, and by him all things consist." Tyndale and the sixteenth-century versions had "in him all things exist." Rheims rendered the clause, "in him all things consist," and KJ adopted this, changing "in" to "by." RSV has a literal rendering of the Greek, "in him all things hold together."

**CONSORT WITH** means to associate or keep company with. "Consort" was a relatively new word when the KJ translators were at work; as a verb, its earliest occurrences recorded in OED were in 1588. Shakespeare used it often, as well as the related verb "sort."

> "They wilfully themselves exile from light,
> And must for aye consort with black-brow'd night."
> *A Midsummer Night's Dream*, III, 2, 386–387
> "What will you do? Let's not consort with them."
> *Macbeth*, II, 3, 141

The one appearance of the word in KJ is in Acts 17.4: "And some of them believed, and consorted with Paul and Silas." Its use was an innovation. Wyclif and Rheims had "joyned to"; Tyndale and the Great Bible, "came and companyed with"; Coverdale and the Bishops' Bible, "joyned with"; the Geneva Bible, "joyned in companye with."

Except for the revised versions of 1881–1901, no modern English translators retain "consorted with," which falls short of the meaning of the Greek. John Wesley in 1755 translated it "were joined to"; Alexander Campbell in 1826, "adhered to." The Twentieth Century New Testament (1904), taking its clue from the etymology of the Greek verb, translated it "threw in their lot with Paul and Silas," and this has been accepted by Moffatt, Knox, and Phillips. Weymouth and Ballantine have "attached themselves to." Goodspeed returns to the word which was used by most of the sixteenth-century versions, and reads, "joined Paul and Silas." This simple, direct translation of the Greek is used also by Confraternity, Williams, and RSV.

**CONSTANT** and **CONSTANTLY,** as used in the Bible, are more than time words; they mean "with constancy," that is, with firmness, steadfastness, consistency. When Rhoda "constantly affirmed" that Peter was at the door, the Greek does not mean continually, but confidently—"she insisted that it was so" (Acts 12.15). "These things I will that thou affirm constantly" (Titus 3.8) means "I desire you to insist on these things." "If he be constant to do my commandments and my judgments, as at this day" (1 Chronicles 28.7) is reworded by RSV, "if he continues resolute in keeping my commandments and my ordinances, as he is today."

**CONSULT** is used twice in the obsolete sense of plan or devise. "Thou hast consulted shame to thy house" (Habakkuk 2.10) means "You have devised shame to your house." "What Balak . . . consulted" (Micah 6.5) means what Balak planned. The verse reads in RSV:

"O my people, remember what Balak king of Moab devised,
and what Balaam the son of Beor answered him,
and what happened from Shittim to Gilgal,
that you may know the saving acts of the LORD."

**CONTAIN.** "If they cannot contain" (1 Corinthians 7.9) has reference to sexual behavior, and means cannot be continent and chaste. A literal translation of the Greek is given by RSV, "if they cannot exercise self-control, they should marry." (See BURN)

**CONTENT.** The mild imperative "Be content" occurs four times in KJ, in the obsolete sense of "Be pleased." When Gehazi, the servant of Elisha, ran after Naaman's chariot and asked him for a talent of silver, Naaman replied, "Be content, take two talents" (2 Kings 5.23). It is obvious that Naaman was not advising Gehazi to restrain his desires or urging him to be contented with only two talents. His reply is an immediate and generous gift of twice what Gehazi asked. RSV translates it, "Be pleased to accept two talents." This was the language of polite diplomacy, between the commander of the army of the king of Syria and the servant of the man of God who represented the king of Israel.

The other passages, in the wording of RSV, are: "Be pleased to spend the night" (Judges 19.6); "Be pleased to go with your servants" (2 Kings 6.3); "But now, be pleased to look at me" (Job 6.28). In present-day language, "be pleased to" would be cut to "please," and Job would say, "But now, please look at me." There are interesting discussions of this idiom in OED, under the adjective *Content*, I, 3 and the verb *Please*, I, 4 and II, 6.

**CONTRARIWISE** is a mild word in the Bible, meaning simply on the other hand, on the contrary. It does not refer to contrary dispositions, to contradictions, or to perverse, self-willed opposition—all of which it may connote in appropriate contexts. The three passages where it appears in KJ are 2 Corinthians 2.7, Galatians 2.7, and 1 Peter 3.9. RSV deletes it as redundant in the first of these passages, and translates the Greek by "on the contrary" in the other two.

**CONTROVERSY.** The phrase "without controversy," a literal translation of the Latin *sine controversia,* was current in the sixteenth century in the sense of undeniably, unquestionably. The KJ translators used it in their Preface, when they referred to "S. Hierome, a most learned Father, and the best linguist without controversy of his age, or of any that went before him." They used it in 1 Timothy 3.16, "without controversy great is the mystery of godliness." The Greek adverb here means confessedly, most certainly, as all would agree. The Latin Vulgate translates it by *manifeste.* And the statement is not about godliness in general but about the religion which is the subject of the entire letter to Timothy. RSV translates, "Great indeed, we confess, is the mystery of our religion."

**CONVENIENT** originally meant fitting, becoming, appropriate, proper, right. But these meanings of the word are now obsolete, and "convenient" is applied to what suits one's personal ease or comfort or lies near at hand. It was used in the older sense in KJ, and is not used in RSV.

"Feed me with food convenient for me" (Proverbs 30.8) means "feed me with the food that is needful for me." When Jeremiah is told that he may "go wheresoever it seemeth convenient unto thee to go" (Jeremiah 40.5; compare verse 4), the meaning is "go wherever you think it right to go." "Not convenient" (Ephesians 5.4) translates Greek which means "not fitting." "To enjoin thee that which is convenient" (Philemon 8) means "to command you to do what is required." "To do those things which are not convenient" (Romans 1.28) is expressed by RSV "to improper conduct."

In four New Testament passages, the Greek word underlying the use of "convenient" or "conveniently" means "opportunity" (Mark 6.21; 14.11; Acts 24.25; 1 Corinthians 16.12).

**CONVERSATION** in KJ always refers to conduct, behavior, or manner of life, and is never used in the sense that it has today as a term for the give-and-take of talk. "The end of *their* conversation" (Hebrews 13.7) is now translated, "the outcome of their life." The "vain conversation *received* by tradition from your fathers" (1 Peter 1.18) is "the futile ways inherited from your fathers." Lot is said to have been "vexed with the filthy conversation" of Sodom and Gomorrah (2 Peter 2.7), but it means that he was "greatly distressed by the licentiousness" of these cities.

The injunction to the Christian wives of unbelieving husbands expressed in KJ 1 Peter 3.1–2 is confusing to the reader of today: "Likewise, ye wives, *be* in subjection to your own husbands; that, if any obey not the word, they also may without the word be won by the conversation of the wives; While they behold your chaste conversation *coupled* with fear." That conveys the impression that these wives are to talk their husbands into becoming Christians, though it seems strange that husbands are to behold the conversation rather than listen to it, and one can only wonder what being coupled with fear has to do with it. But there is no word in the Greek for "coupled," and no justification for dragging it in; the word "fear" stands for the reverent fear of God which is the mark of a good Christian; and the "conversation" of these wives is their behavior. RSV translates the passage: "Likewise you wives, be submissive to your husbands, so that some, though they do not obey the word, may be won without a word by the behavior of their wives, when they see your reverent and chaste behavior."

Writing to the Corinthians Paul, referring to himself as "we," expresses rejoicing in "the testimony of our conscience, that in simplicity and godly sincerity, not with fleshly wisdom, but by the grace of God, we have had our conversation in the world, and more abundantly to you-ward" (2 Corinthians 1.12). Note how much more clearly this reason for rejoicing is expressed in RSV: "the testimony of our conscience that we have behaved in the world, and still more toward you, with holiness and godly sincerity, not by earthly wisdom but by the grace of God."

The archaic use of the word "conversation" is so misleading that it will be well to cite other examples, quoting the renderings of RSV and stating in parentheses the archaic phrases which they have displaced. In Galatians 1.13 Paul refers to his "former life in Judaism" ("conversation in time past in the Jews' religion"). He reminds the Ephesians (2.3) how "we all once lived" ("we all had our conversation in times past") as children of wrath; and he urges them (4.22) to "put off your old nature which belongs to your former manner of life" ("put off concerning the former conversation the old man"). He exhorts the Philippians (1.27) to let their "manner of life be worthy of (conversation be as it becometh) the gospel of Christ," and declares that "our commonwealth (conversation) is in heaven" (3.20).

Timothy is encouraged, in spite of his youth (1 Timothy 4.12), to "set the believers an example in speech and conduct" ("be thou an example of the believers, in word, in conversation"). Among the injunctions in the Letter to the Hebrews is (13.5) "Keep your life free from love of money" (*"Let your* conversation *be* without covetousness"). If a man is wise and understanding (James 3.13), "by his good life let him show his works" ("let him shew out of a good conversation his works").

Peter counsels his readers (1 Peter 1.15; 2.12) to be holy "in all your conduct" ("in all manner of conversation"), and to "maintain good conduct among the Gentiles" ("having your conversation honest among the Gentiles"). He warns (3.16) that some may "revile your good behavior in Christ" ("falsely accuse your good conversation in Christ"). He encourages them (2 Peter 3.11) to "lives of holiness and godliness" ("holy conversation and godliness").

In the Old Testament "the strangers that were conversant among them" means "the sojourners who lived among them" (Joshua 8.35); and "as long as we were conversant with them" means "as long as we went with them" (1 Samuel 25.15).

**CONVINCE** occurs seven times in KJ, always in a sense for which it is now obsolete. It is used four times in the sense of convict, prove one to be guilty or in the wrong; it is used three times in the sense of confute, prove one to be in error. The passages are:

John 8.46, "Which of you convinceth me of sin?" (RSV ". . . convicts me of sin?"). 1 Corinthians 14.24, "convinced of all" (RSV "convicted by all"). James 2.9, "If ye have respect to persons, ye commit sin, and are convinced of the law as transgressors" (RSV "If you show partiality, you commit sin, and are convicted by the law as transgressors"). Jude 15, "to convince all that are ungodly" (RSV "to convict all the ungodly").

Job 32.12, *"there was* none of you that convinced Job" (RSV "there was none that confuted Job"). Acts 18.28, "he mightily convinced the Jews" (RSV "he powerfully confuted the Jews"). Titus 1.9, "Holding fast the faithful word as he hath been taught, that he may be able by sound doctrine both to exhort and to convince the gainsayers" (RSV "he must hold firm to the sure word as taught, so that he may be able to give instruction in sound doctrine and also to confute those who contradict it").

Shakespeare uses "convince" in the sense of "convict" in *Troilus and Cressida*, II, 2, 129:

> "Else might the world convince of levity
> As well my undertakings as your counsels."

He uses "convince" in its literal sense of conquer, overcome, in *Macbeth*, I, 7, 64:

> "his two chamberlains
> Will I with wine and wassail so convince
> That memory, the warder of the brain,
> Shall be a fume, and the receipt of reason
> A limbeck only."

**CORN** means "grain," first as a small granular object, and second as a cereal crop. The word is used once by KJ in the sense of a single seed: "Except a corn of wheat fall into the ground and die, it abideth alone" (John 12.24). The revised versions use "a grain of wheat." We still refer to a "barleycorn" or a "peppercorn," and formerly it was common to refer to a corn of gunpowder, an apple corn, or a corn of salt—from which we retain "corned beef."

An outstanding difference between British usage and American usage is that "corn" in America means maize or Indian corn, while in British usage it is a general term for grain, including all the cereal plants and their seed. For this reason "corn" occurs in KJ 101 times and in RSV not at all, while "grain" occurs in KJ 8 times and in RSV 117 times. Where KJ has "corn fields" RSV has "grainfields."

**CORRUPT** originally referred to physical decay, but in this sense has become archaic; it is now generally used of moral taint or dishonesty, or of whatever tends to impair the integrity of a person, an institution, or a document. The word is used in both senses in KJ, standing for a wide variety of Hebrew and Greek terms.

"Where moth and rust doth corrupt" is better translated, "where moth and rust consume" (Matthew 6.19). "Neither moth corrupteth" is "and no moth destroys" (Luke 12.33). "Your riches are corrupted" means "Your riches have rotted" (James 5.2).

The distinction in Romans 1.23 between "the uncorruptible God" and "corruptible man" is not, according to the Greek terms, the difference between God as morally incorruptible and man as corruptible, but the difference between God as imperishable and man as perishable. The same distinction between *phthartos,* "perishable," and *aphthartos,* "imperishable" appears in 1 Corinthians 9.25; 15.42, 50–54; 1 Peter 1.4, 18, 23. These passages are concerned with the resurrection of the dead to eternal life. "For this corruptible must put on incorruption, and this mortal must put on immortality" means "For this perishable nature must put on the imperishable, and this mortal nature must put on immortality" (1 Corinthians 15.53).

The KJ translators seem to have missed the meaning of some passages: "They are corrupt" should be "They scoff" (Psalm 73.8). In place of "My breath is corrupt," Job 17.1 reads "My spirit is broken." The meaning of the first clause of Malachi 2.3 is not clear, but certainly the verb means "rebuke" rather than "corrupt."

Where KJ uses "corrupt" in a moral sense, it is usually retained in the revised versions. In Genesis 6.12 we still read that God saw the earth, and behold, it was corrupt; for all flesh had corrupted their way upon the earth." And the latest of the books of the New Testament writes of men who are "slaves of corruption; for whatever overcomes a man, to that he is enslaved" (2 Peter 2.19).

**COUNTERVAIL** means to compensate or make up for. When Esther protests to the king against the edict to destroy her people, she adds, "If we had been sold for bondmen and bondwomen, I had held my tongue, although the enemy could not countervail the king's damage" (Esther 7.4). Modern translations regard the last clause as causal rather than concessive, and its subject as "distress" or "affliction" rather than "enemy." Hebrew has two nouns, from different roots, but spelled alike, *tsar,* one of which means "distress" while the other means "adversary." The conjunction *ki* may sometimes mean "though," but much more commonly means "when," "because," or "for." RSV reads "for our affliction is not to be compared with the loss to the king." The Basic Bible has "for our trouble is little in comparison with the king's loss."

**COUNTRY.** KJ reads "a" in John 11.54, where RSV has "the"— "Jesus therefore no longer went about openly among the Jews, but went from there to the country near the wilderness." "A country" seems to mean a different land or nation; "the country" is equivalent to "the countryside." All English translations from Wyclif on had "a" here until the Rheims version (1582) used "the." KJ reverted to the misleading expression in spite of the fact that the Greek has "the country." This has been corrected by John Wesley (1755) and Alexander Campbell (1826), by the revised versions, and by modern translations generally. Most of them have "the country"; Weymouth has "the district," and Phillips "the countryside."

**COUSIN,** as used in KJ, simply means a relative, a kinsman or kinswoman. When the angel told Mary that her "cousin" Elizabeth had also conceived a son, the Greek word meant "kinswoman" (Luke 1.36). When Elizabeth gave birth to her son, it was not "her neighbors and her cousins" that rejoiced with her, but "her neighbors and kinsfolk" (1.58). For "uncle's son" RSV substitutes "cousin" in Leviticus 25.49 and Jeremiah 32.8, 9, 12. The Greek word used to describe Mark's relation to Barnabas does not mean "sister's son" but "cousin" (Colossians 4.10).

**COVER HIS FEET.** The literal translation of a Hebrew euphemism for evacuating the bowels. It was derived from the posture assumed, screening the feet with long garments (Oxford Hebrew Lexicon, 697). RSV translates it, "relieve himself" (Judges 3.24; 1 Samuel 24.3).

**COVET** means to have inordinate desire for what belongs to someone else. Covetousness is consistently denounced in the Bible, from the Ten Commandments (Exodus 20.17; Deuteronomy 5.21) to the Second Epistle of Peter (2.3, 14). The characteristic word for covetousness in the Old Testament is *betsa,* which means unjust gain; and in the New Testament it is *pleonexia,* which means greed, the desire for more and more. Bishop Lightfoot, commenting on Romans 1.29, defined *pleonexia* as "the disposition which is ever ready to sacrifice one's neighbour to oneself in all things, not in money dealings merely."

Yet the verb "covet" has been used in the simple sense of desire or long for, without any sinister implications. It appears twice in this good sense, in Paul's first letter to the Corinthians. "Covet earnestly the best gifts" (12.31). "Wherefore, brethren, covet to prophesy" (14.39). The Greek verb here is *zēloute,* an imperative which means desire, strive for. The noun *zēlos* has entered the English language as "zeal." In these two texts the revised versions reject "covet," and translate by "earnestly desire."

**CRACKNEL** is defined by OED as "a light, crisp kind of biscuit," with citations which show that the word has been used in England for five hundred years. When King Jeroboam sent his wife in disguise to consult the prophet Ahijah, he said she should take with her "ten loaves, some cakes, and a jar of honey" (1 Kings 14.3). Just what the cakes (*neqqudim*) were is a mystery. The word is translated "mouldy" in Joshua 9.5, and the Hebrew dictionary inclines toward "crumbly." An adjective from the same Hebrew root describes the "speckled" sheep and goats that Jacob acquired (Genesis 30.32–31.12). The conjecture has been made that *neqqudim* may have been cakes sprinkled on the surface with aromatic seeds. But we do not know. It is clear, however, that to call these cakes "cracknels" was a piece of modernization about as justifiable as it would be to call them "pretzels" or "ginger snaps" today.

**CREATURE.** In Romans 8.19–23, 37–39 the word "creature" is employed in the now obsolete sense of the created universe —"the whole creation," as KJ itself translates the same Greek word in verse 22. The revised versions use "creation" throughout this passage, which closes with Paul's great affirmation of faith: "We are more than conquerors through him who loved us. For I am sure that neither death, nor life, nor angels, nor principalities, nor things present, nor things to come, nor powers, nor height, nor depth, nor anything else in all creation, will be able to separate us from the love of God in Christ Jesus our Lord."

"Creature" means anything created, and is not limited to living beings unless it is so stated or implied. RSV makes this clear by changing "every creature of God is good" to "everything created by God is good" (1 Timothy 4.4). It also reads "a new creation" in 2 Corinthians 5.17 and Galatians 6.15.

The article on *Creature* in OED makes interesting reading, and stirs one to reflection upon the varied play of language. The words of invocation in the order for Holy Communion, "bless and sanctify, with thy Word and Holy Spirit, these thy gifts and creatures of bread and wine," doubtless remain clear and meaningful to those who partake. But the man who speaks of "creature comforts" is probably not thinking of the God who created them, but of himself as the creature who is comforted by them.

**CREEK.** In Great Britain a creek is a narrow inlet of the sea; but in America and in the British colonies a creek is a small tributary or branch of a river. In any case "a certain creek with a shore" is an inaccurate translation of the Greek, which means "a bay with a beach" (Acts 27.39).

**CUMBER.** "Martha was cumbered about much serving" (Luke 10.40) is reworded by RSV, "Martha was distracted with much serving." The owner of the barren fig tree is represented as saying, "Cut it down; why cumbereth it the ground?" RSV has "Cut it down; why should it use up the ground?" (Luke 13.7). The Greek verbs are quite different, and these are examples of felicity in literal translation.

**CUMBRANCE** appears once (Deuteronomy 1.12): "How can I myself alone bear your cumbrance, and your burden, and your strife?" "Cumbrance" was Tyndale's word here. It is now obsolete, and its successor, "encumbrance," savors so much of an acquired impediment that it is hardly a good translation for the Hebrew word *torah,* which simply means burden. In this verse *torah* is coupled with the more common word for "burden," *massa'*. RSV translates: "How can I bear alone the weight and burden of you and your strife?"
The word *torah* is used in one other passage (Isaiah 1.14):
"Your new moons and your appointed feasts
my soul hates;
they have become a burden to me,
I am weary of bearing them."

**CUNNING** is used in a good sense in the Old Testament of the King James Version, and in a bad sense in the New Testament. It refers in the Old Testament to practical knowledge or skill. As this use of the word is now almost, if not quite, obsolete, the revised versions replace it usually with "skilled" or "skilful." Esau was a "skilful" rather than a "cunning" hunter (Genesis 25.27). David was "skilful in playing the lyre" (1 Samuel 16.16). Hiram of Tyre was "full of wisdom, understanding, and skill" (1 Kings 7.14). The "cunning artificer" of Isaiah 3.3 was a "skilful magician."
In the chapters of Exodus and Chronicles dealing with the furnish-

ings of the tabernacle and the temple, "cunning men" are "skilled men," "cunning workmen" are "skilful craftsmen" or "skilled designers," and "of cunning work" is "skilfully worked."

In the New Testament "cunning" is used in the bad sense which is now its prevalent meaning; the passages are Ephesians 4.14 and 2 Peter 1.16.

**CURIOUS** is used in its now obsolete sense of made with care and art.
            The "curious girdle of the ephod" (Exodus 28.8) was a "skilfully woven band to gird it on." The "curious works" which Bezalel devised were "artistic designs" (Exodus 35.32).

*The Bible Word-Book,* 1884, quotes from an old concordance the following statement concerning the expression "curiously wrought in the lowest parts of the earth" (Psalm 139.15): "the word is the same which is usually translated 'embroidered'; the adjusting and formation of the different members of the human body being by a bold and beautiful metaphor compared to the arranging the threads and colours in a piece of tapestry."

In the New Testament "curious" appears once only, in an obsolete sense defined by OED as "recondite, occult." This is in the account of Paul's successful ministry at Ephesus, Acts 19.1–20. In verse 19, "them which used curious arts" means "those who practiced magic arts."

**DAMNATION, DAMNED.** The word "damnation" is used 10 times, and "damned" 3 times, as translations of words connected with the Greek *krinō,* which means to judge, pass sentence, or condemn. But for these same Greek words KJ uses "judge" 87 times, "judgment" 41 times, "condemn" 22 times, and "condemnation" 8 times. The revised versions eliminate "damnation" and "damned" in the 13 contexts, and use the same terms which are used elsewhere. There is no special significance in these passages to call for the heavier English words. We must remember, too, that in 1611 "damn" was a general word which meant condemn, and "damnation" meant condemnation—senses in which these words are now obsolete.

The scribes who devour widows' houses do not receive "greater damnation," but "greater condemnation" (Matthew 23.14; Mark 12.40; Luke 20.47). The penalty of resisting the authorities is not to "receive damnation" but to "incur judgment" (Romans 13.2). In the KJ rendering of 1 Corinthians 11.29, "he that eateth and drinketh unworthily, eateth and drinketh damnation to himself," the word which is rendered "damnation" is the same as that which is rendered "condemnation" in verse 34. RSV has "eats and drinks judgment upon himself."

The younger widows who wish to marry do not incur "damnation, because they have cast off their first faith"; they incur "condemnation for having violated their first pledge" (1 Timothy 5.12). "How can ye escape the damnation of hell?" (Matthew 23.33) means "How are you to escape being sentenced to hell?"

**DAMSEL** was spelled "damsell" and more often "damosell" in the 1611 edition of KJ. It appears 51 times, representing Hebrew and Greek words which mean young woman, child, little girl, maiden, or maid. Since the seventeenth century "damsel" is not in ordinary spoken use; it is archaic and literary or playful (OED). RSV uses "maiden" for Rebecca and Dinah (Genesis 24 and 34), "young woman" in Deuteronomic law (22.15–29), "girl" for Salome (Matthew 14.11; Mark 6.22, 28), and either "child" and "girl," following the Greek, in the account of the healing of the daughter of the ruler of the synagogue (Mark 5.39–42). For the Greek *paidiskē*, a maidservant, it uses "maid" (Matthew 26.69; John 18.17; Acts 12.13) and "slave girl" (Acts 16.16).

**DANGER.** "Whosoever shall kill shall be in danger of the judgment" (Matthew 5.21–22). The phrase "in danger of" in this and the succeeding clauses means "liable to." It expresses, not casual peril, but legal liability. The word "danger" is used in its original meaning as the power that an authority has over those subject to it. This is now obsolete English, but it was in 1611 an admirable translation of the Greek *enochos,* which was a legal term meaning "bound by," "liable to," or "subject to." In Shakespeare's *Merchant of Venice,* IV, 1, 180, Portia's first question to Antonio is concerning Shylock's bond: "You stand within his danger, do you not?"

In the translation of the New Testament which Alexander Campbell published in 1826, he used in Matthew 5.21 what seems to us now to be a strange word—"whosoever commits murder shall be obnoxious to the judges." "Obnoxious" once meant subject or answerable to, but that meaning is now obsolete.

In Mark 3.29, "is in danger of eternal damnation" does not represent the original Greek text, which means "is guilty of an eternal sin." KJ translates *enochos* by "subject to" in Hebrews 2.15, and by "guilty of" in four other cases. (See GUILTY OF)

**DARLING.** In Psalms 22.20 and 35.17 "my darling" represents the
               Hebrew word which means "my only." It is the word
which is used for Abraham's only son Isaac and for Jephthah's only
child, and also occurs repeatedly in references to mourning for an only
son. In Psalms 22 and 35, however, the psalmist is not praying for an
only son or a loved one, but for himself. "My only" is parallel to "my
soul" in the first line of Psalm 22.20. It is a poetic expression for "my
life," according to the Hebrew lexicon, "as the one unique and price-
less possession which can never be replaced."

**DAYSPRING** means daybreak, dawn, "the spring of the day." It
               occurs in Job 38.12, where RSV substitutes "dawn"
and reads:
    "Have you commanded the morning since your days began,
        and caused the dawn to know its place?"
The well-known line in the Benedictus, "whereby the dayspring from
on high hath visited us," reads in RSV, "when the day shall dawn
upon us from on high" (Luke 1.78).

    In Milton's *Samson Agonistes,* 11, the blind Samson, led out into
the open air for a brief rest, expresses joy in "the breath of heaven
fresh blowing, pure and sweet, with dayspring born." (See SPRING)

**DEAD CORPSES.** "Then the angel of the LORD went forth, and smote
                in the camp of the Assyrians a hundred and four-
score and five thousand: and when they arose early in the morning,
behold, they *were* all dead corpses" (Isaiah 37.36 = 2 Kings 19.35).
This picture of the Assyrian soldiers whom the angel smote arising early
and discovering that they were dead corpses has awakened amusement.
The revised versions clear up the ambiguous "they" and rid the "dead
corpses" of redundancy. RSV reads: "And the angel of the LORD
went forth, and slew a hundred and eighty-five thousand in the camp
of the Assyrians; and when men arose early in the morning, behold,
these were all dead bodies."

    It must be admitted that in this case the Hebrew itself has the
redundant equivalent of "dead corpses." It is also true that redundancy
was a common form of emphasis in Elizabethan language. Witness
Shakespeare's report of the death of Mortimer: "Upon whose dead
corpse there was such misuse" (*King Henry IV, Part I,* I, 1, 43). But
these facts afford no sufficient reason for retaining the expression.

**DEARTH** means a scarcity of something. In the sixteenth century it had the sense of a general scarcity of food, a famine. Tyndale, portraying the plight of the prodigal son, translated Luke 15.14: "And when he had spent all that he had, ther rose a greate derth thorow all that same londe, and he began to lacke." Tyndale was followed by the subsequent sixteenth-century versions, but KJ substituted the word "famine." There remain 6 passages in KJ where "dearth" is used for the Hebrew and Greek words which KJ translates "famine" in 92 other passages. These passages are Genesis 41.54; 2 Kings 4.38; 2 Chronicles 6.28; Nehemiah 5.3; Acts 7.11; 11.28.

In Jeremiah 14.1 "the dearth" translates a different Hebrew word, and it is clear from the context that it means "the drought."

**DEBATE** is now a decorous word, with no suggestion of bad temper or violent disorder, yet KJ lists debate along with envy, murder, deceit, and malignity among the characteristics of the reprobate mind in Romans 1.29. It stands there, and in 2 Corinthians 12.20, as a translation of the Greek word *eris,* which means "strife." In Greek legend Eris was the goddess of strife, who threw the golden apple which awakened the jealousy of Hera, Athene, and Aphrodite, and brought on the Trojan War. Isaiah 58.4 reads "ye fast for strife and debate" (RSV "you fast only to quarrel and to fight"). In Shakespeare's *King Henry IV, Part II,* IV, 4, 2, the king refers to Northumberland's insurrection as "This debate that bleedeth at our doors."

Jesus' answer to his own question, "Do you think that I have come to give peace on earth?" (Luke 12.51) was translated by Tyndale, Coverdale, and Geneva: "I tell you nay, but rather debate." The Great Bible, the Bishops' Bible, and KJ say "division," and are followed by the revised versions. Among modern translators, Weymouth, Moffatt, Ballantine, Torrey, and Knox agree with the Greek lexicon in using "dissension."

**DECAY** is used five times in the obsolete sense to dwindle or cause to dwindle. It stands for four different Hebrew verbs, each with its own meaning. "*As . . .* the flood decayeth and drieth up" means "As . . . a river wastes away and dries up" (Job 14.11). "The decayed places thereof" means "their ruins" (Isaiah 44.26). At Ecclesiastes 10.18, "By much slothfulness the building decayeth; and through idleness of the hands the house droppeth through," the concrete Hebrew terms are translated more accurately by the revised versions. RSV has:

"Through sloth the roof sinks in,
and through indolence the house leaks."
"Decay" twice refers to persons. "The strength of the bearers of
burdens is decayed" means "the strength of the burden-bearers is failing" (Nehemiah 4.10). "If thy brother be waxen poor, and fallen in
decay with thee; then thou shalt relieve him" means "if your brother
becomes poor, and cannot maintain himself with you, you shall maintain him" (Leviticus 25.35).

A strange use of "decayeth" occurs in Hebrews 8.13: "In that he
saith, A new *covenant,* he hath made the first old. Now that which
decayeth and waxeth old *is* ready to vanish away." No one reading
that translation without prior knowledge of the Greek would imagine
that the word for "hath made old" and the word for "decayeth" are
simply active and passive forms of the same verb. The active form
means "make old, treat as obsolete"; the passive form means "become
old, become obsolete." Tyndale's translation was: "In that he sayth a
new testament he hath abrogat the old. Now that which is disannulled
and wexed olde, is redy to vannyshe awaye." Geneva accepted this, but
substituted "Covenant" for "testament." Coverdale, the Great Bible,
and the Bishops' Bible had, with some variations, the rendering which
appears in the second edition of the Bishops' Bible: "In that he saith
a new Covenant, he hath worne out the first: for that which is worne
out and waxed old is ready to vanish away." KJ was the first to introduce the idea of "decayeth" into this verse. The term has been
repudiated by the revised versions and most modern translations.
RSV has: "In speaking of a new covenant he treats the first as obsolete. And what is becoming obsolete and growing old is ready to vanish
away."

**DECLARE** meant originally to make clear or plain, hence to explain
or to recount in detail. It is no longer used in these senses,
but has become a verb for formal, studied, public utterance or for
emphatic statement or legal procedure. This shift in meaning makes
"declare" no longer the appropriate word in many of the contexts
where it occurs in KJ. When Pharaoh told Joseph about his dream and
said *"there was* none that could declare *it* to me," the meaning is "there
was no one who could explain it to me" (Genesis 41.24). The statement in Deuteronomy 1.5, "On this side Jordan, in the land of Moab,
began Moses to declare this law," is more accurately translated, "Beyond
the Jordan, in the land of Moab, Moses undertook to explain this
law." In the statement of procedure at the cities of refuge, "declare
his cause" means "explain his case" (Joshua 20.4). The request of the

disciples that Jesus "declare unto us the parable" meant "explain to us the parable" (Matthew 13.36; 15.15).

In other cases "tell" is a sufficient translation of the Hebrew or Greek —examples are: Judges 14.12–15; Jeremiah 36.13; Micah 1.10; Colossians 4.7. For other Greek verbs RSV uses "disclose" (1 Corinthians 3.13), "report" (Acts 15.3), "relate" (15.12, 14; 21.19), "make known" (John 1.18; 17.26; Colossians 1.8).

The suggestion of the messenger sent to summon Micaiah reads in KJ: "Behold now, the words of the prophets *declare* good unto the king with one mouth: let thy word, I pray thee, be like the word of one of them, and speak *that which is* good" (1 Kings 22.13 = 2 Chronicles 18.12). In this rendering "declare" and "that which is" were inserted by the translators, and "now" and "I pray thee" represent the Hebrew particle *na'*, an enclitic syllable of polite entreaty or exhortation which has no English equivalent. RSV translates: "Behold, the words of the prophets with one accord are favorable to the king; let your word be like the word of one of them, and speak favorably."

In Numbers 1.18 "declared their pedigrees after their families" is translated by RSV "registered themselves by families."

**DECLINE.** The verb "decline" now means to slope or move downward, to refuse, or to fall off in mental or physical vigor. In the sixteenth and seventeenth centuries it was also used with reference to moral standards, and meant to turn aside, turn away, swerve, deviate, or depart, from the right. Thus "declined *neither* to the right hand, nor to the left" (2 Chronicles 34.2) means that Josiah "did what was right in the eyes of the LORD, and walked in the ways of David his father; and he did not turn aside to the right or to the left." Job's protest, "his way have I kept, and not declined" (23.11), means "I have kept his way and have not turned aside." The Psalms declare: "I do not turn away from thy law" (119.51), "I do not swerve from thy testimonies" (119.157), "nor have our steps departed from thy way" (44.18). "Thou shalt not follow a multitude to *do* evil; neither shalt thou speak in a cause to decline after many to wrest *judgment*" (Exodus 23.2) is more clearly stated, "You shall not follow a multitude to do evil; nor shall you bear witness in a suit, turning aside after a multitude, so as to pervert justice."

**DEGREE.** Whatever was the form of the sundial of Ahaz, the "degrees" upon it were "steps" (2 Kings 20.9–11; Isaiah 38.8). The Hebrew word means an ascent, step, or stair; and the word "degree" was employed by the KJ translators in the sense, now obsolete, defined by OED as "a step in an ascent or descent; one of a flight of steps; a rung of a ladder."

Applied to persons, the term "degree" meant social or official rank. "What is thy degree?" asks King Henry VI of the man who brings him the head of Jack Cade. "A poor esquire of Kent, that loves his king" is the answer, and the esquire is forthwith created knight and given a post in the royal retinue (*King Henry VI, Part II,* V, 1, 73–80). "You know your own degrees; sit down," says Macbeth to his guests at the banquet at which he will see the ghost of Banquo (*Macbeth,* III, 4, 1). RSV has retained the expression "exalted those of low degree" in Luke 1.52, but uses "the lowly brother" in James 1.9. "Purchase a good degree" means "gain a good standing" (1 Timothy 3.13).

The KJ rendering of Psalm 62.9 is: "Surely men of low degree *are* vanity, *and* men of high degree *are* a lie: to be laid in the balance, they *are* altogether *lighter* than vanity." RSV has:

> "Men of low estate are but a breath,
>  men of high estate are a delusion;
> in the balances they go up;
>  they are together lighter than a breath."

**DELICACY** and **DELICIOUSLY** are used in Revelation 18.3, 7, 9 in the obsolete sense of voluptuous, sensual luxury. This chapter portrays the judgment of God upon "Babylon the great." "The abundance of her delicacies" does not refer to a plentiful supply of dainties; the phrase translates Greek which means "the wealth of her sensual luxury." The kings who "lived deliciously with her" were indulging their lust and greed. Tyndale and his successors translated it, "lived wantonly with her." The revised versions have returned to Tyndale's word. RSV has "the wealth of her wantonness" (vs. 3); "as she . . . played the wanton" (vs. 7); "the kings of the earth, who committed fornication and were wanton with her" (vs. 9).

**DELICATELY** is used three times in the obsolete sense of sumptuously, luxuriously. For "They that did feed delicately" (Lamentations 4.5) RSV reads "Those who feasted on dainties." For "they which are gorgeously apparelled, and live delicately" (Luke 7.25) it has "those who are gorgeously appar">led and live in luxury." "He that delicately bringeth up his servant from a child" (Proverbs 29.21) means "He who pampers his servant from childhood."

The account of Agag coming to Samuel is more difficult. "Then said Samuel, Bring ye hither to me Agag the king of the Amalekites. And

Agag came unto him delicately" (1 Samuel 15.32). Here "delicately" was an innovation of the Bishops' Bible which KJ adopted. Since then readers have wondered just what "delicately" meant. Various ideas have been suggested—mincingly, tottering, trembling, in fear, cautiously, slowly, haughtily, walking in state. Most of these are simply attempts to define "delicately," and have no clear relation to the Hebrew. The revised versions return to the view of the Geneva Bible, which had "pleasantly," and of Martin Luther's German Bible, which had *getrost* (confidently). RSV translates "Agag came to him cheerfully." This agrees with RV and ASV, and with recent German translations. Agag did not fear the prophet after he had been spared by Saul and his soldiers. But Samuel "hewed Agag in pieces before the LORD."

**DEMAND** means to ask with authority or as a right, or to ask peremptorily, imperiously, urgently. As used in KJ, however, "demand" does not have these stronger connotations, but is a simple equivalent for "ask." Shakespeare occasionally used the word in this weaker sense.

> "*Miranda.* Wherefore did they not
> That hour destroy us?
> *Prospero.* Well demanded, wench:
> My tale provokes that question."
> *The Tempest*, I, 2, 139
> "We'll mannerly demand thee of thy story,
> So far as thou wilt speak it."
> *Cymbeline*, III, 6, 92

"When Uriah was come unto him, David demanded *of him* how Joab did" (2 Samuel 11.7) is better translated: "When Uriah came to him, David asked how Joab was doing." Herod "inquired," rather than "demanded," where the Christ was to be born (Matthew 2.4). When we read concerning John the Baptist that "the soldiers . . . demanded of him, saying, And what shall we do?" (Luke 3.14), we get an impression of peremptoriness that is not justified by the Greek, which means "asked him." So also in Luke 17.20 and Acts 21.33.

"I will demand of thee" (Job 38.3; 40.7; 42.4) means "I will question you." In Exodus 5.14 "were beaten, *and* demanded" is ambiguous, for it suggests that the same persons who were beaten made a demand. RSV has "were beaten, and were asked."

**DENOUNCE.** Except for its technical sense, to give formal notice of the termination of an armistice or a treaty, the verb "denounce" now means to declare that something is bad, or to accuse persons of evil. But it was used in a wider, more general sense up to the seventeenth century, meaning simply to proclaim or announce, without implication of evil.

A publication of 1581 is quoted in OED as saying: "I suppose no man will deny, but that Paule doth denounce men to be Justified by fayth." Wyclif's translation of the instruction to the Levites concerning the tithes (Numbers 18.26) begins: "Commande thou, and denounce to the dekenes . . ." Tyndale and later translators have "Speak unto the Levites, and say . . ." Following Wyclif, the Rheims New Testament (1582) had Paul say, "we denounced to you, that if any will not work, neither let him eat" (2 Thessalonians 3.10). Tyndale, the Great Bible, and the Geneva Bible have "we warned you . . ." and KJ "we commanded you . . ."

The word "denounce" is used only once in KJ, where Moses delivers his final exhortation to the people of Israel, warning them what will happen if they turn away from God: "I denounce unto you this day, that ye shall surely perish" (Deuteronomy 30.18). It is used here to represent a general Hebrew verb, *nagad,* which KJ translates "declare" 62 times, "shew" 60 times, and "tell" 189 times. The use of the word "denounce" in this verse was an innovation of the KJ translators. Coverdale had used "certify"; Tyndale, the Great Bible, the Geneva Bible, and the Bishops' Bible had used "pronounce"; and the Douay Bible had "foretell." RSV reads, "I declare to you this day, that you shall perish."

**DEPUTY** means a person appointed to act for another, or elected to represent a constituency. It is correctly used for a regent in Moab (1 Kings 22.47). But in Esther 8.9 and 9.3 "deputy" is wrongly used for a word which means "governor" and is so translated by KJ in 23 other occurrences. It is wrongly used in Acts 13 for the official title of Sergius Paulus, proconsul of Paphos, and in 18.12 for the official title of Gallio, proconsul of Achaia. In Acts 19.38 the town clerk reminds Demetrius and his fellow craftsmen that "the courts are open, and there are proconsuls" before whom legal charges may be brought.

**DESCRY** means to get sight of, discover, perceive. It is used in the obsolete sense of investigate, spy out, reconnoiter, in Judges 1.23, "the house of Joseph sent to descry Bethel." The revised versions read, "the house of Joseph sent to spy out Bethel."

**DESIRE** in one instance among more than two hundred in KJ has a rare old connotation of regret. 2 Chronicles 21.18–20 records the death of Jehoram, smitten in the bowels with an incurable disease, in punishment for his evil ways and his infidelity to the LORD. "Thirty and two years old was he when he began to reign, and he reigned in Jerusalem eight years, and departed without being desired." RSV reads "he departed with no one's regret." This is a passage in which the KJ translators showed their sound literary judgment. The preceding English versions had failed to grasp the meaning of the last clause. The Geneva Bible translated it "and lived without being desired"; Coverdale "and walked not well"; Matthew's Bible "and he walked not pleasantly"; the Great Bible and the Bishops' Bible "and lived wretchedly."

**DESPITE** is an old word for contempt or scorn, growing into malice, injury, or outrage. With its adjective and adverb, it appears eight times in KJ. In Ezekiel 25.6, 15 RSV replaces it with "malice," and in 36.5 with "contempt." The adjective "despiteful," in the list of vices in Romans 1.30, stands for the Greek *hubristēs,* which is better translated by "insolent." "Pray for them which despitefully use you" (Luke 6.28) means "pray for those who abuse you."

The account of the visit of Paul and Barnabas at Iconium closes with: "And when there was an assault made both of the Gentiles, and also of the Jews with their rulers, to use *them* despitefully, and to stone them, They were ware of *it,* and fled unto Lystra and Derbe" (Acts 14.5–6a). The word "assault" is too heavy here, for it implies an actual attack, while the first clause of verse 6 implies that the apostles learned of the plot and escaped. RSV translates: "When an attempt was made by both Gentiles and Jews, with their rulers, to molest them and to stone them, they learned of it and fled to Lystra and Derbe."

"To do despite to" is an old idiom which OED defines as "to treat with injury and contumely; to outrage." It appears in Hebrews 10.29: "Of how much sorer punishment, suppose ye, shall he be thought worthy, who hath trodden under foot the Son of God, and hath counted the blood of the covenant, wherewith he was sanctified, an unholy thing, and hath done despite unto the Spirit of grace?" RSV translates: "How much worse punishment do you think will be deserved by the man who has spurned the Son of God, and profaned the blood of the covenant by which he was sanctified, and outraged the Spirit of Grace?"

**DEVICE** is used in the sense of purpose or plan, as it was by Shakespeare:

> "Our wills and fates do so contrary run
> That our devices still are overthrown;
> Our thoughts are ours, their ends none of our own."
>
> *Hamlet*, III, 2, 222

Except in two cases where the purpose or plan is the LORD's (Jeremiah 18.11; 51.11), the purposes are unworthy and the plans underhanded, so that "scheme" or "plot" is sometimes the appropriate word.

When Huram the king of Tyre assured King Solomon that the skilled craftsman he was sending was able "to grave any manner of graving, and to find out every device which shall be put to him," the meaning was "to do all sorts of engraving and execute any design that may be assigned him" (2 Chronicles 2.14). Paul's statement to the men of Athens, "Forasmuch then as we are the offspring of God, we ought not to think that the Godhead is like unto gold, or silver, or stone, graven by art and man's device" (Acts 17.29), is more literally translated, "Being then God's offspring, we ought not to think that the Deity is like gold, or silver, or stone, a representation by the art and imagination of man."

**DEVOTIONS.** The translation of Paul's speech at Athens, as contained in KJ, begins with two misleading expressions (Acts 17.22–23). Paul did not insult his audience by calling them "too superstitious"; he won a sympathetic hearing, and laid a foundation for his appeal, by saying "I perceive that in every way you are very religious."

The statement, "as I passed by, and beheld your devotions," which KJ attributes to him, implies that he beheld a group or groups of Athenians engaged in the act of worship. But this is not implied by the Greek, which is correctly translated by the revised versions, "as I passed along, and observed the objects of your worship."

The Greek word *sebasma*, "object of worship," is used in one other passage (2 Thessalonians 2.3–4) where KJ refers to "the son of perdition, who opposeth and exalteth himself above all that is called God, or that is worshipped; so that he as God sitteth in the temple of God, shewing himself that he is God." That is a strangely confusing translation. The first "God" should not be capitalized; the expression "as God" is a gloss or copyist's insertion which does not appear in the ancient manuscripts; and "shewing himself" means "proclaiming himself." RSV reads; "the son of perdition, who opposes and exalts himself against every so-called god or object of worship, so that he takes his seat in the temple of God, proclaiming himself to be God."

**DIET.** The freeing of King Jehoiachin from prison is described in 2 Kings 25.27–30 and Jeremiah 52.31–34 in almost identical terms. The last verse of the account in 2 Kings reads in KJ: "And his allowance *was* a continual allowance given him of the king, a daily rate for every day, all the days of his life." The corresponding verse in Jeremiah reads in KJ: "And *for* his diet, there was a continual diet given him of the king of Babylon, every day a portion until the day of his death, all the days of his life." Except for the addition of the words for "of Babylon" and "until the day of his death," the Hebrew text of these two verses is identical. The word "diet" is used in the sense, now obsolete, of an allowance of food and living expenses. RSV translates Jeremiah 52:33–34: "So Jehoiachin put off his prison garments. And every day of his life he dined regularly at the king's table; as for his allowance, a regular allowance was given him by the king according to his daily need, until the day of his death as long as he lived."

**DIG UP.** "An ungodly man diggeth up evil" (Proverbs 16.27) may be taken to refer to scandalmongers who claim to unearth and reveal the misdeeds of others. But the Hebrew word refers to the digging of a pit or snare. It is the word used in Proverbs 26.27, "Whoso diggeth a pit shall fall therein." It appears also in Psalms 57.6; 119.85 and Jeremiah 18.20, 22. These passages make clear that "dig up" is a misleading expression here. RV and ASV have "A worthless man deviseth mischief," and RSV has ". . . plots evil."

**DISALLOW** means to refuse to approve, sanction, or accept. The word appears in Numbers 30.3–15, with respect to the vows or pledges made by a woman. RSV uses "express disapproval" (vs. 5, 8) and "oppose" (vs. 5, 11). The entire passage should be read in both versions.

The other appearance is 1 Peter 2.7, where Christ is referred to as "the stone which the builders disallowed." This is strangely inconsistent, for KJ itself has "the stone which the builders rejected" in Matthew 21.42, Mark 12.10, and Luke 20.17. It has "be rejected of the elders" (Mark 8.31; Luke 9.22), "be rejected of this generation" (Luke 17.25), and "was rejected" (Hebrews 12.17). The Greek verb which in all these cases is translated "rejected," is represented by "disallowed" in 1 Peter 2.7.

**DISANNUL** simply means to annul; and "annul" means to abolish, cancel, make null and void. In four of the six passages where "disannul" occurs in KJ, the revisers did little more than delete the prefix "dis-." RSV reads in Isaiah: "For the LORD of hosts has purposed, and who will annul it" (14.27); "your covenant with death will be annulled" (28.18). In Galatians it reads: "no one annuls even a man's will, or adds to it, once it has been ratified" (3.15); "the law . . . does not annul a covenant previously ratified by God, so as to make the promise void" (3.17). The other two passages have required more rewording. "Wilt thou also disannul my judgment?" means "Will you even put me in the wrong?" (Job 40.8). Hebrews 7.18–19 should be compared in KJ and RSV; here two verses are regarded by KJ as independent sentences, which are the correlative parts of one sentence in the Greek.

"Disannul" is an anomaly among English words, for the prefix "dis-" usually means separation, as in "dismiss" and "dissolve," or negation, as in "disobey" and "displease." In "disannul" the "dis-" is repetitive and intensive, like the prefix "un-" in "unloose" and "unravel." Just as in Latin *pereo* means "I perish" and *dispereo* is simply an emphatic or even profane way of saying the same thing, "disannul" is one of the few English words which has no function except to embellish the language.

**DISCERN** is used four times in KJ as translation for a Hebrew verb which means to recognize some person or thing as formerly known. When Jacob presented himself in the guise of Esau, his father Isaac "discerned him not" (Genesis 27.23). When Laban accused Jacob of stealing his gods, Jacob told him to "discern thou what *is* thine with me, and take *it* to thee" (Genesis 31.32). When Tamar returned to Judah the pledges he had left with her, she said, "Discern, I pray thee, whose *are* these" (Genesis 38.25). A wounded man, his face disguised with ashes, condemned Ahab for sparing Benhadad; and when he removed his disguise Ahab "discerned him that he *was* of the prophets" (1 Kings 20.41). RSV uses "recognize" in the first and fourth of these cases, "point out" in the second, and "mark" in the third. When Joseph knew his brothers, but they did not know him (Genesis 42.7, 8), when Obadiah met Elijah and "knew him" (1 Kings 18.7), and when Job's friends "knew him not," the same Hebrew

verb is used which KJ represents by "discern" in the other cases. RSV
retains "knew" in the account of Joseph, but uses "recognized" for
Elijah and Job. Elsewhere KJ and RSV each use "discern" 18 times,
with no marked difference of usage between the two versions.

**DISCOMFIT** is an old military word. Its primary meaning is to
undo, throw into confusion, rout, defeat an army or
other organized body of attack or defense. In non-military contexts, it
means to thwart or defeat the purposes and plans of some individual or
group. Applied to an individual, it may mean little more than to confuse or disconcert him.

"Discomfited" is used nine times in KJ, always in the military sense.
RSV replaces it by "threw into confusion" (1 Samuel 7.10), "threw
into a panic" (Joshua 10.10; Judges 8.12), "routed" (Judges 4.15;
2 Samuel 22.15; Psalm 18.14). In Exodus 17.13 a more literal translation of the Hebrew verb gives, "And Joshua mowed down Amalek
and his people with the edge of the sword." This verb is translated
by "laid low" in Job 14.10 and Isaiah 14.12.

"His young men shall be discomfited" (Isaiah 31.8) fails to convey
the meaning of the Hebrew, which is "his young men shall be put to
forced labor." (See TRIBUTE)

"There was a very great discomfiture" (1 Samuel 14.20) means
"there was very great confusion." The Hebrew word here is *mehumah*,
which means confusion, tumult, panic. This noun and the verb *hum*,
from which it is derived, appear in Deuteronomy 7.23. KJ renders this
verse: "But the LORD thy God shall deliver them unto thee, and shall
destroy them with a mighty destruction, until they be destroyed." ASV
has: "But Jehovah thy God will deliver them up before thee, and
will discomfit them with a great discomfiture, until they be destroyed."
RSV has: "But the LORD your God will give them over to you, and
throw them into great confusion, until they are destroyed."

**DISCOVER.** In the KJ Old Testament the word "discover" is used
34 times, and always in the now obsolete sense of un-
cover or lay bare. It is retained by the revised versions in only one of
these cases, 1 Samuel 22.6, "Saul heard that David was discovered."
It is replaced by "uncover" 13 times. Other typical renderings are:
"exposed your iniquity" (Lamentations 2.14); "do not disclose another's secret" (Proverbs 25.9); "the foundations of the world were
laid bare" (2 Samuel 22.16); "strips the forests bare" (Psalm 29.9);
"we will show ourselves to them" (1 Samuel 14.8). Instead of "I will

discover thy skirts upon thy face" (Nahum 3.5) the RSV has "I will lift up your skirts over your face." Where KJ says concerning leviathan "Who can discover the face of his garment?" (Job 41.13) the revised versions read "Who can strip off his outer garment?"

In other passages containing the same Hebrew words KJ shows that in 1611 the older sense of "discover" was tending to become obsolete. For example, where Wyclif had "His heed he shal not discouer" KJ has "he shall not uncover his head" (Leviticus 21.10). It uses "uncover" 35 times as translation for these Hebrew words, and is followed by the revised versions in most of these cases.

In both cases where "discover" is used in the KJ New Testament it is an inexact translation of the Greek. The meaning of "had discovered Cyprus" (Acts 21.3) is "had come in sight of Cyprus"; and in place of "discovered a certain creek with a shore" (Acts 27.39), RSV reads "noticed a bay with a beach."

**DISHONESTY,** in the one passage where it occurs, is used in the obsolete sense of dishonor, discredit, shame. It represents the Greek word *aischunē*, shame, disgrace. In place of "have renounced the hidden things of dishonesty," RSV reads "have renounced disgraceful, underhanded ways" (2 Corinthians 4.2). "His dishonesty appears in leaving his friend here in necessity and denying him" (*Twelfth Night,* III, 4, 421).

**DISORDERLY** appears in three verses, 2 Thessalonians 3.6, 7, 11, where it is a mistranslation of the Greek, which in this context means be idle, live in idleness. The corresponding adjective is represented by "unruly" in 1 Thessalonians 5.14, but there also means "idle." Paul's exhortation, which KJ renders "warn them that are unruly, comfort the feebleminded, support the weak, be patient toward all *men,*" is translated by RSV, "admonish the idle, encourage the fainthearted, help the weak, be patient with them all."

**DISPUTE** in KJ often carries the meaning of reasonable discussion or argument, rather than that of wordy altercation. The verb and its derivatives appear 15 times in the New Testament. RSV retains "dispute" in Acts 6.9; 9.29; 24.12; Romans 14.1; Jude 9. It uses "discuss" in Mark 9.33–34, "debate" in Acts 15.2, 7 and 1 Corinthians 1.20, and "argue" in Acts 17.17; 19.8–9. It has "questioning" in Philippians 2.14, and "wrangling" in 1 Timothy 6.5—the latter as translation of a quite distinct and rather bitter Greek word.

The one appearance of "dispute" in the KJ Old Testament is in Job's plea for a hearing before God, beginning, "Oh that I knew where I might find him!" (23.3) and ending, "There the righteous might dispute with him; so should I be delivered for ever from my judge" (23.7). RSV translates the passage:

"Oh, that I knew where I might find him,
  that I might come even to his seat!
I would lay my case before him
  and fill my mouth with arguments.
I would learn what he would answer me,
  and understand what he would say to me.
Would he contend with me in the greatness of his power?
  No; he would give heed to me.
There an upright man could reason with him,
  and I should be acquitted for ever by my judge."

**DISQUIETNESS.** "I have roared by reason of the disquietness of my heart" (Psalm 38.8) is the only use of the word in KJ. It is in a context of distress. RSV reads "I groan because of the tumult of my heart."

**DIVERS** and **DIVERSE** were originally two spellings of the same word. Since about 1700 each has had its own pronunciation and meaning—"diverse" meaning "different in character or quality," while "divers" means "various, sundry, several, more than one" without stating how many. In KJ "diverse" appears 8 times, always in the sense of "different" (Leviticus 19.19; Esther 1.7; 3.8; Daniel 7.3, 7, 19, 23, 24).

"Divers" appears 36 times in KJ, and is not used by RSV. *"Divers of the princes of Judah"* (2 Chronicles 21.4) are "some of the princes of Judah," and "divers of Asher" (30.11) are "a few men of Asher." When Jesus expressed compassion on the multitude, "for divers of them came from far" (Mark 8.3), he said that "some of them have come a long way." "When divers were hardened" against Paul's speaking in the synagogue at Ephesus (Acts 19.9), the meaning is that some hardened themselves or were stubborn.

"Thou shalt not sow thy vineyard with divers seeds" (Deuteronomy 22.9) means ". . . with two kinds of seed." The prohibition of "divers weights" and "divers measures" (Deuteronomy 25.13, 14) refers to "two kinds of weights" and "two kinds of measures."

"Divers diseases" are "various diseases" (Matthew 4.24; Mark 1.34;

Luke 4.40), and "divers places" are "various places" (Matthew 24.7; Mark 13.8; Luke 21.11). So also RSV has "various impulses" (2 Timothy 3.6), "various passions" (Titus 3.3), "various miracles" (Hebrews 2.4), "various ablutions" (Hebrews 9.10), "various trials" (James 1.2).

One of the oldest poems in the Bible is the Song of Deborah, Judges 5, which ends with the desperate attempt of the mother of Sisera to still her fears because her son has not yet returned from the battle. She seeks to reassure herself by the thought that he is delaying over the division of booty. KJ reads: "Have they not sped? have they *not* divided the prey; to every man a damsel *or* two; to Sisera a prey of divers colours, a prey of divers colours of needlework, of divers colours of needlework on both sides, *meet* for the necks of *them that take* the spoil?" RSV reads:

"Are they not finding and dividing the spoil?—
    A maiden or two for every man;
  spoil of dyed stuffs for Sisera,
      spoil of dyed stuffs embroidered,
      two pieces of dyed work embroidered for my neck as spoil?"

**DOCTOR.** The word "doctor" originally meant "teacher," and is so used three times in KJ. The revised versions use "teacher," which is the meaning of the Greek *didaskalos* (Luke 2.46; 5.17; Acts 5.34). In 1 Timothy 1.7 KJ uses "teacher of the law" for the same Greek term which it renders "doctor of the law" in Luke and Acts. (See TEACHER)

**DOCTRINE.** The verb *didaskō* appears 97 times in the Greek New Testament, and is always translated "teach." Yet *didachē* and *didaskalia* are translated by KJ as "learning" once, "teaching" once, and "doctrine" 48 times. In 1611 the word "doctrine" denoted the act of teaching as well as the content of teaching. "He said unto them in his doctrine" means "he said to them in his teaching" (Mark 4.2; 12.38). This sense of the word is now obsolete, and the revised versions use "teaching" more often than "doctrine." For *didachē* and *didaskalia* RSV has "teaching" 33 times, "doctrine" 14 times, "instruction" twice, and "lesson" once.

**DOGS** are mentioned in the Bible with contempt. "Am I a dog," says Goliath, "that you come to me with sticks?" (1 Samuel 17.43). "Why should this dead dog curse my lord the king?" growls Abishai when an old retainer of Saul curses David (2 Samuel 16.9). Dogs licked up the blood of Ahab, and ate the body of Jezebel (1 Kings 22.38; 2 Kings 9.30–37). When the author of Ecclesiastes reflects that life at its worst is yet better than death, he writes, "A living dog is better than a dead lion" (9.4). The psalmist compares his enemies to dogs (59.14). (See GRUDGE)

Paul calls his opponents dogs (Philippians 3.2), and John places "the dogs" outside of the holy city, with "sorcerers and fornicators and murderers and idolaters" (Revelation 22.15).

There is no trace in the Scriptures of the friendship and loyalty that so commonly exist between a dog and its owner. "The Eastern street dog is a type of all that is cowardly, lazy, filthy, treacherous, and contemptible," says Hastings' *Dictionary of the Bible*.

The only admiring reference is in Proverbs 30.29–31, which reads in KJ: "There be three *things* which go well, yea, four are comely in going: A lion *which* is strongest among beasts, and turneth not away for any; A greyhound; an he goat also; and a king, against whom *there is* no rising up." But the greyhound here is a precarious guess at the intent of the Hebrew expression, which means "girt in the loins." Other guesses are "war horse" or "cock." The last of these conjectures is supported by the ancient versions. The Septuagint has "a cock walking proudly among the hens."

"The price of a dog" (Deuteronomy 23.18) means "the wages of a dog," and the reference is to the sodomites or male cult prostitutes who were banned by the commandment in verse 17.

**DONE AWAY.** "Why should the name of our father be done away from among his family, because he hath no son?" is the justified question of the daughters of Zelophehad (Numbers 27.4), for which RSV has: "Why should the name of our father be taken away from his family, because he had no son?" Coverdale has "perish"; Tyndale and the other sixteenth-century versions have "taken away."

In 1 Corinthians 13.8–10 prophecies shall "fail," knowledge shall "vanish away," and "that which is in part shall be done away." The three verbs go back to Tyndale; but in each of the three clauses the Greek has the same verb. RSV here follows the Greek strictly, saying of prophecy, knowledge, and the imperfect that it "will pass away."

2 Corinthians 3 is a difficult chapter, which is made somewhat less difficult by the clearer translation and the paragraphing of RSV. The whole chapter should be read in the two versions. "Done away" appears in verses 7, 11, and 14; and is replaced by "fading," "faded away," "taken away."

**DOTE.** To dote is "to be silly, deranged, or out of one's wits; to act or talk foolishly" (OED). One thus afflicted is described as "a dotard," "in his dotage," or "a doting fool." When the LORD in anger checked the incipient rebellion of Miriam and Aaron against Moses, Aaron confessed to Moses, "we have done foolishly" (Numbers 12.11). "The princes of Zoan are become fools," declares Isaiah 19.13. "They are foolish," says Jeremiah of the inhabitants of Jerusalem (5.4). "They shall dote," he says of the "liars" among the inhabitants of Babylon (50.36). In these four cases the Hebrew verb is the same, *ya'al.* The last passage (Jeremiah 50.35–38) should be read in its entirety; RSV translates verse 36:

> "A sword upon the diviners,
> that they may become fools!
> A sword upon her warriors,
> that they may be destroyed!"

"Dote" is used with respect to foolish sexual infatuation in Ezekiel 23, and is retained by the revised versions.

"He is proud, knowing nothing, but doting about questions and strifes of words" (1 Timothy 6.4) does not convey the meaning of the Greek text, for the verb *noseō,* which is here rendered "doting," means "to be sick." Tyndale had "wasteth his braynes." RSV translates: "he is puffed up with conceit, he knows nothing; he has a morbid craving for controversy and for disputes about words."

**DOUBT,** noun. One of the greatest of Horace Bushnell's sermons was entitled "The Dissolving of Doubts." Its text, Daniel 5.12, served simply as a point of departure; and the sermon was in no wise impaired by the fact that King Belshazzar appealed to Daniel not to dissolve doubts, but as one who could solve problems. The literal meaning of the Aramaic is to loosen joints or knots. This Aramaic expression is used literally in 5.6: "the joints of his loins were loosed." It is applied to the knotty problems of the mind in 5.12, 16, where in place of "dissolve doubts" RSV has "solve problems."

**DOUBT,** verb. The multitude on the day of Pentecost were not so much "in doubt" as "perplexed" (Acts 2.12). Later, when the officers report that the apostles are not to be found in the prison into which they had been put, KJ states that "when the high priest and the captain of the temple and the chief priests heard these things, they doubted of them whereunto this would grow" (5.24); RSV has "they were much perplexed about them, wondering what this would come to." When Peter "doubted in himself" what his vision might mean, the meaning is that he "was inwardly perplexed" (10.17). In all these cases the Greek verb is the one which KJ itself translates by "was (were) perplexed" in Luke 9.7 and 24.4.

For a different form of the same verb, "doubting" is replaced by "uncertain" (John 13.22); "Because I doubted of such manner of questions" is rendered "Being at a loss how to investigate these questions" (Acts 25.20); and "I stand in doubt of you" means "I am perplexed about you" (Galatians 4.20).

The question put to Jesus at the feast of dedication, in the winter, as he walked in the temple in Solomon's porch, "How long dost thou make us to doubt?" (John 10.24) means "How long will you keep us in suspense?" In general, the word "doubt" in 1611 stood for indecision, uncertainty, perplexity, suspense of judgment, without as much of weighting toward the negative as it has now acquired.

The final word in the phrase "without wrath and doubting" (1 Timothy 2.8) represents the Greek word *dialogismos,* which in the plural is the last word of the phrase rendered by KJ, "without murmurings and disputings" (Philippians 2.14). In the Timothy context RSV has "without anger or quarreling" and in the Philippians context "without grumbling or questioning."

**DOUBTFUL.** "Him that is weak in the faith receive ye, *but* not to doubtful disputations" (Romans 14.1) is worded in RSV: "As for the man who is weak in faith, welcome him, but not for disputes over opinions." Arndt makes this rendering more explicit: "welcome, but not for the purpose of getting into quarrels about opinions."

Luke 12.29 is parallel to Matthew 6.31, though with different sentence structure, and with different Greek verbs for "do not be anxious." In the rendering "neither be ye of doubtful mind" the word "doubtful" is used in the obsolete sense "full of fear" or "apprehensive." Modern lexicons, relying on evidence from ancient Greek papyri, make it clear that the Greek verb used in Luke means "do not be anxious," as well as that which is used in Matthew. RSV's "nor be of anxious mind" simply reflects its conservatism and possibly a desire to intimate to the English reader that the verbs are different.

**DOUBTLESS** originally meant without any doubt, unquestionably, certainly; but usage has weakened it so that, except where used in a concessive clause, it means little more than probably.

It is more likely to raise doubts than to allay them. In Isaiah 63.16, "Doubtless thou *art* our father," the revised versions have "For thou art our father." In 2 Samuel 5.19, "I will doubtless deliver the Philistines into thine hand," the revised versions use "I will certainly . . ." In 1 Corinthians 9.2 they replace "doubtless" with "at least."

The translation of Philippians 3.7–8a has an ambiguous phrase, "loss for Christ," at the end of verse 7, and an awkward beginning, "Yea doubtless, and . . . ," for verse 8. RSV has: "But whatever gain I had, I counted as loss for the sake of Christ. Indeed I count everything as loss because of the surpassing worth of knowing Christ Jesus my Lord." In the other three cases where "doubtless" appears in KJ, it is omitted by the revised versions as not sustained by the Hebrew or Greek (Numbers 14.30; Psalm 126.6; 2 Corinthians 12.1).

**DRAGON.** The Oxford English Dictionary defines "dragon" as "a mythical monster, represented as a huge and terrible reptile, usually combining ophidian and crocodilian structure, with strong claws, like a beast or bird of prey, and a scaly skin; it is generally represented with wings, and sometimes as breathing out fire." In the New Testament this word occurs only in Revelation, beginning with the appearance in heaven of the "great red dragon" (12.3) and ending with his being bound for a thousand years and thrown into the bottomless pit (20.2–3). It occurs in the KJ Old Testament 22 times, but is retained by RSV only 5 times. In 14 cases it is replaced by "jackal," correcting a mistaken rendering of the Hebrew. (See SEA MONSTER.) In Ezekiel 29.3; 32.2 the word "dragon" refers to the Pharaoh of Egypt; and in Psalm 74.13 and Isaiah 27.1; 51.9 the references are to ancient Semitic mythology.

**DREADFUL** applies properly to persons, things, or events which inspire fear, reverence, or awe. Like "awful" and "horrid," it has been weakened in common usage and may mean little more than bad, ugly, or objectionable. KJ uses "dreadful" in its proper sense, yet RSV usually employs other terms, in the interest of clarity and consistency of translation. Jacob's exclamation when he awoke from his dream—"How dreadful *is* this place!"—now reads, "How awesome is this place!" (Genesis 28.17). The word of the LORD by Malachi, "my name *is* dreadful among the heathen," is better rendered, "my name is feared among the nations" (Malachi 1.14). An identical Hebrew phrase is translated consistently in Joel 2.31 and Malachi 4.5, "the great and terrible day of the LORD" (RSV). The attribute "dreadful" which is applied to God in Daniel 9.4 is changed to "terrible," to be consistent with the KJ rendering of the same Hebrew word as an attribute of God in Deuteronomy 7.21; 10.17; Nehemiah 1.5; 4.14; 9.32; Psalms 47.2; 66.3; 68.35; 76.12; 99.3; and Zephaniah 2.11. (See REVEREND)

**DUKE** is used 57 times in KJ to denote the chiefs of Edom. It is not an hereditary title of nobility, as in Great Britain, but simply an English rendering of the Latin word *dux,* leader. In the lists of the chiefs of Edom (Genesis 36.15–43; 1 Chronicles 1.51–54; compare Exodus 15.15) the Latin Vulgate used *dux* and its plural *duces* as translation for the Hebrew *'alluph,* and both Wyclif and Tyndale took the word over into English as "duke." The Hebrew word may have meant "the leader of a thousand," for it is derived from *'eleph,* the word for "thousand." The only other "dukes" in the Old Testament are the "dukes of Sihon" (Joshua 13.21), for whom the Latin Vulgate has *duces,* though the Hebrew has the plural of *nasik,* prince.

Wyclif translated Matthew 2.6 from the Latin, "And thou bethleem the lond of iuda are not the leest among the princis of iuda, for of thee a duyk schal go out that schal gouerne my puple israel." But Tyndale and his sixteenth-century successors, translating from the Greek, used "captayne" with various spellings. KJ chose "for out of thee shall come a Governor, that shall rule my people Israel."

**DULCIMER.** A musical instrument with strings struck by hammers held in the hands. It was the prototype of the harpsichord and the piano. "Dulcimer" appears in the Bible only as one of the instruments played at the dedication of the golden image which King Nebuchadnezzar had set up (Daniel 3.5, 10, 15). But it is there a mistranslation of the Aramaic *sumponyah,* which was a wind instrument, a kind of bagpipe.

**DURE,** a verb from the Latin *durare,* is now obsolete. Its place has been taken by "endure," from the Latin *indurare.* "Dure" appears only once in KJ, Matthew 13.21: "Yet hath he not root in himself, but dureth for a while." The same Greek appears, in the plural number, in Mark 4.17, where KJ has, "And have no root in themselves, and so endure but for a time." The difference in translation goes back to Tyndale, who had "dureth but a season" in Matthew and "so endure but a time" in Mark. The revised versions use "endure" in both passages

What was originally the present participle of "dure" has survived in living English as the preposition "during." And such derivatives as "durable," "durability," and "duration" seem to possess the qualities which they denote, and will doubtless last for more centuries to come.

**EAR** and **PLOW** are old verbs which have the same meaning, to prepare the soil for sowing by turning it up in furrows. "Ear" was often used by Wyclif and the sixteenth-century versions. For example, Wyclif had "Whether al day shal ere the erere, that he sowe" (Isaiah 28.24). Tyndale had "earynge" in Genesis 45.6, Exodus 34.21, and Deuteronomy 21.4; his version of 1 Corinthians 9.10 had "he which eareth, shuld eare in hope." But he also had "plowe" in Deuteronomy 22.10 and Luke 9.62, and "plowinge" in Luke 17.7.

The King James Version retained *"there shall* neither *be* earing nor harvest" (Genesis 45.6), "in earing time and in harvest" (Exodus 34.21), "neither eared nor sown" (Deuteronomy 21.4), "to ear his ground" (1 Samuel 8.12), "that ear the ground" (Isaiah 30.24); elsewhere it uses "plow." The revised versions do not retain "ear" in this sense. KJ uses "plough" as a noun once, Luke 9.62.

**EARNEST.** (2 Corinthians 1.22; 5.5; Ephesians 1.14.) An earnest is money paid to bind a bargain, serving at once as a first instalment and as a pledge or guarantee that the rest will follow as agreed. Paul is saying in these passages that the gift of the Holy Spirit in our hearts is a foretaste and a guarantee of our heavenly inheritance.

Examples of the use of this word in English literature are Shakespeare's *Cymbeline*, I, 5, 65:

> I prithee, take it;
> It is an earnest of a further good
> That I mean to thee

and Tennyson's *In Memoriam*, xcvii:

> The days she never can forget
> Are earnest that he loves her yet.

**EDIFY, EDIFICATION.** To edify, from the Latin *aedificare*, is to build. The word is rarely used, however, in a material sense. While "edifice" usually refers to a large building of wood or stone or steel, "edify" and "edification" are used in a figurative sense, to refer to intellectual improvement or moral and spiritual upbuilding.

Jesus said, in answer to Peter's confession, "on this rock I will build my church," Matthew 16.18; and Paul took up the verb which Jesus used, and made it one of his most characteristic expressions. KJ sometimes translates it as "build" or "build up" (Acts 20.32; 1 Corinthians 3.10–14; Ephesians 2.20–22; Colossians 2.7; see also 1 Peter 2.5 and Jude 20). But more often KJ translates it as "edify" or "edification."

Archbishop Trench, in his *English Past and Present,* held that "our use of 'edify' and 'edification' first obtained general currency among the Puritans," and cited two quotations. One is from the satirist, John Oldham, 1653–1683:

> "The graver sort dislike all poetry,
> Which does not, as they call it, edify."

The other is from Robert South, 1634–1716, voluble opponent of Non-conformists: "All being took up and busied in the grand work of preaching and holding forth, and that of edification, as the word then went . . ."

There is a measure of irony in these quotations, and it must be admitted that the words lend themselves to ironic use. They may also be used in less than the high moral and religious sense which has come to be their primary meaning. One may speak of an edifying conversation when it is merely informing, or revealing, or even amusing.

For this reason RSV uses "build up" or "upbuilding" in a dozen cases where KJ used "edify" or "edification." It retains the latter terms in 1 Corinthians 14, Romans 15.2, and Ephesians 4.29. But elsewhere it replaces them with such renderings as "the church was built up" (Acts 9.31); "building up the body of Christ" (Ephesians 4.12); "your upbuilding" (2 Corinthians 12.19); "mutual upbuilding" (Romans 14.19); "upbuilds itself in love" (Ephesians 4.16).

**EITHER,** in a usage now obsolete, could be used to introduce the second or any later alternative, as well as the first. "Can the fig tree . . . bear olive berries? either a vine, figs?" (James 3.12) is reworded in RSV, "Can a fig tree . . . yield olives, or a grapevine figs?" "Not as though I had already attained, either were already perfect" (Philippians 3.12) means "Not that I have already obtained this or am already perfect." "Either what woman having ten pieces of silver . . ." (Luke 15.8) begins with an unmistakable word for "Or" in the Greek. So too Luke 6.42, "Either how canst thou say to thy brother . . ." should begin with "Or," as the parallel in Matthew 7.4 does.

The old usage is interestingly shown in Wyclif's phrasing of Matthew 12.33: "ether make ye the tree good and his fruyt good: ether make ye the three yuel and his fruyt yuel, for a tree is knownun of the fruyt." For the second "ether" Tyndale and his successors had "or else."

**EMERODS.** A variant form of "hemorrhoids," a disease also known as "piles," characterized by tumors or painful swellings of the veins about the anus. The three names for this disease were used interchangeably until the seventeenth century, and "emerods" only is used in KJ. All but one of its appearances are in the account of the plague which smote the Philistines when they had captured the ark of the LORD (1 Samuel 5–6). The problem of translation is complicated by the fact that the Philistines are described as making an expiatory offering to the LORD of five golden images of their "emerods" (6.3–5). The phrase "in their secret parts" (5.9) is a mistranslation of the Hebrew verb which means "broke out." There is no good reason for thinking that these were hemorrhoids; it is probable that they were the boils of the bubonic plague. The revised versions use "tumors."

In the context of Deuteronomy 28.27, RSV translates the Hebrew word by "ulcers"—"The LORD will smite you with the boils of Egypt, and with the ulcers and the scurvy and the itch, of which you cannot be healed."

**EMINENT** refers only to physical height in KJ, and not to persons or qualities. The "eminent place" built by the harlot Jerusalem (Ezekiel 16.24, 31, 39) was probably "a vaulted chamber." "An high mountain and eminent" means "a high and lofty mountain" (Ezekiel 17.22).

On the other hand, the noun "preeminence," which occurs three times, refers to persons. "A man hath no preeminence above a beast" (Ecclesiastes 3.19) reads in RSV "man has no advantage over the beasts." In 3 John 9 "Diotrephes, who loveth to have the preeminence among them" is more sharply rendered, "Diotrephes, who likes to put himself first." In Colossians 1.18, speaking of Christ Jesus, the Son of God, KJ has "that in all *things* he might have the preeminence," and RSV "that in everything he might be pre-eminent."

**EMULATION.** The two occurrences of "emulation" are different in tone. In Romans 11.14 Paul writes of stirring his fellow Jews to emulation of the Gentiles; but in Galatians 5.20 "emulations" are included with adultery, idolatry, murder, drunkenness, and a spate of similar evils in a long list of the works of the flesh as contrasted with the fruit of the Spirit.

Like the Latin *aemulatio,* "emulation" could be used in a good sense or a bad sense. It has retained the good sense, its primary meaning, an honest and fair endeavor to equal or surpass others. The bad sense, ambitious rivalry leading to contention and ill will, was current in the sixteenth and seventeenth centuries, and appears a dozen times in Shakespeare's plays.

> "I was advertised their great general slept,
> Whilst emulation in the army crept."
> *Troilus and Cressida,* II, 2, 212
> "My heart laments that virtue cannot live
> Out of the teeth of emulation."
> *Julius Caesar,* II, 3, 14

This bad sense of "emulation" is now obsolete, and the revised versions use "jealousy" in the list of works of the flesh in Galatians 5.20.

Though used in a good sense, "provoke to emulation" is not a correct translation in Romans 11.14. The Greek verb means to make jealous. The same verb appears in 11.11, where KJ translates it "provoke to jealousy"; also in 10.19. The Rheims New Testament was the first to use "emulate" and "emulation" in these texts, taking the words from the Latin. KJ took the Rheims rendering in 11.14, but not in 11.11 or in 10.19.

RSV translates Romans 11.13b–14, "Inasmuch then as I am an apostle to the Gentiles, I magnify my ministry in order to make my fellow Jews jealous, and thus save some of them." The word "jealous" is here used in the sense which is defined by OED as "troubled by the belief, suspicion or fear that the good which one desires to gain or keep for oneself has been or may be diverted to another." This view of the text has the support of the revised versions and of such modern translations as Weymouth, Moffatt, Goodspeed, C. B. Williams, and Phillips. Knox sticks to "emulation," but he is translating the Latin Vulgate.

**ENABLE** appears only in 1 Timothy 1.12, "I thank Christ Jesus our Lord, who hath enabled me." The word is here used in the sense of "strengthen." The Greek verb which it represents is translated "be strong" in Romans 4.20, Ephesians 6.10, and 2 Timothy 2.1; "strengthen" in Philippians 4.13 and 2 Timothy 4.17; and "increased in strength" in Acts 9.22. Tyndale and his successors here translated it "hath made me strong." RSV reads, "I thank him who has given me strength for this, Christ Jesus our Lord."

**END.** The word "end" is much used in the Bible, and its meaning is usually clear. There is one Hebrew word for "end," however, which occasionally entangled the KJ translators. The word is *aharith,* which may mean not only the termination of a period of time, but also the latter part of a period of time, or the future, or prosperity. Which of these meanings it has in a particular case depends upon the context. And the KJ translators got into trouble where *aharith* appears with *tiqwah,* a Hebrew word for "hope."

The word of the LORD to the exiles in Babylon (Jeremiah 29.11) was not that he planned "to give you an expected end," but "to give you a future and a hope." His assurance, two chapters further on (Jeremiah 31.17), that "there is hope in thine end" means "there is hope for your future."

The statement of Proverbs 23.18 seems oddly self-contradictory: "surely there is an end, and thine expectation shall not be cut off." And there is no way for the English reader to know that the same Hebrew words are translated differently by KJ itself in the following chapter: "there shall be a reward, and thy expectation shall not be cut off" (Proverbs 24.14). RSV reads: "Surely there is a future, and your hope will not be cut off." ". . . there will be a future, and your hope will not be cut off."

"There shall be no reward to the evil *man;* the candle of the wicked shall be put out," Proverbs 24.20, means "the evil man has no future; the lamp of the wicked will be put out."

In Psalm 37.37–38 the word *aharith* is used in the sense of "posterity," as was recognized by both the Greek Septuagint and the Latin Vulgate. The KJ renderings, "the end of *that* man *is* peace" and "the end of the wicked shall be cut off," have been replaced in RSV by "there is posterity for the man of peace" and "the posterity of the wicked shall be cut off."

**ENLARGE** means to make larger, extend, widen. It is retained by RSV in more than half the cases where it appears in KJ. Hannah's prayer of Thanksgiving, "my mouth is enlarged over mine enemies" means "my mouth derides my enemies" (1 Samuel 2.1). "Thou hast enlarged my steps under me" (2 Samuel 22.37 = Psalm 18.36) now reads "Thou didst give a wide place for my steps under me." "Thou hast enlarged me *when I was* in distress" means "Thou hast given me room when I was in distress" (Psalm 4.1). "When thou shalt enlarge my heart" is less ambiguously worded, "when thou enlargest my understanding" (Psalm 119.32). For "who enlargeth his desire as hell, and *is* as death, and cannot be satisfied" (Habakkuk 2.5) RSV reads:

> "His greed is as wide as Sheol;
> like death he has never enough."

Chapter 60 of Isaiah, which begins, "Arise, shine; for thy light is come, and the glory of the LORD is risen upon thee"; is great literature —a poem of sustained beauty and strength. It is marred only by the first half of verse 5, "Then thou shalt see, and flow together, and thine heart shall fear, and be enlarged"—a statement which is quite at variance with all else in the chapter. RSV has a sound translation of the Hebrew text:

> "Then you shall see and be radiant,
> your heart shall thrill and rejoice."

The KJ rendering "flow together" results from confusing the verb *nahar,* which means "be radiant," with a different verb *nahar,* which means "flow." The KJ translators followed the Vulgate here, rejecting the truer renderings of the sixteenth-century English versions. The Great Bible and the Bishops' Bible had "Then thou shalt see this and be glorious"; the Geneva Bible had "Then shalt see and shine."

Paul's plea to the Corinthians (2 Corinthians 6.11–13) reads in KJ: "O *ye* Corinthians, our mouth is open unto you, our heart is enlarged. Ye are not straitened in us, but ye are straitened in your own bowels." The Greek of this passage is more accurately translated by RSV: "Our mouth is open to you, Corinthians; our heart is wide. You are not restricted by us, but you are restricted in your own affections. In return —I speak as to children—widen your hearts also."

**ENLARGEMENT** appears once, in Mordecai's counsel to Queen Esther: "if thou altogether holdest thy peace at this time, *then* shall there enlargement and deliverance arise to the Jews from another place" (Esther 4.14). The word is obviously used in the sense of release from confinement, bondage, or distress. The Hebrew, however, has the word for respite or relief. The revised versions agree in using "relief." RSV reads: "if you keep silence at such a time as this, relief and deliverance will rise for the Jews from another quarter."

**ENSUE** was sometimes used in the sixteenth and seventeenth centuries in the sense of pursue, seek after, or strive for. It has this meaning in 1 Peter 3.11: "seek peace, and ensue it." This verse is part of a passage (3.10–12) which quotes, with some adaptation, Psalm 34.12–16, in which KJ had "seek peace, and pursue it." The inconsistent "ensue" comes from Tyndale. The revised versions replace it with "pursue."

**ENTREAT, INTREAT.** The corrected editions of the KJ prepared by Dr. Paris, 1762, and Dr. Blayney, 1769, made a distinction between "entreat," meaning to deal with, and "intreat," meaning to ask or pray. This distinction was not present in the original edition of 1611, where the two spellings are used interchangeably—for example, Job 19.16 has "intreated" and 19.17 has "entreated," Job 24.21 has "intreateth," Jeremiah 15.11 has "intreat" in the text and "entreat" in the marginal note, Philippians 4.3 has "entreat."

The truth is that these are simply different spellings of the same word. They are so handled in OED, which defines "intreat" as an obsolete or archaic form of "entreat."

"Entreat" is used in an obsolete sense in Luke 20.11, Acts 27.3, and 1 Thessalonians 2.2, where the revised versions have "handled" or "treated." The KJ rendering, "Julius courteously entreated Paul," means "Julius treated Paul kindly" (Acts 27.3).

The expression "be entreated" means to be prevailed on or persuaded to grant the object of an entreaty. It is used in KJ only of God, though in now obsolete English it was applied to human beings also. The passages are Genesis 25.21; 2 Samuel 21.14; 24.25; 1 Chronicles 5.20; 2 Chronicles 33.13, 19; Ezra 8.23; Isaiah 19.22. RSV uses "granted his prayer," "heeded their supplications," "granted their entreaty," in forms suitable to the context.

"Easy to be entreated" (James 3.17) represents a Greek word which RSV translates "open to reason."

The successive translations of 2 Corinthians 8.4 reveal the difficulty of finding the right English to express the meaning of very compact Greek. In modern spelling, Tyndale and his successors had: "and prayed us with great instance that we would receive their benefit, and suffer them to be partakers with others in ministering to the saints." KJ took a different interpretation of the last clause: "praying us with much intreaty that we would receive the gift, and *take upon us* the fellowship of the ministering to the saints." The revised versions of 1881–

1901 have a mechanical rendering which is opaque: "beseeching us with much entreaty in regard of this grace and the fellowship in the ministering to the saints." RSV returns to Tyndale's understanding of the verse, and translates it: "begging us earnestly for the favor of taking part in the relief of the saints."

**EQUAL** had a moral meaning in the sixteenth and seventeenth centuries. Like the Latin *aequus,* from which it is derived, the word "equal" was applied to what is fair, just, and therefore right. In this sense it has been superseded by the word "equitable." Ezekiel protests in the name of the LORD: "Yet ye say, The way of the Lord is not equal. Hear now, O house of Israel; Is not my way equal? are not your ways unequal?" (18.25). RSV uses "just." Douay had "right"; Moffatt and Smith use "fair." See also Ezekiel 18.29; 33.17, 20. "Let thine eyes behold the things that are equal" (Psalm 17.2) reads in RSV, "Let thy eyes see the right!" The injunction to masters in Colossians 4.1, "give unto *your* servants that which is just and equal" means "treat your slaves justly and fairly."

The KJ translation of Paul's statement in Galatians 1.13–14 is defective at a number of points: "For ye have heard of my conversation in time past in the Jews' religion, how that beyond measure I persecuted the church of God, and wasted it: And profited in the Jews' religion above many my equals in mine own nation, being more exceedingly zealous of the traditions of my fathers." RSV translates this: "For you have heard of my former life in Judaism, how I persecuted the church of God violently and tried to destroy it; and I advanced in Judaism beyond many of my own age among my people, so extremely zealous was I for the traditions of my fathers." In the KJ rendering the word "equals" is used to represent a Greek noun which means precisely "persons of one's own age."

The verb "equal" is used in the obsolete sense of liken or compare in Lamentations 2.13.

**ESCHEW.** In the sense of avoid or escape a danger or inconvenience, "eschew" is now obsolete, surviving in Shakespeare's proverb, "What cannot be eschewed must be embraced" (*The Merry Wives of Windsor,* V, 5, 251).

In 2 Corinthians 8.20 Tyndale had: "For thys we eschue, that eny man shuld rebuke us in this plenteous distribution that is ministred by us." The Geneva Bible changed to "Avoyding this," which KJ adopted. RSV states Paul's purpose more positively: "We intend that no one should blame us about this liberal gift which we are administering."

In the sense of abstain from, avoid, or shun a course of conduct the word "eschew" is still living English, in literary rather than colloquial use. From Coverdale comes the rendering of Psalm 18.23 which still appears in the Book of Common Prayer: "I was also uncorrupt before him, and eschewed mine own wickedness." KJ changed this to "I was also upright before him, and I kept myself from mine iniquity"; and RSV has "I was blameless before him, and I kept myself from guilt."

"Eschewed" is retained by KJ in two contexts. Job is described as "one that feared God, and eschewed evil" (1.1, 8; 2.3). In 1 Peter 3.11 appears this counsel for one who would love life and see good days: "Let him eschew evil, and do good." RSV uses "turn away from evil" in both these contexts.

**ESPOUSED** is used by KJ in an obsolete sense, meaning "betrothed" rather than "married." The contexts are 2 Samuel 3.14, David and Michal; and Matthew 1.18; Luke 1.27; 2.5, Joseph and Mary. In each of these cases the revised versions use "betrothed." In all other cases, 10 in number, KJ itself, as well as the revised versions, translates as "betrothed" the word used by David.

Another New Testament occurrence is a figure of speech concerning Christ and the church (2 Corinthians 11.2). This reads in KJ: "I have espoused you to one husband, that I may present *you as* a chaste virgin to Christ." RSV translates: "I betrothed you to Christ to present you as a pure bride to her one husband."

On the other hand, the plural "espousals" is used in KJ, as it still is, for the formal celebration of a marriage. It is equivalent to "nuptials" or a "wedding." The contexts are Song of Solomon 3.11 and Jeremiah 2.2.

**EVEN,** as adverb, is used 1,032 times in the KJ Old Testament, and in 928 of these cases there is no corresponding word in the Hebrew text. This surprising fact is due in part to the disposition of the translators in 1611 to write "even so" for "so," "even as" for "as," and "even unto" where we should now say "to" or "up to" or "as far as." It is due chiefly, however, to their use of "even" to introduce an additional word or words intended to explain more clearly or fully some preceding word or words. The word "even" was for them a sign of equivalence or identity; it meant that the person or thing or subject referred to in what followed was the same person or thing or subject referred to in what preceded.

For example, "the men of the city, *even* the men of Sodom" means "the men of the city, the men of Sodom"—the same persons are meant by the two phrases (Genesis 19.4). So also "the man, *even* Lot" means "the man Lot" (Genesis 19.9). "Jacob set up a pillar, *even* a pillar of stone" (Genesis 35.14) has no "even" in the Hebrew. In such cases, the word "even" has a function similar to "namely" or "that is."

The use of "even" in this colorless sense is now obsolete, and it has become a misleading feature of KJ. "Even" is now used to indicate an extreme case or something not to be expected. So the reader of Genesis 10.21 is likely to wonder what was the matter with Shem to occasion the statement that "even to him were *children* born."

The revised versions omit the inserted "even" in most cases. In Genesis, for example, KJ uses "even" 26 times, of which 21 were cases of insertion without a corresponding Hebrew word. RSV retains "even" only in 27.34, 38 and 46.34.

The use of "even" in the KJ New Testament is more restrained, and the cases of sheer insertion are not many. Yet the revised versions are more cautious. KJ uses "even" 273 times in the New Testament; RSV uses it 175 times. "God, even the Father" (1 Corinthians 15.24) means "God the Father." "God, even our Father" (2 Thessalonians 2.16) is "God our Father." "The will of God, *even* your sanctification" (1 Thessalonians 4.3) is "the will of God, your sanctification." Compare also the two versions of John 1.12; Acts 5.37; Romans 9.10; 1 Thessalonians 2.19; Hebrews 5.14.

**EVERY** is sometimes used by KJ in senses now usually expressed by "each." "They received every man a penny" (Matthew 20.9, 10) is an archaic rendering that came from Tyndale; RSV has "each of them received a denarius." An obsolete use of "every" for each of two occurs in 2 Samuel 21.20: "And there was yet a battle in Gath, where was a man of *great* stature, that had on every hand six fingers, and on every foot six toes, four and twenty in number." Modern versions read "each hand" and "each foot."

**EVIDENCE.** When Jeremiah purchased the field in Anathoth, the documents recording the transaction are described as "the evidence of the purchase." In this sense, the word "evidence" is used eight times in Jeremiah 32; the revised versions replace it with the legal term "deed."

The text which opens the great chapter on faith, Hebrews 11, "Now faith is the substance of things hoped for, the evidence of things not seen," is more accurately translated: "Now faith is the assurance of things hoped for, the conviction of things not seen."

**EVIDENT.** "Now therefore be content, look upon me; for *it is* evident unto you if I lie" (Job 6.28) is more accurately translated,
"But now, be pleased to look at me;
for I will not lie to your face."
The KJ translators got "evident unto you" out of the Hebrew for "to your face," and misconstrued the strong Hebrew negative as a condition.

**EVIDENTLY** (See APPARENTLY)

**EXAMPLE, ENSAMPLE.** Examples are typical, or good, or bad. KJ uses "example" nine times, and "ensample" six times, without any distinction of meaning, except that no merely typical instances are included. Of the "examples," five are good and four bad; of the "ensamples," four are good and two bad. The revised versions of 1881–1901 made an effort to use "ensample" for good instances and "example" for bad, but the effort failed—they could not thus arbitrarily limit the word "example." RSV discards "ensample" as archaic, and uses "example" in all cases where the word is called for.

"Now all these things happened unto them for ensamples" (1 Corinthians 10.11) now reads, "Now these things happened to them as a warning." "Lest any man fall after the same example of unbelief" (Hebrews 4.11) means "that no one fall by the same sort of disobedience." In Hebrews 8.5 "Who serve unto the example and shadow of heavenly things" is revised to read "They serve a copy and shadow of the heavenly sanctuary." Timothy is urged, not to "be thou an example of the believers," but to "set the believers an example" (1 Timothy 4.12). In Matthew 1.19 "not willing to make her a publick example" is worded "unwilling to put her to shame." The Greek verb in this case appears also in Hebrews 6.6, where it is translated by KJ "put *him* to an open shame" and by RSV "hold him up to contempt."

**EXCEED** is used at least once in the obsolete sense of pass the bounds of propriety, go too far. The passage is Job 36.9, which KJ renders: "Then he sheweth them their work, and their transgressions that they have exceeded." The Hebrew verb here represented by "exceeded" is the one which is rendered "strengtheneth" in Job 15.25: "he strengtheneth himself against the Almighty." RSV translates this, "bids defiance to the Almighty"; and 36.9, "then he declares to them their work and their transgressions, that they are behaving arrogantly."

When Jonathan sent his lad home with his "artillery," and David came forth from his hiding place, the two friends "kissed one another, and wept one with another, until David exceeded" (1 Samuel 20.41). The Hebrew means simply that he wept greatly, or, as we should now say, bitterly. RSV translates it: "they kissed one another, and wept with one another, until David recovered himself."

**EXCEEDING.** As an adjective, "exceeding" was used in the sixteenth century to connote either surpassing excellence or extreme impropriety. Now obsolete in these senses, the adjective "exceeding" is used only with nouns "denoting quality, condition, or feeling, or including a notion of magnitude or multitude" (OED), and it may mean either surpassing or excessive, in amount or degree. Nowhere in the Bible does it mean excessive or immoderate. In the Old Testament, RSV retains "God my exceeding joy" (Psalm 43.4) and uses "exceeding greatness" (Psalm 150.2) and "exceeding brightness" (Daniel 2.31). In the New Testament, RSV does not use "exceeding" in any of the six passages where it served as an adjective. Varying with the Greek, RSV reads: "beyond all comparison" and "surpassing grace" (2 Corinthians 4.17; 9.14); "immeasurable greatness" and "immeasurable riches" (Ephesians 1.19; 2.7); "rejoice and be glad" (1 Peter 4.13); "with rejoicing" (Jude 24).

RSV does not use "exceeding" as an adverb. "An exceeding high mountain" is "a very high mountain" (Matthew 4.8); "exceeding sorry" is "exceedingly sorry" (Mark 6.26) and "greatly distressed" (Matthew 17.23); "exceeding sorrowful" is "very sorrowful" (Matthew 26.22); and so on.

**EXCELLENCY.** This is one of many words in English derived from Latin words ending in -*ia*—arrogancy, continency, innocency, etc.—which are now commonly spelled with a final "e" instead of "y." "Excellency" appears 25 times in KJ. RSV replaces it by other words in all cases, though in no case by "excellence." It is replaced by "majesty" or "majestic" 9 times, and by "pride" 5 times. "The excellency of Jacob" is "the pride of Jacob" (Psalm 47.4; Amos 6.8; 8.7). "The voice of his excellency" is "his majestic voice" (Job 37.4). In Isaiah 35.2 RSV reads "the majesty of Carmel and Sharon

. . . the majesty of our God." The revised versions have "height" in Job 20.6—"Though his height mount up to the heavens . . ."

Philippians 3.8 reads in KJ, "I count all things *but* loss for the excellency of the knowledge of Christ Jesus my Lord"; and in RSV, "I count everything as loss because of the surpassing worth of knowing Christ Jesus my Lord."

**EXERCISE,** as verb, is like the verb "practice." It is used both for habitual action and for training with a view to establish habits and acquire strength or skill. It appears 18 times in KJ, translating 12 different Hebrew and Greek verbs. Because RSV translates these verbs more literally, it uses other terms in many of these cases. "I exercise myself" means "I occupy myself" (Psalm 131.1) and "I take pains" (Acts 24.16). "The travail which God hath given to the sons of men to be exercised in it" means "the business that God has given to the sons of men to be busy with" (Ecclesiastes 3.10; 1.13). "The people of the land have used oppression, and exercised robbery, and have vexed the poor and needy" is reworded, "The people of the land have practiced extortion and committed robbery; they have oppressed the poor and needy" (Ezekiel 22.29). "Having . . . an heart they have exercised with covetous practices" means "They have hearts trained in greed" (2 Peter 2.14). "Those who by reason of use have their senses exercised to discern both good and evil" means "those who have their faculties trained by practice to distinguish good from evil" (Hebrews 5.14). "Train" and "training" are used by RSV in Hebrews 12.11 and 1 Timothy 4.7, 8. The Greek verb is *gymnazō* and the noun *gymnasia*.

**EXPECT** occurs in the obsolete sense of "wait" (Hebrews 10.13): "From henceforth expecting till his enemies be made his footstool." RSV reads: "then to wait until his enemies should be made a stool for his feet."

**EXPECTATION,** as used in KJ, means "hope." "The expectation of the poor" (Psalm 9.18) is "the hope of the poor." "My soul, wait thou only upon God; for my expectation *is* from him" (Psalm 62.5) is more accurately translated, "For God alone my soul waits in silence, for my hope is from him." "Thy expectation shall not be cut off" (Proverbs 24.14) means "your hope will not be cut off." "To give you an expected end" (Jeremiah 29.11) is "to give you a future and a hope." (See END)

**EXPERIENCE.** Laban asked Jacob to remain with him because, he said, "I have learned by experience that the LORD hath blessed me for thy sake" (Genesis 30.27). But this mistranslates the Hebrew word *nahash,* which means to practice divination, to observe signs or omens. The revised versions of 1881–1901 read "I have divined that . . . ," but this is an ambiguous rendering which may mean nothing more than "I have come to believe that . . ." RSV says clearly, "I have learned by divination that the LORD has blessed me because of you." Goodspeed reads "I have noted the omens"; Moffatt "I have learned from the omens." Compare 1 Kings 20.33, where the verb is *nahash;* KJ has "the men did diligently observe . . ." and RSV reads "the men were watching for an omen. . . ."

Romans 5.3b–5a reads: "we glory in tribulations also: knowing that tribulation worketh patience; And patience, experience; and experience, hope; And hope maketh not ashamed . . ." With this compare RSV: "we rejoice in our sufferings, knowing that suffering produces endurance, and endurance produces character, and character produces hope, and hope does not disappoint us . . ." The Greek word here translated "experience" is *dokimē,* which means character that has been tested and proved.

**FABLE** appears five times as translation for the Greek *mythos.* Since the word "myth" did not enter the English language until the early nineteenth century, "fable" long carried its meaning. But the favor with which the word "myth" was received and its quick establishment in English usage have tended to restrict the word "fable" to stories more or less akin to the fables of Aesop. OED says that the most prominent sense of the word now is "a short story devised to convey some special lesson, especially one in which animals or inanimate things are the speakers or actors."

The word *mythos* in the Greek New Testament does not mean "fable," but "myth," which is defined by OED as "a purely fictitious narrative usually involving supernatural persons, actions, or events, and embodying some popular idea concerning natural or historical phenomena." Paul instructs Timothy to "Have nothing to do with godless and silly myths" and to warn certain persons not to "occupy themselves with myths and endless genealogies" (1 Timothy 4.7; 1.4). He takes, as always, a realistic view of human nature, and says that "the time is coming when people will not endure sound teaching, but having itching ears they will accumulate for themselves teachers to suit their own likings, and will turn away from listening to the truth and wander into myths" (2 Timothy 4.3–4). In the letter to Titus, he warns against "the circumcision party" (1.10) with their "Jewish myths" (1.14). Peter, in his second letter, declares: "We did not follow cleverly devised myths when we made known to you the power and coming of our Lord Jesus Christ, but we were eyewitnesses of his majesty" (1.16).

**FAIN,** as an adverb, means gladly. "He would fain have filled his belly with the husks that the swine did eat" (Luke 15.16) is translated by RSV "he would gladly have fed on the pods that the swine ate." (For "pods" see HUSKS.) The substitution of "fed" for "filled his belly with" marks a return to the Greek text of the best ancient manuscripts.

The only other occurrence of "fain" is in Job 27.22, where "would fain flee" is an attempt, which began with the Geneva Bible, to translate the intensified force of the Hebrew idiom which combines the absolute infinitive and the finite form of the verb for "flee." This is represented in RSV by "flees in headlong flight." The three verses, 21–23, should be compared in the two versions. "East wind" is the subject of verse 21, and RSV takes it as the subject of all three verses. KJ, on the other hand, inserts *"God"* as the subject of verse 22, and *"Men"* as the subject of verse 23. (See GENERALLY and SURELY for explanation of the Hebrew idiom.)

**FAINT,** as used in KJ, means to grow weak, whether in body or in spirit. To lose courage is the basic idea. The word refers to the fainthearted and dispirited more often than to the feeble or exhausted. Shakespeare used it thus in *Richard II*, II, 1, 297:
"But if you faint, as fearing to do so,
Stay and be secret, and myself will go."
The RSV retains "faint" in most of its occurrences in this sense, but replaces it in some. Examples are: Luke 18.1, "ought always to pray and not lose heart"; 2 Corinthians 4.1, 16, "we do not lose heart; Hebrews 12.5, "nor lose courage." See also Galatians 6.9, Ephesians 3.13.

More literal translations of the Hebrew verbs give: "lest the heart of his fellows melt" (Deuteronomy 20.8); "the inhabitants of the land melt away" (Joshua 2.9); "melt in fear" (Jeremiah 49.23); "hearts melt" (Ezekiel 21.15). The Hebrew also expresses bodily weakness or fatigue in Genesis 25.29, 30, "I am famished"; 1 Samuel 30.10, 21, "exhausted"; 2 Samuel 21.15, "David grew weary"; Jeremiah 45.3,

"I am weary." KJ's rendering, "Therefore shall all hands be faint," is literally translated, "Therefore all hands will be feeble" (Isaiah 13.7).

"Faint" does not occur in the sense of swoon, unless Isaiah 51.20, Jonah 4.8, and Daniel 8.27 are to be so construed. The context in Isaiah 51.17–23 does not support this construction, however; and RSV reads "so that he was faint" in the description of Jonah's plight, and "was overcome" in the account of Daniel's vision.

Where Eliphaz says to Job, "But now it is come upon thee, and thou faintest," RSV translates the Hebrew more accurately: "But now it has come to you, and you are impatient" (Job 4.5). A confusion of Hebrew terms underlies the KJ rendering of Isaiah 10.18, "they shall be as when a standard-bearer fainteth"; RSV has "it will be as when a sick man wastes away." In the rendering of Psalm 27.13, *"I had fainted,* unless I had believed to see the goodness of the LORD in the land of the living," the words "I had fainted" are an insertion of the translators for which there is no good reason. RSV makes the positive affirmation, "I believe that I shall see the goodness of the LORD in the land of the living!"

The reason given for Jesus' compassion on the multitudes, "because they fainted, and were scattered abroad" (Matthew 9.36) is mis-worded as the result of an eighth-century error in copying the manuscript of the Greek text. RSV translates: "When he saw the crowds, he had compassion for them, because they were harassed and helpless, like sheep without a shepherd." "Harassed" is the meaning of the Greek word in the ancient manuscripts, which had been miscopied. "Helpless" translates a Greek participle which means literally "lying down."

**FAME.** The primary meaning is what people say, current talk, a report, rumor, or item of news, whether good or bad. The word is now rarely used in this sense, however; and is generally applied to a widespread reputation derived from notable achievements. KJ uses "fame" 24 times; RSV retains it in 13 of these cases and changes it to "renown" in one. In the other 10 cases KJ uses "fame" in the older, primary sense, and RSV expresses the meaning by "report" 9 times and "rumor" once. Examples are: "When the report was heard in Pharaoh's house" (Genesis 45.16); "your wisdom and prosperity surpass the report which I heard" (1 Kings 10.7 = 2 Chronicles 9.6); "we have heard the report of it" (Jeremiah 6.24). With respect to Jesus, RSV uses "fame" in Matthew 4.24; 9.31; 14.1; Mark 1.28; and it uses "report" in Matthew 9.26 and Luke 4.14, 37; 5.15, as fits the context in each case.

The one use of "rumor" is in the Hymn to Wisdom which constitutes Job 28. Verse 22 reads:

> "Abaddon and Death say,
>     'We have heard a rumor of it with our ears.' "

The entire chapter, verses 1–28, should be read in the RSV, which is more accurate and clear than the KJ rendering of this chapter. The exegesis by Samuel Terrien in *The Interpreter's Bible* (vol. 3, pp. 1099–1105) is excellent.

Examples of Shakespeare's use of "fame" in the older sense are:

> "Shame hath a bastard fame, well managed;
>     Ill deeds are doubled with an evil word."
>                 *Comedy of Errors*, III, 2, 19–20
> "So is the fame."
>                 *Antony and Cleopatra*, II, 2, 166
> "When fame had spread their cursed deed."
>                 *Pericles*, V, 3, 95


**FAMILIARS** (Jeremiah 20.10) means "familiar friends." The Hebrew expression means literally "men of my peace," and occurs also in Psalm 41.9, Jeremiah 38.22, and Obadiah 7. In these passages RSV uses "my bosom friend" and "your trusted friends."


**FAMILIAR SPIRIT.** A spirit or demon believed to be in communication with a necromancer and responsive, as a servant (*famulus*), to his call. Those who "have familiar spirits" are often referred to in the Old Testament, nearly always in connection with "wizards." The Law required that both be put to death (Leviticus 20.27). RSV retains the word "wizard," but for those who have familiar spirits uses the term "medium." This is one of the newest words to appear in RSV, for the earliest citation of it in OED is dated 1853, and is concerned with the "spirit-rappings" which excited public interest in the middle of the nineteenth century.


**FAN, FANNER.** The metaphor of the wheat and the chaff occurs a number of times in the Bible, most notably in the words of John the Baptist: "He that cometh after me is mightier than I, whose shoes I am not worthy to bear: he shall baptize you with the Holy Ghost, and *with* fire: Whose fan *is* in his hand, and he will thoroughly purge his floor, and gather his wheat into the garner; but he will burn up the chaff with unquenchable fire" (Matthew 3.11–12). RSV translates verse 12: "His winnowing fork is in his hand, and he will clear his threshing floor and gather his wheat into the granary, but the chaff he will burn with unquenchable fire."

"Fan" appears six times and "fanners" once in the KJ Old Testament. RSV replaces these terms with "winnow," "winnowing fork," and "winnowers" (Isaiah 30.24; 41.16; Jeremiah 4.11; 15.7; 51.2). The winnowing fan was a six-pronged wooden fork or a perforated wooden shovel to toss the grain in the air and let the wind blow the lighter chaff away.

Shakespeare wrote in *Cymbeline*, I, 6, 177:

> "The love I bear him
> Made me to fan you thus, but the gods made you,
> Unlike all others, chaffless."

**FASHION.** "Rear up the tabernacle according to the fashion thereof" (Exodus 26.30), means "erect the tabernacle according to the plan for it." When Solomon's temple was finished "according to all the fashion of it," this was "according to all its specifications" (1 Kings 6.38). King Ahaz, seeing at Damascus an altar that took his fancy, "sent to Urijah the priest the fashion of the altar, and the pattern of it, according to all the workmanship thereof." What he sent was "a model of the altar, and its pattern, exact in all its details" (2 Kings 16.10). "Model" here represents a different Hebrew noun, which is usually translated "likeness." In Ezekiel 43.11, "the fashion thereof" means "its arrangement," translating yet another Hebrew noun.

In the New Testament RSV replaces "fashion" with "appearance" (Luke 9.29); "form" (1 Corinthians 7.31; Philippians 2.8); "pattern" (Acts 7.44). "The grace of the fashion of it" (James 1.11) means "its beauty." "On this fashion" (Mark 2.12) is "like this."

Dr. William Aldis Wright, in *The Bible Word-Book*, 1884, said, "The verb is now rarely used." If that was so, the revisers sixty years later were not aware of it, for they treated the verb "to fashion" as still living English, retaining it in most, though not all, of the cases where it was used in KJ. The outstanding examples of change are 1 Peter 1.14, where "not fashioning yourselves according to the former lusts in your ignorance" has been replaced by "do not be conformed to the passions of your former ignorance"; and Philippians 3.21, where "be fashioned like unto" is "be like."

**FAST** means close or near in Ruth 2.8, 21, 23: "abide here fast by my maidens"; "so she kept fast by the maidens of Boaz." This is an archaic meaning of the word, carried on occasionally in such poetic forms as "fast by." Milton refers to "the snaky Sorceress that sat fast by Hell-gate" (*Paradise Lost*, II, 725). Keats' *Lamia*, 17, reads "Fast by the springs . . . were strewn rich gifts." In Ruth RSV uses "close to" or "close by."

**FAT,** adjective. "Fat and flourishing" is a phrase that comes to the tongue as readily as "fat and sleek" (Horace, *Epistles*, I, 1, 15), "fat and greasy" (Shakespeare, *As You Like It,* II, 1, 55), or "fat, fair, and forty." But it is not an accurate translation of the Hebrew in Psalm 92.12–15, where the righteous are compared to trees.
"They still bring forth fruit in old age,
they are ever full of sap and green."

**FAT,** noun. The King James Version uses "fats" for "vats" in Joel 2.24; 3.13, and "winefat" for "wine press" in Isaiah 63.2 and Mark 12.1. Both "fat" and "vat" are old words, but "fat" is the original and "vat" the variant. The song to Bacchus in Shakespeare's *Antony and Cleopatra* (II, 7, 120) contains the lines:
"In thy fats our cares be drown'd,
With thy grapes our hairs be crown'd:
Cup us, till the world go round!"
The Oxford English Dictionary quotes from Bishop Gervase Babington's *Exposition of the Commandments,* 1583: "They would have every fatte . . . stand on his owne bottome," and from Bunyan's *Pilgrim's Progress,* 1678: "Every Fatt must stand on his own bottom." It quotes from Nathan Bailey's *Dictionary,* 1736: "Every Tub must stand upon it's own Bottom."

**FEEBLEMINDED.** "Comfort the feebleminded" (1 Thessalonians 5.14) does not convey the sense of the Greek, which means "encourage the fainthearted." Those to whom Paul refers were not mentally deficient but discouraged. The verse reads in KJ: "Now we exhort you, brethren, warn them that are unruly, comfort the feebleminded, support the weak, be patient toward all *men*." RSV translates: "And we exhort you, brethren, admonish the idle, encourage the fainthearted, help the weak, be patient with them all." The term "idle," as well as "fainthearted," is justified by the evidence of the Greek papyri.

**FENCED** comes from "defence." The word is often used in the Old Testament, chiefly in the phrase "fenced cities," for which RSV has "fortified cities." More care to express the specific meanings of the Hebrew verbs replaces "fenced" in the following RSV translations: "He digged it and cleared it of stones" (Isaiah 5.2); "Thou didst . . . knit me together with bones and sinews" (Job 10.11); "He has walled up my way, so that I cannot pass" (Job 19.8); "the man who touches them arms himself with iron and the shaft of a spear" (2 Samuel 23.7).

**FERVENT,** in the physical sense, means boiling, glowing, burning. It occurs in this literal physical sense in one passage of KJ, where it is twice said that "the elements shall melt with fervent heat" (2 Peter 3.10, 12). RSV says "with fire."

The word is more often used with reference to the passions, aspirations, or actions of persons. It then means ardent, glowing, intensely earnest. In 1 Peter 1.22 and 4.8 the Greek words carry the idea of constancy and earnestness, rather than hot ardor. The first of these verses reads in KJ: "Seeing ye have purified your souls in obeying the truth through the Spirit unto unfeigned love of the brethren, *see that ye love one another with a pure heart fervently.*" The phrase for "through the Spirit" is a medieval addition which is not in the ancient Greek manuscripts. RSV reads, "Having purified your souls by your obedience to the truth for a sincere love of the brethren, love one another earnestly from the heart." The KJ rendering of 1 Peter 4.8 is, "And above all things have fervent charity among yourselves: for charity shall cover the multitude of sins." Here KJ's substitution of "charity" for "love" is misleading. (See CHARITY.) RSV translates, "Above all hold unfailing your love for one another, since love covers a multitude of sins."

In three other passages the Greek words carry the idea of glowing zeal. For "your fervent mind toward me" (2 Corinthians 7.7), RSV has "your zeal for me." Apollos is described by KJ as "fervent in the spirit" and by RSV as "fervent in spirit" (Acts 18.25). Paul enjoins the Christians at Rome, according to KJ, to be "not slothful in business; fervent in spirit; serving the Lord" (Romans 12.11). RSV translates this, taking the participles as imperatives: "Never flag in zeal, be aglow with the Spirit, serve the Lord." Note how the difference in context makes "in spirit" appropriate concerning Apollos, and "in the Spirit" a sound translation in the Letter to the Romans.

Paul's message to the Colossians that Epaphras was "always labour-

ing fervently for you in prayers" is translated by RSV "always remembering you earnestly in his prayers" (Colossians 4.12). There is
no Greek word for "fervent" in James 5.16, "The effectual fervent
prayer of a righteous man availeth much." RSV has "The prayer of a
righteous man has great power in its effects."

**FETCH ABOUT.** An obsolete expression, according to OED and Webster, for contrive or devise. In some parts of Amer-
ica it is used colloquially, however, with the same meaning as "bring
about," that is, effect or accomplish. Just what sense the KJ translators attached to it in 2 Samuel 14.20 is not clear. Their rendering,
"To fetch about this form of speech hath thy servant Joab done this
thing," misapprehends the meaning of three Hebrew words. The revised versions of 1885 and 1901 give a literal translation: "to change
the face of the matter. . . ." RSV reads: "In order to change the
course of affairs your servant Joab did this."

**FETCH A COMPASS** appears five times in KJ, and means to turn,
take a roundabout course, make a circuit. The
invention and wide use of the magnetic compass have caused the
phrase to become ambiguous and fall into disuse. The revised versions
of the Bible substitute other renderings. In the description of boundaries RSV uses "turn" (Numbers 34.5) and "turns about" (Joshua
15.3). "Fetch a compass behind them" means "go around to their
rear" (2 Samuel 5.23). When the kings of Israel, Judah, and Edom
joined forces against the king of Moab and "fetched a compass of seven
days' journey," they "made a circuitous march of seven days" through
the wilderness of Edom (2 Kings 3.9). After Paul's shipwreck, he and
his guards and companions remained three months on the island of
Malta, then sailed to Syracuse, where they stayed three days. "From
thence we fetched a compass, and came to Rhegium," according to KJ.
RSV has "from there we made a circuit and arrived at Rhegium" (Acts
28.13).

**FINE,** as a verb, is used in KJ only in the sense of to make fine or
pure, to refine. "Surely there is a vein for the silver, and a
place for gold *where* they fine *it*" (Job 28.1) reads in RSV, "Surely
there is a mine for silver, and a place for gold which they refine."
"Take away the dross from the silver, and there shall come forth a
vessel for the finer" (Proverbs 25.4) is reworded in RSV ". . . and

the smith has material for a vessel." The "fining pot" is a "crucible" in which silver is refined (Proverbs 17.3; 27.21).

**FINE,** as an adjective, is used 100 times in KJ, always in the sense of finished, pure, of superior quality. We read in it of "fine flour," "fine meal," "fine linen," "fine gold," "fine brass." These expressions are retained by RSV, except for "fine brass," which is "burnished bronze" (Revelation 1.15; 2.18). The revised versions use the word also in the sense of very small, of minute particles. "Small dust" (Exodus 9.9) is "fine dust"; and "as small as dust" (Deuteronomy 9.21) means "as fine as dust."

The revised versions use "fine clothing" in James 2.2, 3 for "goodly apparel" and "the gay clothing." The diverse renderings came from Tyndale, and it would not hurt to keep them; but the Greek is the same in the two verses, and "gay" is used in an obsolete sense.

RSV introduces "fine" in an ironic sense in Mark 7.9, "You have a fine way of rejecting the commandment of God, in order to keep your tradition!"

**FLAGON.** "Stay me with flagons, comfort me with apples; for I *am* sick of love," if taken out of context, seems to be the cry of a disillusioned lover who is seeking solace in drink (Song of Solomon 2.5). But here, and in 5.8, the speaker is a young woman who is sick with love and longing for her beloved. The "of" simply perpetuates a loose rendering, probably without realization that as early as 1597 to be sick of something meant to be "thoroughly tired and weary of it" (OED). The word represented by "flagon" is *'ashishah,* which means a pressed "cake of raisins" such as King David distributed to the people when he brought the ark of the LORD into the city (2 Samuel 6.19; 1 Chronicles 16.3), and such as were used in Canaanite sacrificial feasts (Hosea 3.1).

By a mistake in interpreting the Hebrew, KJ has "covers to cover withal" in the list of utensils for the table of shewbread in the tabernacle. The revised versions correct this; RSV has "flagons with which to pour libations" (Exodus 25.29; 37.16) and "flagons for the drink offering" (Numbers 4.7).

**FLANKS** is the word used by KJ for the loins of a sacrificial animal (Leviticus 3.4, 10, 15; 4.9; 7.4). For the loins of a man it has "flanks" in Job 15.27 and "loins" in Psalm 38.7. The Hebrew word is the same, and the revised versions have "loins" in all these cases, except that RV retains "flanks" in the passage from Job.

**FLOOD** means a flow of water. It refers to the flowing in of the tide and to flowing rivers, as well as to deluge, overflow, and inundation. The flood of Noah's time has a special name in Hebrew, *mabbul* (Genesis 6–11; Psalm 29.10), though "the waters of Noah" are referred to in Isaiah 54.9. Outside of these passages and the New Testament references to Noah, "flood" has in KJ almost the variety of meanings recorded in OED. It stands for "streams" (Psalm 78.44; Isaiah 44.3) and "rivers" (Psalms 24.2; 66.6). "The flood decayeth and drieth up" (Job 14.11) means "a river wastes away and dries up." It refers on occasion to a particular river, the Nile, the Euphrates, or the Jordan. "On the other side of the flood" (Joshua 24.2) means "beyond the Euphrates"; in verses 3, 14, 15 RSV has "beyond the River."

"Thou didst cleave the fountain and the flood" (Psalm 74.15) means "thou didst cleave open springs and brooks." The hymn concerning wisdom (Job 28) is one of the great poems of the Bible, which should be read as a whole, comparing KJ and RSV. The rendering of verse 4 in KJ is puzzling: "The flood breaketh out from the inhabitant; *even the waters* forgotten of the foot: they are dried up, they are gone away from men." The revised versions are clearer. RSV has, "They open shafts in a valley away from where men live; they are forgotten by travelers, they hang afar from men, they swing to and fro." In verse 11, "He bindeth the floods from overflowing" means "He binds up the streams so that they do not trickle."

Shakespeare used "flood" in a full variety of meanings. Examples are:

"What need the bridge much broader than the flood?"
*Much Ado About Nothing*, I, 1, 318

"Three times did they drink,
Upon agreement, of swift Severn's flood."
*King Henry IV, Part I*, 1, 3, 103

"Through flood, through fire,
I do wander every where."
*A Midsummer Night's Dream*, II, 1, 5

**FLOOR** in the sense of the floor of a room or building occurs only 7 times in KJ. It appears 13 times, however, in the sense of a threshing floor. The Hebrew word for threshing floor, *goren,* is translated by KJ "threshing floor" 19 times and "floor" 11 times. There are scattered other renderings: "barn" (Job 39.12); "barnfloor" (2 Kings 6.27); "corn" (Deuteronomy 16.13); "threshingplace" (2 Samuel 24.16); "void place" (1 Kings 22.10 = 2 Chronicles 18.9). "Cornfloor" appears in Hosea 9.1, representing Hebrew which adds the word for "corn" to that for "floor." RSV uses "threshing floor" for all of these cases. (For "floor" in Matthew 3.12 and Luke 3.17 see PURGE.)

**FLOWERS,** derived from the Latin *fluor* (a flowing) rather than from *flos, floris* (a flower), is an old term, now obsolete, for menstrual discharges. It appears twice in the list of uncleannesses in Leviticus 15. The Hebrew *niddah* is translated by "flowers" in verses 24 and 33, but by "separation" in verses 20, 25, and 26 of the same chapter as well as in 12.2, 5. RSV uses "menstruation" for *niddah* in chapter 12, and "impurity" throughout chapter 15.

**FLUX.** The "bloody flux" which afflicted the father of Publius (Acts 28.8) was an early English name for dysentery, and is here used as translation for the Greek word *dysenteria*.

**FOLLOW** is a word that often occurs in the narratives of the Old Testament and of the Gospels, and is in most cases a correct translation and easily understood. The outstanding exception is Jeremiah 17.16, which appears in KJ, "As for me, I have not hastened from *being* a pastor to follow thee." The Hebrew of this clause is translated by RSV "I have not pressed thee to send evil." (See PASTOR)

In KJ "follow" sometimes represents the Hebrew word which means to pursue; and in these cases RSV uses stronger terms, as: "pursues righteousness" (Proverbs 21.21); "pursues the east wind" (Hosea 12.1); "runs after gifts" (Isaiah 1.23); "run after strong drink" (Isaiah 5.11); "let us press on to know the LORD" (Hosea 6.3). "Because I follow *the thing that* good *is*" (Psalm 38.20) is now translated "because I follow after good."

In a few cases KJ uses "follow hard" to represent the Hebrew verb which means cling or overtake. In place of "My soul followeth hard after thee," RSV has "My soul clings to thee" (Psalm 63.8). In 1 Samuel 31.2 and 1 Chronicles 10.2 the meaning is "the Philistines overtook Saul and his sons."

In the Epistles the Greek words for "pursue" or "imitate" are generally used. The RSV therefore has "pursue righteousness" (Romans 9.30, 31); and "Let us then pursue what makes for peace and for mutual upbuilding" (Romans 14.19). In place of "Follow peace with all *men*" it reads "Strive for peace with all men" (Hebrews 12.14); and in place of "Follow after charity" (1 Corinthians 14.1) now reads "Make love your aim." "Aim at righteousness" appears in 1 Timothy 6.11 and 2 Timothy 2.22.

The KJ rendering of 1 Thessalonians 5.15 is: "See that none render evil for evil unto any *man;* but ever follow that which is good, both among yourselves and to all *men.*" This verse is more accurately translated, "See that none of you repays evil for evil, but always seek to do good to one another and to all."

In place of "I follow after, if that I may apprehend that for which also I am apprehended of Christ Jesus," RSV has "I press on to make it my own, because Christ Jesus has made me his own" (Philippians 3.12). The same Greek verb which is here rendered "I follow after" is translated "I press" in verse 14 by KJ.

"Some men's sins are open beforehand, going before to judgment; and some *men* they follow after" (1 Timothy 5.24) is now translated "The sins of some men are conspicuous, pointing to judgment, but the sins of others appear later." (See IMITATE)

**FOOTMEN** in the Bible are not servants or lackeys but men who are in or available for military service. RSV retains the word only in 2 Kings 13.7, where it stands in context with "horsemen." Elsewhere the Hebrew term is translated "foot soldiers" or "men on foot." In 1 Samuel 22.17 a different Hebrew term is translated "guard," as KJ itself does 14 times in 1 Kings 14, 2 Kings 10 and 11, and 2 Chronicles 12. This means the company of foot soldiers assigned to protect the king, the king's house, or the house of the LORD.

**FORASMUCH AS** is a conjunctional phrase meaning in view of the fact that, inasmuch as, since, because. It appears 43 times in KJ, and is retained by RSV only in Jonathan's farewell words to David, "Go in peace, forasmuch as we have sworn both of us in the name of the LORD, saying, 'The LORD shall be between me and you, and between my descendants and your descendants, for ever'" (1 Samuel 20.42). Elsewhere it is replaced by less archaic terms, in most cases by "since" or "because."

In the following examples the KJ reading appears first, then that of RSV: "Forasmuch therefore as your treading *is* upon the poor" (Amos 5.11); RSV "Therefore because you trample upon the poor." "Forasmuch as thou sawest" (Daniel 2.41, 45); RSV "just as you saw." "Forasmuch as he had not to pay" (Matthew 18.25); RSV "as he could not pay." "Forasmuch as Lydda was nigh to Joppa" (Acts 9.38); "Since Lydda was near Joppa."

A more literal translation of the Greek is afforded by RSV in Acts 11.17: "If then God gave the same gift to them as he gave to us when we believed in the Lord Jesus Christ, who was I that I could withstand God?" More literal, again, are the participles in Acts 17.29, "Being God's offspring"; Acts 24.10, "Realizing that for many years you have been judge over this nation"; 1 Corinthians 15.58, "knowing that in the Lord your labor is not in vain." The revised versions use nothing to replace "forasmuch as" in Jeremiah 10.6, 2 Corinthians 3.3, and 1 Peter 1.18 because it is not called for by the Hebrew or Greek.

The phrase appears once in the obsolete form FORSOMUCH AS. This is in Jesus' word to Zacchaeus, "forsomuch as he also is a son of Abraham" (Luke 19.9). RSV has "since he also is a son of Abraham."

**FORETELL** means more than "predict" in 2 Corinthians 13.2. The word is used in the sense, now obsolete, of enjoining or warning someone beforehand. In the KJ rendering which follows, "told you before" and "foretell" simply represent different tenses of the same Greek verb: "I told you before, and foretell you, as if I were present, the second time; and being absent now I write to them which theretofore have sinned, and to all other, that, if I come again, I will not spare." RSV translates the Greek text as found in the ancient manuscripts, which have no word for "I write": "I warned those who sinned before and all the others, and I warn them now while absent, as I did when present on my second visit, that if I come again I will not spare them."

Examples of Shakespeare's use of "foretell" in the sense of "warn" are:

> "many men that stumble at the threshold
> Are well foretold that danger lurks within."
> *King Henry VI, Part III*, IV, 7, 11
> "These our actors,
> As I foretold you, were all spirits, and
> Are melted into air, into thin air."
> *The Tempest,* IV, 1, 149

**FORTH OF** means out of or from. God's command to Noah, "Go forth of the ark," is worded in the revised versions, "Go forth from the ark" (Genesis 8.16). The prophecy of Amos 7.17,

"Israel shall surely go into captivity forth of his land," means ". . . into exile away from its land."

Jehoiada's command concerning Queen Athaliah, "Have her forth without the ranges" (2 Kings 11.15) appears in 2 Chronicles 23.14 as "Have her forth of the ranges." The Hebrew is the same, and neither rendering conveys a clear meaning. RSV has "Bring her out between the ranks." (See RANGE)

In Shakespeare's plays Prospero "was thrust forth of Milan" (*The Tempest*, V, 1, 160) and the poet Cinna had "no will to wander forth of doors" (*Julius Caesar*, III, 3, 3).

**FOR THAT** is an archaic expression for "because" or "since" in such passages as Romans 5.12, 1 Timothy 1.12, and Hebrews 5.2. It appears occasionally in Shakespeare; for example,

> "for that
> It is not night when I do see your face,
> Therefore I think I am not in the night."
> *A Midsummer Night's Dream*, II, 1, 220

**FOR TO** is an obsolete conjunctive phrase indicating purpose; RSV usually replaces it with "to." "They pressed upon him for to touch him, as many as had plagues" (Mark 3.10) is reworded "all who had diseases pressed upon him to touch him." "All their works they do for to be seen of men" (Matthew 23.5) reads in RSV "They do all their deeds to be seen by men." "For to make in himself of twain one new man" (Ephesians 2.15) means "that he might create in himself one new man in place of the two."

**FORWARD, FORWARDNESS.** As applied to a person's disposition and behavior, these words have an air of pertness or presumption. Not so in the Bible, where they stand for earnestness, readiness, or desire in a good cause. They are used, in fact, only in relation to one particular good cause, the offering for the relief of the saints in Jerusalem in which Paul enlisted the interest of the churches he founded or visited. Paul himself was "forward to do" this—"which very thing I was eager to do" (RSV Galatians 2.10). The other four occurrences are in Paul's "money letter" (2 Corinthians 8–9), which are concerned entirely with the plans for the collection of this offering. In a more accurate rendering of the various Greek words, RSV has "earnestness" (8.8); "desire" (8.10); "very earnest" (8.17); and "readiness" (9.2).

**FRAME,** as verb, is used once in the obsolete sense of manage, contrive. This is in the famous Shibboleth passage (Judges 12.6): "Say now Shibboleth; and he said Sibboleth: for he could not frame to pronounce *it* right." The Hebrew text of this verse, however, has no word for "frame," and is best translated by omitting it. RSV simply says "for he could not pronounce it right." There was no second trial, no time for contriving to reshape his sibilants. If he did not pronounce it right, "they seized him and slew him."

In Shakespeare's *King Henry VI, Part II,* III, 1, 52, the Duke of Suffolk accuses Humphrey, Duke of Gloucester, of planning "by wicked means to frame our sovereign's fall." In *King Henry VI, Part III,* III, 2, 182, another Duke of Gloucester, the hunchback who later became King Richard III, soliloquizes concerning his ambition and his readiness to do anything to get the crown:

"Why, I can smile, and murder whiles I smile,
And cry 'Content' to that which grieves my heart,
And wet my cheeks with artificial tears,
And frame my face to all occasions."

In Hosea 5.4, "They will not frame their doings to turn unto their God," the revised versions and most modern translations regard "their doings" as the subject of the verb. RSV reads, "Their deeds do not permit them to return to their God."

**FRANKLY** appears just once in the Bible (Luke 7.42), "he frankly forgave them both." It is used, not in the modern sense of openly or candidly, but in the older sense of freely, generously, unconditionally. OED cites Shakespeare's *Measure for Measure,* III, 1, 106:

"O, were it but my life,
I'd throw it down for your deliverance
As frankly as a pin."

The insertion of the word "frankly" before "forgave" is a peculiar feature of KJ. There is no corresponding adverb in the Greek, and it is not required to convey the meaning of the verb, which KJ translates in nine other cases with a simple "forgive." The prior versions, from Tyndale on, used no adverb; and the revised versions have dropped it. Why the KJ translators inserted it is not clear.

**FRAY,** as used in KJ, is a shortened form of the verb "affray," which meant frighten, make afraid. The familiar adjective "afraid" is simply the modern form of the past participle "affrayed." In Moses' declaration of blessings and curses, the punishment of the disobedient

ends with the abandonment of their dead bodies to be carrion—"thy
carcase shall be meat unto all fowls of the air, and unto the beasts of
the earth, and no man shall fray *them* away" (Deuteronomy 28.26).
RSV translates: "your dead body shall be food for all birds of the air,
and for the beasts of the earth; and there shall be none to frighten
them away." The same punishment is declared in Jeremiah 7.33. In
Zechariah's vision (1.18–21), the four "carpenters" who came to
"fray" the four horns which had scattered Judah were "smiths" who
came to "terrify" them. Compare Ezekiel 21.31, where the phrase "skilful to destroy" translates Hebrew which means literally "smiths of
destruction."

Shakespeare uses the verbs "affright" and "fright," but not
"frighten." He uses "fray" only as a noun signifying a brawl or fight.
He uses "affray" only once, and as a verb.

"Since arm from arm that voice doth us affray."
*Romeo and Juliet,* III, 5, 33

**FREELY.** One meaning of "freely" is without restraint or stint, plenti-
fully, abundantly. The word is so used, however, only
twice in the Bible—in Genesis 2.16, "You may freely eat of every tree
of the garden"; and in 1 Samuel 14.30, "How much better if the
people had eaten freely." It has a different meaning in Numbers 11.5,
where it represents the Hebrew word which means free, gratis, without
payment. The Israelites who longed in the desert for the fish they had
eaten in Egypt spoke particularly of the fact that it had cost them
nothing.

In five passages of the New Testament "freely" is used to translate
the Greek word which means gratis. "Freely ye have received, freely
give" (Matthew 10.8) does not refer to the quantity or size of the
gifts to be made, but to the fact that they are to be free gifts—"You
received without pay, give without pay." "Whosoever will, let him
take the water of life freely" (Revelation 22.17) means "let him who
desires take the water of life without price" (so also 21.6; compare
Isaiah 55.1). The other passages are Romans 3.24, "they are justified
by his grace as a gift"; and 2 Corinthians 11.7, "I preached God's
gospel without cost to you."

The word "freely" refers to freewill offerings in Psalm 54.6 and
Ezra 2.68; 7.15. In Acts 2.29 it represents the Greek phrase which
means "with confidence" or "with boldness," and which is so translated by KJ itself in Acts 4.29, 31 and 28.31.

The phrases "freely give" (Romans 8.32) and "freely given" (1 Corinthians 2.12) are an attempt to express the fact that God's gifts to us are at his initiative and of his grace. The verb in these phrases is related to the noun which is translated "free gift" in Romans 5.15–17. RSV omits the adverb "freely" from the verses as unnecessary and ambiguous. Its translation is: "He who did not spare his own Son but gave him up for us all, will he not also give us all things with him?" (Romans 8.32). "Now we have received not the spirit of the world, but the Spirit which is from God, that we might understand the gifts bestowed on us by God" (1 Corinthians 2.12).

**FRET** occurs four times in the obsolete sense of eat into, gnaw, corrode, or be eaten away, become corroded, decay. "A fretting leprosy" appears in Leviticus 13.51, 52; 14.44, and "it *is* fret inward" in Leviticus 13.55. These are Tyndale's terms, accepted by later versions. For the first of these terms RSV has "a malignant leprosy." The Hebrew word represented by "fret inward" is a noun which means leprous decay; RSV translates it "the leprous spot."

**FROWARD, FROWARDNESS, FROWARDLY.** "Froward" is a variant of "fromward," like "to and fro" for "to and from." It is the opposite of "toward," but has been most used as an adjective rather than as a preposition. It means opposed, contrary, perverse, and in KJ is used also in the sense of tortuous, crooked, devious—the opposite of sincere, frank, and straightforward.

Seventeen of the 24 appearances of "froward" and "frowardness" are in Proverbs, where RSV usually has "crooked" or "perverse."

In the context of Job 5.12–13, "the counsel of the froward is carried headlong" is better translated, "the schemes of the wily are brought to a quick end." In 1 Peter 2.18 some masters are referred to as "froward." The Greek here means harsh or unjust. RSV translates the verse: "Servants, be submissive to your masters with all respect, not only to the kind and gentle but also to the overbearing."

"Frowardly" appears once (Isaiah 57.17), "he went on frowardly." RSV translates "he went on backsliding." (See BACKSLIDING)

**FURNITURE** is used in the KJ Old Testament for any means of equipment. It refers to the furnishings and utensils of the tabernacle in Exodus 31.7, 8, 9; 35.14; 39.33. When Rachel stole her father's images, "and put them in the camel's furniture, and sat upon them" (Genesis 31.34), she put them in the camel's saddle. "Take ye the spoil of silver, take the spoil of gold: for *there is* none end of the store *and* glory out of all the pleasant furniture" (Nahum 2.9) reads in RSV:

> "Plunder the silver,
>     plunder the gold!
> There is no end of treasure,
>     or wealth of every precious thing."

**GAIN LOSS.** This joining of contradictory terms occurs in the account of the tempest which beset the ship carrying Paul toward Rome. When all hope was abandoned, Paul came forward and said that an angel of God had assured him that no lives would be lost, but only the ship. He began by reminding them that he had advised against making the voyage so late in the season: "Sirs, ye should have hearkened unto me, and not have loosed from Crete, and to have gained this harm and loss" (Acts 27.21).

The primary meaning of the Greek verb *kerdainō* is to gain, to derive profit or advantage. But it is also used in a general sense, meaning to get or obtain; and even in a bad sense, to reap a disadvantage or to gain someone's ill will. Most scholars regard it as used in a general sense here. Tyndale's translation was "brought unto us this harm and loss," in which he was followed by Coverdale, the Great Bible, and the first edition of the Bishops' Bible; the revised versions of 1881 and 1901 use "gotten." RSV uses "incurred," as do Alexander Campbell, the Twentieth Century New Testament, Ballantine, and Goodspeed.

The word "gained" was introduced by the Geneva Bible, where it was accompanied by an explanatory note: "That is, ye should have saved the loss by avoiding the danger."

John Wesley translated the clause, "and so have avoided this injury and loss." Other modern translators use "escaped" or "have been spared."

It has been suggested that we have here an oxymoron, that is, a "pointedly foolish" saying, a deliberate conjoining of contradictory terms to sharpen the speaker's point. But oxymoron is usually a matter of wit or irony, satire or reproach; and it is a figure of speech that does not fit the situation here. Paul did not begin with a wry joke or a bitter jibe as he carried to his shipmates God's assurance that their lives would be saved.

**GAINSAY, GAINSAYING, GAINSAYERS.** "Gainsay" is not yet obsolete, but it has become a purely literary word, slightly archaic. It is the only word that remains of a set of compound verbs which were common in the middle ages. These verbs were formed by prefixing "gain" or "again" (both meaning "against") to the verb root: "again-call" (to revoke), "again-rise" (to rebel), "gainstand" (to resist).

"Gainsay" means to speak against, hence to deny, contradict, oppose. RSV replaces the term in each of its five KJ appearances. "Without gainsaying" (Acts 10.29) is "without objection." "A disobedient and gainsaying people" (Romans 10.21) is "a disobedient and contrary people." For "perished in the gainsaying of Core" (Jude 11) RSV reads "perish in Korah's rebellion." ". . . able by sound doctrine both to exhort and to convince the gainsayers" (Titus 1.9) is more accurately translated ". . . able to give instruction in sound doctrine and also to confute those who contradict it." In Luke 21.15 RSV follows the ancient Greek manuscripts, in which the order of the words differs from the medieval manuscripts available to the KJ translators; it therefore changes "which all your adversaries shall not be able to gainsay nor resist," to read "which none of your adversaries will be able to withstand or contradict."

**GALL** means bile, the secretion of the liver; but the word has long been used for anything bitter to taste or to endure, or for rankling bitterness of spirit. It is retained by RSV in Job 16.13; 20.14, 25 and Acts 8.23. A familiar phrase is kept in Lamentations 3.19:
"Remember my affliction and my bitterness,
the wormwood and the gall!"
Following the ancient manuscripts, RSV translates Matthew 27.34, "they offered him wine to drink, mingled with gall." Here the word "gall" simply means something bitter; Mark's gospel is more definite, saying that the drink which Jesus refused was "wine mingled with myrrh" (15.23).

In more than half of its occurrences in KJ, "gall" has the now obsolete sense of poison or venom (paragraph 5 of OED's treatment of the first noun "Gall"). It is in these cases used as a translation of the Hebrew word *rosh,* which means a bitter, poisonous herb, or the venom of a serpent. RSV uses "poison" (Deuteronomy 32.32; Psalm 69.21; Amos 6.12); "poisoned water" (for "water of gall," Jeremiah 8.14; 23.15); "poisonous" (Deuteronomy 29.18; Jeremiah 9.15).

**GARDEN HOUSE** is defined in OED as a summerhouse, and this in turn as "a building in a garden or park, usually of very simple and often rustic character, designed to provide a cool shady place in the heat of summer." When KJ says that King Ahaziah fled from Jehu "by the way of the garden house" (2 Kings 9.27), the English translation gives a more intimate picture of the scene than is warranted by the context. Scholars are in general agreed that the Hebrew here represents the name of a place, Beth-haggan, which is probably to be identified with En-gannim ("spring of gardens," Joshua 19.21; 21.29). Ahaziah fled toward Beth-haggan, and was shot in his chariot near Ibleam. The charioteer turned toward Megiddo, where Ahaziah died, and from where his body was carried by chariot to Jerusalem.

**GARNISH** means to furnish, fit out, adorn, decorate. Originally it was of heavy import, meaning to furnish a place with the means of defense, to garrison a town or city. Applied to persons, its passive participle meant to be furnished with a retinue of attendants or to be adorned with any property or quality. Richard Chancellor, visiting Moscow in 1553, learned to address Ivan the Terrible as "the right High, right Mighty and right Excellent Prince, garnished with all gifts of Nature by God's grace . . ."

But these senses are now obsolete, and, except for its meaning in the language of the law, the word applies to the lighter embellishments of appearance. A cook will season a stew with onions, but she will garnish potatoes with parsley. In three of its occurrences in KJ "garnish" is replaced in RSV by "adorn." Solomon adorned the house of God with settings of precious stones (2 Chronicles 3.6). In the Revelation to John (21.19) "the foundations of the wall of the city were adorned with every jewel." Jesus' accusation of the Pharisees (Matthew 23.29–30), reads in RSV: "Woe to you, scribes and Pharisees, hypocrites! for you build the tombs of the prophets and adorn the monuments of the righteous, saying, 'If we had lived in the days of our fathers, we would not have taken part with them in shedding the blood of the prophets.' "

In Jesus' parable of the Unclean Spirit that returns to the house from which he had gone out, and finds it "empty, swept, and garnished," the meaning of the Greek is better translated, "empty, swept, and put in order" (Matthew 12.44; Luke 11.25).

Job's statement concerning the Almighty, "By his spirit he hath garnished the heavens" (26.13), is translated by RSV, "By his wind the heavens were made fair."

**GATHER,** with its various inflections, appears 461 times in the sense of collect or assemble, and once in the sense of infer, deduce, conclude. This one occurrence is in the account of the vision which led Paul to carry the gospel to Europe. "And after he had seen the vision, immediately we endeavoured to go into Macedonia, assuredly gathering that the Lord had called us for to preach the gospel unto them" (Acts 16.10). The two words "assuredly gathering" represent the participle of the Greek verb *symbibazō,* which is translated by "proving" in Acts 9.22. This Greek verb, like the Latin *colligo* and the English "gather," applies to the minds' decisions as well as to physical bringing or coming together. The KJ translators sought to convey its certainty by the word "assuredly." The revised versions replace "assuredly gathering" by "concluding." RSV reads: "And when he had seen the vision, immediately we sought to go on into Macedonia, concluding that God had called us to preach the gospel to them."

**GAY.** The man in "the gay clothing" (James 2.3) is not wearing anything inappropriate to his presence at worship in a Christian church; he is simply clothed in "goodly apparel," as verse 2 has it. "Gay" is here used in the obsolete sense of excellent, fine. The clothing is described by the same Greek words in the two verses. The change from "goodly apparel" to "the gay clothing" was one of Tyndale's characteristic touches, and was retained by KJ. The revised versions use "fine clothing" in both verses.

**GENDER,** as a verb, refers to the breeding of cattle in Leviticus 19.19 and Job 21.10. "Which gendereth to bondage" (Galatians 4.24) means "bearing children for slavery." "Foolish and unlearned questions avoid, knowing that they do gender strifes" (2 Timothy 2.23) is translated by RSV: "Have nothing to do with stupid, senseless controversies; you know that they breed quarrels."

**GENERALLY.** Repetition of words is a characteristic device of the Hebrew language to give emphasis or added intensity of meaning. "Justice, justice shalt thou follow" begins Deuteronomy 16.20, which KJ translates "That which is altogether just. . . ." In Ecclesiastes 7.24 the Hebrew "deep, deep" is translated "exceeding deep." In both of these cases RSV retains the repetition—"Justice, and only justice, you shall follow" and "deep, very deep."

In the case of verbs, this repetition consists of the absolute infinitive plus a finite form. For example, in Genesis 2.17 a literal translation would be "to die shall die"; in Exodus 21.17 "to be put to death shall be put to death." KJ has "shall surely die" and "shall surely be put to death." (See SURELY)

When Joseph tells his dream to his brothers, they say, literally, "To reign, shall you reign over us? or to have dominion, shall you have dominion over us?" Here KJ represents the emphasis of the absolute infinitive by the word "indeed"—"Shalt thou indeed reign over us? or shalt thou indeed have dominion over us?" (Genesis 37.8).

In the one case where the word "generally" is used (2 Samuel 17.11), its status is like that of "surely" and "indeed." A literal translation of the Hebrew would be "I counsel to be gathered be gathered to you all Israel." KJ represents this by "I counsel that all Israel be generally gathered unto thee." The word "generally" is here employed in the sense of "including every individual without exception"—a sense in which it is now obsolete. The sixteenth-century translations, from Tyndale to the Bishops' Bible, made no attempt to represent the infinitive; and the word "generally" represents it so poorly that the RSV has followed their example.

**GENERATION** appears almost 200 times in the fifth sense defined by OED: "the whole body of individuals born about the same period; also the time covered by the lives of these." This is not its meaning, however, in Matthew 1.1 where KJ uses it to translate the Greek word *genesis*. "The generation of Jesus Christ" in 1.1 and "the birth of Jesus Christ" in 1.18 represent the same Greek words. RSV uses "the genealogy of Jesus Christ" in 1.1.

In 1 Peter 2.9 "a chosen generation" means "a chosen race"—the Greek word here is *genos*.

The term "generation of vipers" which appears in a saying of John the Baptist (Matthew 3.7; Luke 3.7) and twice in sayings of Jesus (Matthew 12.34; 23.33) means offspring or brood of vipers—here the Greek word is *gennēma*.

Tyndale translated Paul's quotation from the Greek poet Aratus, "For we are also his generation" (Acts 17.28); and he was followed by subsequent versions up to and including the Geneva Bible. The Bishops' Bible changed it to read, "For we are also his offspring," and the KJ translators accepted this rendering—one of the comparatively few good contributions made by the Bishops' Bible.

**GHOST.** Except for the term "Holy Ghost," the word "ghost" appears in KJ only in the phrases "give up the ghost" (16 times) and "yield up the ghost" (3 times). There is no difference in meaning between these phrases, which in most of the cases simply represent a single Hebrew or Greek word, a verb meaning "die." For example, in Acts 5.5, it is said that Ananias "gave up the ghost," and in verse 10 of the same chapter that his wife "yielded up the ghost." The difference in wording was Tyndale's, and was retained by the authorized versions including KJ. Yet there is no word here for "ghost"; and the Greek verb, which is exactly the same in the two verses, means "died."

In 1611 the expression "Holy Ghost" meant what "Holy Spirit" means now. Then the word "ghost" meant the spirit, or immaterial part of a person, as distinct from the body; and "ghostly" meant spiritual. Romeo called Friar Laurence "a ghostly confessor" (*Romeo and Juliet,* III, 3, 49), and the literature of the period abounds in references to priests as ghostly father, ghostly adviser, ghostly director, or ghostly instructor. Ghostly counsel was spiritual counsel, and a ghostly day was a day set apart for worship. Hobbes' *Leviathan* refers to "a Ghostly Authority" set up "against the Civill." These meanings of "ghost" and "ghostly" are now obsolete and by most people forgotten. The American revisers in 1901 used "Holy Spirit" instead of "Holy Ghost," and this more meaningful translation has gained wide acceptance.

It should be added that the Greek word *pneuma* is by KJ itself translated as the "spirit" of man 151 times and as the "Spirit" of God 137 times, while it has retained the expression "Holy Ghost" 89 times.

The Greek word *phantasma,* which means apparition or phantom, is used in Matthew 14.26 and Mark 6.49 to express the fear of the disciples when they saw Jesus walking on the sea. Following Tyndale, KJ has them say "It is a spirit." The Rhemish Version of 1582 used "ghost," as do the revised versions of 1881–1901 and nearly all modern translations.

**GIN** is a contraction of "engine," which at first meant ingenuity, then its products, implements, or tools. "Gin" occurs five times in KJ in the sense of a snare or trap to catch birds or other game, and refers in four of these passages to the snares which beset people. It is replaced in RSV by "snares" (Psalms 140.5; 141.9) and "trap" (Job 18.9; Isaiah 8.14; Amos 3.5). In Shakespeare's *King Henry VI, Part III,* I, 4, 61, when the Duke of York struggles as his enemies lay hands on him, they comment,

> "Ay, ay, so strives the woodcock with the gin."
> "So doth the cony struggle in the net."

In *King Henry VI, Part II*, III, 1, 261, Suffolk counsels that Humphrey, Duke of Gloucester, be put to death:

> "And do not stand on quillets how to slay him:
> Be it by gins, by snares, by subtlety,
> Sleeping or waking, 'tis no matter how,
> So he be dead."

A "quillet" is an old word for a quibble.

The King James Bible of 1611 had "ginne" in Isaiah 8.14 and Amos 3.5, but had "grinne" in Job 18.9 and "grinnes" in Psalms 140.5; 141.9. "Grinne" is an Old English word, of independent origin, which means a snare with a running noose. This reading remained in KJ until the revision by Dr. Paris in 1762, when "gin" and "gins" were substituted in these three texts.

**GIVE PLACE** is an archaic phrase which has a different meaning in each of its four occurrences in KJ. In Isaiah 49.20 it means "make room." RSV translates the verse:

> "The children born in the time of your bereavement
> will yet say in your ears:
> 'The place is too narrow for me;
> make room for me to dwell in.' "

In Matthew 9.24 "Give place" represents the Greek verb which means "go away." Jesus said to the crowd of mourners in the ruler's house, "Depart; for the girl is not dead but sleeping." In Ephesians 4.27 "give place" stands for two Greek words; RSV translates "give no opportunity to the devil." In Galatians 2.5 the verb means "yield"; and RSV translates "we did not yield submission even for a moment."

**GLASS.** Except for the book of Revelation, the word "glass" in KJ means "mirror." And mirrors in ancient times were made of polished metal rather than of coated glass. In Exodus 38.8 we read that the "looking glasses" of the women were used as material for the making of the "laver of brass" and its base. In Job 37.18 the sky is said to be "strong, *and* as a molten looking glass." The italics indicate that no word for "and" is in the Hebrew; and the verse is accurately translated:

> "Can you, like him, spread out the skies,
> hard as a molten mirror?"

The "glasses" which are listed by Isaiah among the articles of female finery (3.23) may have been hand mirrors, as the revised versions of 1881–1901 translate the word *gillayonim*; but the Septuagint understood it to mean garments of gauzy transparent material, in Laconian style.

While the reference to Laconia is probably an anachronism, the adjective which means transparent or translucent fits the context; and many scholars agree with Ewald in accepting it as a correct rendering. RSV has "garments of gauze."

The revised versions use "mirror" in two notable New Testament passages. "If any one is a hearer of the word and not a doer, he is like a man who observes his natural face in a mirror" (James 1.23). "Now we see in a mirror dimly, but then face to face" (1 Corinthians 13.12). The point of these passages will be missed unless we remember that the mirrors to which they refer were simply polished metal surfaces, incapable of the clear, sharply defined reflections from a mirror made of glass.

In 2 Corinthians 3.18 the Greek verb may mean "beholding" or "reflecting." The English phrase "as in a glass" or "as in a mirror" is not required by the Greek, and has been dropped by RSV in the interest of a clear translation: "And we all, with unveiled face, beholding the glory of the Lord, are being changed into his likeness from one degree of glory to another."

**GLISTERING.** "Glisten," "glister," and "glitter" are old verbs with a common Teutonic base, and at first with no apparent difference of meaning. "Glisten" does not appear in KJ; "glistering" appears twice, "glitter" once, and "glittering" six times. KJ had "glistering sword" (Job 20.25) in 1611; but in 1762 this was changed to "glittering sword." Shakespeare quoted an old proverb, "All that glisters is not gold" (*Merchant of Venice,* II, 7, 65); but in Boswell's *Life of Samuel Johnson* it appears as "All is not gold that glitters."

The "glistering stones" listed among the materials that David had provided for the building of the house of God represent the Hebrew term for "antimony" (1 Chronicles 29.2; compare Isaiah 54.11).

Each of the Synoptic Gospels has its own language to describe the appearance of Jesus' raiment when he was transfigured in the presence of Peter and James and John. The one word on which the three Gospels agree is "white." The KJ rendering of Luke 9.29 has "white *and* glistering"; RSV translates "and his raiment became dazzling white." The Greek word here is the participle of the verb which means to flash or gleam like lightning.

**GLORY.** Moses began his reply to Pharaoh (Exodus 8.9) with the words "Glory over me: when shall I intreat . . . to destroy the frogs . . . ?" His first phrase means "Glorify yourself over me." The verb is the one which is translated "vaunt themselves" (Judges 7.2) and "boast itself" (Isaiah 10.15). Moses is saying, "Assume the honor over me (to decide) when. . . ." RSV translates it: "Be pleased to command me when I am to entreat . . . that the frogs be destroyed." It is not simply a polite form of address; the real reason for leaving to Pharaoh the decision concerning the time for the destruction of the frogs was to manifest more clearly the omnipotence of God. When Pharaoh said, "Tomorrow," Moses answered, "Be it as you say, that you may know that there is no one like the LORD our God" (Exodus 8.10).

**GO ABOUT.** "He who goes about gossiping reveals secrets" (Proverbs 20.19). "They went about through all the cities of Judah and taught among the people" (2 Chronicles 17.9). "He went about doing good" (Acts 10.38). These are three of a dozen passages where "go about" is used in the natural sense of moving hither and thither or traveling in various places. In other passages it is not so naturally used; "Their imagination which they go about, even now" (Deuteronomy 31.21) means "the purposes which they are already forming." In 1 Samuel 15.12 "is gone about" means "turned"; and in 2 Kings 3.25 "went about *it*" means "surrounded it." "How long wilt thou go about, O thou backsliding daughter?" (Jeremiah 31.22) is translated by RSV, "How long will you waver, O faithless daughter?" "Both the prophet and the priest go about into a land that they know not" (Jeremiah 14.18) means "both prophet and priest ply their trade through the land, and have no knowledge."

"Go about" with a following infinitive is used seven times in the New Testament in the obsolete sense of endeavor or plan. Jesus is represented as asking "Why go ye about to kill me?" (John 7.19). On Paul's first visit to Jerusalem after his conversion, his opponents "went about to slay him" (Acts 9.29). When the Jews caught him in the temple on his last visit, they "went about to kill" him (Acts 26.21). In these cases "go about" is used as translation for Greek verbs which mean seek, try, or attempt. Indeed, the same Greek verb which KJ represents by "go about" in Jesus' question is translated by "seek" a few verses later—"Is not this he, whom they seek to kill?" (John 7.25).

**GO ASIDE** has a special meaning in Numbers 5.12, 20, 29, where it refers to the behavior of an unfaithful wife. RSV uses "go astray." The same Hebrew verb appears in Proverbs 7.25, at the close of a vivid description of the seductive wiles of a loose woman. "Go not astray in her paths," counsels KJ; and RSV is more stringent, "Do not stray into her paths."

**GO BEYOND** means "transgress" in 1 Thessalonians 4.6, and the KJ phrase "in *any* matter" should be corrected to read "in this matter." The view held by Tyndale and other sixteenth-century translators that verses 3–5 refer to the relations of the sexes, but that verse 6 refers to bargaining or to business in general, has been given up by most modern translations based upon the Greek rather than the Latin Vulgate. Verses 3–8 belong together, and deal with the same subject—abstention from immorality and the sanctity of Christian marriage. RSV reads (vs. 4–6a): "that each one of you know how to take a wife for himself in holiness and honor, not in the passion of lust like heathen who do not know God; that no man transgress, and wrong his brother in this matter." (See VESSEL.) There is an admirable discussion of this passage in *The Interpreter's Bible*, vol. 11, pp. 294–295.

**GOD FORBID.** An expression of strong dissent, used as translation of Hebrew and Greek expressions which do not refer to the Deity. The Hebrew expression is an exclamation, *halilah*, derived from the verb *halal*, which means to pollute, defile, violate, profane. The exclamation means that the suggestion which calls it forth is so utterly wrong or impious that it is immediately and decisively rejected. The Latin Vulgate usually translated it by *Absit a me* (*te*, etc.), "Far be it from me (you," etc.). But Tyndale took "God forbid" as the English translation in the majority of cases, and was followed by KJ, which has "God forbid" in Genesis 44.7, 17; Joshua 22.29; 24.16; 1 Samuel 12.23; 14.45; 20.2; Job 27.5. It has "The LORD forbid" in 1 Samuel 24.6; 26.11; 1 Kings 21.3, and "My God forbid" in 1 Chronicles 11.19; but in these four texts the word LORD or God is added to *halilah* in the Hebrew. KJ translates *halilah* "Be it far from" or "Far be it from" in Genesis 18.25; 1 Samuel 2.30; 20.9; 22.15; 2 Samuel 20.20; 23.17; Job 34.10.

The Septuagint used various Greek phrases to represent *halilah*. Of these, the one which is most often used in the New Testament is *mē genoito*, which means literally "May it not be so!" This expression appears 10 times in Paul's epistle to the Romans, where it marks the onward course of his argument, as he rejects various wrong inferences and suggestions. It appears also in 1 Corinthians 6.15 and Galatians 2.17; 3.21; 6.14. Tyndale and following versions used "God forbid" in all these cases. RSV uses "By no means!" in Romans, "Never!" in 1 Corinthians, and "Certainly not" and "far be it from me" in Galatians —the choice of English expressions being determined by the context in each case. In Luke 20.16 RSV retains "God forbid!" and it also uses this expression in Matthew 16.22.

**GOD SAVE THE KING** appears in Shakespeare as a greeting (*Macbeth*, I, 2, 47), a benediction (*King Richard II*, IV, 1, 172), and a cry of loyal acclaim (*King Henry VI, Part II*, IV, 8, 19; 9, 22). It occurs in KJ where the people accept Saul as their king (1 Samuel 10.24), and is used in reference to Absalom, Adonijah, Solomon, and Joash (2 Samuel 16.16; 1 Kings 1.25, 34, 39; 2 Kings 11.12; 2 Chronicles 23.11). In none of these passages does the word "God" appear in the Hebrew, which means simply "may the king live." The same Hebrew expression occurs in 1 Kings 1.31, where the Bishops' Bible had "I pray God that my lord king David may live for ever," which KJ reduced to "Let my lord king David live for ever."

The revisers in 1901 changed "God save the king" to "Long live the king" in all the passages where the expression occurs, and RSV has followed their example.

**GOD SPEED.** To bid one God speed, says OED, is "to express a wish for the success of one who is setting out on some journey or enterprise." The expression is inappropriate in 2 John 10–11, where the context is arrival rather than departure, and the Greek word is the usual one for "Hail!" The revised versions use "greet" and "greeting," as do most modern translations. RSV reads: "If any one comes to you and does not bring this doctrine, do not receive him into the house or give him any greeting; for he who greets him shares his wicked work." Goodspeed has "do not bid him good morning"; Ballantine "do not bid him welcome."

**GOING FORTH** refers to the rising of the sun in Psalm 19.6 and Isaiah 13.10. The plural "goings forth" occurs in Micah 5.2, and is best translated "origin." This prophecy reads in RSV:

"But you, O Bethlehem Ephrathah,
who are little to be among the clans of Judah,
from you shall come forth for me
one who is to be ruler in Israel,
whose origin is from of old,
from ancient days."

In Ezekiel 43.11, the phrases "the goings out thereof, and the comings in thereof" mean "its exits and its entrances." In 44.5 "mark well the entering in of the house, with every going forth of the sanctuary" is not so clear; but a slight emendation of the Hebrew words warrants the rendering, "mark well those who may be admitted to the temple and all those who are to be excluded from the sanctuary." The emendation is explained in *The Interpreter's Bible*, vol. 6, p. 308.

**GOINGS.** The plural of the verbal noun "going" is used six times to render Hebrew words which KJ elsewhere translates "steps" or "paths." Following the Hebrew, RSV has "steps" in Job 34.21; Psalms 17.5; 40.2; Proverbs 20.24, and "paths" in Proverbs 5.21; Isaiah 59.8. The meaning in each of these cases is figurative, referring to a course of life. In Psalm 140.4 "who have purposed to overthrow my goings" is more accurately rendered "who have planned to trip up my feet." "Thy goings, O God" (Psalm 68.24) refers either to the procession of worshipers or to the manifestation of God—probably to both. RSV translates verses 24–26:
"Thy solemn processions are seen, O God,
    the processions of my God, my King, into the sanctuary—
the singers in front, the minstrels last,
    between them maidens playing timbrels:
'Bless God in the great congregation,
    the LORD, O you who are of Israel's fountain!' "
"The sound of a going in the tops of the mulberry trees" (2 Samuel 5.24; 1 Chronicles 14.15) means "the sound of marching in the tops of the balsam trees."
The expression "goings out" in Numbers 34 and Joshua 15, 16, 18 stands for the Hebrew word which KJ renders by "outgoings" in Joshua 17, 18, 19; and means the same. (See OUTGOINGS)

**GO IT UP.** "For by the mounting up of Luhith with weeping shall they go it up" (Isaiah 15.5) does not imply that the fugitives scamper up in haste. This clause is simply an example of the awkward English that besets translators. The revised versions deleted the unnecessary "it." RSV reads:
            "For at the ascent of Luhith
                they go up weeping."

**GOODLY** is used 36 times in KJ, and represents 19 different Hebrew and Greek terms. RSV retains "I have a goodly heritage" (Psalm 16.6); "when she saw that he was a goodly child" (Exodus

2.2); "goodly hill country," "goodly cities," "goodly houses" (Deuteronomy 3.25; 6.10; 8.12); and uses the word in seven other contexts. It uses the word "handsome" to describe the physical appearance of Joseph (Genesis 39.6), Saul (1 Samuel 9.2), David (1 Samuel 16.12), Adonijah (1 Kings 1.6), and the Egyptian whom Benaiah slew with his own spear (2 Samuel 23.21). It has "a noble cedar" (Ezekiel 17.23) and "the mighty cedars" (Psalm 80.10). The "goodly Babylonish garment" which Achan coveted (Joshua 7.21) was "a beautiful mantle from Shinar." RSV has "the precious vessels of the house of the LORD" (2 Chronicles 36.10, 19), "rich treasures" (Joel 3.5), and "fine pearls" (Matthew 13.45).

"Goodliness" appears once: "All flesh *is* grass, and all the goodliness thereof *is* as the flower of the field" (Isaiah 40.6). RSV has, "All flesh is grass, and all its beauty is like the flower of the field."

**GOODMAN.** A "goodman" is a husband or the male head of a household. The word is archaic except in Scotland. It is one word, accented on the first syllable; and it should never be printed as two words, "good man," though it did so appear in four passages of the 1611 edition of KJ.

In Proverbs 7.19, a harlot tells her quarry, "the goodman *is* not at home." This translation began with Coverdale. The Geneva Bible and the Douay Bible have "my husband is not at home," which is the reading of RSV.

"Goodman of the house" is used 5 times in the Synoptic Gospels to translate the Greek *oikodespotēs*, which means "master of the house" (Matthew 20.11; 24.43; Mark 14.14; Luke 12.39; 22.11). "Master of the house" is used 3 times (Matthew 10.25; Luke 13.25; 14.21), and "householder" 4 times (Matthew 13.27, 52; 20.1; 21.33). RSV uses "householder" in all of these passages except Matthew 10.25, where "master of the house" is obviously required by the context.

In the *Concordance to Shakespeare* "good man" and "goodman" are separately listed. The two-word phrase appears in the plays of Shakespeare 37 times, and the word "goodman" 13 times.

**GO TO.** A mild imperative, used to introduce an exhortation or command, and having the force of "Come" in "Come, let us go" (1 Samuel 9.10); "Come on, let us deal wisely with them" (Exodus 1.10); or "Come, and let us go up to the mountain of the LORD" (Micah 4.2). The passages where KJ uses "Go to" rather than the more natural "Come" are Genesis 11.3, 4, 7; 38.16; James 4.13; 5.1. The revised versions omit it in 2 Kings 5.5 and Judges 7.3 as an obsolete expression which is not called for by the Hebrew.

As an expression of remonstrance, protest, incredulity, or derision "go to" may still be archaic English, as the dictionaries imply. It does not have this sense in the Bible, however.

**GOVERNOR** is used (James 3.4) in the obsolete sense of the pilot or steersman of a ship. In Galatians 4.1–2, "the heir, as long as he is a child . . . is under tutors and governors until the time appointed of the father," the Greek terms are better translated "under guardians and trustees."

In the account of the marriage at Cana, "the governor of the feast" and "the ruler of the feast" (John 2.8–9) are the same person, the *architriklinos*. He was not the toastmaster or "master of the feast"; the Greek word for that was *sumposiarchēs*. He was the head waiter or steward, whose duty it was to manage all of the properties and procedures of the affair—tables, seating, courses, and the serving of food and wine.

In 1 Kings 18.3, "Ahab called Obadiah, which *was* the governor of *his* house." The revised versions give a literal translation of the Hebrew, which has simply the preposition for "over." RSV reads ". . . who was over the household." Following the Hebrew, it uses a general term, "officer," in 1 Chronicles 24.5 and Jeremiah 20.1.

**GRIEF, GRIEVE.** The word "grief" was widely applied in Old English. It could mean any hardship or cause of hardship, any harm or damage, any bodily injury, ailment, disease or pain, any mental pain or distress. Most of these meanings are now obsolete, and "grief" is used only for deep sorrow or regret. The colloquial idiom "come to grief" is an exception. It means "meet with disaster" and may refer to disaster or frustration of any kind.

The King James Version uses "grief" or "grieve" as translation for 24 different Hebrew words and 4 Greek words, each of which has its own meaning. Job, for example, is not a man overcome with grief, in the modern sense of the term. We understand him better if we read "suffering" in 2.13 and "pain" in 16.5–6. When, after seven days of silence, Job cursed the day of his birth and Eliphaz ventures to speak, his question is not "Wilt thou be grieved?" but "Will you be offended?" (4.2). Job's answer begins in 6.2, "O that my vexation were weighed, and all my calamity laid in the balances!" He uses the Hebrew word which in 10.17 he attributes to God, "thy vexation toward me." KJ has "my grief" in 6.2 and "thine indignation" in 10.17, but the Hebrew word is the same.

The basic meaning of the Hebrew is vexation or anger in such passages as Genesis 34.7; 1 Samuel 1.16; 15.11; Nehemiah 2.10; 13.8; Psalm 112.10; Ecclesiastes 1.18; 2.23. It is bitterness in Genesis 26.35; Ruth 1.13; 1 Samuel 30.6; Psalm 73.21. It is loathing or disgust in Psalms 95.10; 119.158; 139.21. It is dread in Exodus 1.12. It refers to physical attack in Genesis 49.23; and to mere discomfort in Jonah 4.6.

Even more than "heaviness" and "heavy," the words "grief" and "grieve" are used in KJ in a great variety of meanings. With the related adjective and adverb, they appear 120 times. The evidence is too bulky to be marshaled here; the Bible student will find guidance in the concordances by Young or Strong, and in the *Oxford English Dictionary*.

**GRIEVOUS, GRIEVOUSLY.** Like the noun and verb above, the adjective and adverb are used more widely in KJ than in present usage. They are applied not only to wounds, blows, famine, illness, and sin; but in more general senses to what is heavy, severe, stern, harsh, or displeasing. "His ways are always grievous" (Psalm 10.5) is a mistranslation for "His ways prosper at all times." "Speak grievous things" (Psalm 31.18) means "speak insolently." "Grievous revolters" (Jeremiah 6.28) is better rendered "stubbornly rebellious." A more accurate translation of the Greek replaces "grievous" with "fierce" (Acts 20.29), "serious" (Acts 25.7), "burdensome" (1 John 5.3), "irksome" (Philippians 3.1), "painful" (Hebrews 12.11), "evil" (Revelation 16.2). "Grievous to be borne" means simply "hard to bear" (Matthew 23.4 = Luke 11.46).

**GRIEVOUSNESS** occurs twice in KJ. "Woe unto them . . . that write grievousness *which* they have prescribed" (Isaiah 10.1) is more accurately rendered "Woe to . . . the writers who keep writing oppression." "For they fled . . . from the grievousness of war" (Isaiah 21.15) means "For they have fled . . . from the press of battle."

**GRISLED** is not a form of "grisly," which means horrible or ghastly, but is an early form of "grizzled" or "grizzly," which mean gray or grayish, sprinkled, streaked, or mixed with gray. The Hebrew adjective *barod*, which KJ translates by "grisled," means spotted or marked, as if sprinkled with hail (the word for a storm of hail is *barad*). This adjective is applied to Jacob's rams (Genesis 31.10, 12) and to horses in the vision of Zechariah 6.3, 6. RSV uses "mottled" for the rams, and "dappled gray" for the horses.

**GRUDGE** originally meant to murmur, grumble, or complain. Its earlier variant was "grutch"; modern colloquial variants are "grouse" and "grouch." This meaning for "grudge" has been obsolete for more than three centuries; OED records the date of its last appearance for the noun in 1611, and for the verb in 1632. Shakespeare used "grudge" along with a new word, "grumbling" (this is the first record of the word) in *The Tempest,* I, 2, 249, where Ariel reminds Prospero that he has

> "told thee no lies, made thee no mistakings, served
> Without or grudge or grumblings."

The King James Version uses "grudge" twice in this obsolete sense. "Grudge not one against another" (James 5.9) means "Do not grumble against one another." The other case is a little more complicated. Psalm 59 is a prayer for deliverance from the psalmist's enemies—its ancient heading means, "A Miktam of David, when Saul sent men to watch his house in order to kill him" (the meaning of *Miktam,* which appears in the headings of Psalms 16 and 56–60, is uncertain). In two strophes of Psalm 59, verses 6–7 and verses 14–15, he compares his enemies to dogs:

> "Each evening they come back,
>     howling like dogs
>     and prowling about the city."

The first of these strophes he completes with three lines about their bellowing and snarling, the second with two lines about their foraging for food. The latter are rendered by KJ: "Let them wander up and down for meat, and grudge if they be not satisfied." RSV translates:

> "They roam about for food,
>     and growl if they do not get their fill."

In three passages KJ uses "grudge," "grudging," "grudgingly" in their present sense (Leviticus 19.18; 1 Peter 4.9; 2 Corinthians 9.7). RSV uses "grudge" instead of "quarrel" in Mark 6.19. (See DOG, QUARREL)

**GUILTY OF.** In Numbers 35.27, 31 KJ uses "guilty of blood" and "guilty of death" in the sense in which we would naturally understand these phrases today. When it represents the members of the council of Caiaphas, however, as saying of Jesus, "He is guilty of death" (Matthew 26.66), the expression is used in an obsolete sense.

The KJ translators took it from the Rheims translation, which got it from the Latin Vulgate, *reus est mortis*. Tyndale and his successors had translated the Greek "He is worthy to die." The revised versions of 1881 and 1901 have "He is worthy of death." RSV reads "He deserves death." Compare Mark 14.64.

**HABERGEON** means a short, sleeveless hauberk or coat of mail. The term is used in KJ as translation of three Hebrew words, to only one of which it properly applies. That is *shiryon*, which occurs in 2 Chronicles 26.14 and Nehemiah 4.16, where its plural is translated "coats of mail" by RSV. It is the word for the coat of mail worn by Goliath and for that which Saul put on David and David would not wear (1 Samuel 17.5, 38).

A different word, *shiryah*, occurs in the description of Leviathan (Job 41) where KJ renders verse 26: "The sword of him that layeth at him cannot hold: the spear, the dart, nor the habergeon." These are offensive weapons, and "habergeon" is out of place. RSV translates:
"Though the sword reaches him, it does not avail;
nor the spear, the dart, or the javelin."

The other word is *tahara*, which occurs in the description of "the robe of the ephod" which Aaron wore (Exodus 28.32; 39.23). The meaning of this term is uncertain; the Hebrew lexicons state that it probably means a linen corselet. In any case, it is clear that the robe of the ephod was to be put on over the head and slipped down into place on the body, and that *tahara* refers to a garment that had to be put on in the same way. KJ renders Exodus 28.32: "And there shall be an hole in the top of it, in the midst thereof: it shall have a binding of woven work round about the hole of it, as it were the hole of an habergeon, that it be not rent." RSV reads: "It shall have in it an opening for the head, with a woven binding around the opening, like the opening in a garment, that it may not be torn."

In the description of the locusts from the bottomless pit (Revelation 9.1–11) Tyndale and the other sixteenth-century translations said that "they had habbergions, as it were habbergions of yron" (vs. 9). KJ moved in the right direction by changing "habbergions" to "breastplates." But the Greek word *thōrax*, which is here used twice, separated by the Greek word for "like," means not only breastplate but the part of the body which the breastplate covers. RSV translates: "they had scales like iron breastplates." The entire description should be read in both versions. In verses 2, 3, 5, 7c, 8, and 9 the same simple Greek word *hos* occurs, and means "like." KJ uses "as" except in 9a, where it uses "as it were."

**HALE.** To one who has been "haled into court" it may come as a surprise that he was "hauled" or "dragged." Yet "hale" and "haul" are the same word in meaning and origin. "Hale" is the older form, and the only one to appear in KJ or in Shakespeare. "Haul" is a variant spelling which began in the sixteenth century and has now superseded "hale" except in the language of the law court.

"Hale" occurs twice in KJ: "lest he hale thee to the judge" (Luke 12.58); "As for Saul, he made havock of the church, entering into every house, and haling men and women committed *them* to prison" (Acts 8.3). We must not let the legal aura of the terms "judge" and "prison" lead us to think that the word "hale" should be retained here. The Greek verbs imply force rather than law; and RSV properly uses "drag" and "drag off." The verb *surō*, which appears in Acts 8.3, occurs also in John 21.8, "dragging the net full of fish"; Acts 14.19, "they stoned Paul and dragged him out of the city, supposing that he was dead"; Acts 17.6, "they dragged Jason and some of the brethren before the city authorities." The verb *katasurō* (Luke 12.58) is an intensive form of the same word, which means to drag forcibly or even, in some contexts, to ravage and lay waste.

**HALT,** as an adjective, occurs 4 times (Matthew 18.8; Mark 9.45; Luke 14.21; John 5.3), as rendering for the Greek adjective which means lame or crippled, and which KJ translates by "lame" in 10 other passages and by "a cripple" in Acts 14.8.

As an intransitive verb, "halt" is used 7 times in the Old Testament, always to render Hebrew terms which mean to limp, stumble, or fall. For "her that halteth" RSV has "the lame" (Micah 4.6, 7; Zephaniah 3.19). "I *am* ready to halt" (Psalm 38.17) means "I am ready to fall," and "watched for my halting" means "watching for my fall" (Jeremiah 20.10). For "he halted upon his thigh" RSV reads "limping because of his thigh" (Genesis 32.31). Elijah's question to the people of Israel, "How long halt ye between two opinions?" (1 Kings 18.21) means "How long will you go limping with two different opinions?" RSV uses "halt" only in the sense of "stop."

**HAND.** *Take in hand* followed by an infinitive means to undertake or attempt. Tyndale's translation of the preface to Luke's gospel reads "many have taken in hand to . . ." and all subsequent versions in the Tyndale-KJ tradition retained the expression, until RSV replaced it by "many have undertaken to. . . ."

*At the hand(s) of* is an old English idiom, still current, which expresses the immediate source from which something is received or required. "Shall we receive good at the hand of God, and shall we not receive evil?" (Job 2.10). "When ye come to appear before me, who hath required this at your hand, to tread my courts?" (Isaiah 1.12). The Hebrew preposition is *min*, which means "from" in both of these texts; the Hebrew word for "hand" is expressed only in the second.

*Out of hand* means at once, immediately. It appears in Numbers 11.15, where Moses says to the LORD, "If thou deal thus with me, kill me, I pray thee, out of hand, if I have found favour in thy sight: and let me not see my wretchedness." This is a case where the Hebrew uses repetition as a means of emphasis, adding to the finite verb its absolute infinitive. (See GENERALLY and SURELY.) A literal translation would be "kill me, I pray thee, to kill, if I have found favor in thy sight." The translations from Tyndale on, including the Bishops' Bible, simply ignored the repetitive infinitive; the idea of representing it by the idiom "out of hand" originated with the KJ translators. RSV substitutes "at once," which is clearer; but it might have been better to return to the simple, direct emphasis of Tyndale and his sixteenth-century successors.

*"An hand weapon of wood"* means a weapon of wood in the hand (Numbers 35.18). The Hebrew phrase is parallel to that of verse 17, which KJ renders "throwing a stone" but the revised versions translate "a stone in the hand."

*"With a high hand"* is the literal translation of a Hebrew phrase which is applied to the action of the people of Israel in leaving Egypt (Exodus 14.8; Numbers 33.3). It is also applied to the action of one who despises the word of the LORD and deliberately breaks his commandment (Numbers 15.30 RSV). The translations in the Tyndale-KJ tradition used "with an high hand" in the first two cases, and "presumptuously" in the latter. RSV reverses this, using "with a high hand" for the rebel against God, and "defiantly" and "triumphantly" for the departure from Egypt. This reflects the shift in the meaning of the English idiom. "With a high hand" at first simply referred to great power—"High is thy right hand" (Psalm 89.13), "Our hand *is* high" (Deuteronomy 32.27). But it has come to connote an imperious temper and the overbearing, arbitrary exercise of power.

**HAP** means chance or fortune, whether good or bad. The good meanings now cluster about the related words happy, happily, happiness. The neutral meanings are caught up in such terms as happen, happening, haply, perhaps. The one use of "hap" in the Bible is in Ruth 2.3 "her hap was to light on a part of the field *belonging* unto Boaz"—which RSV expresses plainly, if more prosily, "She happened to come to the part of the field belonging to Boaz." In Milton's *Paradise Lost*, 9, 421 the Serpent "sought them both, but wished his hap might find Eve separate." Shakespeare has "Hap what hap may" (*Taming of the Shrew*, IV, 4, 107).

**HAPLY** means by hap or chance, hence "perchance," "perhaps." It is used 6 times in KJ: "if haply" (1 Samuel 14.30; Mark 11.13; Acts 17.27); "lest haply" (Luke 14.29; Acts 5.39; 2 Corinthians 9.4). For some reason the revisers of the New Testament in 1881–1901 joined the word "haply" to "lest" in 20 cases where KJ did not have it. In 7 of these cases "lest haply" was substituted for "lest at any time"; in the other 13 "lest haply" took the place of "lest." The RSV has eliminated "haply." In almost all cases the element of contingency is sufficiently expressed by the simple "if" or "whether" or "lest." RSV uses "perhaps" (Luke 3.15; Matthew 25.9); "might" (Acts 5.39; 27.29); and "in the hope that" (Acts 17.27).

It is an interesting fact that the original edition of KJ (1611) had "happily" in 2 Corinthians 9.4. This then meant the same as "haply," as may be seen in Shakespeare's *Twelfth Night*, IV, 2, 57 or *Hamlet*, II, 2, 402. The latter passage reads:

> *"Hamlet:* That great baby you see there is not yet out of his swaddling clouts.
> *Rosencrantz:* Happily he's the second time come to them; for they say an old man is twice a child."

**HARD** has the variety of meanings in KJ which it has today. We read of hard bondage, hard labor, hard questions, hard sayings, hard language, hard causes, hard men, hard hearts, and things hard to understand. Some dozen times the adverb "hard" is used in the sense of close or near. When Abimelech "went hard unto the door of the tower" (Judges 9.52) he "drew near to the door."

The familiar text from Proverbs 13.15, "the way of transgressors *is* hard" may be understood to mean that the path of transgressors is difficult and that they have hard times ahead, or it may be understood to mean that the conduct of transgressors is unfeeling and cruel. But both of these meanings are far from the Hebrew, which astonishingly asserts that the way of the treacherous (or faithless) is enduring (or permanent). The English translators passed from the idea of "enduring" to the idea of "firm," then from "firm" to "hard"; and their readers have understood "hard" to mean something quite different from firm or enduring.

The Greek Septuagint and the Syriac read "destruction," and the

Latin Vulgate "whirlpool," where the present Hebrew text has *'eythan*, the word for enduring. Biblical scholars in general agree that the Hebrew text must have formerly read *'eydham*, which means "destruction." RSV accepts this emendation, reading "the way of the faithless is their ruin."

**HARDLY** means "with difficulty" in Matthew 19.23, Mark 10.23 = Luke 18.24, and Acts 27.8. In place of "How hardly shall they that have riches enter into the kingdom of God!" RSV has "How hard it will be for those who have riches to enter the kingdom of God!" In Luke 9.39 the meaning is "scarcely," and the word "hardly" is retained.

"Hardly bestead" means "greatly distressed" (Isaiah 8.21). "Sarai dealt hardly with her" (Genesis 16.6) means "Sarai dealt harshly with her." "When Pharaoh would hardly let us go" (Exodus 13.15) is an awkward translation which reduces the verb for "make hard" to the adverb "hardly." Tyndale had (in modern spelling) "when Pharaoh was loath to let us go," in which he was followed by the Great Bible and the Bishops' Bible, the latter saying "very loath." The Geneva Bible had "when Pharaoh was hard hearted against our departing." The margin of the ASV has "hardened himself against letting us go"; and RSV reads "when Pharaoh stubbornly refused to let us go."

**HARDNESS** of heart is a familiar concept which runs throughout the course of Biblical revelation and appears in all translations. As applied to the effect of rain upon dust (Job 38.38) the word "hardness" is inappropriate, and is abandoned by the revised versions. RSV has:

> "Who can tilt the waterskins of the heavens,
>    when the dust runs into a mass
>    and the clods cleave fast together?"

In the injunction to Timothy, "endure hardness as a good soldier of Jesus Christ," the word is employed in the sense of "hardship" (2 Timothy 2.3). But this rendering falls short of the meaning of the ancient Greek text, which is expressed in the RSV:

> "Take your share of suffering as a good soldier of Jesus Christ."

**HARNESS,** as noun, was originally applied to any sort of gear or equipment. The *Promptorium Parvulorum*, in the fifteenth century, gave four meanings: raiment, weapons, household utensils, the trappings of a horse. In KJ the noun is used only in the sense of armor.

"A *certain* man drew a bow at a venture, and smote the king of Israel between the joints of the harness" (1 Kings 22.34 = 2 Chronicles 18.33) is more accurately translated, "A certain man drew his bow at a venture, and struck the king of Israel between the scale armor and the breastplate." In 2 Maccabees 15.28, where KJ reads "they knew that Nicanor lay dead in his harness," RSV reads "they recognized Nicanor, lying dead, in full armor." The Greek word here is *panoplia*, from which we get the English word "panoply."

In the list of presents which King Solomon received from other kings, year by year, KJ has "armour" (1 Kings 10.25) and "harness" (2 Chronicles 9.24) to represent the same Hebrew word. Following the Septuagint, RSV has "myrrh."

**HARNESS,** as verb, is used once for horses (Jeremiah 46.4): "Harness the horses." In Micah 1.13, where KJ has "bind the chariot to the swift beast," RSV reads "Harness the steeds to the chariot."

"The children of Israel went up harnessed out of the land of Egypt" (Exodus 13.18) is reworded in RSV, "the people of Israel went up out of the land of Egypt equipped for battle." The same Hebrew word is translated "armed" by both KJ and RSV in Joshua 1.14; 4.12; Judges 7.11.

Tyndale's translation of Numbers 32.20–22 was "Yf ye will do this thinge, that ye will go all harnessed before the Lorde to warre, and will go all of you in harnesse ouer Iordane before the Lorde . . . then ye shall returne and be without sinne agenst the Lorde and agenst Israel."

In 1 Maccabees 4.7 KJ refers to an enemy camp as "strong and well harnessed"; RSV has "strong and fortified."

**HASTILY** now means hurriedly; it implies being pressed for time, or lack of due consideration. But in Elizabethan language the word could be used in the simple sense of promptly, without delay. It has this meaning in three KJ passages. These passages read in RSV: "The LORD left those nations, not driving them out at once" (Judges 2.23); "Now the men were watching for an omen, and they quickly took it up from him" (1 Kings 20.33); "When the Jews . . . saw Mary rise quickly and go out, they followed her" (John 11.31).

**HAVE,** followed by an adverb of place, is used in the archaic sense of bring, lead, take, put. Amnon's order, "Have out all men from me" (2 Samuel 13.9), means "Send out every one from me."

Jehoiada's command concerning Athaliah, "Have her forth without the ranges" (2 Kings 11.15), is worded by RSV "Bring her out between the ranks." When King Josiah was shot by an archer in battle and said to his servants, "Have me away; for I am sore wounded" (2 Chronicles 35.23), the Hebrew means "Take me away, for I am badly wounded."

**HE** is cited by Wright as redundant in Joshua 22.22, "the LORD God of gods, he knoweth, and Israel he shall know." But the trouble with the KJ rendering of this verse lies deeper. It fails to make clear that this is a solemn invocation of the LORD which has the effect of an oath, and it throws the sentence into confusion by placing "save us not this day" in parentheses. Verses 22–25 go together, and should be compared in the two versions.

KJ has: "The LORD God of gods, the LORD God of gods, he knoweth, and Israel he shall know; if *it be* in rebellion, or if in transgression against the LORD, (save us not this day,) That we have built us an altar to turn from following the LORD, or if to offer thereon burnt offering or meat offering, or if to offer peace offerings thereon, let the LORD himself require *it*; And if we have not *rather* done it for fear of *this* thing, saying, In time to come your children might speak unto our children, saying, What have ye to do with the LORD God of Israel? For the LORD hath made Jordan a border between us and you, ye children of Reuben and children of Gad; ye have no part in the LORD: so shall your children make our children cease from fearing the LORD."

RSV has: "The Mighty One, God, the LORD! The Mighty One, God, the LORD! He knows; and let Israel itself know! If it was in rebellion or in breach of faith toward the LORD, spare us not today for building an altar to turn away from following the LORD; or if we did so to offer burnt offerings or cereal offerings or peace offerings on it, may the LORD himself take vengeance. Nay, but we did it from fear that in time to come your children might say to our children, 'What have you to do with the LORD, the God of Israel? For the LORD has made the Jordan a boundary between us and you, you Reubenites and Gadites; you have no portion in the LORD.' So your children might make our children cease to worship the LORD."

**HEADSTONE,** now the upright stone at the head of a grave, occurs once in the sense of the topstone or capstone of a building (Zechariah 4.7). In the original printing of KJ, 1611, it appeared as two words, "head stone," but some later editor or printer ran the two words together, without a hyphen, into one word. This was kept, even by Scrivener in *The Cambridge Paragraph Bible*, and appears in the present editions of KJ. It has been rejected by the revised versions, which have "the top stone."

The King James Version uses the expression "head *stone* of the corner" in Psalm 118.22. The italic type indicates that the English word "stone" was inserted by the translators, and the difference in type doubtless prevented later editors from running the words together. This expression, too, was kept by Scrivener, with cross-references between Psalm 118.22 and Zechariah 4.7. The cross-references are misleading, for Zechariah has *'eben ro'shah*, and the Psalm has *ro'sh pinnah*, which is literally "head of the corner." RSV translates Psalm 118.22: "The stone which the builders rejected has become the chief cornerstone." This verse was cited by Jesus (Matthew 21.42; Mark 12.10; Luke 20.17) and by Peter (Acts 4.11; 1 Peter 2.6–7). Taken in conjunction with Peter's citation of Isaiah 28.16 and Paul's "household of God, built upon the foundation of the apostles and prophets, Christ Jesus himself being the cornerstone" (Ephesians 2.19–20), the context as a whole clearly refers to a cornerstone which enters into the foundation of a building, rather than to a topstone or capstone.

**HEADY** means precipitate, passionate, headstrong. It occurs once, among the vices listed in 2 Timothy 3.1–5: "In the last days perilous times shall come. For men shall be . . . traitors, heady, highminded, lovers of pleasures more than lovers of God." RSV translates: ". . . treacherous, reckless, swollen with conceit, lovers of pleasure rather than lovers of God." The Greek adjective means rushing headlong, rash, reckless; it occurs also in Acts 19.36, where the town clerk urged the citizens of Ephesus "to be quiet and do nothing rash."

**HEALTH** now refers to the soundness and efficient functioning of body and mind. But it had wider meanings in 1611 and before. It was used as a synonym for healing or cure; used in the sense of safety or deliverance; and used in a moral and spiritual sense as the equivalent of salvation.

Wyclif wrote of Shammah that "he smote the Philistines, and the Lord made a great health" (2 Samuel 23.12), where Tyndale and subsequent versions read "a great victory." Coverdale has the people say of Jonathan, "that hath done so great health in Israel this night" (1 Samuel 14.45), where the Geneva Bible has "who hath so mightily delivered Israel."

Wyclif's version of Acts 28.28 is "Therefore be it known to you that this health of God is sent to heathen men." Tyndale rendered it "this salvation of God is sent to the Gentiles"; but at Luke 19.9 his version has Jesus say to Zacchaeus, "This day is health come unto this house." In Ephesians 6.17 Wyclif had "the helm of health," where subsequent versions have "the helmet of salvation."

In Psalms 42.11 and 43.5 the Geneva Bible reads "my present help and my God"; the Bishops' Bible, "my present salvation and my Lord," which was changed in its second edition to "the help of my countenance and my God." KJ changed this to "the health of my countenance, and my God." RSV returns to Geneva, with the simple rendering "my help and my God."

One of the most familiar verses of the Bible is Psalm 67.2: "That thy way may be known upon earth, thy saving health among all nations." Its wording goes back to Tyndale, and is kept by RSV, except that "saving health" is changed to "saving power."

**HEAR** is used in the sense of hear about, be informed of, in Matthew 11.2—"when John had heard in the prison the works of Christ." RSV has "when John heard in prison about the deeds of the Christ." The elliptical expression "heard say" occurs in Genesis 41.15, where Pharaoh says to Joseph, "I have heard say of thee, *that* thou canst understand a dream to interpret it"; and in 2 Samuel 19.2, "the people heard say that day how the king was grieved for his son." RSV translates: "I have heard it said of you that when you hear a dream you can interpret it"; and "the people heard that day, 'The king is grieving for his son.'" A similar expression "heard tell" appears in Numbers 21.1, "king Arad the Canaanite, which dwelt in the south, heard tell that Israel came by the way of the spies." RSV translates more literally: "the Canaanite, the king of Arad, who dwelt in the Negeb, heard that Israel was coming by the way of Atharim."

These ways of construing "hear" are still in colloquial use. Examples from Shakespeare are:

"We have heard your miseries as far as Tyre."
*Pericles*, I, 4, 88
"I hear say you are of honourable parts."
*Pericles*, IV, 6, 86
"She cannot endure to hear tell of a husband."
*Much Ado About Nothing*, II, 1, 362

**HEAVE OFFERING.** The King James Version translates the Hebrew word *terumah* by "oblation" 18 times, "offering" 28 times, and "heave offering" 24 times. RSV drops "oblation" and "heave offering," and uses "offering" in all cases except a few "contributions" in 2 Chronicles and Nehemiah and the "portion" of the land to be set apart for the LORD in Ezekiel 45 and 48.

The term "heave offering" is ambiguous and misleading. It implies a rite of elevation, which is doubtful. The verb "heave," moreover, now suggests strenuous effort, lifting or throwing something very heavy.

"The shoulder of the heave offering, which is waved, and which is heaved up, of the ram of the consecration" means "the thigh of the priests' portion, which is waved, and which is offered from the ram of ordination" (Exodus 29.27). "When ye come into the land whither I bring you, Then it shall be, that, when ye eat of the bread of the land, ye shall offer up an heave offering unto the LORD. Ye shall offer up a cake of the first of your dough *for* an heave offering: as *ye do* the heave offering of the threshingfloor, so shall ye heave it" (Numbers 15.18–20) is more accurately translated: "When you come into the land to which I bring you and when you eat of the food of the land, you shall present an offering to the LORD. Of the first of your coarse meal you shall present a cake as an offering; as an offering from the threshing floor, so shall you present it." The injunction to the Levites concerning their offering to the LORD a tenth part of the tithes which they receive, concludes with the assurance: "ye shall bear no sin by reason of it, when ye have heaved from it the best of it" (Numbers 18.32). This means: "you shall bear no sin by reason of it, when you have offered the best of it."

**HEAVILY** is used in an obsolete sense in Psalm 35.14, "I bowed down heavily," an ambiguous rendering of the Hebrew which means "bowed down in mourning." The Hebrew word represented by "heavily" is translated "mourning" in Psalms 38.6; 42.9; 43.2. RSV translates this passage:

"I went about as one who laments his mother,
     bowed down and in mourning."

**HEAVINESS** appears 14 times in the Bible, but never in the sense of physical weight. In each case it has a psychological meaning; it denotes a state of mind. More precisely, in each of these cases it denotes one of a dozen different states of mind. For KJ uses "heaviness" to represent 7 different Hebrew words and 3 different Greek words, each of which has its own distinct meaning. The more exact translation of these terms by RSV displaces the word "heaviness" in all of the 14 cases. Listing the terms in the order in which they are given in Young's *Concordance*, "heaviness" is replaced by "anxiety" (Proverbs 12.25), "a faint spirit" (Isaiah 61.3), "sad countenance" (Job 9.27), "moaning" (Isaiah 29.2), "sorrow" (Psalm 119.28; Proverbs 10.1; Romans 9.2), "grief" (Proverbs 14.13), "fasting" (Ezra 9.5), "dejection" (James 4.9), "painful" (2 Corinthians 2.1), "despair" (Psalm 69.20), "distressed" (Philippians 2.26), "have to suffer" (1 Peter 1.6).

The three examples in Proverbs are: "Heaviness in the heart of man maketh it stoop" (12.25); RSV "Anxiety in a man's heart weighs him down." "A foolish son *is* the heaviness of his mother" (10.1); RSV "a foolish son is a sorrow to his mother." "The end of that mirth *is* heaviness" (14.13); RSV "the end of joy is grief."

1 Peter 1.6 reads, "Wherein ye greatly rejoice, though now for a season, if need be, ye are in heaviness through manifold temptations." RSV translates, "In this you rejoice, though now for a little while you may have to suffer various trials."

**HEAVY** is used by KJ more naturally than "heaviness"—we read of heavy yokes, heavy burdens, heavy bondage, heavy hands, heavy hearts, heavy hair, heavy transgression, eyes heavy with sleep, and ears heavy to hear. In Isaiah 58.6 "heavy burdens" does not accurately represent the Hebrew, which means "the thongs of the yoke"; in Proverbs 31.6 "heavy hearts" is not strong enough an expression for "those in bitter distress."

The King James Version uses the same word to express King Ahab's vexation over Naboth's refusal and our Lord's feeling as he approached his agony in the Garden of Gethsemane. Ahab was "heavy," it says, and Jesus began to be "very heavy." This is entirely unjustified, for the Hebrew term used concerning Ahab means "resentful" or "vexed," which is just the opposite of our Lord's attitude in Gethsemane. Compare 1 Kings 20.43; 21.4; Matthew 26.37; Mark 14.33 in KJ and RSV.

**HELPS** means helpful deeds (1 Corinthians 12.28) and refers to the ministry of the deacons, who had care of the poor and the sick. In this list of gifts of the Spirit, Paul uses personal terms for the first three—apostles, prophets, teachers—then turns to impersonal terms—miracles, healings, helps, administrations, tongues. RSV translates by personal terms throughout, hence "helpers."

"They used helps, undergirding the ship" is a literal translation of the Greek in Acts 27.17. The Arndt and Gingrich lexicon says that the word for "helps" is probably a nautical technical term. A correspondingly technical expression in English would be "they frapped the ship" (Conybeare and Hawson, *Life and Letters of St. Paul*, chapter 23). But just exactly what they did is not clear, and RSV is as vague as KJ: "they took measures to undergird the ship." There is a good summary of the alternatives in *The Interpreter's Bible*, vol. 9, p. 336.

**HENCE,** in the sense of "therefore," causes no trouble. It is equally clear in the sense of "away from here." The redundant expression "from hence" has a long history and is used five times in Shakespeare's plays and six times in KJ. RSV substitutes "from here." The devil's third temptation of Jesus was, "If you are the Son of God, throw yourself down from here" (Luke 4.9). Abraham's answer to the rich man in torment was, "between us and you a great chasm has been fixed, in order that those who would pass from here to you may not be able, and none may cross from there to us" (Luke 16.26).

With respect to time, "hence" means "from now on"; with respect to origin, it means "from this (which has just been mentioned)." Jesus' answer to Pilate concludes, "but now is my kingdom not from hence" (John 18.36). RSV avoids ambiguity by repetition of the word "world"; its translation of the full answer is "My kingship is not of this world; if my kingship were of this world, my servants would fight, that I might not be handed over to the Jews; but my kingship is not from the world."

James 4.1 is rendered by KJ: "From whence *come* wars and fightings among you? *come they* not hence, *even* of your lusts that war in your members?" The Greek is more directly and accurately translated: "What causes wars, and what causes fightings among you? Is it not your passions that are at war in your members?"

**HER** is used reflexively, in the sense of "herself," in Genesis 21.16, "she went, and sat her down"; and in 38.14, "she put her widow's garments off from her, and covered her with a vail." In the first of these cases RSV simply omits "her"; in the second it reads "she put off her widow's garments, and put on a veil."

**HEREAFTER** in the Bible, as in Shakespeare, is always an adverb, meaning after this or from now on. It is retained by RSV except in a few cases where the Greek is translated more literally, such as "from now on" (Luke 22.69), "no longer" (John 14.30), "afterward" (John 13.7), "after this" (Revelation 4.1). "Hereafter" is not used in the Bible as a noun, either in the sense of the future on earth or in the sense of life beyond death, the world to come. Its earliest use in the latter sense, as recorded by OED, was in 1702. John Wesley's use of "the hereafter" probably popularized the word.

**HEREUNTO** is an archaic adverb which means "to this." "For even hereunto were ye called" means "For to this you have been called" (1 Peter 2.21). The KJ rendering of Ecclesiastes 2.25 is meaningless: "For who can eat, or who else can hasten *hereunto*, more than I." With the help of the ancient Greek and Syriac versions, RSV joins this verse to 24b, and translates: "This also, I saw, is from the hand of God; for apart from him who can eat or who can have enjoyment?"

**HIGH** is used in the sense of "haughty" in such passages as Psalms 18.27; 101.5; Proverbs 21.4. A typical verse is Isaiah 10.12, where it is said that the Lord "will punish the fruit of the stout heart of the king of Assyria, and the glory of his high looks." This is a literal word-for-word translation of the Hebrew, but it fails to convey the meaning because each of these good terms is used in a bad sense. The Hebrew lexicons, taking into account the context, including comparison with 9.9, declare that here the stout heart is pride, and its fruit is arrogant speech, the high looks are haughty, and the glory is glorying or boasting. RSV translates it, "will punish the arrogant boasting of the king of Assyria and his haughty pride."

"Every high thing that exalteth itself against the knowledge of God" means "every proud obstacle to the knowledge of God" (2 Corinthians 10.5). On the other hand, "the high calling of God in Christ Jesus" is "the upward call of God in Christ Jesus" (Philippians 3.14).

**HIGHMINDED** is now almost always used in a good sense. A highminded person is one who holds and is true to high principles, who is magnanimous, generous, and above any petty feeling or mean action. But in the sixteenth century the word was more often used in a bad sense, and it is so used in KJ. "Be not highminded" was the common translation of Romans 11.20 and 12.16, and 1 Timothy 6.17; but the meaning was "be not haughty." In 2 Timothy 3.4 "highminded" appears as one of a long list of evil dispositions of the ungodly, and represents a Greek word which means "swollen with conceit."

**HIM** is used reflexively, in the sense of "himself," in Matthew 9.22, "Jesus turned him about." RSV has "Jesus turned."

**HIMSELF** is used as the subject of a verb, in place of the nominative pronoun "he," in Matthew 8.17: "Himself took our infirmities, and bare *our* sicknesses." RSV has "He took our infirmities and bore our diseases."

**HIS.** The use of "his" for a neuter possessive pronoun as well as for the masculine (see IT) may lead to ambiguity. That is possible, though perhaps not likely, in 1 Corinthians 15.38, "God giveth it a body as it hath pleased him, and to every seed his own body." Certainly "to each kind of seed its own body" is clearer. Confusion can hardly be avoided in Daniel 7.9, "I beheld till the thrones were cast down, and the Ancient of days did sit, whose garment *was* white as snow, and the hair of his head like the pure wool: his throne *was like* the fiery flame, *and* his wheels as burning fire." RSV has ". . . its wheels were burning fire."

The original edition of KJ had "Asa his heart" (1 Kings 15.14) and "Mordecai his matters" (Esther 3.4), but these phrases were changed in 1762 to the modern form, "Asa's heart" and "Mordecai's matters."

**HITHERTO** usually means up to this time, until now. It formerly was used of space also, meaning up to this place, thus far. When David sat before the LORD, and said, "Who *am* I, O Lord GOD? and what *is* my house, that thou hast brought me hitherto?" the Hebrew adverb is one of place. RSV translates ". . . that thou hast brought me thus far?" (2 Samuel 7.18 = 1 Chronicles 17.16). The LORD's word to the sea, "Hitherto shalt thou come, but no further" (Job 38.11), means "Thus far shall you come, and no farther." The "people terrible from their beginning hitherto" (Isaiah 18.2) are "a people feared near and far." The reader should compare the translations of KJ and RSV for the entire chapter. *The Interpreter's Bible*, vol. 5, pp. 275–278, explains the historical situation.

**HOLD.** The noun "hold" is used 12 times by KJ in the sense of "stronghold," which replaces it in RSV (Judges 9.46; 1 Samuel 22.4; etc.). It is twice replaced by "custody" (Ezekiel 19.9; Acts 4.3). The description of Babylon as "the hold of every foul spirit, and a cage of every unclean and hateful bird" comes from Tyndale, and exhibits his characteristic habit of varying words (Revelation 18.2). In this verse the Greek word for "foul" is the same as that for "unclean," and the Greek word for "hold" is the same as that for "cage." The basic meaning of the latter word is a watch or guard. It does not here refer to a prison where foul spirits are under guard or a cage where unclean birds are confined. It is employed here in the active sense, and means a station or post of guards, a garrison, or police headquarters. The implication is that the very forces of public safety and defense are prostituted to foul purposes; evil is in control, and is not caged or imprisoned. RSV translates the passage:

> "a haunt of every foul spirit,
> a haunt of every foul and hateful bird."

**HOLDEN** is the old past participle of "hold," which began to be displaced by "held" in the sixteenth century. Shakespeare used "held" many times, and "holden" only once ("his majesty's parliament, holden at Bury," *King Henry VI, Part II*, II, 4, 71). Depending upon the Hebrew and the contexts, RSV replaces "holden" with "held" (Isaiah 42.14; Acts 2.24) and "caught" (Job 36.8; Proverbs 5.22). "Holden up" is "supported" (Psalm 18.35) and "upheld" (Romans 14.4). "By thee I have been holden up from the womb" is more accurately translated "Upon thee I have leaned from my birth" (Psalm 71.6). "Thou hast holden *me* by my right hand" is not a statement concerning the past; it means "thou dost hold my right hand" (Psalm 73.23). "Cyrus, whose right hand I have holden" means "Cyrus, whose right hand I have grasped" (Isaiah 45.1). The earlier translations had "kept" or "celebrated" the passover commanded by King Josiah (2 Kings 23.22, 23); the exception was the Geneva Bible, which used "holden" and was followed by KJ. "Their eyes were holden that they should not know him" means "their eyes were kept from recognizing him" (Luke 24.16).

"And this is the cause that they are so holden with pride" is the rendering of Psalm 73.6a in the Book of Common Prayer. It comes from Coverdale, who probably got it from the Latin translation by Münster, which read, *tenet eos constrictos superbia.* The Geneva Bible had "Therefore pride is as a chaine unto them"; and KJ "Therefore pride compasseth them about as a chain." But the word "chain" is ambiguous, and the Hebrew here does not mean a bond or fetter, but an ornament. RSV translates the clause accurately, "Therefore pride is their necklace."

**HOLPEN** is the old past participle of "help." From the fourteenth to the seventeenth century it was also spelled "holpe" or "holp," and it was gradually displaced by "helped." Shakespeare, according to the *Concordance*, used "holp" 17 times and "helped" 6 times, as past tense and participle. Examples are:

"Would I had been by, to have helped the old man!"
*The Winter's Tale*, III, 3, 110
"By foul play, as thou say'st, were we heaved thence;
But blessedly holp hither."
*The Tempest*, I, 2, 63

The King James Version uses "holpen" 5 times and "helped" 6 times, as past participle. "Holpen" appears in Psalms 83.8; 86.17; Isaiah 31.3; Daniel 11.34; Luke 1.54. "Helped" appears as participle in 1 Samuel 7.12; 1 Chronicles 5.20; 2 Chronicles 26.15; Job 26.2; Psalm 28.7; Isaiah 49.8.

The word "holpen" has been kept alive by liturgical use in the Magnificat—"He hath holpen his servant Israel." Its presence in the KJ version of the Magnificat is doubtless due to its use in the Book of Common Prayer. While "holpen" had appeared in Tyndale's first translation (1525) of Luke 1.54, he rejected it in his final edition (1534), and the word was not used at this point by any of the other English versions which preceded KJ. The Great Bible and the Bishops' Bible had "He hath helped his servant Israel, in remembrance of his mercy."

It is hardly possible that the KJ translators saw any value, other than adherence to liturgical custom, in the use of "holpen." It weakens the meter, and dulls the edge of Mary's ascription of praise. If they had deemed the word to possess any special poetic or spiritual value, they would probably have written "Hitherto hath the LORD holpen us" (1 Samuel 7.12), "he was marvellously holpen" (2 Chronicles 26.15), and "in a day of salvation have I holpen thee" (Isaiah 49.8). But they did not; they used "helped" in these and other cases.

**HONEST** occurs seven times in the New Testament, always in the older and wider sense of honored, honorable, worthy of honor. In the parable of the Sower RSV retains "an honest and good heart" (Luke 8.15). It uses "honorable" (2 Corinthians 8.21; Philippians 4.8), "right" (2 Corinthians 13.7), and "noble" (Romans 12.17). "Having your conversation honest among the Gentiles" means "Maintain good conduct among the Gentiles" (1 Peter 2.12); and "men of honest report" means "men of good repute" (Acts 6.3).

"I am no strumpet; but of life as honest
As you that thus abuse me."
*Othello*, V, 1, 122

**HONESTLY** is used for two Greek adverbs, one of which means "honorably" (Hebrews 13.18) and the other "becomingly" (Romans 13.13). The second of these occurs also in 1 Thessalonians 4.12, where KJ reads, "That ye may walk honestly toward them that are without, and *that* ye may have lack of nothing." RSV translates this verse, "so that you may command the respect of outsiders, and be dependent on nobody."

**HONESTY** appears once (1 Timothy 2.2) as translation for the Greek noun which, as applied to God, means holiness and, as applied to men, means reverence, dignity, respectfulness, probity. "That we may lead a quiet and peaceable life in all godliness and honesty" reads in RSV, "that we may lead a quiet and peaceable life, godly and respectful in every way."

**HONORABLE** may refer to a person's character or to his reputation or social status. The emphasis of the word, as used in KJ, is not upon inner principles, but upon an honored position among one's fellow men. Out of 30 occurrences, "honorable" is retained by RSV in 5. In the other cases it is replaced, according to context and varying Hebrew and Greek terms, by such expressions as "honored" (Genesis 34.19; 1 Samuel 22.14; Isaiah 5.13; 23.8, 9; 43.4; Nahum 3.10), "held in honor" (1 Samuel 9.6; 1 Corinthians 4.10; Hebrews 13.4), "renowned" (2 Samuel 23.19, 23; 1 Chronicles 11.21, 25), "in high favor" (2 Kings 5.1), "the man of rank" (Isaiah 3.3), "eminent" (Luke 14.8), "of high standing" (Acts 13.50; 17.12). In the place of "The Lord is well pleased for his righteousness' sake; he will magnify the law, and make *it* honourable" (Isaiah 42.21) RSV reads:
"The Lord was pleased, for his righteousness' sake,
   to magnify his law and make it glorious."

**HOST.** Except for the host of the inn in Jesus' parable of the Good Samaritan (Luke 10.35) and Paul's reference to "Gaius mine host" (Romans 16.23) the word "host" means "army," as used in KJ. Derived from the Latin *hostis*, enemy, it translates three Hebrew words and one Greek word for army. "The host of heaven" means (1) the multitude of angels that serve God, or (2) sun, moon, and stars, either as evidence of God's creative power or as themselves the objects of idolatrous worship. "The Lord of hosts" was used by the Hebrew prophets in the sense of God of the universe, signifying as no other title his supremacy and omnipotence. The expression "Lord of Sabaoth," which KJ has in Romans 9.29 and James 5.4, represents simply the fact that here the Hebrew word for "hosts" was left untranslated into Greek, and that Tyndale took it over untranslated into English. The Greek Septuagint had left "sabaoth" untranslated as part of this title in many passages, especially in Isaiah. It appears, to take the most notable example, in the Greek version of Isaiah 6.3, from which it was taken over by the Old Latin version, and consequently appears in the *Te Deum:*

*Sanctus, Sanctus, Sanctus, Dominus Deus Sabaoth*
"Holy, Holy, Holy, Lord God of Sabaoth"

The "of" was sometimes omitted, and the title was expressed in English as "the Lord Sabaoth." It so appears in the second verse of Hedge's translation of Martin Luther's great hymn, "A Mighty Fortress Is Our God":

> "Did we in our own strength confide,
> Our striving would be losing;
> Were not the right man on our side,
> The man of God's own choosing.
> Dost ask who that may be?
> Christ Jesus, it is he;
> Lord Sabaoth his name,
> From age to age the same,
> And he must win the battle."

**HOUGH** belongs to the "-ough" series of English words, which have such diverse pronunciations as "cough," "though," "through," "plough," "sough," "rough," "tough." When "slough" means a stretch of mire, it rhymes with "how"; when it means a river inlet, with "hue"; and when it means to cast off, with "huff." "Hough" is pronounced "hock," and is generally so spelled. It is used in KJ only as a verb, and means to cut the tendons in the back of the foot of a horse or other animal. The synonym of "hough" or "hock" is "hamstring," and this is the verb used by RSV (Joshua 11.6, 9; 2 Samuel 8.4; 1 Chronicles 18.4).

The KJ rendering in Genesis 49.6, "in their anger they slew a man, and in their selfwill they digged down a wall," is a cryptic statement which results from confusing the Hebrew word for "ox" with the word for "wall" and consequent failure to recognize the Hebrew verb for "hamstring." The revised versions correct this. RSV translates, "in their anger they slay men, and in their wantonness they hamstring oxen."

**HOUSE.** The Hebrew *bayith* and the Greek *oikos*, like the English word "house," may mean (1) a building, (2) a household, (3) an immediate family of parents and children, (4) a family of ancestors and descendants, distinguished by continuity of residence or by occupation, position, or renown. The context generally makes the meaning clear, even in chapters like 2 Samuel 7, where "make a house" (vs. 11) and "build a house" (vs. 27) refer to the dynasty of David, and "build a house" (vs. 5, 13) refers to what was in due time Solomon's temple. In the corresponding chapter, 1 Chronicles 17, the phrase "build a house" is used throughout, with reference to the dynasty in verses 10 and 25, and with reference to the temple in verses 4 and 12. RSV usually retains the word "house," but occasionally replaces it to avoid ambiguity. For example, "thou shalt be saved, and thy house" (Acts 16.31) now reads "you will be saved, you and your household." The comment concerning the Hebrew midwives, "because the midwives feared God, . . . he made them houses" (Exodus 1.21), now reads ". . . he gave them families."

**HOUSE, TO.** When the Levite from Ephraim, with his concubine and servant, turned aside to Gibeah to spend the night, "he sat him down in a street of the city; for *there was* no man that took them into his house to lodging" (Judges 19.15). When an old man, who was also an Ephraimite, asked him in friendly fashion where he was going and whence he had come, he answered in detail and ruefully added, "and there *is* no man that receiveth me to house" (19.18).

Except for the difference between "them" and "me" and the omission of the phrase "to lodging," the last clause of verse 18 and the last clause of verse 15 are identical in the Hebrew. The elliptical phrase "to house" is an oddity that appeared first in Matthew's Bible, 1537, which means that it was part of Tyndale's translation of the books from Joshua to Chronicles, first published in this volume edited by John Rogers under the pseudonym "Thomas Matthew." The clause "receiveth me to house" was kept by the Great Bible, the Geneva Bible, the Bishops' Bible, and KJ.

Where did Tyndale get "to house"? Wright says that it "is probably due to the *zu Hause* of some German version." But Luther's German Bible, which Tyndale used, does not have *zu Hause*. Moreover, the German idiom *zu Hause* means "at home" rather than "into the house," and is not likely to be used here by any German version.

The truth is, more probably, that Tyndale got the phrase "to house" from no other version. It is simply an example of his characteristic freedom of rendering and lack of care for mechanical consistency. There is no archaic English idiom "to house" corresponding to the German *zu Hause*. It is even possible that when Tyndale wrote "to house" as the closing words of verse 18 he meant them to be the infinitive of the verb "to house" rather than to be a preposition and a noun.

**HOW, HOW THAT.** The archaic combination "how that" appears frequently in KJ. It usually means simply "that." Examples are: "We will not hide *it* from my lord, how that our money is spent" (Genesis 47.18); RSV "We will not hide from my lord that our money is all spent." "Ye may know how that I *am* the LORD" (Exodus 10.2); RSV "you may know that I am the LORD." "She had heard in the country of Moab how that the LORD had visited his people" (Ruth 1.6); RSV "she had heard in the country of Moab that the LORD had visited his people." "Know ye not . . . how that the law hath dominion over a man as long as he liveth?" (Romans 7.1); RSV "Do you not know . . . that the law is binding on a person only during his life?" "Ye see then how that by works a man is justified, and not by faith only" (James 2.24); RSV "You see that a man is justified by works and not by faith alone." Other cases are: Exodus 9.29; Joshua 9.24; 2 Samuel 18.19; 1 Kings 5.3; Acts 7.25; 13.32; 15.7; 23.30; 1 Corinthians 1.26; 10.1; 15.3; 2 Corinthians 12.4; 13.5; Ephesians 3.3; Hebrews 12.17; James 2.24.

In seven cases "how that" means "how." "Thou hast seen how that the LORD thy God bare thee" (Deuteronomy 1.31) means "you have seen how the LORD your God bore you." "How that beyond measure I persecuted the church of God, and wasted it" (Galatians 1.13) means "how I persecuted the church of God violently and tried to destroy it." The other cases are: Ruth 2.11; 1 Samuel 24.10, 18; 2 Kings 9.25; Acts 10.28.

In one case "how that" is replaced in RSV by "for." This is in 2 Corinthians 8.2, which begins with the same Greek word *hoti* with which the next verse (8.3) begins. The statements are parallel, and "for," which KJ uses in verse 3, is the correct word for both verses.

The word of the LORD in Jeremiah 9.7, "Behold, I will melt them, and try them; for how shall I do for the daughter of my people," represents Hebrew which is more clearly translated,

"Behold, I will refine them and test them,
for what else can I do, because of my people?"

Protests or requests for explanation which begin with "How say ye . . .?", "How saidst thou . . .?", and the like, are better expressed with "How can you say . . .?" or "How is it that you say . . .?" (Genesis 26.9; Psalm 11.1; Isaiah 19.11; Luke 20:41; John 8.33; 12.34; 14.9).

In the account of the birth of Tamar's twins (Genesis 38.27–30), the midwife's exclamation, "How hast thou broken forth? *this* breach *be* upon thee" is an unnecessarily awkward representation of Hebrew which means, "What a breach you have made for yourself!"

"How think ye?" (Matthew 18.12) means "What do you think?" and is so translated by KJ in Matthew 17.25; 21.28. "How he would have him called" (Luke 1.62) is properly translated, "What he would have him called."

When the Greek words *pōs ouchi* which mean "How not?" or "Why not?" introduce a question, no answer is expected or needed. It is a rhetorical question, which is in effect a strong affirmation. The best way to express this idiom in English is to put the question directly—"Will he not . . .?"—leaving the initial *pōs* without representation by a "how" or "why." This idiom appears in Romans 8.32 and 2 Corinthians 3.8. The whole of Romans 8.31–35, 37–39 should be read to convey the force of the series of rhetorical questions with which Paul leads up to the confession of faith that is one of the greatest passages in all literature. Again, the whole of 2 Corinthians 3.1–11 must be read as a basis for understanding the rhetorical question in verse 8. Here, unfortunately, RSV changes "how" to "why." It would have been better to deal with the idiom as in Romans. The verse would then read: "will not the dispensation of the Spirit be attended with greater splendor?"

**HOWBEIT** is an archaic word for however, nevertheless, be that as it may. It seems to have served the KJ translators as a general, all-purpose connective, for it appears 41 times in the Old Testament, and in only 5 of these cases is there a corresponding word in the Hebrew, other than the ubiquitous conjunction *w* with which most sentences and clauses begin. It appears 23 times in the New Testament, with a corresponding Greek word in only 10 of these cases.

RSV does not use "howbeit." It uses "but" (Judges 18.29), "only" (1 Samuel 8.9), "nevertheless" (2 Samuel 12.14), "however" (1 Kings 11.13), "and so" (2 Chronicles 32.31)—each of these passages has a different Hebrew conjunction. In the New Testament it uses "however" (John 6.23; 1 Corinthians 8.7), "yet" (John 7.13, 27; Acts 7.48), "but" (1 Corinthians 8.7; 1 Timothy 1.16); and it simply omits "howbeit" in 1 Corinthians 14.20, Galatians 4.8, and Hebrews 3.16 as not called for by the Greek text.

As evidence of the studied archaism of the revised versions of 1881–1901 is the fact that they use "howbeit" in 31 cases where KJ had used other terms. An interesting example is Philippians 4.14, where KJ reads "Notwithstanding ye have well done, that ye did communicate with my affliction." RV and ASV have "Howbeit ye did well that ye had fellowship with my affliction." RSV has "Yet it was kind of you to share my trouble."

**HUSBANDMAN** is a word not used by Shakespeare, though he uses "husbandry." It appears 26 times in KJ, but is not retained by RSV. "Noah was the first tiller of the soil" (Genesis 9.20), and "I am a tiller of the soil" (Zechariah 13.5), are translations close to the Hebrew. "O tillers of the soil" is better poetic cadence in Joel 1.11. "Farmer" is used for *'ikkar* in 2 Chronicles 26.10; Jeremiah 14.4; 31.24; 51.23; Amos 5.16, and "plowmen" in 2 Kings 25.12 (= Jeremiah 52.16) and in Isaiah 61.5.

For the Greek *geōrgos* the general word "farmer" is used in 2 Timothy 2.6, "It is the hard-working farmer who ought to have the first share of the crops," and in James 5.7, "the farmer waits for the precious fruit of the earth." In Jesus' parable of the Vineyard it is obvious that the "husbandmen" were "tenants"—the point of the parable turns upon that fact (Matthew 21.33–41; Mark 12.1–9; Luke 20.9–16). With Weymouth, Moffatt, Confraternity, Phillips, RSV translates *geōrgos* by "vinedresser" in the quite different context of John 15.1–2. Goodspeed dissents in favor of "cultivator." RSV has: "I am the true vine, and my Father is the vinedresser. Every branch of mine that bears no fruit, he takes away, and every branch that does bear fruit he prunes, that it may bear more fruit."

**HUSBANDRY.** It is said of King Uzziah that "he loved husbandry" (2 Chronicles 26.10). But the literal translation of the Hebrew is more effective—"he had farmers and vinedressers in the hills and in the fertile lands, for he loved the soil."

The KJ translation of Paul's statement to the Corinthians, "ye are God's husbandry," is needlessly abstract and ambiguous (1 Corinthians 3.9). The Greek word here, *geōrgion,* means cultivated land or field. RSV reads: "For we are fellow workers for God; you are God's field, God's building." In justice to the KJ translators it should be said that among the various meanings of "husbandry" in the sixteenth century was "land under cultivation," and that they probably used the word in that sense—a sense now obsolete.

**HUSKS.** The "husks" that the swine ate, Luke 15.16, were the pods of
the carob tree, with a sweetish pulp containing seeds. They
were used not only as fodder for animals, but as food by the poorer
people, who ground and boiled them to extract their sugar, somewhat
as molasses is extracted from sugar cane. The prodigal son could certainly have eaten them.

Wyclif, Tyndale, Coverdale, the Great Bible, and the Bishops' Bible
have "the coddes," for "cod" was the old word for "pod." The word
"husk," which was introduced in the Geneva Bible, is misleading, for it
applies only to the outer covering and not to the whole fruit. It must be
admitted, however, that the husks sharpen the point of the story. Modern English translations, for the most part, forego the sharpening, and
use "pods."

The Hebrew word represented by "husk" in Numbers 6.4 probably
refers to grapeskins. The law for one taking the vow of a Nazirite required strict abstinence: "he shall separate himself from wine and
strong drink; he shall drink no vinegar made from wine or strong drink,
and shall not drink any juice of grapes or eat grapes, fresh or dried. All
the days of his separation he shall eat nothing that is produced by the
grapevine, not even the seeds or the skins" (Numbers 6.3–4 RSV).

In 2 Kings 4.42 "full ears of corn in the husk thereof" is now translated "fresh ears of grain in his sack." The editors of the revised versions agree that the Hebrew word refers not to the husk of the grain
(which, incidentally, was not American corn), but to the sack in which
the man carried it.

**IF SO BE (THAT).** The Oxford English Dictionary describes this as
a somewhat rhetorical equivalent of simple "if."
The expression occurs nine times in KJ, where it represents six different
terms—one Hebrew and five Greek. RSV does not use "if so be," but
the variety of terms and contexts is such as to call for nine distinct
English expressions. The passages are Joshua 14.12; Hosea 8.7; Matthew 18.13; Romans 8.9, 17; 1 Corinthians 15.15; 2 Corinthians 5.3;
Ephesians 4.21; 1 Peter 2.3.

**ILLUMINATE** is used once (Hebrews 10.32), "after ye were illumi-
nated." But the Greek verb here is the same that KJ
translates by "enlightened" in Hebrews 6.4 and Ephesians 1.18. The
Rheims New Testament, translating from the Latin Vulgate, had "illu-
minated" in all three passages. Why the KJ translators took it in one of
the three is a question for which we have no answer.

**IMAGERY** is used once in the Bible, in its older sense as a collective term for images and for pictures. "Every man in the chambers of his imagery" (Ezekiel 8.12) does not refer to the secret recesses of each individual's imagination, but to the scene that has just been described (vs. 10–11)—seventy elders of Israel gathered in secret worship of idols "portrayed upon the wall round about." "The chambers of his imagery" means "his room of pictures." Their action transgressed the commandment, "You shall not make for yourself a graven image, or any likeness of anything that is in heaven above, or that is in the earth beneath, or that is in the water under the earth; you shall not bow down to them or serve them" (Exodus 20.4–5).

**IMAGINATION.** The key to the use of this word is given in Genesis 6.5: "The LORD saw that the wickedness of man was great in the earth, and that every imagination of the thoughts of his heart was only evil continually." Imagination, in the Bible, does not denote a mental faculty or activity, but an evil purpose, plan, scheme, device, or argument. One Hebrew word, *sheriruth*, is translated "lust" in Psalm 81.12 and "imagination" in Deuteronomy 29.19 and in eight passages in Jeremiah (3.17; 7.24; 9.14; 11.8; 13.10; 16.12; 18.12; 23.17). These are mistranslations, for the word means firmness in an evil course. The revised versions use "stubbornness," "stubborn," or "stubbornly" in all its occurrences.

**IMAGINE,** as used in the Bible, means to purpose, plan, contrive. Its object is action; and, rather oddly, it is always directed to action that is evil or futile. Except for Acts 4.25, where "imagine" translates a verb quoted from the Greek Septuagint, the RSV uses other words: "think" (Job 6.26), "meditate" (Psalm 38.12), "propose" (Genesis 11.6), "plan" (Psalm 140.2), "plot" (Psalm 2.1; Nahum 1.9, 11), "devise" (Psalms 10.2; 21.11; Hosca 7.15; Zechariah 7.10; 8.17). Hastings' *Dictionary of the Bible* quotes a sentence from Sir Thomas Elyot, *The Governour,* II, 74, which illustrates this obsolete use of "imagine": "It was reported to the noble emperour Octavius Augustus that Lucius Cinna, which was susters sonne to the great Pompei, had imagined his dethe."

**IMITATE.** In 11 cases KJ uses "follow" or "followers" where the Greek words in the Epistles mean "imitate" or "imitators." Paul did not hesitate to counsel his converts to imitate him. This was not unwarranted pride or self-assertion, because he associated with himself Timothy and Epaphroditus and others, and because the ground of his counsel was that he and his associates sought to imitate Christ. Here are some of the texts: 1 Corinthians 4.16, "I urge you, . . . be imitators of me"; 1 Corinthians 11.1, "Be imitators of me, as I am of Christ"; Ephesians 5.1, "Be imitators of God, as beloved children"; 1 Thessalonians 1.6, "You became imitators of us and of the Lord." Other texts are: Philippians 3.17; 1 Thessalonians 2.14; 2 Thessalonians 3.7, 9; Hebrews 6.12; 3 John 11.

This was necessary counsel, the import of which is somewhat blurred by the KJ use of "follow" and "followers." Professor James Moffatt, writing in the *Expository Times* (vol. 10, p. 446), said: "In the seventh decade of the first Christian century, with the New Testament yet unwritten, the living ideal of the Christ-life was far from being stereotyped in words or habits. Fluid and free, its appeal had to come largely through men's experience and observation of one another, and the inevitable reproduction of character. The channel of education was chiefly the seen or remembered character of definite individuals, the advice and conduct of the best people."

The situation is expressed in the injunction of Hebrews 13.7, which reads in KJ, "Remember them which have the rule over you, who have spoken unto you the word of God: whose faith follow, considering the end of *their* conversation." RSV translates, "Remember your leaders, those who spoke to you the word of God; consider the outcome of their life, and imitate their faith."

**IMPART.** To impart is to share. It is to give to others a part or share of something that we possess. Originally the word was used for the sharing of any sort of possession, but it is now generally applied to nonmaterial goods. We impart knowledge, news, secrets, happiness, loyalty, friendship—such are possessions that one does not lose as he shares them. The word "impart" is used four times in KJ, as translation for a Hebrew verb and a Greek verb which mean to share. RSV reads, "He who has two coats, let him share with him who has none" (Luke 3.11); "we were ready to share with you" (1 Thessalonians 2.8); "God has . . . given her no share in understanding" (Job 39.17). (See SHARE)

RSV retains "impart" in Romans 1.11–12: "I long to see you, that I may impart to you some spiritual gift to strengthen you, that is, that we may be mutually encouraged by each other's faith, both yours and mine." It uses "impart" in three other contexts where KJ had another word: Psalm 119.130; 1 Corinthians 2.6, 7, 13; Ephesians 4.29.

**IMPLEAD** is an archaic word for sue in a court of justice, bring charges against. It occurs only in Acts 19.38, where the town clerk of Ephesus points out that if Demetrius and his fellow craftsmen have a complaint against anyone, the courts are open—"let them implead one another." This is a strangely inept rendering, in view of the fact that the Greek verb occurs in six other passages, and is translated by KJ itself "accused" (Acts 23.28–29; 26.2, 7), "called in question" (Acts 19.40), and "lay to the charge of" (Romans 8.33). It is a lonely rendering, for the prior translations had "let them accuse one another" and the revised versions returned to that. RSV has "let them bring charges against one another" and "we are in danger of being charged with rioting today" (Acts 19.38, 40). Romans 8.33 RSV reads "Who shall bring any charge against God's elect?"

**IMPOTENT** means powerless, unable, helpless, weak, ineffective. It is used in three passages of the New Testament. At the pool of Bethesda, we are told, "lay a great multitude of impotent folk," one of whom "had an infirmity thirty and eight years" and is referred to as "the impotent man" (John 5.3, 5, 7). In each of these three verses, the Greek word means "ill" or "illness," without specification as to the character of the malady. The "impotent man" healed by Peter and John at the gate of the temple had been "lame from his mother's womb" and had to be carried daily to the place where he sat for alms (Acts 4.9; 3.2). The man whom Paul healed at Lystra was "impotent in his feet, being a cripple from his mother's womb, who never had walked" (Acts 14.8). In place of "the impotent man" RSV uses "the sick man" in John 5.7 and "a cripple" in Acts 4.9.

**IN** is occasionally used with a verbal noun where a more direct translation is better. "As her soul was in departing" is more clearly put in the revised versions, "as her soul was departing" (Genesis 35.18). "While the flesh was in seething" (1 Samuel 2.13) means "while the meat was boiling." The phrase "in building" is retained by RSV in Ezra 5.16 but not in 1 Kings 6.7 or John 2.20.

When the angel of God called to Hagar, "Arise, lift up the lad, and hold him in thine hand" (Genesis 21.18), the meaning is not that she should take him in her arms, but that she should hold him firmly and support him. RSV translates, "hold him fast with your hand; for I will make him a great nation."

"They shall amerce him in an hundred *shekels* of silver" (Deuteronomy 22.19) means "they shall fine him a hundred shekels of silver."

"The king of Egypt put him down at Jerusalem, and condemned the land in an hundred talents of silver and a talent of gold" (2 Chronicles 36.3) means that he deposed Jehoahaz in Jerusalem and "laid upon the land a tribute" of that amount.

Paul's statement concerning woman, "she shall be saved in childbearing," means "woman will be saved through bearing children" (1 Timothy 2.15).

**INCONTINENCY** is an obsolete spelling for "incontinence," which means lack of self-control, either in a general sense or, more often, with reference to sexual desire. It has the specific reference in 1 Corinthians 7.5, where "for your incontinency" is more accurately translated, "through lack of self-control."

**INCONTINENT** is used in a general sense in 2 Timothy 3.3, where ASV translates the Greek adjective by "without self-control" and RSV by "profligate."

**INDITE** meant originally to dictate a form of words to be repeated or written down by someone else; it came soon to be used for the act of expressing one's thoughts in words, in any form of literary composition, without implication as to who wrote them down. The original meaning appears in the Preface to the King James Version, 1611, entitled "The Translators to the Reader," where the Scriptures are described as "a fountain of most pure water springing up unto everlasting life. And what marvel? The original thereof being from heaven, not from earth; the author being God, not man; the inditer, the holy spirit, not the wit of the Apostles or Prophets; the Penmen such as were sanctified from the womb, and endued with a principal portion of God's spirit."

The original meaning is implied also in the one occurrence of the word in the text of KJ, Psalm 45.1: "My heart is inditing a good matter: I speak of the things which I have made touching the king: my tongue *is* the pen of a ready writer." The Hebrew verb, however, is more vivid. It means to bubble up, seethe, boil over. The old Greek and Latin translations use similarly strong words. Modern versions generally forsake "indite" for a more literal rendering. RSV reads:

> "My heart overflows with a goodly theme;
> I address my verses to the king;
> my tongue is like the pen of a ready scribe."

A German translation by Catholic scholars (Professors Hamp and Stenzel), published in 1957, reads: *Mein Herz wallt über vor seliger Botschaft, singen will ich mein Lied dem König; meine Zunge ist dem Griffel des hurtigen Schreibers gleich.*

**INFIDEL** appears twice in KJ. "What part hath he that believeth with an infidel?" (2 Corinthians 6.15); RSV "What has a believer in common with an unbeliever?" "If any provide not for his own, and specially for those of his own house, he hath denied the faith, and is worse than an infidel" (1 Timothy 5.8); RSV "If any one does not provide for his relatives, and especially for his own family, he has disowned the faith and is worse than an unbeliever."

The Greek word represented by "infidel" is *apistos*, which is applied to persons in 20 other contexts, where KJ translates it by "faithless," "unbelieving," "unbeliever," "that believe not." The use of "infidel" in these two verses dates back to Tyndale, who meant by it one who is without the faith rather than one who denies or deliberately rejects it. In his *Prologe* to the five books of Moses, Tyndale wrote, "Behold how soberly and how circumspectly both Abraham and also Isaac behave themselves amonge the infideles." To the Crusaders the Saracens were "infidels." In *The Merchant of Venice* the Jew Shylock and his daughter Jessica are referred to as "infidel" (III, 2, 221; IV, 1, 334).

In this sense the word "infidel" is now obsolete or of only historical significance. It is now used to denote "a disbeliever in religion or divine revelation generally; especially one in a Christian land who professedly rejects or denies the divine origin and authority of Christianity." This definition is quoted from OED, which adds that the word is "usually a term of opprobrium." In any case it is too loaded with specific applications and currents of feeling to be a sound translation of *apistos* in the New Testament. The revised versions use "unbeliever," as do most modern translations.

**INFINITE** is used twice as a loose translation for the Hebrew words which mean "no end." This expression is exactly translated in Ecclesiastes 4.8, "yet *is there* no end of all his labour," and in Isaiah 9.7, "Of the increase of *his* government and peace *there shall be* no end." But to call Job's iniquities and the strength of Egypt "infinite" is the language of hyperbole (Job 22.5; Nahum 3.9). The one other occurrence of the word "infinite" is appropriate, because it has reference to God: "his understanding *is* infinite" (Psalm 147.5). The Hebrew here means "innumerable" or "beyond measure." The use of the word "infinite" in Job and Nahum was an innovation of the KJ translators, but the prior translations had used it in Psalm 147.

**INFLUENCES.** The sweet influences of the Pleiades (Job 38.31) have been often cited, from Milton's *Paradise Lost* (vii, 374) to Bartlett's *Familiar Quotations*. But they have no basis in the Hebrew text, which is properly translated, "Can you bind the chains of the Pleiades?" The question points to God's creative power and wisdom, as do the references to the Pleiades and Orion in Job 9.9 and Amos 5.8. The Septuagint and the Vulgate translated this text correctly. So did Martin Luther, *Kanst du die bande der sieben Sterne zusammen binden?* Of the sixteenth-century English versions, Coverdale, Matthew, and the first edition of the Bishops' Bible had correct renderings. The expression "sweet influences" was a product of Coverdale's later work upon the Great Bible; it was taken into the Geneva Bible and into the second (revised) edition of the Bishops' Bible, whence it got into KJ.

**INJURIOUS** is used as translation for the Greek adjective *hubristēs*, which means wantonly insolent and insulting (1 Timothy 1.13). Compare Shakespeare's *Coriolanus*, III, 3, 69–74:
> "Call me their traitor! Thou injurious tribune!
> Within thine eyes sat twenty thousand deaths,
> In thy hands clutch'd as many millions, in
> Thy lying tongue both numbers, I would say
> 'Thou liest' unto thee with a voice as free
> As I do pray the gods."

The same Greek adjective at Romans 1.30 is rendered as "despiteful" by KJ and "insolent" by the revised versions.

**INN** meant originally any place to dwell or to lodge overnight. The word is used in Genesis 42.27; 43.21 and Exodus 4.24 as translation for the Hebrew *malon*, which KJ elsewhere translates as "lodging," "lodging place," and "place where they lodged" (Joshua 4.3, 8; 2 Kings 19.23; Isaiah 10.29; Jeremiah 9.2). A building is nowhere implied; the lodging may have been in the open air; and the word "inn" has now become misleading. The revised versions use "lodging place" in its stead.

The inn to which the good Samaritan took the wounded traveler, however, was doubtless a khan or caravanserai to which the term "inn" may properly be applied. It was a *pandocheion*, which means an "all-receiving" place, open to all travelers; and it was under the management of a *pandocheus*, a host or innkeeper.

The inn at Bethlehem in which there was no place for Joseph and Mary (Luke 2.7) was a *kataluma*, a guest room. KJ translates this word as "guestchamber" in Mark 14.14 and Luke 22.11, where it refers to a large upper room in a private house, which the owner afforded to Jesus for the celebration of the Passover with his disciples. This was in accord with a custom which is described in Hastings' *Dictionary of the Bible*, vol. II, p. 474: "At the festivals of Passover, Pentecost, and Tabernacles the people were commanded to repair to Jerusalem; and it was a boast of the Rabbis, that, notwithstanding the enormous crowds, no man could truthfully say to his fellow, 'I have not found a fire where to roast my paschal lamb in Jerusalem,' or 'I have not found a bed in Jerusalem to lie in.' The vast numbers who came for the Passover from all parts were made free of the needed apartments, as far as the capacity of the houses permitted; and for this no payment was taken. It was, however, customary for the guests on departing to leave the skins of the paschal lambs, and the vessels which had been employed in the ceremonies, in token of gratitude for their hospitable entertainment."

The author of this article believes that this custom gives a clue to what happened to Joseph and Mary. He says: "We may reasonably suppose that on such an occasion as the great enrollment, when natives of a town came from afar, the 'guest chambers' of their friends would be thrown open to receive them. Joseph, arriving late, found that in which he had purposed to stay already occupied; and no room elsewhere being available, he betook himself with his charge to the khan. Even this apparently was full; possibly some of the animals were moved to afford them space; and here Jesus was born."

**INNOCENT.** "The blood of the souls of the poor innocents" (Jeremiah 2.34) is misleading because the reader may take "poor innocents" to mean children whose innocence is endearing or older folk whose lack of cleverness is to be pitied. The KJ translators took this wording from the Geneva Bible, and substituted it for the correct translation used by Coverdale, Matthew's Bible, the Great Bible, and the Bishops' Bible, which read "the blood of poor and innocent people." The revised versions of 1885–1901 have "the blood of the souls of the innocent poor," and RSV "the lifeblood of guiltless poor." The reference is to the unjust oppression of the poor.

On the other hand, "the blood of innocents" appears in all these translations at Jeremiah 19.4, where the reference is to the sacrificing of children as burnt offerings to Baal.

"He shall deliver the island of the innocent" (Job 22.30) confuses a word for "island" with a word for "not." RV and ASV have "He will deliver *even* him that is not innocent." RSV, relying upon the Greek Septuagint, the Syriac, and the Latin Vulgate, has "He delivers the innocent man."

**INQUISITION** gets its connotation of persecution and torture from the conduct, especially in Spain, of the Holy Office of the Inquisition organized in the thirteenth century under Pope Innocent III, for the suppression of heresy and the punishment of heretics. Basically, the word means "inquiry"; it is used particularly for judicial or official investigations. For "the judges shall make diligent inquisition" (Deuteronomy 19.18), RSV has "the judges shall inquire diligently." For "when inquisition was made of the matter" (Esther 2.23), RSV has "when the affair was investigated."

The only other occurrence of "inquisition" in KJ is not quite so clear: "When he maketh inquisition for blood, he remembereth them" (Psalm 9.12a). "He" refers to the LORD, and the Hebrew verb for "maketh inquisition" is the one which is translated "require" in a dozen similar contexts. The basic passage is Genesis 9.5–6, which reads in RSV: "For your lifeblood I will surely require a reckoning; of every beast I will require it and of man; of every man's brother I will require the life of man. Whoever sheds the blood of man, by man shall his blood be shed; for God made man in his own image." Psalm 9.11–12 forms a strophe, which RSV translates:

> "Sing praises to the LORD, who dwells in Zion!
> Tell among the peoples his deeds!
> For he who avenges blood is mindful of them;
> he does not forget the cry of the afflicted."

**INSTANT, INSTANTLY.** The noun "instant" refers in the Bible, as in present English, to a moment or point of time. The prophet Isaiah likens the iniquity of Israel to "a break in a high wall, bulging out, and about to collapse, whose crash comes suddenly, in an instant" (Isaiah 30.13).

But the adjective "instant" and the adverb "instantly" refer not to time, but to the spirit or manner of an action. The statement that the elders of the Jews went to Jesus and "besought him instantly" to heal the servant of the centurion, means that they "besought him earnestly"

(Luke 7.4). Paul's statement before King Agrippa, "Now I stand and am judged for the hope of the promise made of God unto our fathers: Unto which *promise* our twelve tribes, instantly serving *God* day and night, hope to come" (Acts 26.6–7), is better translated: "Now I stand here on trial for hope in the promise made by God to our fathers, to which our twelve tribes hope to attain, as they earnestly worship night and day."

"They were instant with loud voices, requiring that he might be crucified" (Luke 23.23) means "They were urgent, demanding with loud cries that he should be crucified." The apostles' charge to Timothy, "be instant in season, out of season," means "be urgent in season and out of season" (2 Timothy 4.2).

This use of "instant" is related to "insistent," which does not appear in KJ. "Insist" and its cognates were still new words in 1611. "Instant" comes from the Latin verb *stare*, to stand erect, and "insistent" from the Latin *sistere*, to stand still; but both of these verbs also mean to stand firm.

**INTELLIGENCE.** The expression "have intelligence with" (Daniel 11.30) means "have an understanding with." The Hebrew is the same as that which KJ translates by the verb "regard" in Daniel 11.37. It is more accurately translated "give heed to" in both cases.

**INTEND.** To intend something now means to hold it in mind as a definite purpose or design. "Intend" is a verb that has had many meanings; OED lists 17 senses that are obsolete before it arrives at the current sense. Some of these are reflected in the KJ renderings which follow. In each case the RSV rendering is a more literal translation of the Hebrew or Greek. "The children of Israel blessed God, and did not intend to go up against them in battle" (Joshua 22.33); RSV "the people of Israel blessed God and spoke no more of making war against them." "Intending to build a tower" (Luke 14.28); RSV "desiring to build a tower." "Ye men of Israel, take heed to yourselves what ye intend to do as touching these men" (Acts 5.35); RSV "Men of Israel, take care what you do with these men."

Psalm 21 should be read through in RSV, that its structure may be understood. The first strophe (vs. 1–7) is addressed to the LORD, in grateful acknowledgment of the blessings he has bestowed upon the king; the second strophe (vs. 8–12) is addressed to the king, in confident promise of future victories; and the psalm ends with a final prayer to the LORD (vs. 13). The KJ rendering of verse 11 does not fit the context as well as that of RSV:

"If they plan evil against you,
if they devise mischief, they will not succeed."

**INTERMEDDLE** was an innocent word in the sixteenth century, meaning to mingle, mix, or take part in. It had not yet acquired the connotation it now has of interfering where one has no business or proper concern. "The heart knoweth his own bitterness; and a stranger doth not intermeddle with his joy" (Proverbs 14.10) means, as in RSV:

"The heart knows its own bitterness,
and no stranger shares its joy."

In Proverbs 18.1, however, "intermeddle" is a mistranslation of a Hebrew verb which means to break or burst out in contention. KJ renders the verse, "Through desire a man, having separated himself, seeketh and intermeddleth with all wisdom." RSV, with the help of the Septuagint and the Vulgate in the first line, translates it:

"He who is estranged seeks pretexts
to break out against all sound judgment."

The word "meddle" is an inadequate translation of this same Hebrew verb in 17.14 and 20.3, where RSV has "quit before the quarrel breaks out" and "every fool will be quarreling."

**INTO** means to a point within a definite space or thing; it implies entrance, the crossing of boundaries, or penetration of surfaces to reach the interior. The word appears in an oddly obsolete sense in five passages in Acts. "Sailed into Syria" (18.18) and "sail into Syria" (20.3) mean ". . . for Syria"; "sailed into Syria" (21.3) means ". . . to Syria"; "sail into Italy" and "sailing into Italy" (27.1, 6) mean ". . . for Italy."

**INWARD.** "All my inward friends abhorred me" (Job 19.19) is better translated "All my intimate friends abhor me." The word "inward" was commonly used in the sixteenth and seventeenth centuries in the sense of intimate, close, belonging to the inner circle of one's friends. This sense, which is now obsolete, appears in Shakespeare:

"Sir, I was an inward of his."
*Measure for Measure*, III, 2, 126
"Who is most inward with the royal duke?"
*King Richard III*, III, 4, 8

"For what is inward between us, let it pass."
*Love's Labour's Lost*, V, 1, 102
Shakespeare also uses the noun "inwardness" in a similar sense:
"You know my inwardness and love
Is very much unto the prince and Claudio."
*Much Ado about Nothing*, IV, 1, 247–248

**INWARDS,** as noun, is used 20 times in Exodus 29 and in Leviticus 1, 3, 4, 7, 8, 9 to denote the entrails of an animal offered in sacrifice. RSV replaces it with "entrails."

**IT,** neuter pronoun, was originally spelled "hit." The masculine pronoun "he" and the neuter pronoun "hit" then had the same possessive form "his." In the sixteenth century a tendency arose to restrict "his" to males. "It" was used as a possessive, then "it's" began to be used, and finally "its" came into common use in the first half of the seventeenth century.

The Geneva Bible, 1560, had "That which groweth of it owne accorde" in Leviticus 25.5, and "whiche opened to them by it owne accorde" in Acts 12.10. The KJ translators used "his owne accord" in Acts, but retained "it owne accord" in Leviticus 25.5.

This is, however, the only case in KJ where "it" is used in the possessive case, and this was changed to "its" by later publishers. Except for this verse, the word "its" does not appear in KJ. The translators used "his," "her," "of it," or "thereof" when they needed a neuter possessive. Examples are "the fruit tree yielding fruit after his kind" (Genesis 1.11–12), "the tree of life, which . . . yielded her fruit every month" (Revelation 22.2), "the sea ceased from her raging" (Jonah 1.15), "if the salt have lost his savour" (Matthew 5.13), "stamped the residue with the fect of it" (Daniel 7.7), "the fruit thereof" (Genesis 3.6), "the furrows thereof" (Psalm 65.10). Longer passages that illustrate the expedients to which the translators resorted, because they did not use the new word "its," are Exodus 37.17–24 and Daniel 4.10–14. (See HIS)

**JANGLING** is now used of noisy, quarrelsome, wrangling speech, but in the Bible it means talk that is empty and useless (1 Timothy 1.6). The same Greek word underlies the expression "empty talkers" in Titus 1.10 (RSV). It was in this now obsolete sense that King Henry VIII used "jangle" in his last appearance before Parliament, when he said that he was "very sorry to know and hear how irreverently that precious jewel, the Word of God, is disputed, rimed, sung, and jangled in every alehouse and tavern, contrary to the true meaning and doctrine of the same."

**JOT.** Tyndale represented the Greek *iōta hen,* in Matthew 5.18, by "one iott," and was followed by the other sixteenth-century translators. In the 1611 KJ the word was spelled "iote," pronounced in one syllable, and this in time was changed to "jot." *Iōta* is the smallest letter in the Greek alphabet; and *yod,* the corresponding letter in Hebrew, is still smaller. In any case, whether Jesus referred to the Greek letter or to the Hebrew, "jot" means the smallest letter or least part of any writing, hence stands for the very least whit of anything. Portia declares to Shylock, in Shakespeare's *Merchant of Venice,* IV, 1, 306: "This bond doth give thee here no jot of blood."

"Not an iota" is as clear an English idiom as "not a jot." Among OED's examples are a sentence from the correspondence of Edmund Burke, 1771, "Not an iota should be yielded of the principle of the bill"; and a declaration by John Adams, 1786, "I would . . . demand, in a tone that could not be resisted, the punctual fulfilment of every iota of the treaty."

RSV translates Matthew 5.18: "For truly, I say to you, till heaven and earth pass away, not an iota, not a dot, will pass from the law until all is accomplished." (See TITTLE)

**JUDGE,** as verb, is used in the obsolete sense of condemn, sentence to punishment, in the nobleman's answer to his servant's excuse for having kept his pound laid away in a napkin: "Out of thine own mouth will I judge thee, *thou* wicked servant" (Luke 19.22). RSV translates it: "I will condemn you out of your own mouth, you wicked servant!" The *Greek-English Lexicon of the New Testament* edited by Arndt and Gingrich states that the meaning is "I will punish you on the basis of your own statement."

The KJ rendering of 2 Corinthians 5.14 is: "For the love of Christ constraineth us; because we thus judge, that if one died for all, then were all dead." This is misleading, not only because "judge" is too weak for the meaning of the Greek, but especially because what Paul stated as a fact is here expressed hypothetically, seeming to be a condition contrary to fact. The word for "if" was present in the Greek text used by the KJ translators, but it is an insertion that has no sound basis in the ancient Greek manuscripts. The effect of this inserted "if" is mischievous. It casts doubt upon the death of Christ, and compels KJ to insert the word "that" at the beginning of verse 15 in order to return to the world of fact. RSV translates the two verses: "For the love of Christ controls us, because we are convinced that one has died for all; therefore all have died. And he died for all, that those who live might live no longer for themselves but for him who for their sake died and was raised."

Another error in the Greek text, based upon medieval manuscripts, which was used by the KJ translators, led to the omission of the noun "judge" from James 4.12. KJ renders the verse, "There is one lawgiver, who is able to save and to destroy: who art thou that judgest another?" RSV, relying on the ancient manuscripts, has, "There is one lawgiver and judge, he who is able to save and to destroy. But who are you that you judge your neighbor?"

**KERCHIEF** is a cloth to cover the head. It is the word from which "neckerchief" and "handkerchief" have been derived. But it is the wrong word in the one passage where it appears in KJ—Ezekiel 13.17–23. This is an oracle of the LORD against women who pose as prophets, practicing magic and divination for their own profit. The entire passage should be read in RSV, where its meaning is more clearly stated than in KJ. Verse 18a (KJ) reads: "Woe to the *women* that sew pillows to all armholes, and make kerchiefs upon the head of every stature to hunt souls." RSV translates: "Woe to the women who sew magic bands upon all wrists, and make veils for the heads of persons of every stature, in the hunt for souls!" The "kerchiefs" were long veils thrown over the head and reaching down to the feet, covering the whole person, hence made in various sizes to fit "every stature." Just what was the significance of the bands and veils we do not know, or whether the veils were worn by the practitioner of divination or her clients. Probably they were worn by both. (See ARMHOLE, PILLOW)

**KIDNEYS.** The Hebrews regarded the fat as the choicest and best part of the animal, not to be eaten by men but to be burned upon the altar as an offering by fire to the LORD. "The two kidneys, with the fat that is on them at the loins" are especially mentioned in the law of sacrifice recorded in Leviticus 3 and 7. Hence the best part of anything was called its "fat." "The fat of the land" which Joseph promised to his father and brothers meant the choicest products of the land (Genesis 45.18). "All the best of the oil, and all the best of the wine and of the grain" (Numbers 18.12), "the finest of the wheat" (Psalms 81.16; 147.14) are phrases in which "best" and "finest" represent the

Hebrew word for "fat." Therefore the strange expression, "the fat of kidneys of wheat," does not imply that there are any kidney-shaped grains of wheat; it means the kidney-fat, the best of the fat, the best of the best, of the wheat. RSV translates it, "the finest of the wheat" (Deuteronomy 32.14). (See REINS)

**KNOP** is an archaic word for the bud of a flower or for an ornamental knob or boss. It is used in Exodus 25.31–36 and 37.17–22 as part of the description of the "candlestick" or lampstand of pure gold which Bezalel made, under Moses' direction, for the tabernacle. It there represents the Hebrew word *kaphtor*, which occurs also in Amos 9.1 and Zephaniah 2.14, where it is translated "lintel" with a marginal note, "or knops or chapiters." RSV uses "capital" in all these cases. These were the rounded capitals of the pillars of the temple at Bethel, and of the columns in the ruins of Nineveh, and the rounded capitals in the framework of the golden lampstand and its branches.

In 1 Kings 6.18; 7.24 the word "knops" represents a quite different Hebrew word *peqa'im*, which means "gourds." The reference is to the carved ornamentation of the cedar-lined walls of the house of the LORD, and similar ornamentation of the molten sea, cast with the sea when it was cast. This ornamentation may have been based upon the shape of the "wild gourds" mentioned in 2 Kings 4.39.

**KNOW** has as wide a range of meanings in Hebrew as in English, and its use in KJ calls for little revision. RSV has kept the word when it means to have sexual intercourse, for this idiom is natural not only to Hebrew but to many languages—Greek, Latin, French, German, for example—and remains living English in the language of the law, if not of current colloquial usage. Passages are: Genesis 4.1, 17, 25; 19.8; 24.16; Numbers 31.17, 18, 35; Judges 11.39; 19.25; 21.12; 1 Samuel 1.19; 1 Kings 1.4; Matthew 1.25. An exception is Genesis 38.26. The word is also kept in the sense of homosexual behavior (Genesis 19.5; Judges 19.22).

The Hebrew word for "know," in various contexts, may carry the connotation of regard, care for, pay heed to, approve. In these contexts, again, it is usually kept by RSV, since "know" in English may convey similar extensions of meaning. In Genesis 39.6–8, however, the statements concerning Potiphar are stated more clearly: "he knew not ought he had, save the bread which he did eat" (RSV "he had no concern for anything but the food which he ate"). In Psalm 31.7 "thou hast known my soul in adversities" means "thou hast taken heed of my adversities."

The force of Job's protestation is blunted by the KJ rendering of Job 9.20–21: "If I justify myself, mine own mouth shall condemn me: *if I say,* I *am* perfect, it shall also prove me perverse. *Though* I *were* perfect, *yet* would I not know my soul: I would despise my life." RSV translates:

> "Though I am innocent, my own mouth would condemn me;
> though I am blameless, he would prove me perverse.
> I am blameless; I regard not myself;
> I loathe my life."

**LADE.** Except with reference to the lading of a ship, current English uses the verb "load" rather than "lade." But it retains the passive participle "laden" as well as "loaded" or "loaden." In both respects it is following Shakespearian usage. RSV uses "load," "loaded," and "laden," the last of these forms appearing in 1 Samuel 16.20, Isaiah 1.4, Ezekiel 27.25, and Matthew 11.28. It also appears in Nehemiah 4.17: "Those who carried burdens were laden in such a way that each with one hand labored on the work and with the other held his weapon."

In Psalm 68.19, KJ reads: "Blessed *be* the Lord, *who* daily loadeth us *with benefits.*" But the verb here means not to load, but to carry a load. RSV translates: "Blessed be the Lord, who daily bears us up."

Habakkuk 2.6–7 should be read in the three versions, KJ, ASV, and RSV. The major error of the KJ rendering is the clause "ladeth himself with thick clay," which RSV replaces with "loads himself with pledges."

**LANCET.** Coverdale's description of the behavior of the prophets of Baal at Mount Carmel includes: "And they hopped about the altar, as their use was to do . . . And they cried aloud, and provoked themselves with knives and botkins (as their manner was) till the blood flowed" (1 Kings 18.26–28). Subsequent sixteenth-century versions used "leapt" and "cut themselves," and instead of "botkins" had "lancers," with various forms of spelling. KJ, as published in 1611, used "lancers" here, which was changed to "lancets" in 1762. The change was unfortunate, for if "lancet" ever meant a small lance that meaning has long been obsolete. Since the fifteenth century the word "lancet" has been applied to an instrument used in surgery.

But all of these attempts to get a word for a small weapon—bodkin, lancer, lancet—were beside the point. The Hebrew word here is *romah,* which means spear or lance. KJ translates this word 12 times as "spear" and once as "javelin." It was the weapon with which Phinehas transfixed the bodies of the shameless man of Israel and his Midianite paramour (Numbers 25.6–9). Its plural is the word used for the spears with which Nehemiah armed his men as they built the wall of Jerusalem (Nehemiah 4.13, 16, 21). There is no reason to think that the priests of Baal were indulging in minor surgery. The word for which KJ has "knives" means "swords." RSV translates: "they . . . cut themselves . . . with swords and lances, until the blood gushed out upon them" (1 Kings 18.28).

**LARGE.** The chief priests "gave large money unto the soldiers," to get them to spread a false report concerning the resurrection of Jesus (Matthew 28.12). The adjective "large" is used here in the obsolete sense of "ample" or "liberal." Compare the word "largess," which is still used for a liberal gift. The Greek text, however, does not state or imply any munificence on the part of the priests. Translated literally, it states that they gave the soldiers "enough" money. RSV has simply "a sum of money"; Phillips "a considerable sum of money."

**LASCIVIOUSNESS** is used six times by KJ as translation for the Greek word *aselgeia* (Mark 7.22; 2 Corinthians 12.21; Galatians 5.19; Ephesians 4.19; 1 Peter 4.3; Jude 4), which it elsewhere translates as "wantonness" (Romans 13.13; 2 Peter 2.18), "pernicious ways" (2 Peter 2.2), and as the adjective "filthy" in the expression "filthy conversation" (2 Peter 2.7). In all these cases RSV uses "licentiousness" or "licentious," as connoting a broad range of unbridled passions, including greed, drunkenness, and debauchery as well as sexual lust. Yet even this does not convey the full meaning of *aselgeia,* which has a note of insolent pride. Those who "have given themselves up to *aselgeia*" are "greedy to practice every kind of uncleanness," and are proud of their emancipation from the restraints of personal conscience or public opinion. They have lost all sense of shame.

**LATCHET** is an old word for a shoelace, a thong used to fasten a shoe or sandal. It does not represent a diminutive latch. In Genesis 14.23 Abraham tells the king of Sodom, "I would not take a thread or a sandal-thong or anything that is yours." Isaiah 5.27 describes the disciplined army that is coming to punish Israel:

"None is weary, none stumbles,
        none slumbers or sleeps,
    not a waistcloth is loose,
        not a sandal-thong broken."
John the Baptist declared: "After me comes he who is mightier than I,
the thong of whose sandals I am not worthy to stoop down and untie"
(Mark 1.7; Luke 3.16; John 1.27).


**LAY** is part of many idioms, most of which are generally understood.
        Among those which may be misunderstood are:
*Lay at* is defined as to strike at, attack, assail. But it is used by KJ
(Job 41.26) as translation for the Hebrew verb which means "reach."
The RSV rendering is
    "Though the sword reaches him, it does not avail;
        nor the spear, the dart, or the javelin."
*Lay away* (or *by* or *from*). "Lay away their robes" means simply
"remove their robes" (Ezekiel 26.16). So also "laid his robe from him"
means "removed his robe" (Jonah 3.6), and "laid by her vail from her"
means "took off her veil" (Genesis 38.19).
*Lay out* in the sense of expend money is still a current English
idiom. But "they laid it out to the carpenters and builders" (2 Kings
12.11) is better expressed by "they paid it out to the carpenters and
the builders."


**LEASING.** An old English word for lying or falsehood. Wyclif's
        translation had "lesyngmongers" in 1 Timothy 1.10, but
Tyndale and subsequent versions used "liars." Coverdale's version of
2 Esdras 14.18 reads "The truth is fled far away, and leasing is hard
at hand," which was retained by KJ. "Seek after leasing" appears in
Psalm 4.2, and "them that speak leasing" in Psalm 5.6. RSV uses "lies"
in the Psalms, and "falsehood" in the passage in 2 Esdras.


**LET.** There are two English verbs which are spelled and pronounced
        exactly alike, "let," but which come from two distinct Anglo-
Saxon roots. The one verb "let" means to hinder, impede, or prevent;
the other means just the opposite, to permit or allow. Both were in
current use in 1611; both are used in the Bible and in Shakespeare.
But only the second remains a part of living English today; the first
survives only as a noun in the legal phrase "without let or hindrance"
and in the game of tennis, where anything that interrupts or hinders
the game and requires a point to be played again is called a "let."

In Shakespeare's *King Henry V* (V, 2, 64–67), the Duke of Burgundy, suing for peace with England, and speaking of the ruin that continued war entails, says:

"my speech entreats
That I may know the let, why gentle Peace
Should not expel these inconveniences
And bless us with her former qualities."

When Hamlet's friends seek to restrain him from following the beckoning ghost of his father, he cries:

"Unhand me, gentlemen;
By heaven, I'll make a ghost of him that lets me."

*Hamlet,* I, 4, 85

This obsolete use of the verb "let" appears three times in KJ. In Isaiah 43.13 God speaks through the prophet: *"There is* none that can deliver out of my hand: I will work, and who shall let it?" The revised versions have "who can hinder it?" Paul, writing to the Romans (1.13) tells that he had "oftentimes purposed" to come to them, but that he "was let hitherto"; RSV renders this, "I have often intended to come to you, but thus far have been prevented."

The other occurrence is in 2 Thessalonians 2.6–7, where KJ reads: "And now ye know what withholdeth that he might be revealed in his time. For the mystery of iniquity doth already work: only he who now letteth *will let,* until he be taken out of the way." The obscurity of these verses is increased by the use of the word "letteth" in verse 7 for the Greek word which was translated "withholdeth" in verse 6. RSV reads: "And you know what is restraining him now so that he may be revealed in his time. For the mystery of lawlessness is already at work; only he who now restrains it will do so until he is out of the way."

**LEWD and LEWDNESS** are used in the KJ Old Testament with the reference to lascivious behavior that remains their modern meaning. But in Acts 17.5 "certain lewd fellows of the baser sort" represents Greek which means "some wicked fellows of the rabble"; and in 18.14 "a matter of wrong or wicked lewdness" is better translated "a matter of wrongdoing or vicious crime."

**LIBERTINES** appears once: "Then there arose certain of the synagogue, which is called *the synagogue* of the Libertines . . . disputing with Stephen" (Acts 6.9). These were not men of dissolute, licentious lives, but respectable freedmen. They were probably descendants of the Jews who had been taken as prisoners to Rome by

Pompey in 63 B.C., and there sold as slaves. RSV reads: "Then some of those who belonged to the synagogue of the Freedmen (as it was called) . . . arose and disputed with Stephen."

**LIGHT,** whether as noun, adjective, or verb, is easily understood in KJ. The adjective "light," however, is twice applied by KJ to persons, in the obsolete sense which OED defines as "not commanding respect by position or character; of small account." Abimelech is said to have "hired vain and light persons, which followed him" (Judges 9.4). The prophets of Jerusalem are condemned as "light *and* treacherous persons" (Zephaniah 3.4). There is a more serious defect, however, in the KJ rendering of these two passages. The adjective "light" is too trivial a term to express the meaning of the Hebrew, which in both cases has the participle of the verb *paḥaz*, which means to be wanton or reckless. RSV translates, "Abimelech hired worthless and reckless fellows, who followed him"; and "Her prophets are wanton, faithless men."

The Hebrew noun *paḥaz*, which means "wantonness, recklessness, unbridled license" (BDB), appears in an adjectival phrase concerning Reuben, which KJ translates "Unstable as water"; and this rendering is retained by the revised versions.

In Numbers 21.5, "the people spake against God, and against Moses, Wherefore have ye brought us up out of Egypt to die in the wilderness? for *there is* no bread, neither *is there any* water; and our soul loatheth this light bread." The "light bread" was the manna which the LORD rained from heaven (Exodus 16). But "light" is not only ambiguous; it undertranslates the Hebrew, which means contemptible or worthless. RSV translates the latter half of the verse, "For there is no food and no water, and we loathe this worthless food."

**LIGHTLY.** This adverb does not clearly express the sense of the original text in any of the five passages where it appears. It comes nearest to the meaning in Genesis 26.10, where the revised versions replace it with "easily." In Mark 9.39 the Greek means "quickly" or "soon." "Lightly" is too slight a term for the movement of the hills in Jeremiah 4.24. "Lightly esteemed" falls considerably short of the meaning in Deuteronomy 32.15: "he forsook God who made him, and scoffed at the Rock of his salvation."

The KJ rendering of Isaiah 9.1 misconceives the meaning of the verse, as a comparison with any of the revised versions or modern translations from the Hebrew will make apparent. KJ reads: "Nevertheless the dimness *shall* not *be* such as *was* in her vexation, when at the first he lightly afflicted the land of Zebulun and the land of Naphtali, and afterward did more grievously afflict *her by* the way of the sea, beyond Jordan, in Galilee of the nations." RSV reads: "But there will be no gloom for her that was in anguish. In the former time he brought into contempt the land of Zebulun and the land of Naphtali, but in the latter time he will make glorious the way of the sea, the land beyond the Jordan, Galilee of the nations." The contrast between "brought into contempt" and "will make glorious" was lost in KJ by rendering the verbs "lightly afflict" and "grievously afflict" and regarding these as successive stages of "her vexation." The great Messianic prophecy contained in Isaiah 9.1–7 is marred in KJ by its inept renderings of verses 1, 3, and 5.

**LIGHTNESS.** The LORD condemns the false prophets who "cause my people to err by their lies, and by their lightness." RSV translates: "lead my people astray by their lies and their recklessness" (Jeremiah 23.32). The Hebrew word is *paḥazuth*, an abstract noun derived from the verb *paḥaz*. (See LIGHT)

Paul's question, "When I therefore was thus minded, did I use lightness?" (2 Corinthians 1.17) means "Was I vacillating when I wanted to do this?"

**LIKE,** as a verb, is used three times in the obsolete sense of "be pleasing to." For "where it liketh him best" (Deuteronomy 23.16), RSV has "where it pleases him best." For "as it liketh you" (Esther 8.8), RSV has "as you please." In Amos 4.5, "for this liketh you," the Hebrew has the verb for "love"; RSV translates "for so you love to do." Shakespeare wrote "the music likes you not" (*Two Gentlemen of Verona,* IV, 2, 56).

The adjective "like" is twice used in the archaic or colloquial sense of "likely." The first occurrence is in Ebed-melech's report to the king after Jeremiah has been cast into the dungeon, "he is like to die for hunger in the place where he is" (Jeremiah 38.9). RSV translates "he will die there of hunger." The second occurrence is in Jonah 1.4, "there was a mighty tempest in the sea, so that the ship was like to be broken." RSV translates, ". . . so that the ship threatened to break up." When Juliet directs her nurse to ask the name of Romeo, she says,

"If he be married,
My grave is like to be my wedding bed."
*Romeo and Juliet,* I, 5, 137

**LIKE UNTO** is an archaic equivalent of "like." "Who *is* like unto
thee, O Lord, among the gods? who *is* like thee . . . ?"
(Exodus 15.11) has an "unto" for which there is no warrant. The Hebrew wording of the initial clauses of the two questions is the same,
and is so translated by RSV:

> "Who is like thee, O Lord, among the gods?
>
> Who is like thee, majestic in holiness,
>
> terrible in glorious deeds, doing wonders?"

"Like unto" occurs most frequently in Matthew (6.8; 11.16; 13.33,
44, 45, 47, 52; 20.1; 22.2, 39; 23.27) and in Revelation (1.13, 15;
2.18; 4.3, 6; 9.7, 10, 19; 11.1; 13.2, 4; 14.14; 18.18; 21.11, 18). Modern translations omit the "unto." (See UNTO)

"Like to" is another archaic expression which occurs less often.
"Like to a bear" (Daniel 7.5) means "like a bear." The "to" is cumbrous and not needed in Song of Solomon 7.7; 8.14. The KJ rendering
of Psalm 144.4 is: "Man is like to vanity: his days *are* as a shadow that
passeth away." RSV translates: "Man is like a breath, his days are like
a passing shadow."

"Like as" is a redundant expression from which either "like" or "as"
should be dropped. (See AS, where examples are given.)

**LIKING** was formerly used both as a noun and as an adjective to denote bodily condition. The chief of the eunuchs feared that,
if he granted the request of Daniel and his friends, the king would "see
your faces worse liking than the children which *are* of your sort"
(Daniel 1.10). RSV translates his reply: "I fear lest my lord the king,
who appointed your food and your drink, should see that you were in
poorer condition than the youths who are of your own age."

Concerning the mountain goats and the hinds, KJ reads in Job 39.4:
"Their young ones are in good liking, they grow up with corn." Here
the translators confused Hebrew words for "corn" and "open country,"
and used "are in good liking" for the verb which means "be healthy
and strong." RSV translates: "Their young ones become strong, they
grow up in the open."

**LIMIT.** "They limited the Holy One of Israel" (Psalm 78.41) is a
rendering taken from the Geneva Bible, which adds the marginal note, "As thei all do that measure the power of God by their
capacitie." The first edition of the Bishops' Bible had "prescribed
boundes to," but the second edition returned to "moved," which was
the translation of Coverdale and the Great Bible. One modern scholar

proposed "set a mark for," but most agree that the Hebrew here means "provoked" or "pained." This was the sense of the ancient Greek, Syriac, and Latin translations.

"He limiteth a certain day" is an ambiguous rendering which the KJ translators took from the Rheims New Testament (Hebrews 4.7). In so doing they rejected the true rendering which had appeared in all translations from Tyndale to the Bishops' Bible—"appointeth" or "appointed." While the Greek verb may mean limit or bound, it also means determine, define, appoint, or set, and the latter is the sense here.

In the place of "dost thou restrain wisdom to thyself?" (Job 15.8) the revised versions read "do you limit wisdom to yourself?"

In Ezekiel 43.12 "the whole limit" means "the whole territory."

**LINEN YARN** occurs four times, in the rendering of 1 Kings 10.28 and 2 Chronicles 1.16: "And Solomon had horses brought out of Egypt, and linen yarn: the king's merchants received the linen yarn at a price." The phrase "linen yarn" is a conjecture as to the meaning of the Hebrew word *miqweh*—a conjecture derived from the Geneva Bible (1560), which rendered it "fine linen." The Great Bible (1539) had a quite different conjecture, "the collection of the wares." But Coverdale (1535) and the Matthew Bible (1537) had a geographical rendering, "from Keua." This means that Coverdale and Tyndale agreed, for the Matthew Bible contains Tyndale's translations from Genesis to 2 Chronicles.

Assyrian cuneiform records uncovered by archaelogy have now shown that Tyndale and Coverdale were correct. RSV has, "And Solomon's import of horses was from Egypt and Kue, and the king's traders received them from Kue at a price." Kue was the fertile coastal plain in the southeast portion of Asia Minor, known in the New Testament as Cilicia.

**LIST** appears four times in KJ as a verb meaning to desire or wish. "Whatsoever they listed" (Matthew 17.12 = Mark 9.13) is now translated "whatever they pleased." For "the wind bloweth where it listeth" (John 3.8), RSV has "the wind blows where it wills"—which might better be "where it pleases." In James 3.4 the Greek is different, and "whithersoever the governor listeth" is replaced by "wherever the will of the pilot directs." This sense of the word "list" is now archaic, though it survives in the word "listless."

**LIVELY** was just gaining its present meaning of "spirited" or "sprightly" when the KJ translation was made. It appears in the Bible only in its earlier meaning of "living" or "vigorous." In Exodus 1.19 the meaning of the Hebrew is "vigorous"; RSV translates: "the Hebrew women are not like the Egyptian women; for they are vigorous and are delivered before the midwife comes to them." In Psalm 38.19 RSV reads the Hebrew *hinnam*, "without cause," in place of *hayyim*, "living." It translates the verse:

"Those who are my foes without cause are mighty,
and many are those who hate me wrongfully."

In the New Testament "lively" represents the Greek participle which means "living." Moses received "living oracles" from God (Acts 7.38). Peter writes that "we have been born anew to a living hope through the resurrection of Jesus Christ from the dead," and exhorts his readers as sharers in that hope: "Come to him, to that living stone, rejected by men but in God's sight chosen and precious; and like living stones be yourselves built into a spiritual house, to be a holy priesthood, to offer spiritual sacrifices acceptable to God through Jesus Christ" (1 Peter 1.3; 2.4–5).

**LOATHE** appeared seven times in the 1611 edition of KJ, and the older spelling LOTHE five times. For some reason not apparent, the spelling was changed to "lothe" in four passages, so that even Scrivener, in *The Cambridge Paragraph Bible*, retains "loathe" in only three passages (Numbers 21.5; Job 7.16; Proverbs 27.7). The four passages which were changed are Exodus 7.18; Jeremiah 14.19; Ezekiel 6.9; Zechariah 11.8. Those which had "lothe" in the first edition are Ezekiel 16.5, 45; 20.43; 36.31. ASV and RSV use only "loathe."

The 1611 KJ had "flotes" in 1 Kings 5.9 and 2 Chronicles 2.16. This was changed to "floats" in Kings but not in Chronicles, and most current editions of KJ retain the inconsistency. Most of them also retain the obsolete spelling "sope" (Jeremiah 2.22; Malachi 3.2).

**LOFT** means an upper room or story, an attic, an upper floor without partitions, a hayloft, an organ loft. The word is not a good translation in either of its two occurrences in KJ. When Elijah carried the sick boy up "into a loft, where he abode" (1 Kings 17.19), it was "into the upper chamber where he lodged." The Hebrew word signifies a roof chamber, such as the "roof chamber with walls" which the wealthy woman of Shunem made for Elisha (2 Kings 4.10 RSV). Such chambers, built upon the flat roof of a house, were prized for their coolness and seclusion.

In Acts 20.9 "the third loft" represents a Greek word which means "the third story." RSV translates: "A young man named Eutychus was sitting in the window. He sank into a deep sleep as Paul talked still longer; and being overcome by sleep, he fell down from the third story and was taken up dead."

**LONGSUFFERING** means "patient endurance of provocation or trial" (OED). As noun and adjective it appears 17 times in KJ, but is not retained by RSV. It is replaced three times by a literal translation of the Hebrew, "slow to anger." The proclamation in Exodus 34.6 reads in RSV: "The LORD, the LORD, a God merciful and gracious, slow to anger, and abounding in steadfast love and faithfulness." Compare Numbers 14.18 and Psalm 86.15; and look up "slow to anger" in the Concordance.

"Forbearance" is used by RSV in Jeremiah 15.15; 2 Corinthians 6.6; 2 Peter 3.15, and "forbearing" in 2 Peter 3.9. In the rest of the Epistles "patience" is the word which best translates the meaning of the Greek *makrothumia*. "Charity suffereth long, *and* is kind" means "Love is patient and kind" (1 Corinthians 13.4). (See PATIENCE)

In Luke 18.7 "though he bear long with them" is a mistaken translation. RSV reads: "And will not God vindicate his elect, who cry to him day and night? Will he delay long over them? I tell you, he will vindicate them speedily."

**LOOK FOR** in the sense of expect, watch for, is a well-established English idiom. The Greek verb *prosdokaō* is translated by KJ "look for" (Matthew 11.3; Luke 7.19–20), "wait for" (Luke 1.21; 8.40), "were in expectation" (Luke 3.15), "expecting" (Acts 3.5); and the revised versions retain these renderings. RSV changes "looketh not for *him*" to "does not expect him" (Matthew 24.50; Luke 12.46), and "Cornelius waited for them" to "Cornelius was expecting them" (Acts 10.24).

In the account of Paul's voyage and shipwreck this Greek verb occurs three times. KJ represents it by "tarried" in Acts 27.33: "While the day was coming on, Paul besought *them* all to take meat, saying, This day is the fourteenth day that ye have tarried and continued fasting, having taken nothing." RSV translates: "As day was about to dawn, Paul urged them all to take some food, saying, 'Today is the fourteenth day that you have continued in suspense and without food, having taken nothing.' "

The other two occurrences are in 28.6, expressing the surprise of the people of Malta when Paul suffered no harm from the viper that fastened on his hand. Here KJ has "looked." It reads: "Howbeit they looked when he should have swollen, or fallen down dead suddenly: but after they had looked a great while, and saw no harm come to him, they changed their minds, and said that he was a god." RSV translates: "They waited, expecting him to swell up or suddenly fall down dead; but when they had waited a long time and saw no misfortune come to him, they changed their minds and said that he was a god."

The corresponding Hebrew verb, *qavah*, is usually translated "look for" or "wait for." An exception is Isaiah 5.2, 4, "looked that it should bring forth grapes." Here "look" has the sense of expect, and is followed by a clause. This is an old English usage, now obsolete. RSV translates as elsewhere, "looked for it to yield grapes."

**LOOK TO.** When Jesse brought his youngest son before Samuel, the boy was "goodly to look to" (1 Samuel 16.12). This is an early usage in the sense of "to look at." The same usage appears in Ezekiel 23.15—"all of them princes to look to." RSV says that the young David was "handsome," and describes the Chaldeans as "all of them looking like officers."

Nebuchadnezzar's command concerning Jeremiah was "Take him, and look well to him, and do him no harm; but do unto him even as he shall say unto thee" (Jeremiah 39.12). RSV has "Take him, look after him well and do him no harm, but deal with him as he tells you." The two versions agree on the first clause of 2 John 8, "Look to yourselves," and RSV goes on, "that you may not lose what you have worked for, but may win a full reward."

"Look to" expresses trust and reliance in Micah 7.7, which RSV translates:

> "But as for me, I will look to the LORD,
> I will wait for the God of my salvation;
> my God will hear me."

**LOVE** in the New Testament. There are three Greek words for love. *Eros* and its verb *eraō*, which refer primarily to sexual love, do not appear in the New Testament. *Philia* and its verb *phileō*, which refer primarily to personal friendship, occur only 26 times; and the noun *philos*, which means friend, occurs 29 times. But the noun *agapē* is used 114 times, the verb *agapaō* 136 times, and the adjective *agapē-tos* 62 times—a total of 312 occurrences. In KJ the verb is translated "love" in 130 cases, and its participle "beloved" in 6 cases. The adjective is translated "beloved" 59 times and "dear" 3 times. But a strange thing has happened to the noun. Excluding 2 cases where its plural is used in the sense of love feasts, there remain 112 occurrences. Of these 85 are translated "love," but in 26 the rendering is "charity," and in one case a prepositional phrase is rendered by the adverb "charitably."

Except in the one case when he too uses the adverb "charitably" Tyndale always translated *agapē* by the word "love." When rebuked by More, who wished to retain the Latin-derived, ecclesiastically sanctioned word "charity," Tyndale answered that "charity is not known English, in that sense which *agapē* requireth," and that in common use it means either almsgiving or patience and mercifulness in the judgment of others. He called attention, finally, to the fact that "charity" is a noun that has no correlative verb or adjective, as *agapē* has. "I say not, charity God, or charity your neighbor; but, love God, and love your neighbor."

In his translation of *agapē* by "love," Tyndale was followed by all sixteenth-century versions up to 1568—Coverdale, Matthew, Taverner, the Great Bible, and the Geneva Bible. He was followed by the Bishops' Bible also, except for one verse, Romans 13.10, where the word "charity" was introduced. The result was a bit absurd, for the preceding verse ends with the second great commandment, and the change causes the passage to close with a startling shift of language. Romans 13.8–10 reads as follows in the Bishops' Bible: "Owe nothing to no man, but to love one another: For he that loveth another hath fulfilled the law. For this: Thou shalt not commit adultery, thou shalt not kill, thou shalt not steal, thou shalt not bear false witness, thou shalt not lust and if there be any other commandment it is comprehended in this saying: namely, thou shalt love thy neighbor as thyself. Charity worketh no ill to his neighbor, Therefore the fulfilling of the law is charity."

In 1572 came a real break. The advocates of Catholic Latinity had in some way gathered strength, for in the second edition of the Bishops' Bible, published in that year, the word "charity" is substituted for "love" in 32 cases. The word "love" remained in the other cases, and of course in the translation of the verb *agapaō*.

When the committee appointed by King James revised the Bishops' Bible to make the Authorized Version of 1611, they restored the word "love" in 6 of the 32 cases. But they kept the word "charity" in 26 cases. Just why they did that, we can only conjecture.

Even an attempt to attribute the 26 divergent cases to differences in the Latin Vulgate, fails to explain them. There are 3 Latin words for "love"—*amor, dilectio,* and *caritas.* The first of these is never used to represent *agapē* in the Latin New Testament; *dilectio* is used in about one fifth of the cases of its occurrence, and *caritas* is used in the rest. The Rheims New Testament, which was made by translation from the Latin, reproduces this divergence. It always uses the English word "love" for *dilectio,* and "charity" for *caritas.* The distinction was not justified by anything in the original Greek; but the procedure of the Rheims translators was at least consistent. It resulted in such translations as these: "My dearest, let us love one another, because charity is of God. . . . He that loveth not, knoweth not God; because God is charity" (1 John 4.7–8).

But in this matter the KJ translators are no more consistent with the Latin than with the Greek. Of the 26 cases where they use "charity," 3 have *dilectio* in the Latin and 23 *caritas.* Of the 85 cases where they use "love," 20 have *dilectio* and 65 *caritas.*

The truth is that it is futile to look for a distinction here, for no valid distinction can be found. If Jerome had any distinction in his mind when he used the Latin word *dilectio* to represent *agapē* in a few cases and *caritas* in the rest, it was a distinction that he did not get from the Greek. There is evidence, moreover, that no such distinction was maintained in the usage of the English Church in the 1570's. The *Catechism* by Alexander Nowell, Dean of St. Paul's, sanctioned by the Convocation of Canterbury, written in Latin and then translated into English by Thomas Norton, was published in both languages in 1570. It shows that in Latin *caritas, dilectio,* and even *amor* were used interchangeably, and so were "charity" and "love" in English. Take, for example, this clause from the answer to the question regarding our duty toward Christ: "That we with all our affection, love, esteem, and embrace Christ our Savior, which showed us such dear love while we were yet his enemies, as his most entire love toward us could not possibly be increased." In the Latin of this passage the verb for love was *amo,* and the verb for esteem *diligo;* while the first noun for love was *caritas,* and the second *amor.*

The distribution of the 26 cases in which KJ kept the word "charity," which had been introduced by an unknown reviser of the Bishops' Bible, is peculiar. There are no such cases before 1 Corinthians 8.1. Of the 26 cases, 11 are in 1 Corinthians, 6 in the Pastoral Epistles,

4 in the epistles of Peter, and one each in Colossians, 1 Thessalonians, 2 Thessalonians, 3 John, and Revelation. Eight of them are in one chapter, 1 Corinthians 13. None of them is in 1 John, the epistle of love.

As to why these particular places should have been chosen for the change to "charity," we can only guess. Two guesses may not be wholly wrong. 1 Corinthians 13 was one of the most familiar parts of the New Testament; English versions of it had appeared in primers and aids to devotion; many people doubtless had committed it to memory, both in Latin and in English. Here the word "charity" was established in the public mind. And it was perhaps natural, too, to retain the Latin-derived word in the Pastoral Epistles, as an echo of the language of the confessional.

The second edition of the Bishops' Bible and KJ stand alone in this strange substitution of "charity" for love in less than 10 per cent of the cases of the occurrence of *agapē* and its correlatives. The revised versions of 1881 and 1901 returned to the practice of the earlier sixteenth-century versions, and used "love" throughout; and they have been followed in this by all modern translations based upon the original Greek. Even the Catholic translations from the Vulgate by Father Knox and the Confraternity of Christian Doctrine break away from the supposed distinction between *dilectio* and *caritas;* and they use "love" as the translation for *caritas* in the crucial passages contained in the epistles of John.

By so doing, the modern translations give a surer undergirding to the basic Christian doctrine of God and man than does KJ. The basic principle and ultimate motive of both the Christian gospel and the Christian ethic is love. God is love, and we love because he first loved us. In the translation of the Greek word *agapē*, we are dealing not with a mere exhortation to feeling and action, or even with a statement of human duty, but with the ultimate grounding of human duty and destiny in the very nature and eternal purpose of God. Whatever would tend to separate human love from divine love, or to weaken the essential connection between the Christian ethic and the Christian gospel, is wrong. Yet that is just what KJ does, in those 26 cases which it tears out of the total fabric of the New Testament teaching.

**LOVER** is used occasionally in its basic sense of one who loves. "Hiram was ever a lover of David" means "Hiram always loved David" (1 Kings 5.1). "My lovers and my friends stand aloof from my sore" is better translated "My friends and companions stand aloof from my plague" (Psalm 38.11).

Tyndale used the word often. "For the very sinners love their lovers" was his translation of Luke 6.32, and this was retained in successive versions up to and including the two editions of the Bishops' Bible. The Rheims New Testament changed to the rendering which KJ adopted, "for sinners also love those that love them." Other translations by Tyndale are: "When she hath found it she calleth her lovers and her neighbours" (Luke 15.9); "and yet thou gavest me never so much as a kid to make merry with my lovers" (Luke 15.29); "The lovers salute thee. Greet the lovers by name" (3 John 14). In the first and third of these passages "lovers" was changed to "friends" by the Geneva Bible; in the second, by the Great Bible.

The word "lover" is used by the prophets Jeremiah, Ezekiel, and Hosea in the sense of the male party to an illicit sexual relation. It is an interesting fact that the word "lover" does not appear in the KJ Song of Solomon, where the young woman is referred to as "my love" and the man as "my beloved."

**LOVINGKINDNESS.** Although "loving" and "kindness" are words that go back to Old English, the term "lovingkindness" was introduced by Coverdale as translation for the Hebrew *ḥesed.* At first spelled as two words, it in time came to be printed as "loving-kindness" and later as "lovingkindness."

Tyndale, following the Greek Septuagint, took "mercy" as his translation for *ḥesed* when that denotes an attribute of God in his dealing with men. Coverdale was on the right track when he made the combination "loving kindness," but he did not use it consistently. Any English reader may observe this by comparing the Psalter in the Book of Common Prayer with the Psalms as printed in ASV, where "lovingkindness" appears more than five times as often. KJ uses "mercy" 163 times and "lovingkindness" 28 times to translate *ḥesed* as an attribute of God. ASV uses "lovingkindness" in all cases where it denotes God's attitude toward men.

Research in recent years, however, has made clear that neither Tyndale's word "mercy" nor Coverdale's word "lovingkindness" is adequate to convey the meaning of *ḥesed* when it is asserted of God. *Ḥesed* is a covenant word. Its original use was to denote that attitude of loyalty and faithfulness which both parties to a covenant should maintain toward each other. So says Professor Norman Snaith in *The Distinctive Ideas of the Old Testament* (Allenson, 1953, p. 99). But he goes on to say: "When the word came to be used predominantly of the Covenant between Jehovah and Israel, it was realized by the prophets that such a covenant could be maintained only by that persistent, determined, steadfast love of God, which transcends every other love by its nature and depth. . . . The most important of all the distinctive ideas of the Old Testament is God's steady and extraordinary persistence in continuing to love wayward Israel in spite of Israel's insistent waywardness."

This idea is expressed in Isaiah 54.8, 10, where KJ reads: "In a little wrath I hid my face from thee for a moment; but with everlasting kindness will I have mercy on thee, saith the LORD thy Redeemer. . . . For the mountains shall depart, and the hills be removed; but my kindness shall not depart from thee, neither shall the covenant of my peace be removed, saith the LORD that hath mercy on thee." RSV reads:

> "In overflowing wrath for a moment
>     I hid my face from you,
> but with everlasting love I will have compassion on you,
>     says the LORD, your Redeemer. . . .
> For the mountains may depart
>     and the hills be removed,
> but my steadfast love shall not depart from you,
>     and my covenant of peace shall not be removed,
>     says the LORD, who has compassion on you."

Sir George Adam Smith once suggested "leal love" as a translation for *hesed*. Others have suggested "sure love." The RSV committee, after much study and debate, adopted "steadfast love," and no longer uses "lovingkindness" in the Old Testament. This has one important theological result, Professor Millar Burrows notes in the *Introduction to the RSV Old Testament* (Thomas Nelson & Sons, 1952, p. 61): "the word 'love' now appears far more often in the Old Testament than it did in previous translations, counteracting the erroneous impression of many Christians that the God of the Old Testament was not a God of love." (See MERCY)

**LUCRE** means "gain," and is used in the Bible only for unworthy or dishonest gain. It appears once in the Old Testament, where it is recorded that Samuel's sons, as judges, "walked not in his ways, but turned aside after lucre, and took bribes, and perverted judgment" (1 Samuel 8.3). RSV uses "gain."

In 1 Peter 5.2, the elders are exhorted to "feed the flock of God which is among you, . . . not by constraint, but willingly; not for filthy lucre, but of a ready mind." RSV reads "Tend the flock of God that is your charge, not by constraint but willingly, not for shameful gain but eagerly."

The expression "filthy lucre" appears also in KJ 1 Timothy 3.3, 8 and Titus 1.7, 11. In each case it stands for a combination in some form of the Greek words *aischron kerdos*, which mean dishonest, unworthy, or shameful gain. There is no warrant in the Bible for the modern jocular habit of referring to money as "filthy lucre" or as "the filthy."

**LUNATICK.** Some of those brought to Jesus to be healed were described as "lunatick" (Matthew 4.24; 17.15). The Greek means "moon-struck," for which the Latin was *lunaticus*. Intermittent nervous and mental disorders were formerly thought to be influenced by the changes of the moon. The revised versions read "epileptic," which fits the father's description of his son's malady (17.15). The first recorded use of "epilepsy" as an English word was in 1578; the first recorded use of "epileptic," in 1605.

**LUST** was used in the sixteenth century for any desire or wish for something pleasing; but it soon began to be limited, as it now is, to inordinate or lawless desires, and especially to those associated with sexual pleasure. The word appears 53 times in KJ, and 15 times in RSV. The "lust" of the children of Israel for meat is better described as a "craving" (Numbers 11.4, 34; Psalms 78.18, 30; 106.14). ". . . whatsoever thy soul lusteth after" means "as much as you desire" (Deuteronomy 12.15, 20, 21). On the other hand, "transgressors shall be taken in *their own* naughtiness" is rightly replaced by "the treacherous are taken captive by their lust" (Proverbs 11.6).

The Greek noun *epithumia* is rendered by KJ "concupiscence" 3 times, "desire" 3 times, and "lust" 32 times. RSV drops "concupiscence," retains "lust" in 6 passages, and uses "desire(s)" or "passion(s)" in varying contexts. Examples that may be cited are: "the lusts of other things" = "the desire for other things" (Mark 4.19); "the flesh lusteth against the Spirit, and the Spirit against the flesh" = "the desires of the flesh are against the Spirit, and the desires of the Spirit are against the flesh" (Galatians 5.17); "flee youthful lusts" = "shun youthful passions" (2 Timothy 2.22). In Romans 7.7, 8 the context calls for "covet" and "covetousness."

A notable passage is James 1.13–15, which RSV translates: "Let no one say when he is tempted, 'I am tempted by God'; for God cannot be tempted with evil and he himself tempts no one; but each person is tempted when he is lured and enticed by his own desire. Then desire when it has conceived gives birth to sin; and sin when it is full-grown brings forth death."

"The spirit that dwelleth in us lusteth to envy" is not as sound a translation of the Greek as "He yearns jealously over the spirit which he has made to dwell in us" (James 4.5). There is an excellent discussion of this passage in *The Interpreter's Bible*, vol. 12, p. 56.

**MAD** is a word for insane, out of one's mind. It has a tinge of contempt or disgust, and is applied also to cases of wild excitement, infatuation, uncontrolled anger, or extreme folly. There is no difference between KJ and RSV in the use of this term except in translation of the Hebrew verb which means "make foolish" or "make a fool of." In Job 12.17, KJ has, speaking of the LORD, "he . . . maketh the judges fools," with which RSV agrees. But the same verb is ambiguously translated "Surely oppression maketh a wise man mad" (Ecclesiastes 7.7) and "the LORD . . . maketh diviners mad" (Isaiah 44.24–25). RSV has "Surely oppression makes the wise man foolish," and "the LORD . . . makes fools of diviners."

**MAGNIFY.** In the sense of rendering praise or honor to God, the word "magnify" has become established in liturgical use, and is retained in the Magnificat by such modern translations as Moffatt, Ballantine, Rieu, and the RSV (Luke 1.46). It is also retained by RSV in David's prayer (2 Samuel 7.26 = 1 Chronicles 17.24) and in Psalms 34.3 and 69.30. The expression is replaced elsewhere by "Great is the LORD!" (Psalms 35.27; 40.16; Malachi 1.5) or "God is great!" (Psalm 70.4). "Extol" is used in less liturgical passages (Job 36.24; Acts 10.46; 19.17) and "honor" in Acts 5.13 and Philippians 1.20.

In the sense to make great, to cause to be respected and honored, the word "magnify" is retained by RSV in Isaiah 42.21, but elsewhere such terms are used as "exalt" (Joshua 3.7; 4.14; 2 Chronicles 32.23; Psalm 138.2), "gave great repute" (1 Chronicles 29.25), "made him exceedingly great" (2 Chronicles 1.1), "make much of him" (Job 7.17). "Thou hast magnified thy mercy, which thou hast shewed unto me in saving my life" means "you have shown me great kindness in saving my life" (Genesis 19.19). "The enemy hath magnified *himself*" means "the enemy has triumphed" (Lamentations 1.9).

In Ezekiel 38.23 "magnify myself" appears in the word of the LORD. KJ renders the verse: "Thus will I magnify myself, and sanctify myself;

and I will be known in the eyes of many nations, and they shall know that I *am* the LORD." RSV renders it: "So I will show my greatness and my holiness and make myself known in the eyes of many nations. Then they will know that I am the LORD."

In the sense of unwarranted pretension or aggressive action the expression "magnify (one's) self" is usually retained in RSV (Psalm 35.26; Job 19.5; Jeremiah 48.26, 42; Daniel 8.11, 25; 11.36, 37). An interesting example is Isaiah 10.15, which reads in KJ: "Shall the ax boast itself against him that heweth therewith? *or* shall the saw magnify itself against him that shaketh it? as if the rod should shake *itself* against them that lift it up, *or* as if the staff should lift up *itself, as if it were* no wood." The revised versions translate this more accurately: RSV reads:

> "Shall the axe vaunt itself over him who hews with it,
>> or the saw magnify itself against him who wields it?
> As if a rod should wield him who lifts it,
>> or as if a staff should lift him who is not wood!"

In a few contexts "magnify (one's) self" is replaced by "boast" or "deal insolently" (Psalms 38.16; 55.12; Zephaniah 2.8). Nowhere in the Bible does the word "magnify" have the modern meaning, to increase the apparent size of an object by artificial means such as a lens or microscope.

**MAKE.** When the five explorers from the tribe of Dan recognized the voice of the young Levite in the house of Micah, and asked him, "What makest thou in this *place*?" they did not imply that he was constructing or manufacturing anything. Their question was simply, "What are you doing in this place?" Except for the difference between the singular and plural forms, the Hebrew verb is the same as that in his later question to them: "What are you doing?" (Judges 18.3, 18). The idiom "What make you here?" in the sense of "What are you doing here?" was common in the sixteenth and seventeenth centuries. Examples from Shakespeare are:

> "And what make you from Wittenberg, Horatio?"
>> *Hamlet*, I, 2, 164
> "Thou frantic woman, what dost thou make here?"
>> *King Richard II*, V, 3, 89

"She was in his company at Page's house; and what they made there, I know not."
> *Merry Wives of Windsor*, II, 1, 244

**MAKE FOR** is an old and well-established idiom in the sense of be favorable to, tend toward, operate in aid of. Tyndale's translation of Romans 14.19 was "Let us folowe tho thinges which make for peace," and the idiom has remained through all revisions. When applied to a person, however, "make for" is awkward and ambiguous. "Neither shall Pharaoh with *his* mighty army and great company make for him in the war" (Ezekiel 17.17) is relieved of ambiguity by the revised versions' reading, "help him."

**MALICIOUSNESS** is the equivalent of "malice," which RSV uses in Romans 1.29. It occurs also in 1 Peter 2.16, "As free, and not using *your* liberty for a cloke of maliciousness, but as the servants of God." RSV translates this verse: "Live as free men, yet without using your freedom as a pretext for evil; but live as servants of God."

**MANNER** is used 234 times in KJ, and in more than one third of these cases is unnecessary. There is, in these cases, no corresponding Hebrew or Greek word to call for its use, and the meaning of the text can be conveyed more directly and simply without it.

This is in part because "manner" is used most often in the archaic sense of "kind" or "sort," and in part because of such periphrastic expressions as "no manner of" for "no," and "all manner of" for "all."

"No manner of work shall be done" (Exodus 12.16) is simply "no work shall be done." In Leviticus, "ye shall do no manner of work" (23.31) is "you shall do no work"; so likewise "no manner of fat" is "no fat" (7.23), "no manner of blood" is "no blood" (7.26), and "any manner of blood" is "any blood" (7.27; 17.10).

"All manner of beasts" (Numbers 31.30) is "all the cattle." "All manner of plague of leprosy" is "any leprous disease" (Leviticus 14.54). In 1 Chronicles, "all manner of service" is "all the service" (6.48) and "each service" (28.14); "all manner of instruments of war" is "all the weapons of war" (12.37); "all manner of work" is "all the work" (29.5).

In the Gospels, "all manner of disease" means "every disease" (Matthew 4.23; 10.1); "all manner of sin" is "every sin" (Matthew 12.31); "all manner of herbs" is "every herb" (Luke 11.42).

In some cases, real differences of meaning may be inferred between the periphrastic "manner of" and the simple translation. "Two manner of people" may be taken to mean something quite different from "two peoples" (Genesis 25.23). "No manner of similitude" does not convey the meaning "no form" (Deuteronomy 4.15). The Jews' question concerning Jesus' meaning (John 7.36) and Jesus' question to the two disciples walking to Emmaus (Luke 24.17) are complicated unduly by the insertion of the word "manner." In 1 Peter 1.15 "be holy in all manner of conversation" falls short of the more direct translation, "be holy in all your conduct."

In Revelation 18.12 "all manner vessels" occurs twice—an archaism inherited from Tyndale, who spelled it "almanner vessels." See OED, paragraph 9b under *Manner*. RSV translates "all articles."

**MANSIONS.** A correspondent accuses the RSV translators of taking the glory out of the Scriptures, citing as evidence the wording of John 14.2: "In my Father's house are many rooms; if it were not so, would I have told you that I go to prepare a place for you?" KJ had promised him "mansions," and he complains bitterly that these have shrunk to "rooms." The glory, he says, is left out!

But the word "mansion," as used by Tyndale and KJ, had no reference to a manor house or a pretentious residence. It meant simply a place to stay, a place of abode. The Greek word which it translates is *monē*, which comes from the verb *menō*, to stay or abide. The Latin noun is *mansio*, from the verb *maneo*, which means to stay or abide. Jesus simply promised to his disciples a place to dwell in his Father's house.

The basic trouble of this correspondent lies deeper than his failure to understand the Biblical use of the word "mansion." He is looking for the wrong kind of glory.

The word *monē* is also used in verse 23 of this same chapter, where KJ translates it "abode," and RSV translates it "home." The entire verse reads in RSV: "Jesus answered him, 'If a man loves me, he will keep my word, and my Father will love him, and we will come to him and make our home with him.' "

Jesus also said in his prayer for his disciples (John 17.3): "And this is eternal life, that they know thee the only true God, and Jesus Christ whom thou hast sent."

The real glory of the eternal life in heaven which our Lord has promised to those who love and serve him is that we shall know God, Father, Son, and Spirit, and dwell in our Father's house—at home with him and he with us. The correspondent does not understand what the real glory of life with our Father is.

There is an excellent discussion of these texts in *The Interpreter's*

*Bible*, vol. 8, pp. 699–700, 710–711. This discussion is by two British scholars who had nothing to do with the preparation of the RSV.

**MAR** was a heavy, fatal word in the sixteenth to the eighteenth centuries. It meant to damage beyond repair, to ruin. The impact of the word has become lighter, till it now means simply to disfigure or impair in some respect, to render less perfect or complete. In only two instances is RSV able to retain "mar" in contexts where KJ used it: "mar the corners of thy beard" (Leviticus 19.27); RSV "mar the edges of your beard"; and "his visage was so marred" (Isaiah 52.14); RSV "his appearance was so marred." Elsewhere "mar" must be replaced by heavier terms—"mice that ravage the land" (1 Samuel 6.5); "ruin every good piece of land with stones" (2 Kings 3.19); "ruined their branches" (Nahum 2.2); "the waistcloth was spoiled; it was good for nothing" (Jeremiah 13.7); "so will I spoil the pride of Judah" (Jeremiah 13.9); "the vessel he was making of clay was spoiled in the potter's hand" (Jeremiah 18.4). Closer translations of the Hebrew are: "break up my path" (Job 30.13); "impair my inheritance" (Ruth 4.6).

A rendering which the revised versions were obliged to correct at several points is Mark 2.22: "And no man putteth new wine into old bottles; else the new wine doth burst the bottles, and the wine is spilled, and the bottles will be marred: but new wine must be put into new bottles." RSV has: "And no one puts new wine into old wineskins; if he does, the wine will burst the skins, and the wine is lost, and so are the skins; but new wine is for fresh skins."

**MASTER** appears 100 times in the Old Testament for the Hebrew word *'adon*, which is translated 215 times by "lord." There is general agreement of KJ and RSV in these Old Testament renderings. Two difficult texts call for mention. Ecclesiastes 12.11 reads in KJ: "The words of the wise *are* as goads, and as nails fastened *by* the masters of assemblies, *which* are given from one shepherd." Most twentieth-century translations, including that of the Jewish Publication Society, abandon the rabbinical rendering "masters of assemblies." RSV translates: "The sayings of the wise are like goads, and like nails firmly fixed are the collected sayings which are given by one Shepherd." Malachi 2.12 reads in KJ: "The LORD will cut off the man that doeth this, the master and the scholar, out of the tabernacles of Jacob, and him that offereth an offering unto the LORD of hosts." Here most modern translations reject the rendering "the master and the scholar." RSV reads: "May the LORD cut off from the tents of Jacob, for the man who does this, any to witness or answer, or to bring an offering to the LORD of hosts!" Explanation of these passages may be found in *The Interpreter's Bible*, vol. 5, p. 87 and vol. 6, p. 1135.

In the Gospels the word "Master," as applied to Jesus, stands for the Greek word *epistatēs* 7 times, *rabbi* 8 times, and *didaskalos* 41 times. RSV removes ambiguity by translating *didaskalos* as "teacher." Instead of "Master and Lord" RSV has "Teacher and Lord" in John 13.13, and in verse 14 "your Lord and Teacher." "The disciple is not above *his* master, nor the servant above his lord" (Matthew 10.24) is worded in RSV, "A disciple is not above his teacher, nor a servant above his master." (See TEACHER)

**MAUL** occurs once (Proverbs 25.18): "A man that beareth false witness against his neighbour *is* a maul, and a sword, and a sharp arrow." As here used, "maul" meant the same as "mace," defined by OED as "a heavy staff or club, either entirely of metal or having a metal head, often spiked; formerly a regular weapon of war." Giant Maul, in Bunyan's *Pilgrim's Progress*, was armed with a club, and Mr. Great-heart with a sword. This meaning of "maul" is now obsolete, and it has acquired such associations with heavy industry, and "mace" such associations with the pageantry of public office and academic processions, that neither word is now a suitable translation of the Hebrew.

The Hebrew word *mephits* appears also in Nahum 2.1, where KJ translates it "he that dasheth in pieces," and RSV "the shatterer." With different pointing, it may be read as *mappets*, which appears in Jeremiah 51.20 as "battle ax." RSV uses "hammer" in the Jeremiah context, because of the repeated refrain, "break in pieces"; but it takes the Hebrew dictionary's definition, "war club," in Proverbs.

**MEAN,** as adjective, occurs five times in the sense of common, ordinary, undistinguished. The "mean man" of Isaiah 2.9, 5.15, 31.8 means simply man—man in general, the common man. There is no adjective in the Hebrew text represented by this expression, and the word for man is *'adam*, the generic word for mankind. The more specific word for a man is *'ish*, which is related to *'adam* in much the same way as the Latin *vir* is related to *homo*. The prior English translations did not use the adjective "mean" in these verses; that was an addition made by the KJ translators. In any case they meant by it simply "common"; they did not understand by "the mean man" one who is base or niggardly.

In each of these three verses of Isaiah both *'adam* and *'ish* are used in parallel constructions, and KJ makes a distinction by using "mean man" for *'adam*, and "great man" (2.9) or "mighty man" (5.15; 31.8) for *'ish*. This distinction is not justifiable. RSV translates 2.9, "So man is humbled, and men are brought low . . ." Proverbs 22.29 is a familiar text: "Seest thou a man diligent in his business? he shall stand before kings; he shall not stand before mean *men*." Here the Hebrew text has an adjective which means "obscure." For some reason, the revised versions of 1885–1901 retained the word "mean" in the English text, with a marginal note informing the reader that the Hebrew means "obscure." RSV reads:

> "Do you see a man skilful in his work?
>
> he will stand before kings;
>
> he will not stand before obscure men."

One of the happy innovations of KJ is Paul's claim to be "a citizen of no mean city" (Acts 21.39). This is an admirable translation of the Greek, which means literally ". . . a city not without distinction." Tyndale, the Great Bible, and the Bishops' Bible had ". . . of no vyle citie."

**MEAT** is used in KJ for food in general, anything used as nourishment.

It is applied especially to solid food, to what folk eat, in contrast to what they drink. And it is not limited, as in present common usage, to the flesh of animals used for food.

The clause in Habakkuk 3.17, "the fields shall yield no meat," means "the fields yield no food." The majestic lines of Psalm 145 include these verses (15–16 RSV):

> "The eyes of all look to thee,
>
> and thou givest them their food in due season.
>
> Thou openest thy hand,
>
> thou satisfiest the desire of every living thing."

The "trees for meat" (Ezekiel 47.12) are "trees for food"; instead of "the fruit thereof shall be for meat, and the leaf thereof for medicine," we now read, "Their fruit will be for food, and their leaves for healing."

"Is not life more than food, and the body more than clothing?" said our Lord in the Sermon on the Mount (Matthew 6.25). "Purging all meats" (Mark 7.19) means "Thus he declared all foods clean." The disciples left Jesus at Jacob's well, and went into Samaria "to buy food"; and when they returned he told them, "I have food to eat of which you do not know" (John 4.8, 32).

Jesus' question when he revealed himself to his disciples at the Sea of Tiberias, "Have ye any meat?" is correctly translated, "Have you any fish?" (John 21.5). The sixteenth-century translators seem not to have known that the Greek noun in this question was constantly used for fish, the chief delicacy of the Athenians.

The "meat offering" which is mentioned more than a hundred times in the KJ Old Testament contained no flesh; it consisted of fine flour or meal, and oil. It was a "meal-offering" (RV) or "cereal offering" (RSV). The prostitution of this offering to the worship of idols is the burden of God's accusation of Jerusalem in Ezekiel 16.19: "My meat also which I gave thee, fine flour, and oil, and honey, *wherewith* I fed thee, thou hast even set it before them for a sweet savour." In RSV this verse reads: "Also my bread which I gave you—I fed you with fine flour and oil and honey—you set before them for a pleasing odor."

**MEMORIAL,** as noun, was used in the seventeenth century not only for something by which the memory of a person, thing, or event is preserved, but also for an act of commemoration, and even for memory itself. God's word to the people of Israel through Moses (Exodus 3.15), "this *is* my name for ever, and this *is* my memorial unto all generations," means "this is my name for ever, and thus I am to be remembered throughout all generations." "The LORD *is* his memorial" means "the LORD is his name" (Hosea 12.5). The censers used by Korah and his company were hammered out into plates as a covering for the altar, not "to be a memorial" but as an ever-present "reminder" that no one who is not a priest should burn incense before the LORD (Numbers 16.40).

In the place of "memorial" RSV has "commemoration" (Esther 9.28), "renown" (Psalm 135.13), "memory" (Psalm 9.6). Jesus' comment on the action of the woman who poured costly ointment on his head, closes with the words "Wheresoever this gospel shall be preached throughout the whole world, *this* also that she hath done shall be spoken of for a memorial of her." RSV translates it, "wherever the gospel is preached in the whole world, what she has done will be told in memory of her" (Mark 14.9 = Matthew 26.13).

**MERCHANTMEN** is an archaic word for merchants, occurring in Genesis 37.28 for the Midianites to whom Joseph was sold and in 1 Kings 10.15 for the traders who brought much profit to King Solomon. The latter are called "chapmen" in 2 Chronicles 9.14. (See CHAPMEN.) The Hebrew terms thus translated denote men who travel for the purpose of buying and selling; and that which is used for the traders of Solomon's empire carries the further connotation of seeking, spying out, exploring for profitable ventures. This use of "merchantmen" is in line with the early restriction of the word "merchant" to wholesale traders, especially those dealing with foreign countries. RSV uses "traders" in place of "merchantmen" and "chapmen."

In Matthew 13.45 "merchant man" represents two words in the reverse order—"man merchant"—in the Greek text which the KJ translators used. But the best ancient Greek manuscripts do not have the word for "man." RSV therefore translates, "the kingdom of heaven is like a merchant in search of fine pearls."

"Merchantman" in the sense of a cargo ship is not used in the English Bible.


**MERCY, MERCIES, MERCIFUL** appear 355 times in KJ. The emphasis of the Hebrew and Greek terms thus translated is upon compassion, pity, forbearance, forgiveness, or kindness shown by the merciful rather than upon guilt or lack of deserving on the part of those to whom mercy is extended. Characteristic texts are Jesus' injunction, "Be merciful, even as your Father is merciful" (Luke 6.36 RSV) and the lawyer's description of the good Samaritan as "The one who showed mercy on him" (Luke 10.37 RSV).

"Mercy" is used by RSV in less than half the cases where it appears in KJ. The difference is due to a change in the translation of the Hebrew word *hesed*, for which KJ uses "mercy" 178 times. In 163 of these cases *hesed* denotes a basic attribute of God in relation to his chosen people, for which "mercy" is a partial but inadequate term. RV in some cases, and ASV consistently, use "lovingkindness" to denote this attribute of God. RSV uses "steadfast love." "Mercy" is retained by RSV in the familiar Psalm 23.6, but elsewhere characteristic texts are: "showing steadfast love to thousands of those who love me and keep my commandments" (Exodus 20.6; Deuteronomy 5.10); "I will not take my steadfast love from him" (2 Samuel 7.15); "steadfast love surrounds him who trusts in the LORD" (Psalm 32.10); "The LORD is merciful and gracious, slow to anger and abounding in steadfast love" (Psalm 103.8); "for his steadfast love endures for ever" (Psalm 136.1). "I will make an everlasting covenant with you, *even* the sure mercies of David" (Isaiah 55.3 KJ) is translated by RSV: "I will make with you an everlasting covenant, my steadfast, sure love for David." (See LOVING-KINDNESS)

Where *hesed* is used to denote human attitudes and behavior, it is best translated by "kindness," "loyalty," or "faithfulness." Jonah 2.8 KJ has "They that observe lying vanities forsake their own mercy"; RSV has "Those who pay regard to vain idols forsake their true loyalty." The great summary of human duty in Micah 6.8 reads in RSV:

"He has showed you, O man, what is good;
and what does the LORD require of you
but to do justice, and to love kindness,
and to walk humbly with your God?"

In Deuteronomy 21.8 and 32.43 KJ has "be merciful unto" for the Hebrew verb which means forgive, atone for. RSV reads "Forgive, O LORD, thy people Israel" and "makes expiation for the land of his people."

Three other Hebrew verbs and three groups of Greek words are translated by "mercy" or "be merciful" both in KJ and in the revised versions. These raise no problem. RSV and KJ agree, for example, in Exodus 33.19, "I will be gracious to whom I will be gracious, and will show mercy on whom I will show mercy."

**MESS.** An archaic or colloquial term for a portion, or serving, of food.

Joseph sent "portions" from his own table to his brothers, who could not sit with him because of his station as next to Pharaoh (Genesis 43.34). When David told Uriah to go to his home, "there followed him a present from the king"—there is no indication in the Hebrew that it was "a mess *of meat,*" as KJ has it (2 Samuel 11.8). The Hebrew word in these two cases is the one which is translated "gifts" in the account of the great banquet given by King Ahasuerus to celebrate the coronation of Queen Esther (2.18). It is an interesting fact that the well-worn phrase "a mess of pottage" does not appear in the Biblical account of Esau's sale of his birthright (Genesis 25.29–34) or in the reference to it in Hebrews 12.16.

**METEYARD** appears once (Leviticus 19.35): "Ye shall do no unrighteousness in judgment, in meteyard, in weight, or in measure." RSV translates: "You shall do no wrong in judgment, in measures of length or weight or quantity." "Meteyard" and "metewand" are old words for a rod used to measure length. The KJ rendering of this verse goes back to Tyndale. In the Preface to the King James Version, the translators used the word "meteyard" in the section on "The unwillingness of our chief Adversaries, that the Scriptures should be divulged in the mother tongue." They said: "This seemeth to argue a bad cause, or a bad conscience, or both. Sure we are, that it is not he that hath good gold, that is afraid to bring it to the touchstone, but he that hath the counterfeit; neither is it the true man that shunneth the light, but the malefactor, lest his deeds should be reproved: neither is it the plaindealing Merchant that is unwilling to have the weights or the meteyard brought in place, but he that useth deceit."

**MINISH** is an archaic word for make less or become less. It occurs in Pharaoh's command that the Hebrew people be given no straw for the making of bricks, yet be required to make and deliver the same number of bricks as they had made when straw had been given them (Exodus 5.6–19). In verse 8 KJ reads, "ye shall not diminish *ought* thereof"; and in verse 19, "Ye shall not minish *ought* from your bricks of your daily task." The Hebrew verb is the same in these two verses. RSV reads "you shall by no means lessen it" and "You shall by no means lessen your daily number of bricks."

In Psalm 107.39 "minish" is used intransitively for the Hebrew verb which means become small or few. The meaning of the passage is obscured by the KJ translation of verses 39, 40, and 41 as though each were an independent sentence. RSV regards verses 39–43 as a strophe, and translates verses 39–41 as a single sentence, which reads:

"When they are diminished and brought low
through oppression, trouble, and sorrow,
he pours contempt upon princes
and makes them wander in trackless wastes;
but he raises up the needy out of affliction,
and makes their families like flocks."

**MITE.** A copper coin of very small value. The two mites which the poor widow contributed to the temple treasury were two *lepta*. Mark 12.42 adds, "which make a *kodrantēs*." This is simply the Greek spelling of the Latin *quadrans*, which was a quarter of an *as*. The *as* had suffered successive devaluations throughout Roman history, and was then worth about two thirds of a cent. A *lepton* therefore was worth about one twelfth of a cent. RSV simply says "two copper coins, which make a penny." It might well have retained the word "mite," however, which has been the traditional rendering, beginning with Tyndale.

**MOCK** means to deride, jeer at, tantalize, or ridicule by imitating the speech or action of another. In the sixteenth century it also had a lighter meaning, to jest, trifle, play, or make sport, without implying that it is at the expense of another. This meaning is now obsolete. The latest example of its use which is given by OED is from KJ, Genesis 19.14, where Lot warned his sons-in-law that Sodom would be destroyed, but "he seemed as one that mocked unto his sons in law." The Hebrew verb is *tsaḥaq*, which means to laugh, jest, or play. RSV translates the sentence, "But he seemed to his sons-in-law to be jesting."

From *tsaḥaq* Abraham derived the name for his son, "Isaac," which means "laughter." It is the verb involved in all that is said about laughing in the accounts of God's promise and its fulfilment in the birth of this son (Genesis 18.9–15; 21.1–7). But in the account of the feast to celebrate the weaning of the young Isaac, this same verb is represented by "mocking"—it is said that "Sarah saw the son of Hagar the Egyptian, which she had born unto Abraham, mocking" (Genesis 21.9). The KJ translators may have used the term in the innocent sense which is now obsolete, but "playing" would have been a less ambiguous, truer word. The fact is that a phrase seems to have been lost from the Hebrew text here, for the Septuagint and the Vulgate have "playing with her son Isaac." Most modern translations accept this reading.

A quite different Hebrew verb is used in Jeremiah 38.19, for which "mock" is not strong enough. RSV translates: "King Zedekiah said to Jeremiah, 'I am afraid of the Jews who have deserted to the Chaldeans, lest I be handed over to them and they abuse me.'"

Yet another Hebrew verb appears in Job 13.9, which KJ renders, referring to God: "Is it good that he should search you out? or as one man mocketh another, do ye *so* mock him?" RSV translates this verse:

"Will it be well with you when he searches you out?
Or can you deceive him, as one deceives a man?"

**MODERATION.** "Let your moderation be known unto all men" (Philippians 4.5) is an exhortation that has been turned to the comfort of laziness or mediocrity. It was sometimes used in the days of the prohibition amendment, to justify indulgence in alcoholic liquor. But "moderation" is a mistranslation of the Greek adjective which is here used as a noun. It means gentle, gracious, kind, forbearing. As noun it appears also in Acts 24.4 and 2 Corinthians 10.1; and as adjective in 1 Timothy 3.3, Titus 3.2, James 3.17, and 1 Peter 2.18. The revised versions of 1881–1901 replaced "moderation" with "forbearance." RSV accepted this, but recast the sentence to read: "Let all men know your forbearance." The Greek word for "know" which is used here implies personal contact or experience. Paul is not urging his brethren at Philippi to acquire a worldwide reputation, but to practice forbearance in the give-and-take of everyday living. The text might well be translated, "Let every one feel your forbearing spirit."

**MORE** is used occasionally by KJ in the sense of larger or greater. "To the more ye shall give the more inheritance" (Numbers 33.54) means "to a large tribe you shall give a large inheritance." "These nations *are* more than I" (Deuteronomy 7.17) means "These nations are greater than I." "A people more than thou," in the context of Deuteronomy 20.1, means "an army larger than your own." In the confused assembly in the theater at Ephesus, "the more part," that is, "most of them," did not know why they had come together (Acts 19.32). The captain and owner of the ship on which Paul was being taken to Rome rejected his advice and took the advice of "the more part," that is, "the majority" (Acts 27.12).

**MORTIFY.** The original meaning is to put to death. Wyclif's translation of 1 Samuel 2.6 was "The Lord mortifieth, and quykeneth," for which KJ has "The LORD killeth, and maketh alive." This meaning is now obsolete, and for most people to mortify is to cause a feeling of humiliation or shame. The revised versions use "put to death" in the two passages where "mortify" appears in KJ—Romans 8.13 and Colossians 3.5. "Mortify your members which are upon the earth" is replaced in RSV by "Put to death what is earthly in you."

**MOTIONS.** The verb "move" occurs often in the Bible, but the nouns "move" or "movement" not at all. The noun "motion" occurs once, in the plural, and in the obsolete sense of an inward impulse, passion, or emotion. The passage is Romans 7.5: "For when we were in the flesh, the motions of sins, which were by the law, did work in our members to bring forth fruit unto death." RSV translates: "While we were living in the flesh, our sinful passions, aroused by the law, were at work in our members to bear fruit for death."

In Shakespeare's *Othello*, I, 3, 330, Iago says, "If the balance of our lives had not one scale of reason to poise another of sensuality, the blood and baseness of our natures would conduct us to most preposterous conclusions: but we have reason to cool our raging motions, our carnal stings, our unbitted lusts." In *Cymbeline*, II, 5, 20 Posthumus rails at women:

> "For there's no motion
> That tends to vice in man but I affirm
> It is the woman's part."

**MOUNT** occurs nine times in the sense of a military earthwork, an embankment or heaped-up mound of earth or other material, by which the besiegers fought on a level with the besieged. It is replaced in RSV by "mound," "siege mound," "siegework" (Jeremiah 6.6; 32.24; 33.4; Ezekiel 4.2; 17.17; 21.22; 26.8; Daniel 11.15); and once, for a different Hebrew word, by "towers" (Isaiah 29.3). The usual Hebrew term is three times rendered "bank," and in each case "cast a bank" is replaced by "cast up a mound" (2 Samuel 20.15; 2 Kings 19.32; Isaiah 37.33).

The word "mound" does not appear in KJ. The use of "mount" in this military sense is illustrated by a passage in Bunyan's *Holy War:* "Besides, there were Mounts cast up against it. The Mount *Gracious* was on the one side, and Mount *Justice* was on the other. Further, there were several small banks and advance-grounds, as *Plain-Truth-Hill* and *No-Sin-Banks*, where many of the Slings were placed against the Town."

**MUCH,** as an adjective, was formerly applied to people; and the phrase "much people" appears 25 times in KJ. This usage is recorded as obsolete by OED, which cites no example of it later than 1611. In the Old Testament, RSV replaces it with "many people" or, where the context is that of war, "many men," "many soldiers," "a large army." Joshua 11.4 reads in KJ: "And they went out, they and all their hosts with them, much people, even as the sand that *is* upon the sea shore in multitude, with horses and chariots very many." RSV has: "And they came out, with all their troops, a great host, in number like the sand that is upon the seashore, with very many horses and chariots."

In the Gospels RSV usually replaces "much people" with "a great crowd," which is a literal translation of the Greek. In Acts, it uses "some of the people" (5.37), "a large company" (11.24, 26), "a considerable company" (19.26), and "many people" (18.10). "The great voice of much people in heaven" (Revelation 19.1) is reworded, "the mighty voice of a great multitude in heaven."

In Paul's letter to Philemon, verse 8, "though I might be much bold in Christ to enjoin thee that which is convenient," is now worded, "though I am bold enough in Christ to command you to do what is required."

**MUNITION** is used by KJ in the obsolete sense of a fortification or fortress for the purpose of defense. For "munitions of rocks" RSV has "fortresses of rocks" (Isaiah 33.16), and for "against her and her munition" it has "against her and her stronghold" (Isaiah

29.7). In Nahum 2.1, "keep the munition" is better phrased "man the ramparts." RSV translates this verse:

> "The shatterer has come up against you.
>      Man the ramparts;
>      watch the road;
>    gird your loins;
>        collect all your strength."

**MUSE** is used in the current sense of "meditate" in Psalms 39.3 and 143.5. It is used in the now rare sense of ask oneself some question, wonder whether or how or what, in Luke 3.15, "all men mused in their hearts of John, whether he were the Christ, or not." Shakespeare uses it in this sense in *King John,* III, 1, 317:

> "I muse your majesty doth seem so cold,
> When such profound respects do pull you on."

**NAUGHT,** which appears twice in KJ, is not a synonym for "nought," which appears 36 times. "Nought" is a noun, which means "nothing"; "naught" appears only as an adjective which means "bad." When the men of Jericho told Elisha, "the situation of this city *is* pleasant, . . . but the water *is* naught," they were not complaining that the city lacked water, but that "the water is bad" (2 Kings 2.19–22). "*It is* naught, *it is* naught, saith the buyer" (Proverbs 20.14) is translated by RSV, " 'It is bad, it is bad,' says the buyer." In both cases the Hebrew adjective is *ra‘,* which means bad, evil.

OED cites Pepys' *Diary,* 29 October 1661: "We . . . should have been merry, but their wine was so naught . . . that we were not so." Shakespeare uses "naught" in the sense of morally bad in such passages as:

> "Beloved Regan, Thy sister's naught."
>> *King Lear,* II, 4, 145
>> "There's no trust,
> No faith, no honesty in men; all perjured,
> All forsworn, all naught, all dissemblers."
>> *Romeo and Juliet,* III, 2, 87

**NAUGHTINESS, NAUGHTY.** "Naughtiness" is really bad in KJ; it means downright wickedness. The injunction in James 1.21 to "lay apart all filthiness and superfluity of naughtiness" now reads "put away all filthiness and rank growth of wickedness." The terms "naughty" and "naughtiness" have lost some of their evil through the years; they are now used for the misdeeds of children or the trivial misbehavior of adults who have not matured. The "naughty figs" that Jeremiah saw in his vision (24.2) were simply "bad figs," so bad that they could not be eaten.

Shakespeare used "naughty" frequently, the best-known lines being,
"How far that little candle throws his beams!
So shines a good deed in a naughty world."
*Merchant of Venice*, V, 1, 91

**NECESSITY.** The rendering of Hebrews 8.3, ". . . wherefore *it is* of necessity that this man have somewhat also to offer" is clumsy English and an inaccurate translation. "Of necessity" is a confusing circumlocution for the simple Greek adjective which means "necessary." The translators inserted the word "man" without marking it by italics; the Greek has simply the masculine demonstrative pronoun "this." Since the statement refers to Jesus, the Son of God, our "great high priest" (4.14; 5.5, 10; 6.20; 7.15–8.2), the word "man" is inappropriate; the word "this" should be followed by *"high priest,"* as in the revised versions of 1881–1901, or by "priest," as in RSV. The word for "also" belongs with "this" rather than with "somewhat." The revised versions correct the misleading KJ rendering at these three points; RSV has ". . . hence it is necessary for this priest also to have something to offer."

A similar error is in 7.24, where KJ has "this *man*" to represent the Greek word for "he." It here uses the italics which it fails to use in 8.3, but that is not enough to redeem the mistranslation.

**NEEDS** is an adverb which means necessarily or of necessity, being originally the genitive case of the word "need." The expression "must needs" was common speech in the late sixteenth and early seventeenth centuries; it is cited 85 times in the *Concordance to Shakespeare*. It appears 14 times in KJ, and the revised versions of 1881–1901 use it in three additional passages. RSV eliminates the word "needs" in all these cases, as tautological or not called for by the original Hebrew or Greek. For example, "must needs be circumcised" means "shall be circumcised" (Genesis 17.13); "I must needs go" means "I must go" (Luke 14.18); "Christ must needs have suffered" means "It was necessary for the Christ to suffer" (Acts 17.3); "must needs be subject" means "must be subject" (Romans 13.5). Other cases are Genesis 24.5; 2 Samuel 14.14; Jeremiah 10.5; Matthew 18.7; Mark 13.7; John 4.4; Acts 1.16; 21.22; 1 Corinthians 5.10; 2 Corinthians

11.30; and, in the revised versions of 1881–1901, Matthew 24.6 and Luke 21.9; 24.44.

In colloquial use, the adverb "needs" often has an ironic sense, according to OED, implying a foolish or perverse insistence. Such irony is found in Genesis 19.9, "he will needs be a judge"; and in Genesis 31.30, "thou wouldest needs be gone," where it is laboriously assisted by inserting a "though" and a "yet" which are neither expressed nor implied in the Hebrew. RSV has "he would play the judge!" in the first of the passages, but rejects the attempt at irony in the second. A mistranslation of the Hebrew conjunction *ki* resulted in the curious rendering of the last clause of the question in Numbers 16.13, "except thou make thyself altogether a prince over us?" The revised versions of 1881–1901 changed this to "but thou must needs make thyself also a prince over us?" RSV is more direct: "that you must also make yourself a prince over us?"

**NEESING.** An old word for sneezing, the plural of which appears once in KJ, in the chapter about Leviathan (Job 41.18): "By his neesings a light doth shine." RSV has "His sneezings flash forth light." The Hebrew word is *'atishah*, an almost perfect example of matching sound and sense.

Fnese, nese, neese, neeze, sneeze constitute an interesting chapter in the history of words. OED informs us that "fnese" went out of use early in the fifteenth century. Its place was taken by "nese," a word formed by dropping the initial "f"; and later by "snese," a word formed by misreading or misprinting the initial "f" as a long "s." OED goes on to comment: "The adoption of *sneeze* was probably assisted by its phonetic appropriateness; it may have been felt as a strengthened form of *neeze*."

As published in 1611 and a century and a half thereafter, KJ had, in the account of the miracle wrought through Elisha, restoring to life the young son of the woman of Shunem, "the child neesed seven times" (2 Kings 4.35). This was changed to "sneezed" in 1762, according to Dr. Scrivener. He restored "neesed" in the Cambridge Paragraph Bible of 1873, but the restoration served no useful purpose and has not been followed by other editions.

**NEITHER** is part of a double negative in 2 Samuel 14.7, "shall not leave to my husband *neither* name nor remainder upon the earth." RSV simply leaves out the "not." A rather involved passage in Genesis 21.26 reads, "I wot not who hath done this thing; neither didst thou tell me, neither yet heard I *of it*, but to day." The most ardent admirer of the style of the King James Version might be relieved to have that one reworded as in RSV, "I do not know who has done this thing; you did not tell me, and I have not heard of it until to-day." Matthew 12.32 has another sequence of "not . . . neither . . . neither," which RSV amends to read: "whoever speaks against the Holy Spirit will not be forgiven, either in this age or in the age to come."

Romans 4.19 KJ is based upon a Greek text which says that Abraham did not consider the state of his own body or that of Sarah; but RSV and modern translations generally are based upon the more ancient manuscripts, which say that he did. Phillips, for example, reads: "With undaunted faith he looked at the facts—his own impotence (he was practically a hundred years old at the time) and his wife Sarah's apparent barrenness."

In Luke 14.12 KJ has "not . . . nor . . . neither . . . nor," which RSV changes to "not . . . or . . . or . . . or." In John 1.25 it has "not . . . nor . . . neither" which RSV changes to "neither . . . nor . . . nor."

**NEPHEW** is always used by KJ in an obsolete sense. The 30 "nephews" who rode with Abdon and his 40 sons were, according to the Hebrew, "sons of sons," that is, they were his grandsons (Judges 12.14). "If any widow have children or nephews" (1 Timothy 5.4) means, in the Greek, "If a widow has children or grandchildren." The use of "nephew" to mean "grandson" was common in the seventeenth century, OED informs us; it was also used in the wider sense of a descendant. "He shall neither have son nor nephew among his people" (Job 18.19) is correctly translated, "He has no offspring or descendant among his people." So also "cut off from Babylon the name, and remnant, and son, and nephew" (Isaiah 14.22) means "cut off from Babylon name and remnant, offspring and posterity." The same Hebrew terms are too specifically translated in Abimelech's request to Abraham, "Now therefore swear unto me here by God that thou wilt not deal falsely with me, nor with my son, nor with my son's son" (Genesis 21.23). RSV translates, ". . . that you will not deal falsely with me or with my offspring or with my posterity."

**NOISOME.** Archbishop Trench, in his essay "On the Authorized Version of the New Testament," called attention to the translation of 1 Timothy 6.9 in the versions from Tyndale to the Bishops' Bible—"They that will be rich fall into temptations and snares, and into many foolish and noisome lusts"—and praised the KJ translators for changing "noisome" to "hurtful." In the sixteenth century, he said, "noisome" meant noxious or hurtful, "but in the beginning of the seventeenth century it was acquiring a new meaning, the same which it now retains, namely, that of exciting disgust rather than that of doing actual hurt or harm. Thus a tiger would have been 'noisome' in old English; a skunk would be 'noisome' in modern. Here was reason enough for the change which they made."

But Trench complained that KJ had not made a similar change elsewhere. This has now been done. The revised versions read "deadly pestilence" in Psalm 91.3 and "wild beasts" or "evil beasts" in Ezekiel 14.15, 21.

**NO MAN, ANY MAN.** Indefinite pronouns, referring to any person, use the masculine form in the Greek, just as we in English often use the pronoun "he" in a general statement which includes both men and women. KJ overdoes this masculine habit by its use of "no man" and "any man" where the meaning is "no one" or "any one." This practice limits many statements unduly, and results in occasional infelicities.

For example, in Matthew 11.27 it is said that "no man knoweth the Son, but the Father." The word "but" is ambiguous here, for it may mean that men do not know the Son but do know the Father. That is absurd. But if the meaning is that no man knows the Son except the Father the text involves a worse absurdity by implying that the Father is a man. The Greek is perfectly clear, and the revised versions translate it clearly by using the expression "no one." RSV has: "no one knows the Son except the Father."

Note the wider horizon in such translations as "No one can serve two masters" (Matthew 6.24), "No one puts a piece of unshrunk cloth on an old garment" (Matthew 9.16), "No one after lighting a lamp covers it with a vessel" (Luke 8.16). It was not merely to "any man" but to "any one" that Jesus extended the invitation to eat of the bread of life (John 6.51), to drink of the water of life (John 7.37), to enter the door of the good shepherd (John 10.9), to serve him and follow him (John 12.26).

"If any man love God, the same is known of him" is more accurately translated, "If one loves God, one is known by him" (1 Corinthians 8.3). In spite of the masculine form of the pronouns, it is to women as well as to men that the message of the living Lord is addressed:

"Behold, I stand at the door and knock; if any one hears my voice and opens the door, I will come in to him and eat with him, and he with me" (Revelation 3.20).

**NONE EFFECT** is used eight times, "no effect" once, and "without effect" once. The revised versions take more care to express the meaning of the several verbs with which these phrases are associated. RSV has "make void her vow" (Numbers 30.8), "make void the word of God" (Matthew 15.6; Mark 7.13), "the promise is void" (Romans 4.14), "make the promise void" (Galatians 3.17). In various contexts it has "frustrates the plans of the peoples" (Psalm 33.10), "it is not as though the word of God had failed" (Romans 9.6), "be emptied of its power" (1 Corinthians 1.17), "you are severed from Christ" (Galatians 5.4), "Does their faithlessness nullify the faithfulness of God?" (Romans 3.3).

**NOTABLE** may mean (1) capable of being noted, (2) easily noted, (3) worth noting. That is, it may be the equivalent of (1) perceptible, (2) conspicuous, (3) excellent, eminent, of outstanding importance or worth. The second of these meanings was in common use in the sixteenth and seventeenth centuries, but is now obsolete. The "notable" horns of the he-goat in Daniel's vision were "conspicuous" (Daniel 8.5–8); and Barabbas was "a notorious prisoner" rather than "a notable prisoner" (Matthew 27.16). RSV has "a notable sign" in Acts 4.16, however; and Paul refers to Andronicus and Junias as "men of note among the apostles" (Romans 16.7).

In his address to the people on the day of Pentecost, Peter cited the prophecy of Joel (Acts 2.16–21, quoting Joel 2.28–32). In verse 20 his quotation reads "before that great and notable day of the Lord come," but in Joel 2.31 the prophecy has "before the great and the terrible day of the LORD come." The difference is due to the fact that Peter quoted the Septuagint, the Greek translation of the Old Testament. Because they confused the Hebrew words for "fear" and "see," the translators of the Septuagint, not only in Joel 2.31 but also in Habakkuk 1.7 and Malachi 1.14, used the Greek word *epiphanēs*, which means appearing to the sight, coming into open view, manifest, notable, illustrious.

The translation in Acts 2.20, "before that great and notable day of the Lord come," goes back to Tyndale and was used by subsequent sixteenth-century versions made from the Greek. The Latin Vulgate had *dies Domini magnus et manifestus*, so the Rheims New Testament translated the clause, "before the great and manifest day of our Lord doth come."

The Revised Standard Version agrees with Rheims in using the adjective "manifest," not because it is translating the Latin, but because here that is a sound translation of the Greek *epiphanēs*. The verb *epiphainō* means to appear, become visible, show oneself (Acts 27.20; Titus 2.11; 3.4). The noun *epiphaneia* is used six times to denote our Lord's appearing (2 Thessalonians 2.8; 1 Timothy 6.14; 2 Timothy 1.10; 4.1, 8; Titus 2.13). The last of these passages reads in RSV, "awaiting our blessed hope, the appearing of the glory of our great God and Savior Jesus Christ." The noun has become part of the English language as the name of Epiphany, the festival commemorating the manifestation of Christ to the Gentiles in the person of the "wise men from the East," and as the common noun "epiphany," which OED defines as "a manifestation or appearance of some divine or superhuman being."

The title of Antiochus Epiphanes, king of Syria, meant more than "Antiochus the Notable." It meant "Antiochus the Manifest God," for he claimed to be divine. His title was parodied as *Epimanes*, "Antiochus the Mad." Accounts of his attempt to abolish Judaism are to be found in 1 Maccabees 1.10–6.16 and 2 Maccabees 4.7–9.29.

**NOTHING** is occasionally used in KJ as an adverb, meaning not at all, in no way. "Was nothing bettered" means "was no better" (Mark 5.26). "Prevail nothing" means "was gaining nothing" (Matthew 27.24) and "can do nothing" (John 12.19). "Finding nothing how they might punish them" is in RSV "finding no way to punish them" (Acts 4.21). The Spirit told Peter to go with the three men sent by Cornelius, "nothing doubting," which means "without hesitation" (Acts 11.12; compare 10.20). "Nothing wavering" means "with no doubting" (James 1.6). "Differeth nothing from a servant" is translated by RSV "is no better than a slave" (Galatians 4.1). Three occurrences of "profit nothing" in KJ are reworded by RSV thus: "It is the spirit that gives life, the flesh is of no avail" (John 6.63); "Now I, Paul, say to you that if you receive circumcision, Christ will be of no advantage to you" (Galatians 5.2); "If I give away all I have, and if I deliver my body to be burned, but have not love, I gain nothing" (1 Corinthians 13.3).

This adverbial use of "nothing" points to the origin of "not," which is simply the contracted form of "nought."

**NOUGHT, SET AT.** To "set at nought" is to value at nothing, to regard as good for nothing or worthless, hence to despise or reject. "Ye have set at nought all my counsel" means "you have ignored all my counsel" (Proverbs 1.25). "The stone which was set at nought of you builders" is "the stone which was rejected by you builders" (Acts 4.11). Jesus said that it was written of the Son of man that he would be "set at nought" (Mark 9.12), and Herod with his soldiers "set him at nought" (Luke 23.11); RSV translates "treated with contempt." "Why dost thou set at nought thy brother?" means "Why do you despise your brother?" (Romans 14.10). A different body of Greek words and a quite different Greek construction underlie the speech of Demetrius to his fellow craftsmen and their workmen, where KJ has "be set at nought" for Greek which literally means "come into disrepute" (Acts 19.27). His speech reads in RSV: "Men, you know that from this business we have our wealth. And you see and hear that not only at Ephesus but almost throughout all Asia this Paul has persuaded and turned away a considerable company of people, saying that gods made with hands are not gods. And there is danger not only that this trade of ours may come into disrepute but also that the temple of the great goddess Artemis may count for nothing, and that she may even be deposed from her magnificence, she whom all Asia and the world worship."

**NOURISH** usually means in KJ to rear, bring up, care for, nurture, provide for, rather than to feed. For "rear" see Isaiah 1.2; 23.4; Ezekiel 19.2. For "bring up," 2 Samuel 12.3 and Acts 7.20, 21. Daniel and his friends were not merely fed at Nebuchadnezzar's court; "they were to be educated for three years, and at the end of that time they were to stand before the king" (Daniel 1.5 RSV). Joseph "provided for" his father and brothers and their dependents, throughout their life in Egypt (Genesis 45.11; 47.12; 50.21). Tyre and Sidon asked for peace with Herod, "because their country depended on the king's country for food" (Acts 12.20).

A rendering which lacks clarity or any other literary merit is Colossians 2.18–19: "Let no man beguile you of your reward in a voluntary humility and worshipping of angels, intruding into those things which he hath not seen, vainly puffed up by his fleshly mind. And not holding the Head, from which all the body by joints and bands having nourishment ministered, and knit together, increaseth with the increase of God." RSV translates these verses: "Let no one disqualify you, insisting on self-abasement and worship of angels, taking his stand on visions, puffed up without reason by his sensuous mind, and not holding fast to the Head, from whom the whole body, nourished and knit together through its joints and ligaments, grows with a growth that is from God."

**NOVICE.** The qualifications for the office of bishop are stated, both positively and negatively, in 1 Timothy 3.1–7. Among the negative clauses is verse 6, "Not a novice, lest being lifted up with pride he fall into the condemnation of the devil." The Greek word translated by "novice" is *neophutos*, which means "newly planted." It appears in the Latin as *neophytus*, and has passed on into English as "neophyte."

The King James Version and the revised versions of 1881–1901 stand alone in the use of "novice" here. Wyclif had "not newe conuertid to the feith." Tyndale had "He maye not be a yonge skoler" and was followed by the other Protestant versions of the sixteenth century. The Rheims translators used "neophyte," and stoutly defended it in their Preface to the Reader: "If Proselyte be a received word in the English bibles, . . . why may we not be bold to say, Neophyte?" William Fulke, opponent of the Rheims translators, included *neophyte* with *azymes* and *prepuce* among the "ridiculous inkhorn terms" which he accused them of coining.

The twentieth-century translations return to Wyclif's rendering, most of them reading "He must not be a new convert," and others saying the same in slightly different terms, as Phillips' "He must not be a beginner in the faith."

**NURTURE** appears once (Ephesians 6.4): "Ye fathers, provoke not your children to wrath; but bring them up in the nurture and admonition of the Lord." It is here a translation of the Greek *paideia*, which means education, training, discipline. The emphasis in *paideia* is not upon the free self-expression of the child, but upon his training through correction and discipline. The noun and verb are translated by "chastening," "chasten," "chastisement," "chastise" in KJ Hebrews 12.5–11; Luke 23.16, 22; 1 Corinthians 11.32; 2 Corinthians 6.9; Revelation 3.19. RSV uses "discipline" in the passage in Hebrews, and translates the verse in Ephesians: "Fathers, do not provoke your children to anger, but bring them up in the discipline and instruction of the Lord."

**OBSERVE.** When Herod seized John the Baptist and put him in prison because of the enmity of Herodias, we are told in Mark

6.20, "Herod feared John, knowing that he was a just man, and an holy, and observed him; and when he heard him, he did many things, and heard him gladly."

The word "observe" is here used in the sense of "treat with ceremonious respect or reverence"—a meaning which is now obsolete but was common in Shakespeare's day. In *King Henry IV, Part II* (IV, 4, 30), the King advises his son Thomas to "observe" his older brother, who is heir to the throne:

> "Blunt not his love,
> Nor lose the good advantage of his grace
> By seeming cold or careless of his will:
> For he is gracious, if he be observed."

In *Julius Caesar* (IV, 3, 45), Brutus quarrels with Cassius:

> "Must I budge?
> Must I observe you? Must I stand and crouch
> Under your testy humour?"

In place of "observed him," Tyndale, the Great Bible, the Geneva Bible, and the Bishops' Bible had "gave him reverence." But the Greek word means keep safe, watch over, protect; and this meaning is taken by the Latin Vulgate, by Martin Luther's German Bible, by Wyclif, Coverdale, and Rheims, and by the modern revised versions.

In place of the words for "he did many things," *polla epoiei*, the most ancient Greek manuscripts have the words *polla ēporei*, which mean "he was much perplexed." RSV reads: "Herod feared John, knowing that he was a righteous and holy man, and kept him safe. When he heard him, he was much perplexed; and yet he heard him gladly."

**OCCUPY.** "He called his ten servants, and delivered them ten pounds, and said unto them, Occupy till I come" (Luke 19.13). The Greek verb which is translated "occupy" is *pragmateuomai*, which means "do business." Tyndale and the Geneva Bible translated it, "Buy and sell till I come." But the KJ translators followed Coverdale, the Bishops' Bible, and the Rheims translation in using the word "occupy." RSV has "Trade with these till I come."

The version of Psalm 107.23 in the Book of Common Prayer, "They that go down to the sea in ships, and occupy their business in great waters," goes back to Coverdale. Here the KJ translators changed to a literal rendering ". . . do business in great waters."

In all but two cases, "occupy" is used by KJ in the now obsolete senses of "use" or "trade with." "All the ships of the sea with their mariners were in thee to occupy thy merchandise" means "all the ships of the sea with their mariners were in you, to barter for your wares" (Ezekiel 27.9). The word occurs often in this chapter of Ezekiel, a lamentation over Tyre, which should be read as a whole in the two versions.

When Samson tells Delilah that he would be weak and like other men "if they bind me fast with new ropes that never were occupied," the Hebrew means "with new ropes that have not been used" (Judges 16.11). "All the gold that was occupied for the work" (Exodus 38.24) means "All the gold that was used for the work."

In his warning against "tongues," and urging the use of the understanding, Paul wrote in 1 Corinthians 14.16: "Else when thou shalt bless with the spirit, how shall he that occupieth the room of the unlearned say Amen at thy giving of thanks, seeing he understandeth not what thou sayest?" This is the translation of Tyndale and the sixteenth-century translations generally. "Room" means "place." The Greek word here rendered "unlearned" is *idiōtēs,* which Wyclif simply transliterated as "an idiot" and for which Rheims had "the vulgar." RSV has ". . . can any one in the position of an outsider say the 'Amen' to your thanksgiving when he does not know what you are saying?" (See UNLEARNED)

In Hebrews 13.9 "have been occupied" represents the Greek verb which means "walk" or "live." This is a difficult verse to translate without resort to paraphrase. Rheims was baldly literal—"not with meats, which have not profited those that walk in them." RSV has "not by foods, which have not benefited their adherents." Goodspeed's phrase is clearer—"not through scruples about food. . . ."

**OCCURRENT,** as noun, means an occurrence, something that happens, an incident. The word was in common use in the sixteenth and seventeenth centuries, and appears once in the Bible. In his message to Hiram, king of Tyre, Solomon says, "But now the LORD my God hath given me rest on every side, *so that there is* neither adversary nor evil occurrent" (1 Kings 5.4). The Hebrew word means occurrence or happening. In the only other passage where it appears in the Hebrew Bible, it is translated "chance" by both KJ and the revised versions. This is Ecclesiastes 9.11, where RSV has, "Again I saw that under the sun the race is not to the swift, nor the battle to the strong, nor bread to the wise, nor riches to the intelligent, nor favor to the men of skill; but time and chance happen to them all."

In 1 Kings 5.4 RSV compacts adjective and noun in the one word "misfortune"—"there is neither adversary nor misfortune."

**ODD** appears just once (Numbers 3.48) where it has the meaning of surplus, excess, that which is over and above a certain number. The LORD accepted the service of the Levites instead of requiring such service from all the first-born sons of Israel. There were 22,000 Levites and 22,273 first-born sons, and the "odd number" had to be redeemed by the payment of five shekels apiece—1,365 shekels. RSV uses "excess number" here. The Hebrew word appears in seven other verses, and is translated in almost the same terms by KJ and the revised versions. RSV has "over and above" twice in this same context (Numbers 3.46, 49); elsewhere it reads "had nothing over" (Exodus 16.18), "that is left over" (Exodus 16.23), "that remains" (Exodus 26.12, 13), and "the overpayment" (Leviticus 25.27).

**OF.** The most versatile and ambiguous of the prepositions in KJ is "of." It is used where we would now say "by"—Jesus is said to be baptized *of* John and led *of* the Spirit into the wilderness to be tempted *of* the devil. "To be seen of them" is "to be seen by them," and "have glory of men" is "be praised by men" (Matthew 6.1–2). "Bidden of any *man*" is "invited by any one" (Luke 14.8).

"Which was spoken of the Lord by the prophet" may be understood to mean the prophet's word concerning the Lord; the clause is cleared of ambiguity by the present translation, "what the Lord had spoken by the prophet" (Matthew 2.15). Similarly, in John 8.40, "which I have heard of God" means "which I heard from God."

"The zeal of thine house" is "zeal for thy house" (John 2.17); "zealous of the law" is "zealous for the law" (Acts 21.20); and "a zeal of God" is "a zeal for God" (Romans 10.2). "Of long time" (Acts 8.11) is "for a long time."

The King James Version sometimes uses "of" where we would now use "with." Examples are "in comparison of you" (Judges 8.3) and "provided the king of sustenance" (2 Samuel 19.32). The expression "I *am* sick of love" (Song of Solomon 2.5) now implies surfeit and distaste; the better translation of the Hebrew is "I am sick with love."

To rejoice "more of that *sheep*, than of the ninety and nine" (Matthew 18.13) means to rejoice "over it more than over the ninety-nine." "Power of" means "rule over" in 1 Corinthians 7.4. "Compassion of" (Hebrews 10.34) is "compassion on." Timothy is urged (1 Timothy 4.12) not to "be an example of the believers," but to "set the believers an example."

Occasionally "of" is redundant, and may simply be dropped. Examples are: "Asahel would not turn aside from following of him" (2 Samuel 2.21); and "they thought that he had spoken of taking of rest in sleep" (John 11.13). "They left beating of Paul" (Acts 21.32) means "they stopped beating Paul." The redundant "of" is Shakespearian usage; for example, in *As You Like It* (IV, 3, 10) Silvius, delivering Phoebe's letter, says:

> "I know not the contents; but, as I guess
> By the stern brow and waspish action
> Which she did use as she was writing of it,
> It bears an angry tenour."

**OFFEND.** In addition to its usual meanings, the verb "offend" is used by the KJ New Testament in a peculiar sense, as translation for the Greek verb *skandalizō*. The noun *skandalon* meant a trap or snare, and the verb meant to place something in another's way which would cause him to stumble or fall or sin.

"If thy right eye offend thee, pluck it out. . . . And if thy right hand offend thee, cut it off" is translated in RSV: "If your right eye causes you to sin, pluck it out. . . . And if your right hand causes you to sin, cut it off" (Matthew 5.29, 30 and parallels in Matthew 18.8, 9 and Mark 9.43, 45, 47).

"Whoso shall offend one of these little ones which believe in me, it were better for him that a millstone were hanged about his neck, and *that* he were drowned in the depth of the sea" now begins "whoever causes one of these little ones who believe in me to sin . . ." (Matthew 18.6 and parallels in Mark 9.42 and Luke 17.2).

"It is impossible but that offences will come: but woe *unto him*, through whom they come!" now reads "Temptations to sin are sure to come; but woe to him by whom they come!" (Luke 17.1, with parallel in Matthew 18.7). In Matthew 13.41 "all things that offend" is now "all causes of sin."

Jesus' statement to his disciples as they went together to Gethsemane, "All ye shall be offended because of me this night" means, and is now translated, "You will all fall away because of me this night" (Matthew 26.31, 33 and Mark 14.27, 29). In John 16.1 "that ye should not be offended" means "to keep you from falling away."

Paul's declaration, "Wherefore, if meat make my brother to offend, I will eat no flesh while the world standeth, lest I make my brother to offend," is more accurately translated: "Therefore, if food is a cause of my brother's falling, I will never eat meat, lest I cause my brother to fall" (1 Corinthians 8.13). The climactic question in his spirited defense of himself in 2 Corinthians 11.29, "Who is offended, and I burn not?" means "Who is made to fall, and I am not indignant?"

**OFTEN** is used as an adjective in 1 Timothy 5.23, where a prescription has caused much controversy: "Drink no longer water, but use a little wine for thy stomach's sake and thine often infirmities." RSV: "No longer drink only water, but use a little wine for the sake of your stomach and your frequent ailments." Phillips has a chatty paraphrase: "By the way, I should advise you to drink wine in moderation instead of water. It will do your stomach good and help you get over your frequent spells of illness."

The use of "often" as an adjective was common in the sixteenth and seventeenth centuries. The KJ rendering of this verse comes from Tyndale and was used by all sixteenth-century English versions. *The Interpreter's Bible*, vol. 11, p. 445 has a sound discussion of its meaning.

**OLDNESS** appears in Romans 7.6, "But now we are delivered from the law, that being dead wherein we were held; that we should serve in newness of spirit, and not *in* the oldness of the letter." This is a misleading rendering, which could have been avoided if the translators had given sufficient weight to the prior versions of Tyndale and his successors. The Geneva Bible, for example, reads: "But now we are delivered from the Lawe, being dead unto that wherein we were in bondage, that we should serve in a newe conversation of the Spirit, and not in the olde conversation of the letter" (the reader must remember that the word "conversation" in the sixteenth century meant behavior or manner of life). KJ departed from this sound translation, which had appeared in all the versions based upon the Greek, from Tyndale to the Bishops' Bible, and followed in principle the translation of the Rheims New Testament, which was based upon the Latin Vulgate. It thereby acquired three defects: (1) it says that the law is dead, while Paul said that we are dead to the law; (2) it contrasts "newness of spirit" and "the oldness of the letter" as though "newness" were the principal good; (3) it thus fails to convey to the reader the fact that what is new is the Spirit, "the law of the Spirit of life in Christ Jesus" which Paul goes on to describe in the matchless prose of chapter 8.

RSV rejects these innovations of KJ, and returns to the Greek text and to the Tyndale-Geneva tradition. It reads: "But now we are discharged from the law, dead to that which held us captive, so that we serve not under the old written code but in the new life of the Spirit."

**OLD WIVES' FABLES** is an expression which appears once (1 Timothy 4.7): "refuse profane and old wives' fables." OED defines "old wives' fable, story, tale" as "a foolish story such as is told by garrulous old women." The expression goes back to Tyndale and beyond, has passed into literature, and is dear to those who love clichés. But it does not belong in the English Bible. It perpetuates an obsolete meaning of "wife" and an unrealistic view of age and of women. Moffatt translates the first half of this verse "Shut your mind against these profane, drivelling myths." Phillips has "Steer clear of all these stupid Godless fictions." RSV "Have nothing to do with godless and silly myths." (See FABLE, PROFANE, REFUSE)

**ONCE.** "Woe unto thee, O Jerusalem! wilt thou not be made clean? When *shall it* once *be?*" This is an outcry of Jeremiah (13.27). "Once" is here used in the sense of ever—"When shall it ever be?" The revised versions of 1885–1901 translate: "how long shall it yet be?" RSV compacts the clauses: "How long will it be before you are made clean?"

The Preface to the King James Version, entitled "The Translators to the Reader," in the first sentence of the second paragraph, used the word "once" in the sense of "ever": "in some Commonweales it was made a capital crime, once to motion the making of a new Law for the abrogating of an old, though the same were most pernicious."

**ONE AND OTHER.** ". . . they were afraid both one and other" (Jeremiah 36.16) is a faulty translation of the Hebrew which KJ accepted from the Geneva Bible. Other sixteenth-century translations, from Coverdale to the Bishops' Bible, had been worse: ". . . they were abashed one upon another." The Hebrew idiom is correctly understood by the revised versions of 1885–1901, which have "they turned in fear one toward another." RSV has "they turned one to another in fear," which might be expressed more naturally as "they turned to one another in fear."

**OPEN.** The verb "open" is used twice in the archaic sense of expound or explain (Luke 24.32; Acts 17.3). In the first of these contexts it is retained by RSV: "Did not our hearts burn within us while he talked to us on the road, while he opened to us the scriptures?" In the account of Paul's use of the Scriptures at Thessalonica, "opening and alleging, that Christ must needs have suffered and risen again from the dead," the Greek text is more accurately translated: "explaining and proving that it was necessary for the Christ to suffer and to rise from the dead." (See ALLEGE)

**ORDAIN** means in KJ to arrange, prepare, set up or establish something; to appoint a person to some duty or office; to make an authoritative decision; to decree that some practice or day be observed. OED describes 16 senses of the verb "ordain," of which 13 are obsolete or archaic. The three that remain living English are (*a*) when asserted of God, to appoint as part of the order of nature or history, to predestine or destine; (*b*) when asserted of human authority, to decree or enact what is to be observed or obeyed; (*c*) to appoint or admit to the ministry of the Church, to confer holy orders as priest or minister.

The verb "ordain" is used 41 times in KJ, and represents 10 different Hebrew verbs and 12 different Greek verbs. RSV retains it in 9 texts; in the other cases the word is used in an obsolete sense, such as appoint, designate, prepare, establish, institute, decide, command. The cases in which it is retained are: "a burnt offering, which was ordained at Mount Sinai" (Numbers 28.6); "ordained a feast" (1 Kings 12.33); "ordained to burn incense" (2 Kings 23.5); "ordained . . . that . . . they would keep . . . these days of Purim" (Esther 9.27–28); "O LORD, thou wilt ordain peace for us" (Isaiah 26.12); "thou hast ordained them as a judgment" (Habakkuk 1.12); "the one ordained by God" (Acts 10.42); "as many as were ordained to eternal life believed" (Acts 13.48); "ordained by angels" (Galatians 3.19).

An interesting case is Acts 1.21–22: "Wherefore of these men which have companied with us all the time that the Lord Jesus went in and out among us . . . must one be ordained to be a witness with us of his resurrection." Tyndale had used "ordeyned" in this passage, and was followed by the other sixteenth-century translations made from the Greek. Wyclif and Rheims, translations from the Latin Vulgate, had "be made a witness." But the Greek verb means "become," and the revised versions translate it literally. RSV has "one of these men must become with us a witness to his resurrection."

RSV uses "ordain" in 15 cases where KJ does not have it. Eight of these refer to the ordination of Aaron and his sons as priests (Exodus 28.41; 29.9, 29, 33, 35; 32.29; Leviticus 8.33; Numbers 3.3). Two refer to ordinances of worship (1 Chronicles 15.13; 2 Chronicles 2.4). Five are concerned with the sovereign will and overruling providence of God: "For the LORD had ordained to defeat the good counsel of Ahithophel" (2 Samuel 17.14); "it was ordained by God that the downfall of Ahaziah should come about through his going to visit Joram" (2 Chronicles 22.7); "my King and my God, who ordainest victories" (Psalm 44.4); "as he ordained long ago" (Lamentations 2.17);

> "Who has commanded and it came to pass,
> unless the Lord has ordained it?"
> (Lamentations 3.37)

**ORDER.** Manoah's question about the son promised by the angel of the LORD, "How shall we order the child?" is more accurately translated "What is to be the boy's manner of life?" (Judges 13.12). When Ahab asked the prophet "Who shall order the battle?" he wished to know whether to take the initiative and attack the enemy or to remain in positions of defense; the simple translation of the Hebrew is, "Who shall begin the battle?" (1 Kings 20.14). In Psalms 37.23; 119.133; Isaiah 9.7 "order" is used for the Hebrew verb which means "establish" and "direct."

"They cannot be reckoned up in order unto thee" (Psalm 40.5) is rejected by most modern translations in favor of "none can compare with thee!", *nichts ist dir zu vergleichen!* and the like. KJ itself translates the same Hebrew verb in Isaiah 40.18 "what likeness will ye compare unto him?"

Detailed instructions concerning the pattern of the tabernacle are recorded in Exodus 25–27, and most of these details are repeated in Exodus 36–38, which describe its making by Bezalel and Oholiab. Each "board" or "frame" for the walls of the tabernacle had two tenons, which are described by identical Hebrew clauses in 26.17 and 36.22. Yet KJ reads in 26.17 "Two tenons *shall there be* in one board, set in order one against another," and in 36.22 "One board had two tenons, equally distant one from another." The revised versions correct this inconsistency, and make the meaning clear. RSV reads: "There shall be two tenons in each frame, for fitting together" and "Each frame had two tenons, for fitting together."

**OR EVER** occurs three times in the sense of "before." "I was set up from everlasting, from the beginning, or ever the earth was" (Proverbs 8.23) is more literally translated in RSV: "Ages ago I was set up, at the first, before the beginning of the earth." The puzzling verse, Song of Solomon 6.12, "Or ever I was aware, my soul made me *like* the chariots of Amminadib," is rendered by RSV, with the help of an emendation, "Before I was aware, my fancy set me in a chariot beside my prince." When Daniel was taken up out of the den of lions and his accusers cast into it, with their wives and children, "the lions had the mastery of them, and brake all their bones in pieces or ever they came at the bottom of the den" (Daniel 6.24). RSV has "before they reached the bottom of the den the lions overpowered them and broke all their bones in pieces."

Tyndale had used "or ever" in John 4.49, "Syr come awaye or ever that my chylde dye," and this was kept by some of the subsequent versions. KJ changed to "Sir, come down ere my child die."

Shakespeare used "or ere" nine times in this sense, and used "or ever" in *Hamlet*, I, 2, 183:

> "Would I had met my dearest foe in heaven
> Or ever I had seen that day!"

**OUCHES** is the plural of an old word which was already becoming obsolete in 1611. Tyndale had used it in his translation of Exodus, published in 1530, with a note explaining its meaning: "ouches, ornaments fit to display jewels or precious stones." Tyndale applied the term to the gold settings of the two jewels on the shoulders of the high priest's ephod, and to the gold settings of the 12 jewels of his "brestlappe" (KJ "breastplate"; RSV "breastpiece").

These settings were not solid bars or capsules of gold. Instead of "ouches of gold," RSV has "settings of gold filigree" (Exodus 28.11, 13, 14, 25; 39.6, 13, 16, 18). Such filigree work had been done by Egyptian goldsmiths from early times. The method is described in Exodus 39.3. The Hebrew term appears also in Psalm 45.13, where KJ says of the king's daughter that "her clothing *is* of wrought gold," and RSV that she "is decked with gold-woven robes."

The word "ouche" was originally "nouche," but before Tyndale's time "a nouche" had become "an ouche," just as "a nadder" became "an adder" and "a napron" became "an apron." "Ouches" appears once in Shakespeare, where Falstaff rallies Doll Tearsheet about "Your brooches, pearls, and ouches" (*King Henry IV, Part II,* II, 4, 53).

**OUTGOINGS.** In the description of the allotment of the land of Canaan to the tribes of Israel, the plural of "outgoing" is used in the obsolete sense of extremity, utmost limit, end (Joshua 17–19). "The outgoings of it were at the sea" means "it ends at the sea" (17.9). "The outgoings of it shall be thine" means "you shall possess it to its farthest borders" (17.18).

In Psalm 65.8—"thou makest the outgoings of the morning and

evening to rejoice"—a different Hebrew word is used, which denotes the act or place of going forth, the source of a spring, the start of a journey.

**OUT OF COURSE.** An obsolete expression with much the same range of meaning that "out of order" now has. In Psalm 82.5 it is said that "all the foundations of the earth are out of course." This is a mistranslation of the Hebrew, which means "are shaken." The revised versions have "all the foundations of the earth are shaken."

**OUTLANDISH** is used once (Nehemiah 13.26) to represent the Hebrew word which KJ elsewhere translates by "alien," "foreigner," "strange," or "stranger." The passage refers to Solomon: "among many nations was there no king like him, who was beloved of his God, and God made him king over all Israel: nevertheless even him did outlandish women cause to sin." RSV has: ". . . nevertheless foreign women made even him to sin." For the same Hebrew phrase KJ has "strange women" in 1 Kings 11.1, and "strange wives" in 1 Kings 11.8 and Nehemiah 13.27. Coverdale had the word "outlandish" in all these passages, meaning by it "from a foreign land."

**OUTWENT** means "went faster than." In its one occurrence (Mark 6.33) "outwent" is a loose translation of the Greek. Wyclif had "camen bifor hem," Tyndale and subsequent translations "came thither before them," Rheims "prevented them." (See PREVENT.) RSV translates: "Now many saw them going, and knew them, and they ran there on foot from all the towns, and got there ahead of them." The Greek for "and came together unto him" does not appear in the best ancient manuscripts.

**OVER.** "We were comforted over you" (1 Thessalonians 3.7) does not seem to be as natural English as "he beheld the city, and wept over it" (Luke 19.41). The latter of these texts was new in KJ, for preceding versions from Wyclif to the Bishops' Bible had "wept on it." The Bishops' Bible was the first to use "comforted over you" in Thessalonians; earlier versions had "consolation in you." RSV has "we have been comforted about you."

Coverdale had "to comfort him over his father" (1 Chronicles 19.2). The Great Bible and the Bishops' Bible said "over the death of his father"; Geneva "for his father"; KJ "concerning his father," which has been retained by RSV.

**OVERCHARGE** occurs once in the sense of overburden, and once in the obsolete sense of accuse too strongly. Luke 21.34 reads: "Take heed to yourselves, lest at any time your hearts be overcharged with surfeiting, and drunkenness, and cares of this life, and *so* that day come upon you unawares." Here "overcharged" is too heavy for the Greek verb, "unawares" represents the Greek word for "suddenly," and the best manuscripts join the phrase for "like a snare" to this verse rather than to the next. RSV translates: "Take heed to yourselves lest your hearts be weighed down with dissipation and drunkenness and cares of this life, and that day come upon you suddenly like a snare."

In 2 Corinthians 2.5 KJ reads: "But if any have caused grief, he hath not grieved me, but in part: that I may not overcharge you all." Here mistaken punctuation, attaching "but in part" to "me," misled the sixteenth-century translators. RSV translates: "But if any one has caused pain, he has caused it not to me, but in some measure—not to put it too severely—to you all." This understanding of the verse is shared by modern translations generally, beginning with the revised versions of 1881–1901.

**OVERLIVE** means to live longer than or after the death of, to survive, to outlive. The same Hebrew words which mean "prolonged (their) days after Joshua" are translated "overlived Joshua" in Joshua 24.31, and "outlived Joshua" in Judges 2.7. This difference in rendering goes back to Tyndale. The revised versions have "outlived Joshua" in both passages. Shakespeare uses "outlive" in 18 passages and "overlive" just once, *King Henry IV, Part II*, IV, 1, 15.

**OVERPASS** is used once in the obsolete sense of go too far, go beyond limit or restriction, transgress. The passage is Jeremiah 5.28: "They are waxen fat, they shine: yea, they overpass the deeds of the wicked: they judge not the cause, the cause of the fatherless, yet they prosper; and the right of the needy do they not judge." The Hebrew of the second line of this verse means "they overflow with wicked things." RSV attaches the first line to the preceding verse, and translates 27c and 28 thus:

"therefore they have become great and rich,
    they have grown fat and sleek.

> They know no bounds in deeds of wickedness;
>> they judge not with justice
> the cause of the fatherless, to make it prosper,
>> and they do not defend the rights of the needy."

**OVERPAST, BE** is used twice in the sense of be ended, be past, be over and gone. "Until *these* calamities be overpast" (Psalm 57.1) is better translated "till the storms of destruction pass by." "Come, my people, enter thou into thy chambers, and shut thy doors about thee: hide thyself as it were for a little moment, until the indignation be overpast" (Isaiah 26.20) is more simply rendered by RSV:

> "Come, my people, enter your chambers,
>> and shut your doors behind you;
> hide yourselves for a little while
>> until the wrath is past."

**OVERRUN** in 2 Samuel 18.23 means to run faster than, to outrun. RSV reads "Then Ahimaaz ran by the way of the plain, and outran the Cushite." The only other occurrence of the word is in Nahum 1.8, where its participle means overflowing. RSV translates 1.7–8:

> "The LORD is good,
>> a stronghold in the day of trouble;
>> he knows those who take refuge in him.
> But with an overflowing flood
>> he will make a full end of his adversaries,
>> and will pursue his enemies into darkness."

The two versions agree in Genesis 49.22, "his branches run over the wall"; and in Luke 6.38, "good measure, pressed down, shaken together, running over." In Psalm 23.5, for "my cup runneth over," RSV has "my cup overflows." This change was made to preserve the rhythm of the poetic line, since RSV does not use "-eth" as an inflection denoting the third person of verbs.

**PADDLE** occurs once (Deuteronomy 23.13): "Thou shalt have a paddle upon thy weapon; and it shall be, when thou wilt ease thyself abroad, thou shalt dig therewith, and shalt turn back and cover that which cometh from thee." Tyndale's version was more intelligible: "thou shalt have a sharpe poynt at the ende of thy wepon." Geneva was the first to use "paddle"—"thou shalt have a paddle among thy weapons." In adopting the word, KJ further strained the reader's imagination by putting the paddle *upon* the weapon. The word "paddle" as used in the fifteenth and sixteenth centuries is thus defined by OED: "a small spade-like implement with a long handle, used for cleaning a ploughshare of earth or clods, digging up thistles, etc."

In this Deuteronomic code "paddle" is a bit of sixteenth-century modernization similar to the use of the word "candlestick" for a lampstand. The Hebrew word, *yathed,* means a tent peg or stake. KJ and RSV agree in translating it "stake" in Isaiah 33.20; 54.2, and "pin" in the story of Samson and Delilah (Judges 16.13–14). Elsewhere, KJ uses "nail" or "pin" and RSV uses "tent peg" or "peg." In this text from Deuteronomy, RSV translates "you shall have a stick with your weapons . . ."

**PAINED.** "There appeared a great wonder in heaven; a woman clothed with the sun, and the moon under her feet, and upon her head a crown of twelve stars: And she being with child cried, travailing in birth, and pained to be delivered" (Revelation 12.1–2). The word "pained" is ambiguous here, for it may be taken in the obsolete sense of took pains, endeavored, strove. But the Greek has here the passive participle of the verb which KJ usually translates as "torment." This woman was in anguish. RSV gives a faithful English translation of the terse Greek: "she was with child and she cried out in her pangs of birth, in anguish for delivery."

**PALMERWORM.** A palmer was one who had returned from a visit to the Holy Land as a crusader or pilgrim, in token of which he carried a leaf of palm. The term was also applied to itinerant monks who went from shrine to shrine, under a perpetual vow of poverty. In the sixteenth century "palmer" and "palmerworm" appear in English literature as names for a migratory caterpillar which swarms in great numbers, devouring vegetation. OED quotes from Edward Topsell's *The historie of serpents,* 1608: "There is another sort of these Caterpillars, who have no certain place of abode, nor yet cannot tell where to finde their food, but like unto superstitious Pilgrims, do wander and stray hither and thither, . . . these have purchased a very apt name among us Englishmen, to be called Palmer-worms, by reason of their wandering and roguish life, for they never stay in one place, but are ever wandering."

"Palmerworm" is used in Joel 1.4; 2.25; Amos 4.9 as rendering for the Hebrew *gazam*, which means a cutting, destructive locust. The theme of the book of Joel is an unparalleled plague of locusts, which the prophet takes as a judgment of God, and a warning of "the great and terrible day of the LORD."

There are nine Old Testament Hebrew words for locust, four of which appear in Joel 1.4. This reads in KJ: "That which the palmerworm hath left hath the locust eaten; and that which the locust hath left hath the cankerworm eaten; and that which the cankerworm hath left hath the caterpiller eaten." And in RSV:

"What the cutting locust left,
the swarming locust has eaten.
What the swarming locust left,
the hopping locust has eaten,
and what the hopping locust left,
the destroying locust has eaten."

The four names in this verse, in the judgment of modern scholars, probably denote four stages in the life and development of the locust. There is a brief but clear discussion in *The Interpreter's Bible*, vol. 6, p. 737. For a vivid description of the depredations of locusts in Bible lands see Hastings' *Dictionary of the Bible*, vol. III, pp. 130–131.

**PALSY** is a contraction of the older English "paralysie," derived from the French. In the sixteenth century "paralysie" was passing out of use, and "paralysis" was coming in, while "palsy" was the common term. RSV uses "paralytic" and "paralyzed" (Matthew 4.24; 8.6; 9.2, 6; Mark 2.3–10; Luke 5.18, 24; Acts 8.7; 9.33). These references justify the surmise that there may have been polio epidemics in Palestine in New Testament times.

In modern English, "palsy" carries a connotation of muscular tremor which is not necessarily implied by "paralysis"; and it is often used figuratively. In Ezekiel 7.27, "the hands of the people of the land shall be troubled" falls far short of the meaning of the Hebrew. RSV translates: "The king mourns, the prince is wrapped in despair, and the hands of the people of the land are palsied by terror."

**PAPS.** An old word for breasts or nipples. It was used by Tyndale in three passages of the New Testament (Luke 11.27; 23.29; Revelation 1.13), where it was retained by KJ. The revised versions use "breasts." The KJ rendering of Ezekiel 23.21 reflects a probable error in the transmission of the Hebrew text, which RSV clears by an emendation.

**PART,** as a transitive verb, is used by KJ nine times in the archaic
sense of divide among a number of recipients, distribute. The
outstanding example is the scene at the crucifixion of Jesus: "And
when they had crucified him, they parted his garments, casting lots
upon them, what every man should take" (Mark 15.24). RSV translates: "And they crucified him, and divided his garments among them,
casting lots for them, to decide what each should take." Similarly, RSV
has "divide my garments" (Psalm 22.18), "divide him up" (Job 41.6),
"have divided up my land" (Joel 3.2). The practice of the early believers (Acts 2.45) is thus stated by RSV: "And all who believed were
together and had all things in common; and they sold their possessions
and goods and distributed them to all, as any had need."

As an intransitive verb, "part" is used once in the obsolete sense of
participate in a division into shares. The passage is 1 Samuel 30.24,
where "part" is used twice as a noun and in the final clause as a verb.
KJ reads: "But as his part *is* that goeth down to the battle, so *shall*
his part *be* that tarrieth by the stuff: they shall part alike." RSV
reads: "For as his share is who goes down into the battle, so shall his
share be who stays by the baggage; they shall share alike."

**PARTAKER** means one who takes a part or share, hence a partner
or participator. The word is used 30 times in the KJ
New Testament, and presents no real difficulty, though RSV retains it in
only 8 of these cases. The one occurrence in the Old Testament, Psalm
50.18, is ambiguous: "When thou sawest a thief, then thou consentedst
with him, and hast been partaker with adulterers." A literal translation of the Hebrew of the last clause is "and with adulterers is your
portion," that is, your chosen, habitual companionship and way of life.
RSV translates: "If you see a thief, you are a friend of his; and you
keep company with adulterers." An example of Shakespeare's use of
the term is *King Henry VI, Part I,* II, 4, 100:

> "For your partaker Pole and you yourself,
> I'll note you in my book of memory,
> To scourge you for this apprehension."

**PARTICULAR.** The phrase "in particular" appears twice in the sense
of individually, each, one by one. For "ye are the body
of Christ, and members in particular" (1 Corinthians 12.27), RSV has
"you are the body of Christ and individually members of it." For "let
every one of you in particular so love his wife even as himself"
(Ephesians 5.33), it has "let each one of you love his wife as himself."

The adverb "particularly" has this same older, almost obsolete sense in its two occurrences. Paul's report to James and the elders at Jerusalem is described in Acts 21.19 RSV: "After greeting them, he related one by one the things that God had done among the Gentiles through his ministry." In Hebrews 9.5, "of which we cannot now speak particularly" is reworded "Of these things we cannot now speak in detail."

**PASSAGE** means the act of passing only in Numbers 20.21—"Edom refused to give Israel passage through his territory." Elsewhere it means a place of passage. It denotes "the pass of Michmash," the scene of the exploit of Jonathan and his armor-bearer (1 Samuel 13.23; 14.4), and three centuries later a stage in the advance of an invading army from the north (Isaiah 10.29). It denotes "the fords of the Jordan" where the men of Gilead put the Ephraimites to the test of pronouncing "Shibboleth" (Judges 12.5, 6), and the fords, far to the eastward, seized by the enemies of Babylon (Jeremiah 51.32). In Jeremiah 22.20 the Hebrew word represented by "passages" is a proper name, "Abarim." Professor James Hyatt, in *The Interpreter's Bible,* vol. 5, p. 984 says, "The prophet imaginatively summons Jerusalem to wail over her own fate on three high mountains: Lebanon in Syria, to the north; Bashan in upper Trans-Jordan, to the northeast; and Abarim in Moab, to the southeast (where Moses died, identical with or including Mount Nebo)."

**PASSENGER** is used in the old sense of a passer-by, a traveler or wayfarer. The word is not used in KJ for one who is carried by a vehicle or vessel. The foolish woman who sits at the door of her house "to call passengers" is "calling to those who pass by" (Proverbs 9.15). In the Gog and Magog oracles (Ezekiel 38–39), "the valley of the passengers" is "the valley of the travelers" or "the valley of Abarim," and "it shall stop the *noses* of the passengers" is "it will block the travelers" (39.11). See *The Interpreter's Bible,* vol. 6, pp. 272–282. (See PASSAGE)

**PASTOR** appears once in the New Testament, Ephesians 4.11, where it means a shepherd of souls, a Christian minister. Tyndale and Coverdale used "shepherd" at this point; the Geneva Bible was the first to use "pastor," which all subsequent versions have retained. In the Old Testament "pastor" appears 8 times, all in Jeremiah, as a translation of the Hebrew word which elsewhere is translated "shepherd" 62 times and "herdman" 7 times. These 8 passages are Jeremiah 2.8; 3.15; 10.21; 12.10; 17.16; 22.22; 23.1, 2, all of which refer to those who care or should care, for the people. Here, again, the Geneva Bible took the initiative. But the word "shepherd" appears in 12 other passages of Jeremiah, and in 10 of these the shepherds care for people rather than for animals. The revised versions reject the attempt to select 8 groups of men who should be called "pastors," and use the word "shepherd."

The KJ translation of Jeremiah 17.16, "I have not hastened from *being* a pastor to follow thee," is rejected by most modern scholars. RSV reads "I have not pressed thee to send evil." The issue is whether the Hebrew has here the participle of the verb *ra'ah,* to shepherd, or the noun *ra'ah,* evil. Both readings are possible; the latter is more natural, and fits the context better. See *The Interpreter's Bible,* vol. 5, pp. 952, 957–958 on Jeremiah 17.9–10, 14–18; and *A Catholic Commentary on Holy Scripture* (Thomas Nelson & Sons, 1953), Section 458 f.

**PATIENCE.** The Greek New Testament has two words for patient endurance. KJ usually translates *makrothumia* by "long-suffering" and *hupomonē* by "patience." RSV replaces "longsuffering" by "patience" or "forbearance." (See LONGSUFFERING.) And in most cases it translates *hupomonē* by "endurance," "patient endurance," "perseverance," or "steadfastness."

"In your patience possess ye your souls" (Luke 21.19) seems to be a counsel of resignation; but it is an exhortation and a promise, "By your endurance you will gain your lives" (RSV). "Tribulation worketh patience" (Romans 5.3) means "suffering produces endurance." "The patience of the saints" (Revelation 13.10; 14.12) means "the endurance of the saints"; in the letters to the seven churches "patience" means "patient endurance" (Revelation 1.9; 2.2, 3, 19; 3.10).

"Ye have need of patience, that, after ye have done the will of God, ye might receive the promise" (Hebrews 10.36), seems to imply that patience is needed because of delay on the part of God. But that is not what the text means. RSV translates: "you have need of endurance, so that you may do the will of God and receive what is promised." "Let us run with patience the race that is set before us" (Hebrews 12.1) means "let us run with perseverance the race that is set before us."

James 5.11 reads in KJ: "Behold, we count them happy which endure. Ye have heard of the patience of Job, and have seen the end of the Lord; that the Lord is very pitiful, and of tender mercy." This rendering fails to indicate that the verb for "endure" and the noun for "patience" (*hupomenō* and *hupomonē*) have the same meaning. And two of its English words, "end" and "pitiful," are ambiguous. RSV translates: "Behold, we call those happy who were steadfast. You have heard of the steadfastness of Job, and you have seen the purpose of the Lord, how the Lord is compassionate and merciful."

William Barclay, in *A New Testament Wordbook,* has admirable chapters on *"Makrothumia,* the divine patience" and *"Hupomonē,* the manly virtue."

**PATTERN** means that which is to be copied. In the sixteenth and seventeenth centuries the word was also used for a copy. This obsolete sense appears twice in KJ. In Joshua 22 the men of the tribes of Reuben, Gad, and Manasseh protest that the altar which they had built by the Jordan was not for burnt offering or sacrifice, but was simply a copy of the altar of the LORD, to serve as a reminder and a witness. Verse 28 puts it, "Behold the pattern of the altar of the LORD, which our fathers made, not for burnt offerings, nor for sacrifices; but it *is* a witness between us and you." RSV has, "Behold the copy of the altar of the LORD, which our fathers made, not for burnt offerings, nor for sacrifice, but to be a witness between us and you."

In Hebrews 9.23 "the patterns of things in the heavens" means "the copies of the heavenly things." The verse reads in RSV: "Thus it was necessary for the copies of the heavenly things to be purified with these rites, but the heavenly things themselves with better sacrifices than these." In Hebrews 8.5 the same Greek word is rendered by "example"—"Who serve unto the example and shadow of heavenly things." This reads in RSV "They serve a copy and shadow of the heavenly sanctuary." (See EXAMPLE)

**PECULIAR.** It seems strange to the reader of today that the Bible calls God's chosen people "a peculiar people" (Deuteronomy 14.2). And it is no less strange that the same designation is applied by Paul and by Peter to those who are redeemed by our Savior Jesus Christ (Titus 2.14; 1 Peter 2.9). The word "peculiar" is so commonly used in the sense of odd or eccentric that it seems to be inappropriate in these contexts.

But in 1611 the word had not yet gotten that meaning. It meant "one's very own," and was applied to private personal property as distinguished from what is owned in common.

The same Hebrew word which is translated "peculiar" in Deuteron-

omy 14.2 and 26.18 is translated "special" in Deuteronomy 7.6, which
reads: "For thou *art* an holy people unto the LORD thy God: the LORD
thy God hath chosen thee to be a special people unto himself, above
all people that *are* upon the face of the earth." The word is *segullah*.
KJ elsewhere translates it as "peculiar treasure" (Exodus 19.5;
Psalm 135.4; Ecclesiastes 2.8), "own proper good" (1 Chronicles
29.3), and "jewels" (Malachi 3.17).

The revised versions have given up the use of the word "peculiar" in
these passages. They use "treasure" in 1 Chronicles and Ecclesiastes;
but elsewhere use "my (*or* his *or* God's) own possession" as the translation of *segullah*. The phrase "a peculiar people" has disappeared.
In Titus 2.13–14 RSV reads: "awaiting our blessed hope, the appearing of the glory of our great God and Savior Jesus Christ, who gave
himself for us to redeem us from all iniquity and to purify for himself
a people of his own who are zealous for good deeds." In 1 Peter 2.9
it reads: "You are a chosen race, a royal priesthood, a holy nation,
God's own people, that you may declare the wonderful deeds of him
who called you out of darkness into his marvelous light."

**PEELED** is used as passive participle for the Hebrew verb which
means to make smooth, bare, or bald; to scour, polish. In
Ezekiel 29.18 it is an understandable rendering: "every shoulder *was*
peeled." RSV translates more literally: "every shoulder was rubbed
bare." The same Hebrew participle is applied to a sword in Ezekiel
21.9, 10, 11, 28, where KJ translates it "furbished" and RSV "polished."
It is also used for the temple utensils, which KJ says were of "bright
brass," and RSV of "burnished bronze" (1 Kings 7.45).

In Isaiah 18.2, 7 "scattered and peeled," according to OED, "is a
doubtful translation; but the expression has become a literary common-
place, *peeled* being vaguely associated with one or more of the senses
above."

In these verses, KJ refers to Ethiopia as "a nation scattered and
peeled, a people terrible from their beginning hitherto; a nation meted
out and trodden down, whose land the rivers have spoiled!" The revised versions, and modern translations generally, quite reverse this
picture. RSV reads:

> "Go, you swift messengers,
>> to a nation, tall and smooth,
> to a people feared near and far,
>> a nation mighty and conquering,
>> whose land the rivers divide."

Chapter 18 of the book of Isaiah is not, like chapters 13–17 and 19–

23, a prophecy of doom. It is a word of reassurance to the Ethiopians, who had sent ambassadors to the king of Judah to induce him to combine with them in a league against the Assyrians. "Isaiah sends them back," says Driver (*Introduction to the Literature of the Old Testament,* p. 215) "with the assurance that their anxiety is needless: the plans of the Assyrians will be intercepted, and their host overthrown, independently of the arms of Ethiopia. Hereupon the Ethiopians will do homage to the God of Israel."

The older translators misconceived the situation. They began the chapter with "Woe" without remembering that the Hebrew interjection is sometimes quite as properly translated "Ho," as KJ does in Isaiah 55.1. And then they continued with doleful epithets on to the final "have spoiled" instead of "divide." "Tall and smooth" is the translation which the revised versions substitute for "scattered and peeled." "Smooth" is here used in the sense of rubbed or burnished with oil. W. R. Harper translated the phrase, "tall and of polished skin"; Smith "Tall and sleek."

**PEEP.** In the passage about "wizards that peep, and that mutter" (Isaiah 8.19) the revised versions use "chirp" rather than "peep." This is to remove ambiguity, since "peep" may refer to sly or prying glances. In Isaiah 10.14 likewise the revised versions use "chirped." For the same Hebrew word KJ uses "whisper" in Isaiah 29.4, and is followed by the revised versions; RSV has

"your voice shall come from the ground like the voice of a ghost,
    and your speech shall whisper out of the dust."

**PERADVENTURE** is a word that pleases purists because it is all Latin in origin, whereas "perhaps" couples Latin "per" with Anglo-Saxon "hap." "Peradventure," "percase," "perchance" are words that came into English through the Norman Conquest; "perhaps" appeared later, but has outlived all three. Shakespeare was fond of "perchance," which he used 45 times to 16 times for "peradventure" and 27 times for "perhaps." KJ does not use "perchance" and has "perhaps" only 3 times, but uses "peradventure" 32 times. The references can be located by the list in Strong's *Concordance,* to which must be added Genesis 24.5; 24.39; 27.12, occurrences which he missed.

"Peradventure" as an adverb is obsolete in the sense of by chance; it is archaic in the sense of perhaps. As a noun it survives in phrases like "beyond all peradventure." RSV does not use "peradventure," and usually replaces it with "perhaps." It uses "suppose" in Abraham's pleading with the LORD for Sodom (Genesis 18.22–33) and "it may be that" (50.15), "I thought that" (31.31), "he feared that" (38.11; 42.4), "I fear to see" (44.34), in other passages in Genesis.

**PERSECUTE** meant originally to pursue, but is now obsolete in this sense. Largely from the use of "persecute," "persecution," and "persecutor" to describe actions and persons in bitter religious strife, a connotation of malignancy taints the words. They are not appropriate to the just pursuit of a felon, but to the persistent and malicious harassment of people of honest conviction.

In the Old Testament the word "persecute" is used in the older sense, and the revised versions replace it with "pursue" in contexts such as: "save me from all my pursuers" (Psalm 7.1), "let the enemy pursue me and overtake me" (Psalm 7.5), "Draw the spear and javelin against my pursuers" (Psalm 35.3), "with the angel of the LORD pursuing them" (Psalm 35.6), "pursue and seize him" (Psalm 71.11), "pursue them with thy tempest" (Psalm 83.15), "I will pursue them with sword, famine, and pestilence" (Jeremiah 29.18), "Thou wilt pursue them in anger and destroy them from under thy heavens, O LORD" (Lamentations 3.66).

"Persecute" and "persecutors" in Psalms 10.2 and 7.13 represent a Hebrew verb which means "burn" or "hotly pursue" (compare Genesis 31.36). RSV reads in 10.2 "the wicked hotly pursue the poor." It translates 7.12–13:

> "If a man does not repent, God will whet his sword;
> he has bent and strung his bow;
> he has prepared his deadly weapons,
> making his arrows fiery shafts."

In the New Testament "persecute," "persecution," and "persecutor" are used in the sense which these words now have. There are two exceptions: in 1 Thessalonians 2.15 the revised versions have "drove us out," and in Revelation 12.13 RSV has "pursued."

**PERSON.** It is confusing for young people today, who are being told that respect for persons is a basic principle of sound democracy and true religion, to read in the Bible that "God is no respecter of persons" (Acts 10.34) and to find that same idea repeated in one form or another in a dozen passages of the Old and New Testaments. The Greek word which is translated "respecter of persons" means "acceptor of the face," and the Latin equivalent is *acceptor personae*, that is, acceptor of the mask that an actor wore or the character that he assumed.

When KJ was published, the English word "person" was still close to this primary meaning of the Latin word *persona,* mask. It referred to the outward appearance or circumstances of men—to physical presence, dress, wealth, position—rather than to intrinsic worth or to the inner springs of conscious, self-determining being. This text and others using similar words mean that God does not regard mere externals.

In Moses' instructions to the men whom he appointed as judges, the meaning of the expression "respect persons" is stated clearly: "Ye shall not respect persons in judgment; *but* ye shall hear the small as well as the great; ye shall not be afraid of the face of man; for the judgment *is* God's" (Deuteronomy 1.17). A pointed exposition of the meaning of the phrase for the life of the early Christians is found in James 2.1–9.

The expressions "respect persons" and "respecter of persons" were kept in the revised versions of 1881–1901, but are given up in all other modern translations. Moffatt's translation is "God has no favorites"; and Goodspeed's "God shows no partiality." RSV follows Goodspeed here, and both are in fact returning to William Tyndale, whose translation was "God is not partial."

**PERSUADE** now implies success; we speak of persuading a man only if our arguments and pleas prevail upon him to accept the judgment or make the decision to which we urge him. Yet in Acts 19.8–9 we read of Paul's "disputing and persuading" at Corinth, with the result that some "were hardened, and believed not, but spake evil of that way." In Acts 28.23 we are told that at Rome "there came many to him into *his* lodging; to whom he expounded and testified the kingdom of God, persuading them concerning Jesus, both out of the law of Moses, and *out of* the prophets, from morning till evening"; but the next verse records that some believed and some did not. RSV uses the terms "arguing and pleading" in the account of his work at Corinth, and it uses "trying to convince them" in the account of the day at Rome.

In *The Merchant of Venice* (III, 2, 281) Salerio describes the unyielding temper of Shylock:

> "twenty merchants,
> The Duke himself, and the magnificoes
> Of greatest port, have all persuaded with him;
> But none can drive him from the envious plea."

On the other hand, "persuade" is used in its full sense in such passages as Matthew 27.20; Acts 14.19; 19.26. And "I am persuaded" is hardly strong enough in most contexts where the passive form of the Greek verb appears. Romans 8.38–39 reads in RSV: "For I am sure that neither death, nor life . . . nor anything else in all creation, will be able to separate us from the love of God in Christ Jesus our Lord." Note also "be convinced" (Luke 16.31); "are convinced" (Luke 20.6); "fully convinced" (Romans 4.21; 14.5); "I am sure" (2 Timothy 1.5, 12); "we feel sure" (Hebrews 6.9).

In the Old Testament, the word "persuade" usually has a bad sense, being used as the equivalent of entice, mislead, or deceive. Compare 1 Kings 22.20, 21, 22 where KJ uses "persuade" for the same Hebrew verb which it translates "entice" in 2 Chronicles 18.19, 20, 21. Or compare the accounts concerning Hezekiah found in 2 Kings 18 and 19, 2 Chronicles 32, and Isaiah 36 and 37.

**PILL,** as verb, means to peel, strip off the skin, rind, or bark. "And Jacob took him rods of green poplar, and of the hazel and chesnut tree; and pilled white strakes in them . . . And he set the rods which he had pilled before the flocks in the gutters in the watering troughs when the flocks came to drink" (Genesis 30.37, 38). "Pilled" was the word used in these verses by Tyndale, Coverdale, and the other sixteenth-century versions made from the Hebrew. It was the word used by Shylock in Shakespeare's *Merchant of Venice*, I, 3, 85, when he recounted the story of Jacob:

"The skilful shepheard pil'd me certaine wands,

And . . . stucke them up before the fulsome Ewes."

Later editions of Shakespeare's play, and the revised versions of the Bible, have changed the word to "peeled."

The King James Version used "pilled" also in one of the books of the Apocrypha, Tobit 11.13. When Tobias, returning from his journey, anointed his blinded father's eyes with gall, "he rubbed them, and the whiteness pilled away from the corners of his eyes." RSV translates: "he rubbed them, and the white films scaled off from the corners of his eyes."

Tyndale used the verb "pill" in quite another sense, meaning to rob, plunder, pillage, extort from. He translated Paul's question in 2 Corinthians 12.17, "Did I pill you by any of them which I sent unto you?" And in the following verse the question is repeated with reference to Titus: "Did Titus defraud you of anything?" In the Greek the same verb is used in each of these questions. Tyndale was followed here by the subsequent sixteenth-century versions made from the Greek. KJ changed to "make a gain of you" in both verses; the revised versions have "take advantage of you."

In 1 Corinthians 6.10 Tyndale includes "pillers" in the list of the unrighteous who shall not inherit the kingdom of God; but just a few verses earlier, in 5.10, 11, he translated the same Greek word "extortioners." Here again, the Great Bible and the Bishops' Bible followed Tyndale. KJ had "extortioners" in all three verses; RSV has "robbers."

**PILLOW** may be applied to whatever is used to support the head in sleeping or reclining. The word is appropriate, therefore, in three of the four KJ passages in which it appears. Jacob used a stone for a pillow (Genesis 28.11, 18), and Jesus a boat cushion (Mark 4.38). Michal furthered her deception by using David's customary pillow of goats' hair (1 Samuel 19.13, 16). One fact that is clear with respect to the obscure passage concerning women who prophesy lies as they hunt souls (Ezekiel 13.17–23) is that "sew pillows to all armholes" is an erroneous rendering of the Hebrew. RSV translates it "sew magic bands upon all wrists." (See ARMHOLE, KERCHIEF)

**PLAIN.** "Esau was a cunning hunter, a man of the field; and Jacob *was* a plain man, dwelling in tents" (Genesis 25.27) may easily be misunderstood by the reader of today. The first clause means "Esau was a skilful hunter, a man of the open country." "Dwelling in tents" implies that Jacob stayed home and attended to his cattle. But in what sense was he a "plain" man?

The Hebrew adjective is *tam,* which means complete, perfect. It is the adjective applied to Job, when the LORD calls him "a perfect and an upright man" (Job 1.8; 2.3). It is the adjective used in Psalm 37.37— "Mark the perfect *man,* and behold the upright." RSV reads "blameless" instead of "perfect" in these verses.

The Great Bible and the Bishops' Bible did not hesitate to call Jacob "a perfect man," in this contrast with Esau. Martin Luther's translation was *ein frommer Mann,* which means pious but may also mean gentle, quiet, steady. The Greek Septuagint had *aplastos,* natural, unaffected; and the Latin Vulgate, *simplex,* simple, plain. Coverdale used "simple"; the Geneva Bible took "plain," and KJ followed it.

It seems clear that Genesis 25.27 is to be taken as a quite objective statement. The writer is not here concerned with the moral character of either of the twins; he is not apportioning praise or blame. He is simply stating the basic difference between their respective interests and ways of life. In contrast with Esau's special craving and skill, Jacob was an *'ish tam,* a complete man, in the sense that he took seriously life's ordinary duties. The RSV translators, after considerable debate, settled on "quiet" as the English word which best conveys the meaning in this context—"Esau was a skilful hunter, a man of the field, while Jacob was a quiet man, dwelling in tents."

**PLEAD** in KJ does not mean to pray, supplicate, beg, or implore. It always has the sense of seeking a judgment, and means to argue for or against a cause, to urge the claim or state the case of a person. This KJ usage survives in legal terminology. "If ye plead against me my reproach" means "If you make my humiliation an argument against me" (Job 19.5). *"There is* none to plead thy cause" means "There is none to uphold your cause" (Jeremiah 30.13). "Plead for a man with God" (Job 16.21) is "maintain the right of a man with God"—the verb here is the one which is translated "reason" in Job 13.3, "I desire to reason with God," and in Isaiah 1.18, "Come now, and let us reason together."

The word "plead" does not appear in the New Testament. It is retained by the RSV Old Testament in no more than one fourth of its occurrences in KJ. The four Hebrew verbs which "plead" represents in KJ have as their basic meanings contend, prove, judge, govern; and each may imply action as well as words. In Judges 6.31–32, Joash answers the men who sought to punish his son Gideon: "Will you contend for Baal? . . . If he is a god, let him contend for himself." Proverbs 31.9 reads, "maintain the rights of the poor and needy." Isaiah 66.16 has "execute judgment"; Jeremiah 2.35, "bring to judgment"; Jeremiah 25.31 and Ezekiel 17.20; 20.35, 36; 38.22, "enter into judgment."

**POINT OUT** appears in Numbers 34.7, 8, 10, in the description of the boundaries of the land of Canaan which the LORD is granting to Israel. The whole of Numbers 34.1–12 should be read in RSV, to get a clearer impression than the archaic language of KJ can convey. The Hebrew verbs which are translated by "point out" in these three verses mean "mark out." RSV reads in 7b–8a: "from the Great Sea you shall mark out your line to Mount Hor; from Mount Hor you shall mark it out to the entrance of Hamath."

**POLL.** The basic meaning of the noun "poll," and its only meaning in the Bible, is the human head. A poll tax is a head tax, and to take a poll is to count heads. The book of Numbers records the census of the people of Israel which was taken by Moses at the command of the LORD, "every male by their polls" (1.2). RSV has "every male, head by head"; so also in verses 18, 20, 22. In 3.47 "five shekels apiece by the poll" is adequately expressed in English by "five shekels apiece." David made a census of the Levites who were thirty years old and upward, and "their number by their polls, man by man, was thirty and eight thousand" (1 Chronicles 23.3). RSV translates the verse, "The Levites, thirty years old and upward, were numbered, and the total was thirty-eight thousand men." In verse 24 "number of names by their polls" is worded by RSV "number of the names of the individuals"— the entire verse should be compared in the two versions.

As a verb "poll" means to cut off the hair of the head. The classic passage is 2 Samuel 14.26, concerning Absalom: "when he polled his head, (for it was at every year's end that he polled *it:* because *the hair* was heavy on him, therefore he polled it)." RSV reads: "when he cut the hair of his head (for at the end of every year he used to cut it; when it was heavy on him, he cut it)." In Micah 1.16 "poll the" means "cut off your hair"; but in Ezekiel 44.20 "they shall only poll their heads" means "they shall only trim the hair of their heads." The Hebrew verb in Ezekiel cannot mean "shave," as the verbs in 2 Samuel and Micah may. It is repeated, moreover, in accordance with the Hebrew idiom of emphasis, which in this case is best expressed by "only." (See GENERALLY, SURELY)

**POMMEL.** In 2 Chronicles 4.12–13 "the two pommels of the chapiters which *were* on the top of the pillars" represents the same Hebrew text which in 1 Kings 7.41–42 is translated "the two bowls of the chapiters which *were* upon the top of the pillars." The word "pommel" was used for a spherical or bowl-like ornament at the top of a pillar. The revised versions have made the translation consistent by using "the two bowls" in both passages. The Hebrew word *gullah* is translated "bowl" in Ecclesiastes 12.6 and Zechariah 4.3 also.

**PORT** appears once in KJ, where Nehemiah is said to have gone to the "dung port" in his inspection by night of the walls of Jerusalem (Nehemiah 2.13). But in three other cases this is called the "dung gate" (3.13, 14; 12.31). The Hebrew word *sha'ar* means "gate," and is so translated by KJ in 361 out of 370 occurrences. The revised versions have corrected the few inconsistencies.

**PORTER.** The Hebrew word *sho'er* means "gatekeeper," but is almost always represented by "porter" in KJ. RSV does not use the word "porter" because of its ambiguity; and substitutes "gatekeeper," except in two cases (Ezra 7.24; Mark 13.34) where the contexts make "doorkeeper" appropriate. In 1 Chronicles 16.42, at the end of the list of those appointed to carry on the services of sacrifice and thanksgiving "before the tabernacle . . . in the high place that *was* at Gibeon," the sons of Jeduthun are "to be at the gate" (revised versions of 1881–1901) or "appointed to the gate" (RSV). OED lists this verse in Wyclif's version as the first usage of "porter" in the sense of a luggage porter. But that only shows that even the editors of that great work could sometimes be led astray by ambiguity. The duties of the men at the gate, in this context, were those of gatekeepers.

**PORTION** is used in the Bible, not only in the sense of a part, share, or allowance of something, but in the sense of one's lot or destiny or rightful heritage. Job and his friends speak of "the wicked man's portion from God, the heritage decreed for him by God" (20.29; 27.13); and Job speaks of "my portion from God above, and my heritage from the Almighty on high" (31.2). Moses declares that "the LORD's portion is his people, Jacob his allotted heritage" (Deuteronomy 32.9). The psalmist sings, "The LORD is my portion" (119.57); "God is the strength of my heart and my portion for ever" (73.26).

In Jeremiah 10.16 (=51.19) God is referred to as "the portion of Jacob." These identical texts read in KJ: "The portion of Jacob *is* not like them: for he *is* the former of all *things;* and Israel *is* the rod of his inheritance: The LORD of hosts *is* his name." The first half of this verse can be misunderstood, even by careful readers, to mean that Jacob rather than God is the former of all things. The ambiguity is cleared up by the translation in RSV:

> "Not like these is he who is the portion of Jacob,
>     for he is the one who formed all things,
> and Israel is the tribe of his inheritance;
>     the LORD of hosts is his name."

**POSSESS** is used 54 times in the book of Deuteronomy, and nearly 100 times more in the rest of the Bible. In almost all these cases it has the sense of seize, acquire, gain, or take possession of. Deuteronomy 1.8 sets the key for that book: "go in and possess the land."

Shakespeare used the word in this sense. In *King Henry VI, Part III* (I, 1, 26), the Earl of Warwick encourages the ambition of Richard Plantagenet, Duke of York, to gain Henry's throne:

> "Possess it, York;
> For this is thine, and not King Henry's heirs'."

In *The Tempest* (III, 2, 100), Caliban tells Stephano how to oust Prospero from control of the island:

> "Remember
> First to possess his books; for without them
> He's but a sot, as I am, nor hath not
> One spirit to command."

The Greek verb which KJ translates by "purchased" in Acts 1.18 and 8.20, and by "obtained" in Acts 22.28, is rendered as "possess" in three other New Testament passages, with the result that the English reader is not aware of their true meaning. "In your patience possess ye your souls" (Luke 21.19) is correctly translated "By your endurance you will gain your lives." The Pharisee's statement, "I give tithes of all that I possess" (Luke 18.12), is properly "I give tithes of all that I get"—that is, the tithe is based upon income rather than upon capital. Paul's counsel to the Thessalonians that each should "know how to possess his vessel" (1 Thessalonians 4.4) means "know how to take a wife."

The last of these passages has been so much misunderstood that it will be well to quote it more fully: "This is the will of God, your sanctification: that you abstain from immorality; that each one of you know how to take a wife for himself in holiness and honor, not in the passion of lust like heathen who do not know God." (See VESSEL)

**POST** is used eight times as translation of the Hebrew participle which means running or a runner. RSV uses "couriers" in 2 Chronicles 30.6, 10 and Esther 3.13, 15; 8.10, 14, where the context indicates that these were royal messengers; and expressly states in the last instance that they were "mounted on swift horses that were used in the king's service." In place of "my days are swifter than a post" (Job 9.25), RSV has "My days are swifter than a runner." So also in Jeremiah 51.31, "One runner runs to meet another." The word survives in "posthaste," which means with all possible speed.

> "came there a reeking post,
> Stew'd in his haste, half breathless."
> *King Lear*, II, 4, 30
> "Our posts shall be swift and intelligent betwixt us."
> *King Lear*, III, 7, 11

**POWER** is used in the archaic sense of "army" in 2 Chronicles 32.9— "Sennacherib . . . *laid siege* against Lachish, and all his power with him." RSV has "Sennacherib . . . was besieging Lachish with all his forces." Shakespeare used the word in this sense frequently. For example *King Lear* has "Are my brother's powers set forth?" (IV, 5, 1); "draw up your powers" (V, 1, 51); "He led our powers" (V, 3, 63).

Another strange use of the word "power" is in Genesis 32.28—"Thy name shall be called no more Jacob, but Israel: for as a prince hast thou power with God and with men, and hast prevailed." No less a scholar than William Aldis Wright said that the phrase "to have power with" here signifies "to have influence over." But that is not what the Hebrew means, and the revised versions have gotten rid of the misleading "prince" and "power." RSV translates, "Your name shall no more be called Jacob, but Israel, for you have striven with God and with men, and have prevailed."

**PRANSING** is a survival of 1611 spelling in the present editions of KJ which cannot be located in the dictionaries except under "prance." It is the wrong word in the Song of Deborah (Judges 5.22) and in Nahum's prophecy of the downfall of Nineveh (Nahum 3.2). A prancing horse puts on a show at parade, but would be of no use in a cavalry charge. The Hebrew verb in these two passages means rush, dash, gallop. The KJ rendering of the first passage is mistaken at several points: "Then were the horsehoofs broken by the means of the pransings, the pransings of their mighty ones." RSV translates:
> "Then loud beat the horses' hoofs
> with the galloping, galloping of his steeds."

Again, the vivid, staccato Hebrew of Nahum's picture of battle is poorly represented by "The noise of a whip, and the noise of the rattling of the wheels, and of the pransing horses, and of the jumping chariots." RSV has:
> "The crack of whip, and rumble of wheel,
> galloping horse and bounding chariot!"

**PREFER** now generally denotes an attitude of mind. We prefer something when we like it better, esteem it more highly, than something else. The Bible's one example of "prefer" in this sense is Psalm 137.6—"if I prefer not Jerusalem above my chief joy" (RSV "if I do not set Jerusalem above my highest joy"). Elsewhere the word is used in the older sense of actual advancement or promotion. The officer in charge of the harem of King Ahasuerus "advanced" Esther and her maids to the best place (Esther 2.9). Daniel "became distinguished above all the other presidents and satraps" (Daniel 6.3). John the Baptist pointed to Jesus as "a man which is preferred before me" (John 1.30); RSV "a man who ranks before me." Paul counseled the Romans to "outdo one another in showing honor" (Romans 12.10). Timothy is solemnly charged to "observe these things without preferring one before another, doing nothing from partiality" (1 Timothy 5.21); RSV "keep these rules without favor, doing nothing from partiality." The point is not that he is to refrain from preference among the rules, but from favoritism in their administration.

**PRESENTLY** is used in KJ in the sense of at once, immediately, without delay. This meaning is now obsolete, and "presently" is most often used in the sense of soon, shortly, in a little while. When Jesus said to the barren fig tree, "May no fruit ever come from you again!" the Greek of Matthew 21.19 records that the fig tree withered at once; the KJ statement that it withered "presently" was an accurate translation in 1611, but is so no longer.

When Jesus rebuked one of his followers for drawing a sword and striking out in defense of his Master in the Garden of Gethsemane (Matthew 26.52–53), he said, "Put your sword back into its place; for all who take the sword will perish by the sword. Do you think that I cannot appeal to my Father, and he will at once send me more than twelve legions of angels?" Jesus used a clear, strong word which means "right now" or "at once." But KJ imports a more leisurely air to the saying by using the word "presently"—"he shall presently give me more than twelve legions of angels."

"A fool's wrath is presently known: but a prudent *man* covereth shame" is one of the realistic observations of the Book of Proverbs (12.16). But it is clearer and more realistic in the present translation:

"The vexation of a fool is known at once;
but the prudent man ignores an insult."

"Presently" appears also in KJ 1 Samuel 2.16 and Philippians 2.23. These passages should be compared as they appear in KJ, ASV, and RSV.

**PREVENT** is used 15 times in the Old Testament and twice in the New Testament, but always in the now obsolete sense of go before, anticipate, or precede (a meaning immediately derived from the Latin *prae* before + *venire* to come). When the psalmist says (119.147), "I prevented the dawning of the morning," the present-day reader of KJ is mystified. He may then consult ASV, where he will read, "I anticipated the dawning of the morning"—by which he will probably understand that the writer eagerly looked forward to the dawn. RSV expresses the meaning of the Hebrew clearly, "I rise before dawn." This is a part of the description of the devotional habits of a pious Hebrew who rises before the dawn to begin the day with meditation and prayer. In the following verse, 148, "Mine eyes prevent the *night* watches" is now translated "My eyes are awake before the watches of the night."

When Peter came to Jesus to report that they were asked to pay the half-shekel tax (Matthew 17.25), KJ says that Jesus "prevented him." That does not mean that he kept Peter from speaking; it means simply that Jesus spoke to him first. When Paul tells the Thessalonians, anxious to know what will happen on the last great day, that "we which are alive *and* remain unto the coming of the Lord shall not prevent them which are asleep" (1 Thessalonians 4.15), he is not thinking of a possible attempt to keep the dead in their tombs; he is saying simply that those who are alive will not precede the dead to the triumphant meeting with the Lord.

In the other cases RSV replaces "prevent" with "meet" (Psalms 21.3; 59.10; Isaiah 21.14; Amos 9.10), "come to meet" (Job 30.27; Psalm 79.8), "come before" (Psalm 88.13), "come upon" (2 Samuel 22.19 = Psalm 18.18), "confront" (2 Samuel 22.6 = Psalm 18.5), "receive" (Job 3.12), "has given to" (Job 41.11). The Hebrew word thus translated is *qadam,* the basic idea of which is to come or be in front or beforehand. The appropriate English word therefore depends upon the context. KJ translated *qadam* in 11 other instances by "meet" (Deuteronomy 23.4; Nehemiah 13.2), "come before" (2 Kings 19.32; Psalm 95.2; Isaiah 37.33; twice in Micah 6.6), "go before" (Psalms 68.25; 89.14), "disappoint" (Psalm 17.13), "before" (Jonah 4.2).

The expression "fled before," in Jonah 4.2, is misleading. Tyndale, Coverdale, and the Bishops' Bible had "hasted to flee," and the revised versions have restored this rendering.

**PREY.** In many passages, especially in Numbers, Joshua, Judges, and Esther, the noun "prey" means "booty," "spoil," or "plunder," and is so rendered by RSV. Examples are: "the spoil thereof, and the cattle thereof, shall ye take for a prey unto yourselves" (Joshua 8.2); RSV "its spoil and its cattle you shall take as booty for yourselves." *"Take* the spoil of them for a prey" (Esther 3.13); RSV "plunder their goods." "On the prey they laid not their hand" (Esther 9.15); RSV "they laid no hands on the plunder." In the Song of Deborah the mother of Sisera is depicted as eagerly awaiting his return, and answering her own question why he is so long in coming: "Have they not sped? have they *not* divided the prey?" (Judges 5.30); RSV "Are they not finding and dividing the spoil?"

Jeremiah 21.9b reads: "he that goeth out, and falleth to the Chaldeans that besiege you, he shall live, and his life shall be unto him for a prey." RSV translates: "he who goes out and surrenders to the Chaldeans who are besieging you shall live and shall have his life as a prize of war." The use of "prey" in this sense is afforded a special paragraph in OED, with the definition "that which one brings away or saves from any contest, etc.," marked as "in Scriptural use." The idiom occurs also in Jeremiah 38.2; 39.18; 45.5.

Zephaniah 3.8 reads: "Therefore wait ye upon me, saith the LORD, until the day that I rise up to the prey." The Hebrew word for "prey" is ʿad, and the word for "witness" is ʿed; the consonants are the same, the only difference is in the vowel points, where a short underline means "a" and two underlined dots mean "e." In view of the context, and in view of the fact that the Greek Septuagint and the Syriac read "to witness," RSV translates:

> " 'Therefore wait for me,' says the LORD,
> 'for the day when I arise as a witness.' "

Most modern translators concur in this view of the text—among them W. R. Harper, J. M. P. Smith, H. Menge, the translators of the Basic Bible and those of the Zurich Bible. Moffatt has "wait till the day of my challenge." The LORD is represented as a witness in Jeremiah 29.23, Micah 1.2, Malachi 3.5.

**PRINT.** "Oh that my words were now written! oh that they were printed in a book! That they were graven with an iron pen and lead in the rock for ever!" (Job 19.23–24). The modern reader gets a vivid picture of three stages of desire—a written record, a printed and permanently bound volume, a memorial cut into rock as nearly eternal as the earth. Unfortunately, the second of these stages existed only in the imagination of the KJ translators. The Hebrew word does not mean printed, but cut, engraved, or inscribed. The Greek Septuagint translated it by the word for "put," the Latin Vulgate by another word for "written." Martin Luther, Coverdale, the Great Bible, and the Bishops' Bible followed the Greek, and the Geneva Bible followed the Latin. The modern revised versions say "inscribed." It is an anachronism to depict Job as speaking of a printed book, but from the literary point of view it is an inspired anachronism.

On the other hand, there is nothing to be said in favor of the KJ rendering, "thou settest a print upon the heels of my feet" (Job 13.27), which conveys to the reader the impression that Job is accusing God of branding his heels. The revised versions have "thou settest a bound to the soles of my feet," which would be improved by using "for" instead of "to." The meaning is that God fixes limits beyond which Job's feet may not tread.

**PRIVILY** is an archaic word for "secretly" (Psalm 101.5; Matthew 2.7; Acts 16.37; 2 Peter 2.1) or "stealthily" (1 Samuel 24.4). KJ uses it for Hebrew which means "in the dark" (Psalm 11.2). Modern translations read "at Arumah" instead of "privily" at Judges 9.31, restoring what was almost certainly the original Hebrew text. RSV says of Joseph and Mary that "her husband Joseph, being a just man and unwilling to put her to shame, resolved to divorce her quietly" (Matthew 1.19).

**PRIVY.** To be privy to is to share in the knowledge of something private or secret. Sapphira was "privy *to*" Ananias' attempted deception (Acts 5.2); RSV says that it was "with his wife's knowledge." King Solomon's word to Shimei, as he condemned him to death, was "You know in your own heart all the evil that you did to David my father" (1 Kings 2.44). A man's "privy member" (Deuteronomy 23.1) is his external genital organ. "It *is* the sword of the great *men that are* slain, which entereth into their privy chambers" is generally regarded as a mistaken rendering (Ezekiel 21.14); most modern translations agree in the meaning which RSV expresses "it is the sword for the great slaughter, which encompasses them."

**PROFANE.** The Oxford English Dictionary lists three major meanings of the adjective "profane," which may be summarized as (1) secular, lay, common; (2) unholy, unhallowed, ritually unclean or polluted; (3) irreverent, blasphemous, irreligious. Each of these meanings is found in KJ, and they are now distinguished in RSV.

The difference between "the holy and profane" is between "the holy and the common" (Ezekiel 22.26; 44.23; compare 42.20). ". . . shall be a profane *place* for the city, for dwelling, and for suburbs" means ". . . shall be for ordinary use for the city, for dwellings and for open country" (48.15).

The command not to marry a woman that is "profane" translates a Hebrew word that means "has been defiled" (Leviticus 21.7, 14). The epithet "profane," as applied to King Zedekiah, means "unhallowed" (Ezekiel 21.25).

In the letters to Timothy, "profane" is retained in 1 Timothy 1.9, but "godless" is used elsewhere (1 Timothy 4.7; 6.20; 2 Timothy 2.16). Esau is termed "irreligious" in Hebrews 12.16.

**PROFIT,** as noun and verb, and PROFITABLE are used 70 times in KJ and 45 times in RSV. The two versions agree on such translations as "What profit is it if we slay our brother?" (Genesis 37.26); "it is not for the king's profit" (Esther 3.8); "what does it profit a man, to gain the whole world and forfeit his life?" (Mark 8.36); "Can a man be profitable to God?" (Job 22.2); "All scripture is inspired by God and profitable for teaching . . ." (2 Timothy 3.16). On the other hand, there are contexts in which RSV finds it better to use such terms as gain, advantage, benefit, avail, or value.

Esau's answer to Jacob's proposal, as rendered in KJ, comes from Tyndale: "I *am* at the point to die; and what profit shall this birthright do to me?" RSV's translation is closer to the compact Hebrew: "I am about to die; of what use is a birthright to me?" (Genesis 25.32). In Job 35.8, "Thy wickedness *may hurt* a man as thou *art;* and thy righteousness *may profit* the son of man," the italicized verbs are an unnecessary complication introduced by the translators. RSV has: "Your wickedness concerns a man like yourself, and your righteousness a son of man." Compare also the two versions of Job 35.1–3, where KJ's insertions becloud Elihu's words and twist their meaning. Another passage where an inserted "if any" misleads the reader is Job 33.27–28. "Wisdom *is* profitable to direct" is an obviously true statement, but the sense of the Hebrew is expressed by RSV, "wisdom helps one to succeed" (Ecclesiastes 10.10).

The verb "profit" is twice employed in the obsolete sense of advance, go forward, improve, make progress. Paul's statement that he had "profited in the Jews' religion above many my equals in mine own nation" represents Greek which means "I advanced in Judaism beyond many of my own age among my people" (Galatians 1.14). Again, the exhortation to Timothy, "Meditate upon these things; give thyself wholly to them; that thy profiting may appear to all" (1 Timothy 4.15), is of different temper and import when correctly translated by the revised versions. RSV has: "Practice these duties, devote yourself to them, so that all may see your progress." This returns to Tyndale's under-standing of the verse, which began, "These things exercise . . ."—a rendering in which he was followed by the other sixteenth-century trans-lations made from the Greek. KJ got "meditate" from the Rheims New Testament, which took it from the Latin Vulgate *Haec meditare,* with-out regard for the fact that *meditare* means exercise, practice, rehearse as well as think about and meditate upon.

The adjective "profitable" is rarely applied to persons, but two of these rare occurrences are in KJ. "Take Mark, and bring him with thee: for he is profitable to me for the ministry" (2 Timothy 4.11) is translated by RSV: "Get Mark and bring him with you; for he is very useful in serving me." Paul, writing to Philemon, describes Onesimus as one "which in time past was to thee unprofitable, but now profitable to thee and to me" (vs. 11). RSV has "Formerly he was useless to you, but now he is indeed useful to you and to me."

Examples of Shakespeare's use of "profit" in the sense of advance or progress are: "Sir Hugh, my husband says my son profits nothing in the world at his book" (*Merry Wives of Windsor,* IV, 1, 15); "My brother Jaques he keeps at school, and report speaks goldenly of his profit" (*As You Like It,* I, 1, 7).

**PROFOUND** appears once (Hosea 5.2) in the clause, "the revolters are profound to make slaughter"—a clause without meaning in the context, and so inept that OED is driven to explain that "profound" here apparently means "deep or subtle in contrivance, crafty, cunning." Most modern translations accept the emendation in the Hebrew text which RSV translates "they have made deep the pit of Shittim." The snare at Mizpah, the net upon Tabor, and the pit of Shittim were centers of seductive Baal worship against which judg-ment is declared. *The Interpreter's Bible,* vol. 6, pp. 615–616, gives a detailed explanation of verses 1 and 2.

**PROLONGED** is used twice in the obsolete sense of delayed, post-poned, put off. The verses are Ezekiel 12.25, 28. The latter of these reads, "There shall none of my words be prolonged any more, but the word which I have spoken shall be done, saith the Lord GOD." RSV has, "None of my words will be delayed any longer, but the word which I speak will be performed, says the Lord GOD."

Among the examples cited by OED are this from a sermon by Bishop Thomas Watson (1558): "Wee saye with the wicked seruant, my Lord prolongeth his commynge," and this from William Lisle (1623): "Prolong not to turne unto God, lest the time passe away through thy slow tarrying."

**PROPER GOOD.** When King David announced to the assembly of Israel his plans for the building of the temple, and entrusted these plans to Solomon together with the store of materials he had provided, he made also a personal gift of three thousand talents of gold and seven thousand talents of silver. He referred to this, according to KJ, as "mine own proper good." The word "proper" is here used in the archaic sense of "owned as property," and "good" is archaic for "goods." The Hebrew is simply, "I have a *segullah* of gold and silver," which the revised versions translate, "I have a treasure of my own of gold and silver." The entire sentence (1 Chronicles 29.3–5) should be read in RSV, as the KJ rendering is unnecessarily confusing. (For the meaning of *segullah* in various contexts see PECULIAR.)

"Proper" is used in the sense of "one's own" in Acts 1.19 and 1 Corinthians 7.7, and in the archaic sense of "beautiful" in Hebrews 11.23.

A proper noun is one's own name, the name used to designate a particular individual, whether a person, animal, place, or object. A common noun, on the other hand, applies to all individuals of the class it denotes.

**PROVIDE** meant originally to foresee, then to exercise foresight in making provision for the future; but in usage the idea of foresight has waned, and "provide" now commonly means simply to furnish or supply. As the word is used in the Bible, the element of foresight is usually present or implied, and there is no marked difference between KJ and the revised versions. The effort to express more clearly the specific meaning of various Hebrew and Greek terms has brought about such changes as: "provide out of all the people able men" (Exodus 18.21); RSV "choose able men from all the people." "He provided the first part for himself" (Deuteronomy 33.21); RSV "he chose the best of the land for himself." "Then whose shall those things be, which thou hast provided?" (Luke 12.20); RSV "and the things you have prepared, whose will they be?" "Provide things honest in the sight of all men" (Romans 12.17); RSV "take thought for what is noble in the sight of all." "Providing for honest things" (2 Corinthians 8.21); RSV "we aim at what is honorable." "God having provided some better thing for us" (Hebrews 11.40); RSV "since God had foreseen something better for us."

**PROVIDENCE** appears once, Acts 24.2, where the "orator" employed by the high priest to present the accusation against Paul began: "Seeing that by thee we enjoy great quietness, and that very worthy deeds are done unto this nation by thy providence, We accept *it* always, and in all places, most noble Felix, with all thankfulness." The more literal translation of the RSV reads: "Since through you we enjoy much peace, and since by your provision, most excellent Felix, reforms are introduced on behalf of this nation, in every way and everywhere we accept this with all gratitude." The important changes here are "peace," "reforms," and "in every way."

The debatable question is whether to use "providence" or "provision." The Greek word is *pronoia,* which occurs in one other passage, Romans 13.14, and is there translated by KJ "make not provision for the flesh, to *fulfil* the lusts *thereof*," and by RSV "make no provision for the flesh, to gratify its desires."

One is tempted to fall back upon etymology in Acts 24.2, and to use the term "foresight." But foresight does not express the full meaning of the Greek *pronoia* or the Latin *providentia.* They stand for the kind of foresight which issues in sound provision for the future, in "prudent or wise management, government, or guidance" (OED). From the first, both "providence" and "provision" have meant this; but "providence" has come to be the more general term, while "provision" usually refers to specific needs or materials. "Providence," moreover, is chiefly used of the providence of God, and "provision" is more likely to refer to human forethought, planning, and care. For both of these reasons, RSV chose "provision." Had he been addressing the emperor, the spokesman for the Jews would doubtless have included a discreet reference to his divinity, but he would hardly risk that in presenting a case to the governor of a Roman province.

**PROVOKE.** This verb and the noun PROVOCATION occur some 60 times in KJ in the sense of inciting to anger. But "provocation" is also used for "blasphemies" (Nehemiah 9.18, 26) and "rebellion" (Hebrews 3.8, 15); and "provoke" is used for the Hebrew words which mean "despise" (Numbers 14.11, 23; 16.30; Deuteronomy 31.20; Isaiah 1.4) and "rebel" (Exodus 23.21; Psalms 78.40, 56; 106.7, 43). "To provoke the eyes of his glory" (Isaiah 3.8) is now translated "defying his glorious presence."

The King James Version states in 2 Samuel 24.1 that the LORD "moved" David to number Israel, and in 1 Chronicles 21.1 that Satan "provoked" David to number Israel; but the Hebrew verb is the same in the two cases, and means to move or incite. It may not have seemed proper to the KJ translators to use the same verb for the LORD and for Satan.

In 2 Corinthians 9.2 and Hebrews 10.24 "provoke" is used in the simple sense of to call forth. "Your zeal hath provoked very many" is misleading, for Paul is saying to the Corinthians that their zeal has stirred up similar zeal on the part of the people of Macedonia. "Let us consider one another to provoke unto love and to good works" means "let us consider how to stir up one another to love and good works."

**PSALTERY.** The Greek verb *psallō* means pluck, pull, twitch. Applied first to the string of a bow, drawn to propel the arrow, it came to be used for the strings of a musical instrument, played by plucking with the fingers rather than by striking with a plectron. So a *psalma* became a tune played on a harp, *psalmos* a song or psalm sung to the accompaniment of a harp, *psaltēs* a harper, and *psaltērion* a harp. The word passed into Latin as *psalterium* and into English as "psaltery." In KJ the word occurs only in the Old Testament, where it is used as translation for the Hebrew *nebel*, while "harp" is used for the Hebrew *kinnor*. In the judgment of present-day scholars, however, *kinnor* is to be translated as "lyre," and *nebel* as "harp."

"Psaltery" does not appear in the New Testament, but the noun *psalmos* and the verb *psallō* do. The Psalms of the Old Testament are referred to, and songs of praise and thanksgiving are encouraged. The key passages, as RSV translates them, are: "I will sing with the spirit and I will sing with the mind also" (1 Corinthians 14.15); "be filled with the Spirit, addressing one another in psalms and hymns and spiritual songs, singing and making melody to the Lord with all your heart" (Ephesians 5.18–19); "Let the word of Christ dwell in you richly, as you teach and admonish one another in all wisdom, and as you sing psalms and hymns and spiritual songs with thankfulness in your hearts to God" (Colossians 3.16).

The Greek word in the New Testament which corresponds to "psaltery" in the Old Testament is *kithara*, translated "harp." It appears in 1 Corinthians 14.7, where KJ reads: "And even things without life giving sound, whether pipe or harp, except they give a distinction in the sounds, how shall it be known what is piped or harped?" RSV translates: "If even lifeless instruments, such as the flute or the harp, do not give distinct notes, how will any one know what is played?" Harps accompany the song of the redeemed before the throne of God, in the vision of John recorded in the book of Revelation (5.8; 14.2; 15.2). "I heard the voice of harpers harping with their harps" is not as clear or pleasing in English as the corresponding words in Greek; RSV translates, "the voice I heard was like the sound of harpers playing on their harps" (Revelation 14.2).

**PUBLICAN** is derived from the Latin *publicanus,* a man who farmed the public revenue—that is, who leased the right to collect the taxes and customs in a particular district, with the understanding that he might retain the revenue in excess of a fixed annual sum but would make good any deficiency. The Greek term for such a man was *telōnēs,* a word which appears in the Synoptic Gospels and is translated "publican." The status of these "publicans" is described clearly and with restraint by Arndt and Gingrich, *A Greek-English Lexicon of the New Testament,* p. 820: "The *telonai* in the synoptics are not the holders of the 'tax-farming' contracts themselves, but subordinates hired by them; the higher officials were usually foreigners, but their underlings were taken from the native population as a rule. The prevailing system of tax collection afforded the collector many opportunities to exercise his greed and unfairness. Hence they were particularly hated and despised as a class. The strict Jew was further offended by the fact that the tax-collector had to maintain continual contact with Gentiles in the course of his work; this rendered a Jewish tax-collector ceremonially unclean."

Zacchaeus is described as "a chief tax collector, and rich" (Luke 19.2). He was probably the head of the tax and customs organization for Jericho, an important center of trade. But that does not mean that he was himself the *publicanus,* the man who held the contract with the Roman government. RSV uses "tax collector" in all cases.

**PULSE** is a collective noun for "the edible seeds of leguminous plants cultivated for food, as peas, beans, lentils, etc." (OED). Though not in common use, the word is neither obsolete nor archaic. It is not the right word, however, in the one passage where it is used in the English Bible, Daniel 1.12, 16. Daniel did not ask that his diet be restricted to beans and other legumes, but that he and his friends be permitted to refrain from meat and eat vegetables only. The word which KJ translates "pulse" is a much wider term which means "vegetables." Daniel's reason for the request for a vegetarian diet was that he might not "defile himself," that is, incur ceremonial uncleanness by eating non-kosher food. The Jewish dietary law is stated in Leviticus 20.24–26. That Daniel's strict conscience in this matter was not exceptional for a pious Jew may be seen in the Apocryphal books of Judith, Tobit, and Maccabees. See *The Interpreter's Bible,* vol. 6, pp. 368–370.

**PURCHASE.** To purchase now means to buy. It involves the payment of a price, usually of money. But in 1611 it was still a general word that meant to acquire, obtain, or gain. In Shakespeare's *Tempest* (IV, 1, 14) Prospero agrees to the marriage of Ferdinand and Miranda, in these words:

"Then, as my gift, and thine own acquisition
Worthily purchased, take my daughter."

The revised versions of the Bible retain the word "purchase" only where the context implies the payment of a price. Elsewhere it is replaced by "gotten" (Psalm 74.2); "won" (Psalm 78.54); "obtain" (Acts 8.20; 20.28). "Purchased possession" is a misleading expansion of the Greek word for "possession" (Ephesians 1.14).

"They that have used the office of a deacon well purchase to themselves a good degree" (1 Timothy 3.13) is a sentence that does not refer to men who use an office for their own profit or men who try to buy honorary degrees. Its meaning is: "Those who serve well as deacons gain a good standing for themselves."

**PURGE,** as verb, is used 31 times, representing 7 different Hebrew words and 5 different Greek words. It is retained by modern translations in the 3 cases where it means what the term still means in a political sense: Josiah purged the land of idolatry (2 Chronicles 34.3, 8) and the word of the LORD to Ezekiel was that he would purge out the rebels (Ezekiel 20.38). It is retained also in the great penitential psalm of David (51.7):

"Purge me with hyssop, and I shall be clean;
wash me, and I shall be whiter than snow."

In nearly all other cases "purge" has a moral sense or refers to a ceremonial ritual of moral significance. Nine times it represents the Hebrew word for "forgive," "atone for," or "expiate" (1 Samuel 3.14; Psalms 65.3; 79.9; Proverbs 16.6; Isaiah 6.7; 22.14; 27.9; Ezekiel 43.20, 26). Twelve times it means "cleanse" or "purify." Twice the underlying Hebrew terms are figures of speech drawn from the refining of metals (Isaiah 1.25; Malachi 3.3).

"Throughly purge his floor" (Matthew 3.12; Luke 3.17 KJ) contains the old spelling "throughly" for "thoroughly" and is misleading because it may be taken to mean that the floor is in need of physical cleansing or ceremonial purification. The more ancient manuscripts of Luke 3.17 read, as rendered in RSV: "His winnowing fork is in his hand, and he will clear his threshing floor and gather his wheat into the granary, but the chaff he will burn with unquenchable fire." The cleaning up of the threshing floor is not preliminary to the threshing, but part of the process.

In John 15.2 "purge" means "prune"; in the sixteenth century men spoke either of purging or of pruning a tree or vine, and except for this one verse KJ uses "prune" and "pruning hooks."

The translation of Mark 7.19 is mystifying. Fortunately, the most ancient Greek manuscripts of Mark's gospel, as well as the writings of Origen and Chrysostom, are more intelligible. Following them, the RSV reads: " 'Do you not see that whatever goes into a man from outside cannot defile him, since it enters, not his heart but his stomach, and so passes on?' (Thus he declared all foods clean.)" Similar renderings are in the modern translations made by the Twentieth Century group, Weymouth, Moffatt, Ballantine, Goodspeed, Confraternity, Knox, Basic Bible, Zurich, New Dutch, Williams, Rieu. Neither in this verse nor anywhere else in the Bible does the word "purge" refer to the purging of the intestines.

**PURTENANCE** is a shortened form of "appurtenance," and means whatever pertains or belongs to something larger or of more consequence. In its one occurrence (Exodus 12.9) "purtenance" was Tyndale's word for the "inwards" of the passover lamb. RSV uses "its inner parts."

**PUSH.** In the law concerning fatal injuries inflicted by cattle (Exodus 21.28–32, 35–36) the word "gore" is used in verses 28 and 31, "push with his horn" in 29, and "push" in 32 and 36. The Hebrew verb is the same in all these cases, and the revised versions use "gore" throughout. Tyndale and Coverdale were responsible for some of the inconsistent renderings; the Bishops' Bible introduced "push with his horn."

**QUARREL,** as a noun, appears four times. It is retained by the revised versions where the king of Israel protests, "see how he is seeking a quarrel with me" (2 Kings 5.7). "Quarrel" is used in the obsolete sense of "complaint" in Colossians 3.13, where RSV reads, "forbearing one another and, if one has a complaint against another, forgiving each other." The statement that Herodias had a "quarrel" against John the Baptist means that she had a "grudge" against him (Mark 6.19). Literally, the Greek says that she "had it in for him," and Williams' translation, which states on the title page that it is in the language of the people, uses this colloquialism. "Avenge the quarrel of my covenant" is simply an awkward attempt to put into English a cognate accusative "avenge the vengeance." The word "quarrel" is an intruder, and the revised versions have dropped it (Leviticus 26.25).

RSV uses "quarrel," as noun and verb, 24 times, replacing such words as strive, strife, contention, debate, meddling. Isaiah 58.4, "Behold, ye fast for strife and debate, and to smite with the fist of wickedness," is revised to read,

> "Behold, you fast only to quarrel and to fight
> and to hit with wicked fist."

Proverbs 17.14, "The beginning of strife *is as* when one letteth out water: therefore leave off contention, before it be meddled with," is reworded:

> "The beginning of strife is like letting out water;
> so quit before the quarrel breaks out."

**QUATERNION** means a group or set of four. The Latin word *quaternio* was applied to the number four on dice; the Greek *tetradion* refers to four days in one of the ancient papyri discovered within the last 70 years, and to quires of four sheets of parchment in another. When Herod put Peter in prison, he assigned four quaternions of soldiers to guard him (Acts 12.4). The word "quaternion" was taken by Wyclif, and later by Tyndale, directly from the Latin Vulgate, and was retained by subsequent versions.

"Quaternion" is still living English in the realm of mathematics, and in the field of publishing, where it means a quire of four sheets, doubled so as to make sixteen pages. RSV drops the term and says "four squads of soldiers." The significant fact is not that each squad was made up of four men, but that there were four squads, each to be on duty during one of the four three-hour watches of the night. The squad of soldiers which was detailed to crucify Jesus seems to have consisted of four men (John 19.23). There is an interesting article on Acts 12.4 in Edgar J. Goodspeed, *Problems of New Testament Translation*, pp. 131–132.

**QUESTION,** as noun or verb, raises no difficulty as used in the Old Testament. In more than half its occurrences in the New Testament, however, it does not clearly convey the meaning of the Greek. In Mark 8.11 "to question with him" is used in a sense now obsolete; RSV translates, "The Pharisees came and began to argue with him." In Mark 9.14, 16 RSV has "arguing" and "discussing"; in John 3.25 "a discussion." The words of the town clerk at Ephesus, "For we are in danger to be called in question for this day's uproar," is more exactly translated, "For we are in danger of being charged with rioting today" (Acts 19.40). Instead of "I am called in question" (Acts 23.6; 24.21), Paul cried out in the council, "I am on trial." Instead of "certain questions against him," Festus said that Paul's accusers had "certain points of dispute with him about their own superstition and about one Jesus, who was dead, but whom Paul asserted to be alive" (Acts 25.19). Paul stated that he was glad to appear before King Agrippa, because Agrippa was "especially familiar with all customs and controversies of the Jews" (Acts 26.3 RSV). In 2 Timothy 2.23 KJ reads, "But foolish and unlearned questions avoid, knowing that they do gender strifes"; RSV translates, "Have nothing to do with stupid, senseless controversies; you know that they breed quarrels." Compare the two versions also in 1 Timothy 6.4 and Titus 3.9. In 1 Timothy 1.4 "which minister questions" is replaced by "which promote speculations," on the authority of the best ancient manuscripts.

**QUICK, QUICKEN.** The adverb "quickly" is used in all the English versions of the Bible, and causes no trouble. It translates Hebrew and Greek words which mean speedily, in haste, or soon.

But the adjective "quick" in KJ translates entirely different words, and always means "alive" or "living." It is not retained by the revised versions. In these "the quick and the dead" (Acts 10.42; 2 Timothy 4.1; 1 Peter 4.5) is replaced by "the living and the dead." In Hebrews 4.12, instead of "the word of God *is* quick, and powerful" we now read "the word of God is living and active."

When Korah and his company went down quick into the mouth of the earth, and it swallowed them up, the word "quick" refers not to the immediacy of the catastrophe or the speed of their descent, but to the fact that they were buried alive. The account is in Numbers 16.23–33; it is interesting to note that verse 30 uses "quick" and verse 33 "alive." A similar use of "quick" is found in Psalms 55.15 and 124.3. The word "alive" is now used in all these cases.

The word "quick" is retained by RSV in one passage, Leviticus 13.10, where it refers to the "quick raw flesh" of leprosy.

The verb "quicken" appears 14 times in the Psalms and 11 times in the New Testament; it is replaced in RSV by such terms as revive, give life, preserve life, make alive, life-giving. Examples are: "It is the spirit that quickeneth" (John 6.63); RSV "It is the spirit that gives life." "That which thou sawest is not quickened, except it die" (1 Corinthians 15.36); RSV "What you saw does not come to life unless it dies." "The last Adam *was made* a quickening spirit" (1 Corinthians 15.45); RSV "the last Adam became a life-giving spirit." "Hath quickened us together with Christ" (Ephesians 2.5); RSV "made us alive together with Christ."

**RANGE** does not refer to a range of mountains in Job 39.8, "The range of the mountains *is* his pasture," for the word "range" is here used in the sense which it has in the song, "Home, Home on the Range." It denotes the area over which animals range, that is, move about in search of food. The Bishops' Bible had "seek their pasture about the mountains," and the Geneva Bible "seeketh out the mountain for his pasture." RSV reads "He ranges the mountains as his pasture."

"A ranging bear" (Proverbs 28.15) is too quiet for the Hebrew verb, which means run or rush. The sixteenth-century English versions had "a hungry bear"; RSV has "a charging bear."

When Jehoiada commanded the captains of the guard to seize Queen Athaliah and "Have her forth without the ranges" (2 Kings 11.15), his order was to "bring her out between the ranks." The word "ranges" is here used for ranks of soldiers.

In the command to break everything upon which any part of the carcass of an unclean animal falls, *"whether it be* oven, or ranges for pots" (Leviticus 11.35), the Hebrew term means a very simple stove upon which pots were placed for the cooking of their contents—something much less elaborate, of course, than the kitchen range of today, which includes the oven.

**READY** is used ambiguously in a few cases. "Ready to die" (Luke 7.2) does not mean that the centurion's servant was prepared to die, but that he was "at the point of death." So too Paul's statement in 2 Timothy 4.6, "I am now ready to be offered," means simply that his sacrifice is impending. The Greek literally means "I am already being poured out as a libation" (compare Philippians 2.17). "Ready to depart on the morrow" (Acts 20.7) means "intending to depart on the morrow." "Ready to perish" represents a Hebrew word which is better translated "wandering" in Deuteronomy 26.5; "about to perish" in Job 29.13; and "lost" in Isaiah 27.13.

**REASON,** as noun, occurs once where it seems to be used as an adjective (Acts 6.2): "It is not reason that we should leave the word of God, and serve tables." The Greek has an adjective here which means acceptable, satisfactory; the Latin Vulgate has an adjective which means fair, equitable, just, right. Tyndale and his successors translated the Greek by "mete"; Wyclif translated the Latin by "right," and Rheims by "reason," which was adopted by KJ.

The idiom "it is reason" or "it is not reason," meaning that it is or is not an act or proceeding agreeable to reason, was frequent from about 1400 to 1650, according to OED, but is now rare. RSV in this case returns to Wyclif by using the word "right." It translates the sentence: "It is not right that we should give up preaching the word of God to serve tables."

**REASON,** as verb, appears 23 times in KJ, and is retained by RSV in only one of these cases. This is Isaiah 1.18: "Come now, let us reason together, says the LORD." The same Hebrew verb occurs in Job 23.7, where KJ has the strange rendering, "There the righteous might dispute with him; so should I be delivered for ever from my judge," and RSV has,

"There an upright man could reason with him,
 and I should be acquitted for ever by my judge."

Another case where RSV brings in "reason" is Leviticus 19.17, which reads in KJ, "Thou shalt not hate thy brother in thine heart; thou shalt in any wise rebuke thy neighbour, and not suffer sin upon him." RSV translates: "You shall not hate your brother in your heart, but you shall reason with your neighbor, lest you bear sin because of him."

In 18 cases in the New Testament RSV replaces "reason" with other verbs—"argue," "discuss," "question," "dispute." That, it must be admitted, imparts a somewhat sharper tone to some of the accounts in the Gospels and Acts. But the sharper tone is there; it is implied in the meaning of the Greek, and it was implied in the verb "reason" as this was used by the KJ translators. In each of these cases "reason" had some one of the senses which OED now marks as obsolete—to question, argue, or discuss with one another. The passages are: Matthew 16.7, 8; 21.25; Mark 2.6, 8; 8.16, 17; 11.31; 12.28; Luke 5.21, 22; 20.5, 14;

24.15; Acts 17.2; 18.4, 19; 24.25. The same Greek verbs which are translated by "reason" in these cases, are in 8 other cases translated by "dispute" in KJ—Mark 9.33, 34; Acts 6.9; 9.29; 17.17; 19.8, 9; 24.12.

**REASONING,** as a noun, occurs three times. It is the correct word in Job 13.6—"Hear now my reasoning." But it is not the right word in Luke 9.46, where RSV reads, "An argument arose among them as to which of them was the greatest." Acts 28.29 reads in KJ, "the Jews departed, and had great reasoning among themselves." This verse does not appear in the best ancient Greek manuscripts, but RSV gives it in a footnote, "the Jews departed, holding much dispute among themselves." The Arndt and Gingrich *Greek-English Lexicon of the New Testament* suggests the translation, "disputing vigorously among themselves."

**RECORD,** as noun and verb, appears 34 times, in 27 of which it carries the obsolete meaning of witness, testimony, or testify. "I call heaven and earth to record this day against you" means "I call heaven and earth to witness against you this day" (Deuteronomy 30.19; compare 31.28). "I call God for a record upon my soul" is more accurately translated, "I call God to witness against me" (2 Corinthians 1.23). "God is my record, how greatly I long after you all in the bowels of Jesus Christ" means "God is my witness, how I yearn for you all with the affection of Christ Jesus" (Philippians 1.8). "My record *is* on high" means "he that vouches for me is on high" (Job 16.19). "I took unto me faithful witnesses to record" means "I got reliable witnesses to attest for me" (Isaiah 8.2). Shakespeare uses "record" in this obsolete sense in *King Richard II,* I, 1, 30: "First, heaven be the record of my speech!"

The noun "record" is used 7 times as translation for the Greek noun which means "testimony" (John 1.19; 8.13–14; 19.35; 1 John 5.10–11; 3 John 12). The phrase "bear record" is used 12 times to translate the Greek verb which means "bear witness" or "testify" (John 1.32, 34; 8.13, 14; 12.17; 19.35; Romans 10.2; 2 Corinthians 8.3; Galatians 4.15; Colossians 4.13; 3 John 12; Revelation 1.2).

"I take you to record" (Acts 20.26) is an obsolete phrase which means "I call you to witness." In this case, however, it is an erroneous translation dating back to Tyndale. The revised versions correctly read "I testify to you."

"In all places where I record my name" means "in every place where

I cause my name to be remembered" (Exodus 20.24). The duty of certain Levites, as ministers before the ark of the LORD, "to record, and to thank and praise the LORD God of Israel" was "to invoke, to thank, and to praise the LORD, the God of Israel" (1 Chronicles 16.4). "The book of records" which King Ahasuerus ordered to be read to him when he could not sleep was "the book of memorable deeds" (Esther 6.1).

**RECOVER.** In the story of Naaman, 2 Kings 5, are these expressions: "the prophet . . . would recover him of his leprosy" (vs. 3); "that thou mayest recover him of his leprosy" (vs. 6); "this man doth send unto me to recover a man of his leprosy" (vs. 7); "recover the leper" (vs. 11). While this is still recognized as good English usage, it is becoming rare. We no longer say that the doctor will recover the patient, but that the patient, as a result of the doctor's ministrations, will recover. RSV accordingly uses "cure" in these verses.

"Recover" is used by KJ as translation for 11 different Hebrew verbs, each of which has a distinct meaning. In the following passages, RSV expresses the sense of the Hebrew more literally: Isaiah 38.16, "so wilt thou recover me, and make me to live"; RSV "Oh, restore me to health and make me live!" Psalm 39.13, "that I may recover strength"; RSV "that I may know gladness." Hosea 2.9, "recover my wool and my flax"; RSV "take away my wool and my flax." 2 Samuel 8.3, "recover his border"; RSV "restore his power." 2 Chronicles 14.13, "the Ethiopians were overthrown, that they could not recover themselves"; RSV "the Ethiopians fell until none remained alive."

**REFRAIN,** as a transitive verb meaning to bridle, restrain, or check some person or thing, is obsolete or archaic. The word is now used intransitively, in the sense of abstain, forbear, keep oneself from doing some act or yielding to some feeling. "Refrain" occurs 17 times in KJ, 14 of which are in the obsolete transitive sense. In these 14 cases, RSV uses "control" (Genesis 43.31; 45.1); "restrain" (Esther 5.10; Job 7.11; Psalm 40.9; Proverbs 10.19; Isaiah 42.14; 64.12; Jeremiah 14.10); "hold back" (Psalm 119.101; Proverbs 1.15); "keep" (Jeremiah 31.16; 1 Peter 3.10). In Job 29.9, "the princes refrained talking," RSV simply inserts "from"—"the princes refrained from talking." The only case where KJ and RSV use "refrain" in identical translations is Ecclesiastes 3.5: "a time to embrace, and a time to refrain from embracing." RSV uses "refrain" 15 times, but always intransitively.

**REFUSE.** Isaiah 54.6 reads: "For the LORD hath called thee as a woman forsaken and grieved in spirit, and a wife of youth, when thou wast refused, saith thy God." In current usage the verb "refuse" is so mild a term that it would suggest here a woman pouting because she could not have her way; she had been refused something. To refuse now means to decline a request, suggestion, or offer. It is a simple objective term. If the refusal is made under emotional stress or with more than ordinary vigor, that fact must be expressed in accompanying adverbs. But in Elizabethan English the word was applied to persons, and had a variety of meanings, often with emotional implication, which are now obsolete. These meanings included, among others, to reject, renounce, abandon, forsake, cast off a person, divorce a wife.

The Hebrew verb here is a strong one. Its basic meaning is reject, and KJ translates it by "abhor," "despise," "loathe," "reject," "cast away," "cast off" a total of 60 times, and by "refuse" 10 times. The revised versions use "cast off" in Isaiah 54.6. RSV reads:

"For the LORD has called you
   like a wife forsaken and grieved in spirit,
   like a wife of youth when she is cast off,
      says your God."

This same strong verb is used in Psalm 118.22, which KJ renders, "The stone *which* the builders refused is become the head *stone* of the corner." In the New Testament quotations of this verse (Matthew 21.42; Mark 12.10; Luke 20.17) KJ used "rejected." In other references to it KJ uses "was set at nought" (Acts 4.11) and "disallowed" (1 Peter 2.7). RSV uses "rejected" in all these passages.

"Refuse profane and old wives' fables" (1 Timothy 4.7) is an example of the use of "refuse" in an obsolete sense. The Greek verb here means to shun, avoid. RSV translates: "Have nothing to do with godless and silly myths." (See DISALLOW, OLD WIVES' FABLES)

**REHEARSE** was still used in the sixteenth century in the sense of say, state, declare. It is now obsolete in this sense, and seldom used in the sense of describe or narrate. "Rehearse" appears six times in KJ. It is replaced by "repeat" in Judges 5.11; 1 Samuel 8.21; 17.31, and by "recite" in Exodus 17.14. "They rehearsed all that God had done with them" (Acts 14.27) means "they declared all that God had done with them." In Acts 11.4 KJ has an erroneous translation, "But Peter rehearsed *the matter* from the beginning, and expounded *it* by order unto them." This was taken from the Great Bible and the Bishops' Bible, in spite of the fact that Wyclif, Tyndale, Coverdale, the Geneva Bible, and the Rheims New Testament had translated the verse correctly. In this case Coverdale's later judgment was unsound, for he as editor of the Great Bible misconstrued a clause which he had properly translated in his earlier work. The revised versions have restored the correct rendering. RSV has "But Peter began and explained to them in order."

**REINS** is a name for the kidneys or for the loins, the region of the kidneys. It is a Norman contribution to the English language, a French word derived from the Latin *renes,* which means kidneys. The corresponding Hebrew word is *kelayoth,* which KJ translates "kidneys" 18 times and "reins" 13 times. The former group of passages is concerned with the ritual of animal sacrifice, in which "the two kidneys, and the fat that *is* upon them" had an important part (Exodus 29.13, 22; Leviticus 3.4, 10, 15; 4.9; etc.).

In 11 of the passages using "reins," the word has the figurative meaning for which we now use "heart," as the seat of the feelings and affections. Thus "my reins also instruct me in the night seasons" means "in the night also my heart instructs me" (Psalm 16.7), and "I was pricked in my reins" means "I was pricked at heart" (Psalm 73.21). In his plea to the LORD concerning the prosperity of the wicked, Jeremiah says "thou *art* near in their mouth, and far from their reins," which could be construed to mean far from controlling them; the meaning is "thou art near in their mouth, and far from their heart" (Jeremiah 12.2). "I the LORD search the heart, *I* try the reins" is translated by RSV: "I the LORD search the mind and try the heart" (Jeremiah 17.10). This combination of "heart" and "reins," where the meaning is "mind" and "heart," occurs in 5 other passages: Psalms 7.9; 26.2; Jeremiah 11.20; 20.12; Revelation 2.23. In the one New Testament passage, the Greek *nephros* replaces *kelayoth,* but the thought is that which the Old Testament has made familiar—"I am he who searches mind and heart."

Job's answer to his "miserable comforters" is in the language of deep distress and extravagant metaphor; "he cleaveth my reins asunder" means "he slashes open my kidneys" (Job 16.13). "For thou hast possessed my reins: thou hast covered me in my mother's womb" (Psalm 139.13) is translated by RSV:

"For thou didst form my inward parts,
    thou didst knit me together in my mother's womb."

**REMEMBRANCE** is a lovely word, more likely to be used of memories that are cherished than of those that are bitter. The LORD's "book of remembrance" (Malachi 3.16 RSV) was "of those who feared the LORD and thought on his name." "Do this in remembrance of me," said Jesus in institution of the Lord's Supper (1 Corinthians 11.23–26). "I thank my God in all my remembrance of you," wrote Paul to the Philippians (1.3 RSV).

The word is used in an ironic or disparaging sense, however, in Job's answer to his "comforters." KJ renders Job 13.12: "Your remembrances *are* like unto ashes, your bodies to bodies of clay." RV and ASV translate the Hebrew more correctly: "Your memorable sayings are proverbs of ashes, Your defences are defences of clay." RSV accepts this, but changes "memorable sayings" to "maxims." Job is telling his friends that the old saws which they have dredged up from their memories are dusty answers to his problem.

In Isaiah 57.8 "remembrance" is used in the sense of a love token or a symbol of phallic worship. RSV translates: "Behind the door and the doorpost you have set up your symbol."

**REMOVE** means to take something away from its place, either by transfer to another place or by destruction. In Elizabethan English it was used more widely, in various senses of the verb "move," without implying change of place. Since KJ used "remove" as a rendering for 24 different Hebrew verbs and 7 Greek verbs, it inevitably included some of these now obsolete senses. Out of many instances, the following examples are typical. Only the renderings of the RSV will be quoted, printed as prose, with the obsolete wording of KJ in parentheses. Psalm 104.5, "Thou didst set the earth on its foundations, so that it should never be shaken" ("removed"). Psalm 125.1, "Those who trust in the LORD are like Mount Zion, which cannot be moved ("removed"), but abides for ever." Psalm 46.2, "Therefore we will not fear though the earth should change" ("be removed"). Isaiah 13.13, "Therefore I will make the heavens tremble, and the earth will be shaken out of its place" ("shall remove out of her place"). Exodus 14.19, "Then the angel of God who went before the host of Israel moved ("removed") and went behind them." Exodus 20.18, "the people were afraid and trembled; and they stood afar off" ("removed, and stood afar off"). Lamentations 3.17, "my soul is bereft of peace" ("thou hast removed my soul far off from peace"). Jeremiah 15.4, "I will make them a horror to all the kingdoms of the earth" ("I will cause them to be removed into all kingdoms of the earth"). The last of these sentences appears also in Deuteronomy 28.25 and Jeremiah 24.9; 29.18; 34.17.

**RENDER** is clearly understood in such texts as "Render to Caesar the things that are Caesar's, and to God the things that are God's" (Mark 12.17) and "For he will render to every man according to his works" (Romans 2.6). In other texts it fails to convey the idea of requite, recompense, repay, or return which is connoted by the Hebrew. At the close of the bloody adventure of Abimelech, KJ has the comment: "Thus God rendered the wickedness of Abimelech, which he did unto his father, in slaying his seventy brethren: And all the evil of the men of Shechem did God render upon their heads" (Judges 9.56–57). RSV translates: "Thus God requited the crime of Abimelech, which he committed against his father in killing his seventy brothers; and God also made all the wickedness of the men of Shechem fall back upon their heads." For other examples see 1 Samuel 26.23; Job 34.11; Jeremiah 51.24; Zechariah 9.12.

**REPENT** is a characteristically Biblical word. The verb appears 84 times, almost equally divided between the Old Testament and the New Testament; and the noun REPENTANCE occurs 26 times, all but once in the New Testament.

"Repent" was originally a reflexive verb, but it began early to be used without the reflexive pronoun. Out of 65 occurrences in Shakespeare's plays, only 8 are reflexive, all in the first person—"I repent me." Examples from KJ are "The LORD repented him of the evil" (2 Samuel 24.16, 1 Chronicles 21.15); "no man repented him of his wickedness" (Jeremiah 8.6); "I may repent me" (Jeremiah 26.3); "the LORD will repent him" (Jeremiah 26.13); "the LORD repented him" (Jeremiah 26.19); "I repent me" (Jeremiah 42.10); "repenteth him of evil" (Joel 2.13); "repentest thee of the evil" (Jonah 4.2); "Judas repented himself" (Matthew 27.3). In all these cases RSV omits the reflexive pronoun. In 4 cases it changes the verb to express the meaning more clearly: "the children of Israel repented them for Benjamin"; RSV "the people of Israel had compassion for Benjamin" (Judges 21.6, compare 21.15). "The LORD shall . . . repent himself for his servants"; RSV "the LORD will . . . have compassion on his servants" (Deuteronomy 32.36, compare Psalm 135.14).

The verb "repent" is also used impersonally in KJ. "And it repented the LORD that he had made man on the earth . . . And the

Lord said . . . it repenteth me that I have made them" (Genesis 6.6, 7). RSV reads: "And the Lord was sorry that he had made man on the earth . . . So the Lord said . . . 'I am sorry that I have made them.' " Other examples are: "it repented the Lord because of their groanings"; RSV "the Lord was moved to pity by their groanings" (Judges 2.18). "It repenteth me that I have set up Saul *to be* king"; RSV "I repent that I have made Saul king" (1 Samuel 15.11). "Let it repent thee concerning thy servants"; RSV "Have pity on thy servants" (Psalm 90.13).

In some contexts, "relent" is a more appropriate translation. "I have purposed *it,* and will not repent, neither will I turn back from it"; RSV "I have purposed, I have not relented nor will I turn back" (Jeremiah 4.28). "I am weary with repenting"; RSV "I am weary of relenting" (Jeremiah 15.6). Compare Psalm 106.45; Zechariah 8.14.

**REPLENISH,** in the fifteenth and sixteenth centuries, meant to fill, to make full, to occupy the whole of. It is in this sense that the word is used in Genesis 1.28, "Be fruitful, and multiply, and replenish the earth." This blessing and injunction to Adam and Eve is later repeated, in the same words, to Noah (Genesis 9.1). In both cases, the Hebrew is properly translated by the revised versions, "Be fruitful and multiply, and fill the earth." And this is what the KJ translators meant by their rendering. The present meaning of the word "replenish" is to fill up again, to restore to a former condition of being full or complete. But this meaning did not develop until after the work upon KJ had been done. The first example cited by OED is ambiguous and is dated 1612. The second example, which clearly carries the new meaning, is dated 1666.

**REPORT,** in the sense of rumor, common talk, something generally said or believed, appears in such passages as Eli's remonstrance with his sons (1 Samuel 2.24), the Queen of Sheba's conversation with Solomon (1 Kings 10.6), and various reports of military prowess or disaster (Deuteronomy 2.25; Isaiah 23.5; 53.1). "Thou shalt not raise a false report" means "You shall not utter a false report" (Exodus 23.1); the commandment forbids not only the initiation of a false report but also its further communication.

In the sixteenth century, "report" also meant reputation. Tyndale had "men of honest reporte" (Acts 6.3) and "in evyll reporte and good reporte" (2 Corinthians 6.8), and these phrases passed on to KJ; RSV in these contexts uses "repute." From Tyndale also comes the description of Cornelius as "of good report among all the people (KJ "nation") of the Jews" (Acts 10.22), which RSV translates "well spoken of by the whole Jewish nation." The description of Ananias of Damascus, "having a good report of all the Jews which dwelt *there,*" is ambiguous, as it could be taken to mean Ananias' report concerning the Jews; it means, as RSV has it, that he was "well spoken of by all the Jews who lived there" (Acts 22.12). The requirement that a bishop "must have a good report of them which are without" means that "he must be well thought of by outsiders" (1 Timothy 3.7).

The eleventh chapter of Hebrews, beginning "Now faith is the substance of things hoped for, the evidence of things not seen," goes on in verse 2: "For by it the elders obtained a good report." That translation comes from the Great Bible and the Bishops' Bible. Tyndale had "By it the elders were well reported of," and was followed by Coverdale and the Geneva Bible. Either of these renderings is better than that of the revised versions of 1881 and 1901—"For therein the elders had witness borne to them"—which does not clearly enough carry the idea of attestation and approval.

But whose approval? Some translations imply that it was the approval of their fellow men. "By this the men of old won their fame," says Ballantine. Others, with some variation in the preceding words, say "reputation" (Phillips), "record" (Moffatt), "credit" (Knox), "were renowned" (Twentieth Century). But surely the definite statements of verses 4 and 5, as well as the total argument of the chapter, make it clear that it was the approval of God that these men of old sought and obtained. A thousand years ago, Oecumenius suggested that this be made more explicit; and some modern translations are doing that. Weymouth, Goodspeed, Williams, and the Basic Bible say "God's approval." RSV has "For by it the men of old received divine approval."

**REPROBATE,** as adjective, means rejected because worthless or impure. "Reprobate silver" is a term applied in Jeremiah 6.30 to the people whom the LORD has rejected. The application to morals and religion of figures of speech drawn from the assaying of metals is clearly made in the translation by RSV of verses 27–30:

"I have made you an assayer and tester among my people,
    that you may know and assay their ways.
They are all stubbornly rebellious,
    going about with slanders;
they are bronze and iron,
    all of them act corruptly.

The bellows blow fiercely,
> the lead is consumed by the fire;
in vain the refining goes on,
> for the wicked are not removed.
Refuse silver they are called,
> for the LORD has rejected them."

In the New Testament the Greek word for "reprobate" is *adokimos,* which means failed to meet the test, hence unfit, disqualified, worthless, base. It is the word which Paul uses when he writes of his own self-discipline, "lest that by any means, when I have preached to others, I myself should be a castaway" (1 Corinthians 9.27). RSV has "lest after preaching to others I myself should be disqualified." It translates *adokimos* by "base" (Romans 1.28) and by "fail to meet the test" (2 Corinthians 13.5, 6, 7). In 2 Timothy 3.8 it has "men of corrupt mind and counterfeit faith," and in Titus 1.16 "unfit for any good deed."

**REQUIRE** once meant simply to ask. It is used in that sense in Ezra 8.22, which RSV translates "I was ashamed to ask the king for a band of soldiers and horsemen." Shakespeare uses the word in the request that the defeated Mark Antony sends to Caesar:
> "Lord of his fortunes he salutes thee, and
> Requires to live in Egypt: which not granted,
> He lessens his requests; and to thee sues
> To let him breathe between the heavens and earth,
> A private man in Athens."
> *Antony and Cleopatra,* III, 12, 12

Because the word "required" may be understood to mean "needed," RSV changes to other terms in 2 Samuel 12.20— "when he asked, they set food before him, and he ate"—and in Nehemiah 5.18—"I did not demand the food allowance of the governor, because the servitude was heavy upon this people." A stronger word than "required" is needed in Luke 23.23, where KJ has "they were instant with loud voices, requiring that he might be crucified," and RSV reads, "they were urgent, demanding with loud voices that he should be crucified."

**RESEMBLE** appears twice in KJ. In Judges 8.18 it has its normal meaning and is retained by RSV: "they resembled the sons of a king." But in Luke 13.18—"Unto what is the kingdom of God like? and whereunto shall I resemble it?"—it is used in the sense of "compare." Tyndale and his successors had "wherto shall I compare it?" The same Greek is used in verse 20, where KJ says "liken." The revised versions of 1881–1901 use "liken" in both verse 18 and verse 20; RSV uses "compare" in both.

**REVERENCE.** When Mephibosheth on one occasion, and Bathsheba on another, "did reverence" to King David, it was a gesture of respect and gratitude, an obeisance (2 Samuel 9.6; 1 Kings 1.31). When Haman was promoted by King Ahasuerus to a seat above all the princes who were with him, all the king's servants "did obeisance" to him, except Mordecai (RSV Esther 3.2, 5). When the owner of the vineyard, in Jesus' parable, sent his son to secure the rental due from his wicked tenants, his thought was: "They will respect my son" (RSV Matthew 21.37; Mark 12.6; Luke 20.13). "Respect" rather than "reverence" is the natural translation for the attitude of sons to fathers (Hebrews 12.9), and of the wife to her husband (Ephesians 5.33).

On the other hand, "reverence" is a sound translation of the Hebrew and Greek terms used with reference to God and his sanctuary (Leviticus 19.30; 26.2). Hebrews 12.28 reads in KJ: "Wherefore we receiving a kingdom which cannot be moved, let us have grace, whereby we may serve God acceptably with reverence and godly fear." In RSV: "Therefore let us be grateful for receiving a kingdom that cannot be shaken, and thus let us offer to God acceptable worship, with reverence and awe."

In Psalm 89.7, "to be had in reverence of all *them that are* about him" means "terrible above all that are round about him." (See REVEREND)

**REVEREND** means worthy of deep respect or reverence. As such, it fits naturally into a psalm of praise to the LORD: "holy and reverend *is* his name" (Psalm 111.9). But it is not strong enough to express the Hebrew word in that sentence, and its use as a title for clergymen has tended to blur its significance.

The Hebrew word means "inspiring fear." It appears in three other passages concerning the name of the LORD, where KJ has: "glorious and fearful name" (Deuteronomy 28.58); "great and terrible name" (Psalm 99.3); "my name is dreadful among the heathen" (Malachi 1.14). It appears in Psalm 96.4 (=1 Chronicles 16.25), "he *is* to be feared above all gods"; and in Psalm 130.4, *"there is* forgiveness with thee, that thou mayest be feared." Conjoined with "great" and/or "mighty," it is translated by "terrible," and affirmed as an attribute of God, in Deuteronomy 7.21; 10.17; Nehemiah 1.5; 4.14; 9.32. Daniel prays to "the great and dreadful God" (Daniel 9.4). Jacob exclaims, "How dreadful *is* this place!" (Genesis 28.17). Manoah's wife reports that the countenance of the man who spoke to her was "like the countenance of an angel of God, very terrible" (Judges 13.6). Joel speaks of "the great and the terrible day of the LORD" (Joel 2.31), and Malachi of "the great and dreadful day of the LORD" (Malachi 4.5). In all these passages the Hebrew word is the one which is represented by "reverend" in Psalm 111.9. The rendering comes from Coverdale, and was picked up by the revision of the Bishops' Bible, whence it passed to KJ. The Geneva Bible had "holie and feareful," and the first edition of the Bishops' Bible "holy and terrible." RSV reads "Holy and terrible is his name!"

**RID.** "Rid me, and deliver me . . . from the hand of strange children" (Psalm 144.7, 11) is strange language to the modern reader, which has been changed by RSV to "rescue me and deliver me . . . from the hand of aliens." The use of "rid" in the sense of rescue, save, or deliver someone from some threat or predicament is accounted rare in OED. It occurs in three other contexts in KJ. Reuben advised his brothers to cast Joseph into a pit, "that he might rid (RSV "rescue") him out of their hands" (Genesis 37.22). In the promise of the LORD to the people of Israel, "I will rid you out of their bondage" is parallel to "I will bring you out" and "I will redeem you" (Exodus 6.6); RSV has "I will deliver you from their bondage." The prayer of Psalm 82.4, "Deliver the poor and needy: rid *them* out of the hand of the wicked," is reworded by RSV, "Rescue the weak and the needy; deliver them from the hand of the wicked."

The verb "rid" occurs in a quite different sense in Leviticus 26.6: "I will rid evil beasts out of the land." RSV has "I will remove evil beasts from the land."

**RIDDANCE** is scarcely to be heard now except in the contemptuous "good riddance!" The command in Leviticus 23.22, "thou shalt not make clean riddance of the corners of thy field when thou reapest," means "you shall not reap your field to its very border." Zephaniah's prophecy of the day of the wrath of the LORD, "for he shall make even a speedy riddance of all them that dwell in the land" (1.18), will be better understood if the whole sentence is quoted as in RSV:

"In the fire of his jealous wrath
   all the earth shall be consumed;

for a full, yea, sudden end
he will make of all the inhabitants of the earth."

**RINGSTRAKED** means having stripes of color around the body. It appears in the account of Jacob's dealings with Laban and his flocks (Genesis 30.35, 39, 40; 31.8, 10, 12). This is a word that seems to have originated with the English Bible. Tyndale had "straked" in this passage in Genesis, and was followed by subsequent versions, until the Bishops' Bible used "ringstraked," which was adopted by KJ. The revised versions of 1885–1901 changed to "ringstreaked," which is not quite the same, for a streak may be less firm and regular than a strake or stripe. RSV uses "striped."

**RIOT** and **RIOTOUS** stand in KJ for revelry, extravagance, loose living, or debauchery rather than for scenes of public violence and lawless disorder. "Be not among winebibbers; among riotous eaters of flesh" (Proverbs 23.20) means "Be not among winebibbers, or among gluttonous eaters of meat." "He that is a companion of riotous *men* shameth his father" (Proverbs 28.7) means "a companion of gluttons shames his father." The Hebrew word represented by "riotous" in these texts is translated "glutton" by KJ in Proverbs 23.21 and in Deuteronomy 21.20, *"he is* a glutton, and a drunkard."

The "riotous living" of the prodigal son was "loose living" (Luke 15.13). Paul counsels against "reveling" in Romans 13.13; and 2 Peter 2.13 denounces those who "count it pleasure to revel in the daytime." RSV uses "profligate," "profligacy," and "debauchery" for the Greek word which KJ represents by "riot" or "excess" (Titus 1.6; 1 Peter 4.4; Ephesians 5.18).

**RISING,** as noun, is used in Leviticus 13.2, 10, 19, 28, 43; 14.56 in the sense of a body swelling which is a symptom of disease. RSV uses "swelling." Compare Leviticus 13.28 in the two versions. KJ reads "it *is* a rising of the burning"; RSV has "it is a swelling from the burn."

**ROLL.** The RSV uses "scroll" throughout Jeremiah 36, Ezekiel 2 and 3, and Zechariah 5, where KJ has "roll of a book," "roll," or "book." It also uses "scroll" for the record of the decree of Cyrus, king of Babylon, which was revealed by the search ordered by King Darius (Ezra 6.2). In 6.1, however, "the house of the rolls, where the treasures were laid up" is changed to read, "the house of the archives where the documents were stored." The "great roll" in Isaiah 8.1 is a "large tablet." (See BOOK, VOLUME)

**ROOM.** The "rooms" in Noah's ark (Genesis 6.14) and the "upper room" where the apostles went in Jerusalem were rooms with a floor and walls. Elsewhere in KJ "room" refers to space or place. "No room for them in the inn" (Luke 2.7) is in the Greek "no place for them in the inn." "Thou hast set my feet in a large room" has the Hebrew word for "a broad place" (Psalm 31.8). "Uppermost room," "chief room," and "highest room" translate the same Greek word *prōtoklisia,* which means "the place of honor." It occurs in the singular (Matthew 23.6; Luke 14.8) and in the plural (Mark 12.39; Luke 14.7). "The lowest room" (Luke 14.9, 10) is "the lowest place."

"In the room of Joab" (2 Samuel 19.13) means "in place of Joab"; and "dwelt in their rooms" (1 Chronicles 4.41) means "settled in their place." "In the room of his father Herod" (Matthew 2.22) represents the Greek preposition *anti,* which means instead of, in place of. "Porcius Festus came into Felix' room" (Acts 24.27) stands for Greek which means literally, "Felix received a successor Porcius Festus." RSV translates "Felix was succeeded by Porcius Festus."

In Genesis 24.23, 25; 26.22; Proverbs 18.16; Luke 14.22 both versions use "room" in the sense of space or place. (For a note on 1 Corinthians 14.16 see OCCUPY.)

**RUDE.** When Paul admitted, according to KJ, that he was "rude in speech," it did not mean that he was rough, unrefined, boorish, or discourteous (2 Corinthians 11.6). The word "rude" here goes back to Tyndale, and has the now rare and archaic meaning of inexpert, unskilled. It translates the Greek term *idiōtēs* (see UNLEARNED). What Paul grants is that he is not a professional orator. RSV reads, "Even if I am unskilled in speaking, I am not in knowledge; in every way we have made this plain to you in all things."

**SACKBUT** appears only in the stylized list of musical instruments sounded at the dedication of the golden image which King Nebuchadnezzar had set up (Daniel 3.5, 7, 10, 15), and it appears there only by mistranslation. A sackbut was a bass trumpet, an early form of the slide trombone. But the Aramaic word in this list is *sabbeka',* which means a "trigon," a triangular lyre or harp with four strings. The Greek word for this instrument was *sambukē,* which appears in both Latin and English as "sambuca." For some reason Coverdale thought that a sambuca was a wind instrument, and "the Geneva translators, accepting this view, seem to have chosen the rendering 'sackbut' on account of its resemblance in sound to the Aramaic word" (OED).

**SAFEGUARD,** as noun, occurs in an obsolete sense in 1 Samuel 22.23, where David assures Abiathar, "with me thou *shalt be* in safeguard." RSV reads "with me you shall be in safekeeping."

**SAY ME (THEE) NAY** is to say No to me (thee), to refuse. The expression appears in 1 Kings 2.16–20 as translation of a Hebrew idiom which means literally turn back my (thy) face. This Hebrew idiom is employed twice by Adonijah in making a request of Bathsheba (vs. 16, 17), and twice by Bathsheba in making this request of Solomon (vs. 20). KJ translates by "deny" in verse 16 and "say nay" in the other three cases. The revised versions of 1885–1901 use "deny" in verses 16 and 20, and "say nay" in verse 17. RSV uses "refuse" in each case.

**SCALL** occurs only in Leviticus 13.30–37; 14.54. It translates the Hebrew word *netheq,* which means a scab, an eruption of skin on the head or in the beard. Literally, it means "a tearing off," that is, something which one wants to scratch or tear away. RSV translates it "itch," and for "the plague of the scall" has "the itching disease." OED says that dry scall is psoriasis and that humid scall is eczema.

**SCARCE** is used three times in KJ as an adverb. In two cases RSV substitutes "scarcely": Genesis 27.30, "Jacob had scarcely gone"; and Acts 14.18, "With these words they scarcely restrained the people from offering sacrifice to them." In Acts 27.7 "scarce" has the rare or obsolete meaning "with difficulty." RSV reads, "We sailed slowly for a number of days, and arrived with difficulty off Cnidus." The same Greek adverb occurs in the following verse, where it is translated "hardly" by KJ and "with difficulty" by RSV.

**SCRIP** is defined by OED as "a small bag, wallet, or satchel, especially one carried by a pilgrim, a shepherd, or a beggar." The word, in this sense, is quite lost to common usage, and Webster marks it archaic. KJ uses it for the receptable in which the young David carried the stones for his sling (1 Samuel 17.40) and for the traveling bags which Jesus forbade his disciples to carry (Matthew 10:10, Mark 6.8,

Luke 9.3; 10.4; 22.35, 36). RV retained "scrip" in the account of David's exploit, but changed to "wallet" in the New Testament; ASV in 1901 used "wallet" in the Old Testament story as well. These decisions illustrate one of the many perils of translation, the use of a word in a sense which is already on the decline. OED records N. P. Willis, 1845, as the first to use "wallet" for a pocketbook for holding paper money without folding, or documents. Since the publication of RV and ASV this meaning has replaced all others in common speech.

There is no difficulty in the New Testament passages; RSV here simply says "bag," a word which fits the traveling bags of today as well as those of the first century. But 1 Samuel 17.40 presents a problem. It reads in KJ: "He . . . chose him five smooth stones out of the brook, and put them in a shepherd's bag which he had, even in a scrip." The word for "scrip" is *yalqut,* which occurs only here. Many scholars regard "in the shepherd's bag which he had" as a gloss to explain *yalqut* and "even" as simply the sign of apposition (see EVEN). RSV reads "put them in his shepherd's bag, in his wallet." This lends itself to misunderstanding, however, as the reader may infer that the wallet was a purse kept with other contents in a large shepherd's bag. It would probably be better to omit the gloss, as Smith does, and read "put them in his bag"; or, if the gloss be retained, to read "put them in his shepherd's bag or wallet."

Shakespeare has a fancy use of "scrip" in *As You Like It,* III, 2, 169: "Come, shepherd, let us make an honourable retreat; though not with bag and baggage, yet with scrip and scrippage."

**SEA MONSTER** appears once in KJ: "Even the sea monsters draw out the breast, they give suck to their young ones" (Lamentations 4.3). Its appearance is due to confusion of two Hebrew words which are spelled alike, one meaning dragon or sea monster, and the other meaning jackal. The revised versions and other modern translations use "jackals" here. RSV has:

"Even the jackals give the breast
and suckle their young."

The error has a long history, for the Greek Septuagint here used the word for "dragons" and the Latin Vulgate used *lamiae.* A *lamia,* in Latin, was a witch who was supposed to suck children's blood; and the same word in Greek means a fabulous she-monster who feeds on human flesh, a bugbear to frighten children, or a man-eating shark. The word "lamia" came into English from the Greek and Latin by the way of French and was used in this text by Coverdale and Matthew: "The

Lamyes geue their young ones suck with bare brestes." The Great Bible changed to "dragons," which was retained by the Geneva Bible and the Bishops' Bible. KJ stands alone in the use of "sea monsters" here. "Jackals" was a new word in 1611, and recognition of its proper place in this text had to await the increasing knowledge of Bible lands and languages which the nineteenth century began to bring.

The revised versions use "sea monster" instead of "whale" in Genesis 1.21 and Job 7.12 and instead of "dragon" in Psalm 148.7.

**SECONDARILY** is used in an obsolete sense in 1 Corinthians 12.28, "first apostles, secondarily prophets." The Greek simply means second or secondly, without the connotation of subordinate importance which "secondarily" now conveys. RSV translates, "And God has appointed in the church first apostles, second prophets, third teachers, then workers of miracles, then healers, helpers, administrators, speakers in various kinds of tongues."

Shakespeare's *Much Ado About Nothing,* V, 1, 221, has an example of the use of "secondarily" in this obsolete sense: "they have spoken untruths; secondarily, they are slanders; . . . thirdly, they have verified unjust things; and, to conclude, they are lying knaves."

**SECURE** as used in KJ means without care or anxiety, confident, free from apprehension or distrust. It describes a state of mind, which may or may not be justified by the objective facts. This sense of the word is archaic; when we now use the word "secure," it means more than feeling safe; it means being safe, in so far as men can judge of safety in a precarious world. When KJ says in Judges 8.11 that "the host was secure," the meaning is that "the army was off its guard." The people of Laish, "quiet and secure" (Judges 18.7, 10, 27), were "quiet and unsuspecting." "Thou shalt be secure, because there is hope" (Job 11.18) means "you will have confidence, because there is hope." "Devise not evil against thy neighbour, seeing he dwelleth securely by thee" (Proverbs 3.29) means:

"Do not plan evil against your neighbor
who dwells trustingly beside you."

In Micah 2.8, "them that pass by securely as men averse from war" means "those who pass by trustingly with no thought of war."

**SEEING,** when used as a conjunction, means in view of the fact that, inasmuch as, since, because. In the fifteenth and sixteenth centuries "seen" was also used as a conjunction, in the same sense. The two words were late additions to a group of conjunctions, having the same meaning, which date from Old English—sen, sene, sin, syne, sith, sithen, sithence, since.

"Seeing" appears 112 times in KJ. In 33 cases it is the participle of the verb "see"; it is retained by RSV in 16 of these cases, and elsewhere usually replaced by a clause, "when (one) saw."

The conjunction "seeing" represents corresponding conjunctions in the Hebrew or Greek in 23 cases. It is retained by RSV in Judges 19.23; 1 Samuel 17.36; Ezra 9.13, and elsewhere replaced by "because" (Numbers 15.26; Judges 17.13; Ezekiel 21.4), "for" (Exodus 23.9; Numbers 16.3; Daniel 2.47), "since" (Leviticus 10.17; Judges 21.16; Job 14.5; Luke 1.34; 23.40; Acts 2.15; 13.46; Romans 3.30; 2 Corinthians 11.18; 2 Thessalonians 1.6; Hebrews 4.6; 5.11). Simpler translations are at 1 Corinthians 14.16, where KJ has, "how shall he that occupieth the room of the unlearned say Amen at thy giving of thanks, seeing he understandeth not what thou sayest?" and RSV, "how can any one in the position of an outsider say the 'Amen' to your thanksgiving when he does not know what you are saying?" and at Ecclesiastes 6.11, where KJ has "Seeing there be many things that increase vanity, what *is* man the better?" and RSV, "The more words, the more vanity, and what is man the better?"

In 56 cases the conjunction "seeing" does not represent a corresponding conjunction in the Hebrew or Greek. The list is too long to reproduce here; it can be found in Strong's *Concordance*. "Seeing" is in these cases usually an interpretation of the ubiquitous Hebrew connective *w* or of the causal use of a Greek participle. RSV retains "seeing" in 16 of these cases, and in others replaces it, chiefly by "since." Cases in which RSV deletes "seeing" without replacement are: Job 21.34; 28.21; Isaiah 49.21; Acts 17.24; 2 Corinthians 4.1; 11.19; 2 Peter 3.17. A typical example is 1 Peter 1.22, where KJ has "Seeing ye have purified your souls in obeying the truth through the Spirit unto unfeigned love of the brethren, *see that ye* love one another with a pure heart fervently." Here "through the Spirit" and "pure" have no warrant in the ancient manuscripts, but "seeing" and "see that ye" are the unnecessary elaborations of sixteenth-century English. RSV translates, "Having purified your souls by your obedience to the truth for a sincere love of the brethren, love one another earnestly from the heart."

The Shakespeare *Concordance* cites 53 occurrences of "seeing" in his plays and poems. In 11 of these it is a conjunction. Examples are: "Seeing gentle words will not prevail, Assail them with the army" (*King Henry VI, Part II*, IV, 2, 184); "Seeing thou hast proved so unnatural a father" (*King Henry VI, Part III*, I, 1, 218); "Seeing that death, a necessary end, Will come when it will come" (*Julius Caesar*, II, 2, 36). Shakespeare uses "sith" 22 times, "sithence" 2 times, and "since" 86 times.

**SEETHE, SOD, SODDEN** are always used by KJ in an obsolete sense. "Seethe" is used as a transitive verb meaning to cook food by boiling or stewing; "sod" is used as the past tense of this verb, and "sodden" as its past participle. In eight cases these words refer to the boiling of sacrificial meat that it may be eaten. A typical passage is the account of the behavior of the sons of Eli (1 Samuel 2.12–17). It was specifically stated, however, that the passover lamb should not be boiled: "Eat not of it raw, nor sodden at all with water, but roast *with* fire" (Exodus 12.9); RSV "Do not eat any of it raw or boiled with water, but roasted." This distinction was observed at the great passover commanded by King Josiah at Jerusalem: "They roasted the passover with fire according to the ordinance; but the *other* holy *offerings* sod they in pots, and in caldrons, and in pans, and divided *them* speedily among all the people" (2 Chronicles 35.13); RSV "They roasted the passover lamb with fire according to the ordinance; and they boiled the holy offerings in pots, in caldrons, and in pans, and carried them quickly to all the lay people."

"Thou shalt not seethe a kid in his mother's milk" (Exodus 23.19; 34.26; Deuteronomy 14.21) commands the rejection of a Canaanite pagan practice of preparing a sacrifice by cooking it in milk.

When Jacob "sod pottage" (Genesis 25.29), the meaning is that he "was boiling pottage." "The hands of the pitiful women have sodden their own children" (Lamentations 4.10) means "The hands of compassionate women have boiled their own children."

"Seethe," "sod," and "sodden" began early to acquire the physical and figurative meanings which they have today. "Lovers and madmen have such seething brains," says Theseus in *A Midsummer Night's Dream*, V, 1, 4. In *Troilus and Cressida* Shakespeare has this play on words: "*Pandarus:* I will make a complimental assault upon him, for my business seethes. *Servant:* Sodden business! there's a stewed phrase indeed!" (III, 1, 44). But none of these other meanings appear in KJ, where "seethe" always means "boil," and "sod" and "sodden" mean "boiled."

**SEE TO** means attend to, provide for, take care of. But it does not have this meaning in Joshua 22.10, where the altar erected by the tribes of Israel which settled in Gilead is described—"when they came unto the borders of Jordan, . . . (they) built there an altar by

Jordan, a great altar to see to." The Hebrew means that it was great to look at, great in appearance, great to the sight. RSV translates "an altar of great size." The same Hebrew phrase occurs in Genesis 2.9, where both versions read "every tree that is pleasant to the sight."

**SELFSAME** means the very same. The word is not used by RSV, which substitutes such expressions as "On the very same day" (Genesis 7.13), "that very day" (Deuteronomy 32.48), "at that very moment" (Matthew 8.13). Two New Testament passages in which "selfsame" appears may be cited for comparison. 1 Corinthians 12.11 reads in KJ: "But all these worketh that one and the selfsame Spirit, dividing to every man severally as he will." RSV has: "All these are inspired by one and the same Spirit, who apportions to each one individually as he wills." 2 Corinthians 7.11 reads: "For behold this selfsame thing, that ye sorrowed after a godly sort, what carefulness it wrought in you, yea, *what* clearing of yourselves, yea, *what* indignation, yea, *what* fear, yea, *what* vehement desire, yea, *what* zeal, yea, *what* revenge! In all *things* ye have approved yourselves to be clear in this matter." RSV has: "For see what earnestness this godly grief has produced in you, what eagerness to clear yourselves, what indignation, what alarm, what longing, what zeal, what punishment! At every point you have proved yourselves guiltless in the matter."

**SERVE.** An obsolete idiom appears in Jeremiah 25.14, prophesying punishment for Babylon and the Chaldeans: "Many nations and great kings shall serve themselves of them also." The meaning is expressed in RSV: "Many nations and great kings shall make slaves even of them."

This idiom is described, and examples given, in paragraph 39 of OED's treatment of the verb "serve." Its first appearance was in the Geneva Bible. Other occurrences in KJ are Jeremiah 27.7; 30.8; 34.9, 10; Ezekiel 34.27. In the last three of these cases RSV uses the word "enslave." For example, where KJ has "that none should serve himself of them, *to wit,* of a Jew his brother," RSV reads "that no one should enslave a Jew, his brother."

**SETTLE.** A settle is something to sit on. The word was applied to either of the two ledges of the altar in the temple described in Ezekiel 43.13–17. These ledges were part of the structure of the altar, each a cubit wide, surrounding the altar. The lower ledge was at the height of two cubits, and the upper ledge six cubits, above the base of the altar. The altar hearth was four cubits above the upper ledge, and the four horns of the altar projected one cubit above the hearth. It hardly needs to be said that the priests did not sit upon these ledges while offering sacrifice, and thus the word "settle" is inappropriate.

**SEVEN STARS, THE,** is the term used in Amos 5.8 for the Pleiades. The same Hebrew word is translated "Pleiades" by KJ in Job 9.9; 38.31. In all three passages the Pleiades and Orion are cited as evidence of God's creative power and control. (See INFLUENCES)

**SEVER** means to separate, to cut apart what is normally together, to cut off from the main body or stem. The word appears once in RSV, in the law concerning the priest's procedure when a turtledove is presented as a sin offering: "he shall wring its head from its neck, but shall not sever it" (Leviticus 5.8); KJ "divide it asunder."

"Sever" is not retained by RSV in any of the seven passages where it appears in KJ. "Moses severed three cities" (Deuteronomy 4.41) means "Moses set apart three cities" to be cities of refuge east of the Jordan. "They shall sever out men of continual employment, passing through the land" means "They will set apart men to pass through the land continually" (Ezekiel 39.14). These are examples of the use of "sever" in an obsolete sense which OED describes as "Biblical language."

Passages in which "separate" is the clearer word: "I . . . have severed you from *other* people" (Leviticus 20.26); RSV "I . . . have separated you from the peoples." "Heber . . . had severed himself from the Kenites" (Judges 4.11); RSV "separated from." "Sever the wicked from among the just" (Matthew 13.49); RSV "separate the evil from the righteous."

An identical Hebrew verb is used in Exodus 8.22, "I will sever in that day the land of Goshen"; in Exodus 9.4, "the LORD shall sever between the cattle of Israel and the cattle of Egypt"; and in Exodus 11.7, "the LORD doth put a difference between the Egyptians and Israel." RSV uses "set apart" in the first of these passages, and "make a distinction" in the other two.

**SEVERAL** is used in the obsolete sense of "separate" when it is stated that King Azariah "dwelt in a several house" because he was a leper (2 Kings 15.5; 2 Chronicles 26.21).

"A several tenth deal of flour" is prescribed in Numbers 28.13, to accompany the burnt offering of a lamb. It means the tenth of an ephah of flour, according to verse 5 of the same chapter. Verse 12 prescribes that three tenths of an ephah of flour be offered with a bullock, and two tenths with a ram; verse 13 requires simply "a tenth" with a lamb. The Hebrew has neither the numeral one nor any adjective. The word "several" was inserted by the KJ translators, and was obviously employed in the obsolete sense of "single," "one and only one." This prescription of "a several tenth deal" is repeated in 28.21, 29; 29.10, 15 in a code of sacrificial law to which KJ adds confusion by referring to flour as a "meat offering." RSV strikes out "several" and "deal" wherever they appear in these chapters, and refers to the flour as a "cereal offering."

"Every several gate was of one pearl" is part of the description of the new Jerusalem (Revelation 21.21). Here again the word "several" is a tautology introduced by the translators. A literal translation of the Greek is "each one of the gates." The versions prior to KJ had "every gate"; RSV has "each of the gates."

"To every man according to his several ability" is more directly, and quite as accurately, translated "to each according to his ability" (Matthew 25.15). (For "severally," 1 Corinthians 12.11, see SELF-SAME.)

**SHADE, SHADOW.** The King James Version uses "shade" only once (Psalm 121.5). RSV follows present English usage, which prefers "shade" where the meaning is protection from the light and heat of the sun. Examples are: "a shadow in the daytime from the heat" (Isaiah 4.6); RSV "a shade by day from the heat." "Sat under it in the shadow" (Jonah 4.5); RSV "sat under it in the shade."

**SHAMBLES.** "Whatsoever is sold in the shambles, *that* eat, asking no question for conscience sake" (1 Corinthians 10.25). RSV reads "meat market." The word "shambles" is persistently used to describe a room or scene of wreckage—broken furniture, things overturned and thrown about—and probably will come to have that meaning even though it is not the correct one. It is supposed to mean a place where blood is all over everything, like a slaughterhouse. When King Henry disclaims any thought "to make a shambles of the parliament-house" he means to refrain from making it a scene of bloodshed and carnage (*King Henry VI, Part III*, I, 1, 71).

**SHAMEFACEDNESS.** In 1 Timothy 2.9 the KJ translators wrote "that women adorne themselves in modest apparell, with shamefastnesse and sobrietie." The text thus appeared in 1611 and for sixty years thereafter. Then, as one of various printer's changes, the word "shamefac'dness" appeared. Its spelling was changed to "shamefacedness" in 1743, and this has been kept to the present day. The change is unfair to the KJ translators, for the word which they used, "shamefastness," referred to character, while "shamefacedness" refers to appearance. Paul may be accused of failing to afford to women their full place in the life of the Church, but at least he did not require them to go about shamefacedly. The revised versions of 1881 and 1901 restored "shamefastness." RSV translates, "that women should adorn themselves modestly and sensibly in seemly apparel."

**SHAPEN** is the old past participle of "shape" and appears once in KJ (Psalm 51.5), "I was shapen in iniquity." The word is here used in the obsolete sense of "created." It is, however, a mistranslation of the Hebrew, which means "I was brought forth in iniquity." KJ makes a similar error at Job 15.7, where it uses "made"; but it translates the same Hebrew word correctly in Proverbs 8.24, 25. The revised versions have "brought forth" in each of these passages.

**SHARE** appears only once in KJ (1 Samuel 13.20), where it means a plowshare, the blade of a plow. As a verb meaning to divide a possession with others and as a noun denoting the portions thus allotted, the word was still new in 1611. Shakespeare used it freely, but the KJ translators not at all. They used the nouns "portion" and "part," and the verbs "communicate," "impart," and "partake" or "be partaker of." In the great chapter concerning fasting, they use the verb "deal"—"*Is it* not to deal thy bread to the hungry?" (Isaiah 58.7). RSV reads: "Is it not to share your bread with the hungry?"

**SHEEPMASTER** is an old word for a sheep owner. It is applied to Mesha, king of Moab, with the statement that he "rendered unto the king of Israel an hundred thousand lambs, and an hundred thousand rams, with the wool" (2 Kings 3.4). The Hebrew word used here means a sheep breeder, dealer, or tender. It is the word in Amos 1.1, where Amos is described as "among the shepherds of Tekoa" (RSV). King Mesha was in the business on a large scale. The Hebrew for "rendered" means "used to pay," and the Targum adds "annually." RSV translates: "Mesha king of Moab was a sheep breeder; and he had to deliver annually to the king of Israel a hundred thousand lambs, and the wool of a hundred thousand rams."

**SHEW** is a variant spelling of "show" which is now obsolete except in legal language and in the Bible. OED states that it represents an obsolete pronunciation, rhyming with words like "view" and "true." ASV and RSV use the spelling "show."

"Surely every man walketh in a vain shew" is better translated, "Surely man goes about as a shadow!" (Psalm 39.6; the full context, verses 4–6, should be read). Where it is said that the scribes "for a shew make long prayers" (Luke 20.47) the Greek word is used which both KJ and RSV translate by "in pretense" (Philippians 1.18). In Colossians 2.15, "made a shew of them openly" means "made a public example of them"; and in 2.23 "a shew of wisdom" is "an appearance of wisdom."

The verb "shew" is used in KJ for 18 different Hebrew verbs and for 25 Greek verbs, each of which has its own meaning. "Shew" appears nearly 400 times in KJ, and "show" appears almost 300 times in RSV. Among the replacements of "shew" is "proclaim" (Psalms 19.1; 71.18; Matthew 12.18; Acts 16.17; 26.23). The most beloved passage which uses the verb "shew" is 1 Corinthians 11.26: "For as often as ye eat this bread, and drink this cup, ye do shew the Lord's death till he come." RSV translates, "For as often as you eat this bread and drink the cup, you proclaim the Lord's death until he comes."

An oddly confused rendering is Job 36.32–33: "With clouds he covereth the light; and commandeth it *not to shine* by *the cloud* that cometh betwixt. The noise thereof sheweth concerning it, the cattle also concerning the vapour." RSV translates:

> "He covers his hands with the lightning,
>      and commands it to strike the mark.
> Its crashing declares concerning him,
>      who is jealous with anger against iniquity."

See *The Interpreter's Bible,* vol. 3, p. 1164, for an explanation of this rendering, with which the modern translations by Moffatt, Menge, and Hamp and Stenzel agree, as well as the Zurich Bible. The latter reads:

> *Seine Hände bedeckt er mit Blitzen*
> *und entbietet sie gegen das Ziel.*
> *Ihn kündet an sein Kriegsruf,*
> *den Zorn erregend wider den Frevel.*

**SHIPPING.** To take shipping is an archaic phrase which means to embark. It appears in John 6.24, "they also took shipping." The revised versions translate the Greek literally, "they themselves got into the boats." The passage covers verses 22 to 24, and reads in KJ:

"The day following, when the people which stood on the other side of the sea saw that there was none other boat there, save that one whereinto his disciples were entered, and that Jesus went not with his disciples into the boat, but *that* his disciples were gone away alone; (Howbeit there came other boats from Tiberias nigh unto the place where they did eat bread, after that the Lord had given thanks:) When the people therefore saw that Jesus was not there, neither his disciples, they also took shipping, and came to Capernaum, seeking for Jesus."

This translation is confused by four inaccuracies: (1) the fourth word in verse 22, "when," is not justified by the ancient text; (2) the clause "save that one whereinto his disciples were entered" is an explanatory gloss which does not belong to the ancient text; (3) there is no warrant for placing verse 23 in parentheses; (4) the phrase "took shipping" is inappropriate when the Greek means "got into the boats," that is, the boats which were mentioned in verse 23.

The KJ translators are to blame only for the last of these inaccuracies. Tyndale and the other sixteenth-century translations from the Greek had "took shipping" but they also had "ship" and "ships" in the preceding verses. KJ followed the Rheims New Testament in the more exact rendering "boat" and "boats" in 22 and 23, but failed to follow it in verse 24.

The KJ translators did not have access to the ancient manuscripts which have exposed (1) and (2) above. As for (3), that is an error in punctuation for which they were not responsible. KJ as published in 1611 does not interrupt the narrative by setting verse 23 apart within parentheses. That was first done in the black letter folio edition published by Robert Barker, Printer to the King, in 1634. Barker's folio edition of 1640 did not have the parentheses, but the Cambridge edition of 1638 did, and after 1640 they got established as part of the text. The revisions by Dr. Paris, 1762, and Dr. Blayney, 1769, retained them; so did the revisions of 1881 and 1901. Among the sixteenth-century English versions, only the Great Bible had parentheses here. Twentieth-century translations, almost without exception, do not have them. RSV translates the passage:

"On the next day the people who remained on the other side of the sea saw that there had been only one boat there, and that Jesus had not entered the boat with his disciples, but that his disciples had gone away alone. However, boats from Tiberias came near the place where they ate the bread after the Lord had given thanks. So when the people saw that Jesus was not there, nor his disciples, they themselves got into the boats and went to Capernaum, seeking Jesus."

**SHROUD.** ". . . with a shadowing shroud" is a dismally incongruous item in the picture of a cedar in Lebanon which was the greatest and most beautiful of trees (Ezekiel 31.3). But the word "shroud" is here used in the obsolete sense of shade or protection. The messenger from Caesar to Cleopatra invited her to put herself "under his shrowd" (*Antony and Cleopatra,* III, 13, 71).

The expression "a shadowing shroud" is, however, a double translation, for one of the two Hebrew words which it represents means "shade" and the other is elsewhere translated by KJ as "bough" (Isaiah 17.9), "forests" (2 Chronicles 27.4), and "a (the) wood" (1 Samuel 23.15, 16, 18, 19). The revised versions of 1881–1901 have "a forest-like shade"; RSV has "forest shade."

**SILVERLING.** A piece of silver, a silver coin, a shekel. Tyndale used the word in Acts 19.19: "Many of them which used curious craftes, brought their bokes and burned them before all men, and they counted the price of them and founde it fifty thousande silverlynges." He added the marginal note: "These syluerlinges which we now and then call pence the Jues call sicles, and are worth a x. pence sterlynge." Coverdale and Rheims used "pence" here; the Great Bible and the Geneva Bible, "siluerlynges"; the Bishops' Bible, KJ, and the revised versions, "pieces of silver." In the Old Testament, Coverdale used "silverlings" in Judges 9.4; 16.5; 17.2, 3, 4, 10 and Isaiah 7.23. The Geneva Bible used "pieces of silver" or "shekels of silver" in these passages. KJ followed Geneva except in Isaiah 7.23, where it followed the Bishops' Bible in the retention of "silverlings." Tyndale and Coverdale doubtless got the word from Martin Luther's German Bible, which has *Silberlinge* in all the O.T. passages.

**SIMILITUDE** means the form, likeness, or image of a person or thing. The word appears 12 times in KJ, 6 times in RV, once in ASV, and not at all in RSV. The word concerning Moses, "the similitude of the LORD shall he behold" (Numbers 12.8) means "he beholds the form of the LORD." "Form" is the correct word also in Deuteronomy 4.12, 15, 16. RSV has "one in the likeness of the sons of men" (Daniel 10.16), "in the likeness of Melchizedek" (Hebrews 7.15), "made in the likeness of God" (James 3.9). The description of the ornamentation of the molten sea which is given in 2 Chronicles 4.3 differs from that in 1 Kings 7.24. RSV harmonizes these, and uses "figures" rather than "the similitude." (See KNOP)

"They changed their glory into the similitude of an ox" (Psalm 106.20) is an opaque and misleading statement concerning the Israelites' worship of the molten calf. RSV translates, "They exchanged the glory of God for the image of an ox."

In Psalm 144 verses 1–11 are the prayer of an individual that he may be delivered from his foes, and verses 12–15 are concerned with the welfare of the community. The KJ rendering hides this fact by referring to the psalmist's alien foes as "strange children," and by joining verses 12–14 in one sentence with verse 11. RSV begins a new strophe with verse 12, which it translates:

> "May our sons in their youth
> be like plants full grown,
> our daughters like corner pillars
> cut for the structure of a palace."

Those who have hoped for daughters "polished after the similitude of a palace" may regret the passing of that line, but what does it mean? It is clearly not what the Hebrew means.

"Them that had not sinned after the similitude of Adam's transgression" (Romans 5.14) means "those whose sins were not like the transgression of Adam."

Because the Latin Vulgate sometimes translated the Greek word for "parable" by *similitudo,* the word "similitude" was occasionally used in the sense of parable by Wyclif, Tyndale, and their successors. KJ retains the word only once in this sense, "I have multiplied visions, and used similitudes, by the ministry of the prophets" (Hosea 12.10). RSV has: "it was I who multiplied visions, and through the prophets gave parables."

**SIMPLE.** When Paul wrote to the Romans, "I would have you wise unto that which is good, and simple concerning evil," he was not counseling gullibility or foolishness (16.19). The "simple" is here employed in its oldest meaning, which OED gives as free from duplicity, dissimulation, or guile; innocent and harmless; honest, open, straightforward. The Greek adjective it represents appears also in Jesus' counsel to the twelve as he sent them out to preach and to heal, "be wise as serpents and innocent as doves" (Matthew 10.16 RSV). And Paul used it in urging the Philippians to be "blameless and innocent, children of God without blemish in the midst of a crooked and perverse generation" (2.15). RSV translates his word to the Romans: "I would have you wise as to what is good and guileless as to what is evil."

**SIMPLICITY.** "He that giveth, *let him do it* with simplicity" (Romans 12.8) is a strange exhortation, in view of the fact that the Greek noun here represented by "simplicity" means "liberality." In 2 Corinthians KJ itself translates it by "liberality" (8.2), "bountifulness" (9.11), and "liberal distribution" (9.13). RSV translates these similar contexts consistently.

The primary meaning of this Greek noun is singleness of mind and heart, sincerity. But the KJ rendering of 2 Corinthians 11.3 is hard to understand—"I fear lest . . . your minds should be corrupted from the simplicity that is in Christ." The best ancient manuscripts have also the word for "purity." RSV translates: "I am afraid that . . . your thoughts will be led astray from a sincere and pure devotion to Christ."

**SINCERE** was a new word in the sixteenth century, and was applied to things as well as to persons and motives. "As newborn babes, desire the sincere milk of the word, that ye may grow thereby" (1 Peter 2.2) is a KJ rendering which is now seen to be defective at several points. It is not *as* newborn babes, but *like* newborn babes who long for the mother's breast, that Peter exhorts the exiles to long for the milk of the gospel. The verb has a correlative adjective which KJ translates "my brethren dearly beloved and longed for" (Philippians 4.1). And the aim is not simply to grow, but to "grow up to salvation" —the last phrase appears in the ancient Greek manuscripts, but had been lost from the medieval manuscripts upon which KJ was based. The adjective *adolos,* which modifies the word for "milk," means without deceit, unadulterated, pure, and frequently occurs in the last of these senses in the Greek papyri. RSV accordingly translates, "Like newborn babes, long for the pure spiritual milk, that by it you may grow up to salvation."

In his second epistle Peter says, "I stir up your pure minds by way of remembrance" (3.1). The adjective for "pure" here is *eilikrinēs,* which KJ translates by "sincere," and RSV by "pure," in Philippians 1.10. Both versions translate *eilikrineia* by "sincerity" (1 Corinthians 5.8; 2 Corinthians 1.12; 2.17). RSV has in 2 Peter 3.1, "This is now the second letter that I have written to you, beloved, and in both of them I have aroused your sincere mind by way of reminder."

**SINGULAR.** "A singular vow" (Leviticus 27.2) does not mean a vow that stands alone, or that is eccentric or peculiar. The adjective "singular" here means above the ordinary, especially good or great. It is a sense in which the word was commonly used from about 1500 to 1650, OED records, but is now more rare. This chapter of Leviticus deals with the rates and procedures whereby vows and tithes may be commuted by the payment of money. Verse 2 introduces the section dealing with the dedication of persons to the LORD, as Jephthah's daughter or Samuel had been dedicated, and providing a scale of redemption. RSV reads "a special vow of persons to the LORD." The same Hebrew expression appears in Numbers 6.2, where RSV reads, "When either a man or a woman makes a special vow, the vow of a Nazirite. . . ."

**SITH.** An old word for "since," sharing its several meanings. "Sith" appears once in KJ, and "since" 69 times. (See SEEING)

The one occurrence of "sith" is Ezekiel 35.6: "sith thou hast not hated blood, even blood shall pursue thee." RSV, with the aid of the Septuagint, translates: "because you are guilty of blood, therefore blood shall pursue you."

Shakespeare uses "sith" 22 times. Examples are: "Talk not of France, sith thou hast lost it all" (*King Henry VI, Part III*, I, 1, 110); "Sith there's no justice in earth nor hell, We will solicit heaven" (*Titus Andronicus*, IV, 3, 49); "sith I am enter'd in this cause so far, . . . I will go on" (*Othello*, III, 3, 411).

**SKILL.** The obsolete phrase "can skill" meant to have knowledge, competence, or skill, in some specified field. It is used three times with a following infinitive, in Solomon's message to Hiram, king of Tyre. "*There is* not among us any that can skill to hew timber like unto the Sidonians" (1 Kings 5.6) means "there is no one among us who knows how to cut timber like the Sidonians." So also "can skill to cut timber in Lebanon" (2 Chronicles 2.8) means "know how to cut timber in Lebanon." The preceding verse (2.7) reads in KJ: "Send me now therefore a man cunning to work in gold, and in silver, and in brass, and in iron, and in purple, and crimson, and blue, and that can skill to grave with the cunning men that *are* with me in Judah and in Jerusalem, whom David my father did provide." RSV has: "So now send me a man skilled to work in gold, silver, bronze, and iron, and in purple, crimson, and blue fabrics, trained also in engraving, to be with the skilled workers who are with me in Judah and Jerusalem, whom David my father provided."

In 2 Chronicles 34.12 the phrase "can skill of" occurs: "all that could skill of instruments of musick." OED states that this usage with "of" was common in the period 1525 to 1640. RSV translates "all who were skilful with instruments of music."

The post of Chenaniah is poorly described in 1 Chronicles 15.22:

"Chenaniah, chief of the Levites, *was* for song: he instructed about the song, because he *was* skilful." RSV translates, "Chenaniah, leader of the Levites in music, should direct the music, for he understood it."

The word "skill" and its derivatives are used 16 times in KJ and 56 times in RSV. This is largely because of the frequent use in the Old Testament of "cunning" and "curious" in the sense of skilful or skilfully done. (See CUNNING, CURIOUS.) "Hezekiah spake comfortably unto all the Levites that taught the good knowledge of the LORD" (2 Chronicles 30.22) means "Hezekiah spoke encouragingly to all the Levites who showed good skill in the service of the LORD." The word "wise" appears in KJ occasionally where "skilled" is a more accurate translation. See Jeremiah 4.22; Ezekiel 27.8, 9; 1 Corinthians 3.10. The first of these passages reads in KJ: "For my people *is* foolish, they have not known me; they *are* sottish children, and they have none understanding: they *are* wise to do evil, but to do good they have no knowledge." RSV translates:

> "For my people are foolish,
> they know me not;
> they are stupid children,
> they have no understanding.
> They are skilled in doing evil,
> but how to do good they know not."

**SLEIGHT** is defined by OED, in its primary meaning, as "craft or cunning employed so as to deceive." The word was in common use in the sixteenth and seventeenth centuries, but is now rare or obsolete except in connection with feats of juggling or tricks of legerdemain. "Sleight of hand" remains a familiar expression, but "sleight of man" is not so readily understood. The Greek word translated "sleight" in Ephesians 4.14 means dice playing, gambling, cheating, trickery. The KJ rendering, "by the sleight of men, *and* cunning craftiness, whereby they lie in wait to deceive," is free and somewhat expansive. RSV is closer to the Greek: "by the cunning of men, by their craftiness in deceitful wiles."

**SLIME** was used by Tyndale as a translation for the Hebrew word *chemar,* and the word was kept by KJ. "Slime had they for morter" (Genesis 11.3); "the vale of Siddim *was full of* slimepits" (Genesis 14.10); "she took for him an ark of bulrushes, and daubed it with slime and with pitch" (Exodus 2.3). In the prologue to his translation of the five books of Moses (1530) Tyndale wrote: "That slyme was a fatnesse that issued out of the earth, like unto tarre; and thou mayest call it cement if thou wilt." In fact, it was bitumen, or asphalt, which is what *chemar* means. The Greek Septuagint has *asphaltos*, and the Latin Vulgate *bitumen*, in these three texts. The revised versions of 1885 and 1901 kept "slime" with a marginal note, "That is, bitumen." RSV and Smith dismiss "slime" and use "bitumen" in the text.

**SMELL, SAVOUR.** The nouns and verb which are translated "smell" in KJ denote only what is pleasing; the Hebrew had other words for bad odors. RSV retains "smell" for the verb, and in a few cases for the noun. But it generally uses "fragrance," "scent," "perfume," or "pleasing odor" for the noun, depending upon the context.

"Sweet smelling myrrh" was an error for "liquid myrrh," and "the smell of thy nose" is better translated "the scent of your breath" (Song of Solomon 5.5, 13; 7.8). The "perfume" which Moses was commanded to make was "incense" holy to the LORD; the commandment not to make any like it "to smell thereto" means that none of it should be made "to use as perfume" (Exodus 30.38).

The term "sweet savour" refers to God's pleasure in the odor of burnt offerings, and is now translated "pleasing odor" (Genesis 8.21 and many other occurrences). The word of the LORD through the prophet Amos, "I will not smell in your solemn assemblies" (Amos 5.21) means that the LORD will not take pleasure in the burnt offerings of their solemn assemblies. The revised versions translate the clause, "I take no delight in your solemn assemblies."

The noun "savour" refers to taste in the well-known text about salt (Matthew 5.13; Luke 14.34). The verb "savour" which appears in Jesus' rebuke to Peter at Caesarea Philippi means to have a taste for, to relish, like, or care for (Matthew 16.23; Mark 8.33). The Greek verb for which it is used means to think, to set the mind on, to purpose; it is the verb which is translated "Let this mind be in you, which was also in Christ Jesus" (Philippians 2.5). Jesus told Peter that his mind was not on the purposes of God, but of men.

**SMILE.** A correspondent writes: "Why do they laugh and rejoice and shout with joy in the King James Bible but do not smile? The word is never used, but RSV employs it cautiously in Job 29.24."

This verse reads in KJ: "*If* I laughed on them, they believed *it* not; and the light of my countenance they cast not down." RSV translates it:

"I smiled on them when they had no confidence;
    and the light of my countenance they did not cast down."

This translation is not new; RSV took it from the American Standard
Version of 1901. And there is nothing cautious about it; the revisers
radically recast the whole line, and got rid of an ambiguous rendering. There is no "If" in the Hebrew, and no "it" to serve as the object
of "believed." The KJ translators seem to have been misled by the fact
that *sahaq*, "laugh," frequently implies derision or contempt. But it is
also used as a general word (Ecclesiastes 3.4), and for joking (Proverbs
26.19), for making sport (Judges 16.25, 27; 2 Samuel 2.14), making
merry (2 Samuel 6.5, 21), rejoicing (Proverbs 8.30, 31), merrymakers
(Jeremiah 15.17; 30.19; 31.4), children playing in the streets (Zechariah 8.5). The context here implies a friendly laugh or a smile; and
twentieth-century translations in general agree with the interpretation
of ASV and RSV. Ronald Knox translates the verse: "Were they fainthearted, they found me smiling still, and the encouragement of my
glance never failed them."

**SNORTING** appears once (Jeremiah 8.16). RSV translates the sen-
    tence:

"The snorting of their horses is heard from Dan;
    at the sound of the neighing of their stallions
    the whole land quakes."

The spirited description of the war horse (Job 39.19–25) contains a
verse in which KJ misses the meaning (vs. 20): "Canst thou make him
afraid as a grasshopper? the glory of his nostrils *is* terrible." RSV
translates the Hebrew:

"Do you make him leap like the locust?
    His majestic snorting is terrible."

**SNUFF** is a sixteenth-century verb for purposeful and audible inhal-
    ing the breath. It is probably imitative in origin, like sniff,
sniffle, snuffle, sneeze, and snort. To "snuff at" something or some person was to express disdain or contempt. This expression is now obsolete, as its place began to be taken in the eighteenth century by "sniff
at"—which differs only in being sharper and more audible. Malachi
1.6–14 accuses the priests of neglect of duty and of showing contempt
for the altar and the table of the LORD. In verse 13 KJ "snuffed at it" is
replaced by RSV "sniff at me." "The reading of the RSV," says Professor Robert Dentan, "is based upon a Jewish tradition that the original
reading was changed to *at it* in order to avoid the appearance of ir-

reverence. Either rendering . . . makes good sense" (*The Interpreter's Bible,* vol. 6, p. 1129).

"Snuff up the wind" occurs twice, in translation of a different Hebrew verb. RSV reads, "a wild ass used to the wilderness, in her heat sniffing the wind" (Jeremiah 2.24), and "the wild asses stand on the bare heights, they pant for air like jackals" (14.6).

**SOME** is in the singular number in Romans 5.7. It means one, some-one—a now obsolete usage. KJ reads: "For scarcely for a righteous man will one die: yet peradventure for a good man some would even dare to die." There seems to be a contrast here between "one" in the first clause and "some" in the second clause, but in the Greek the subject of each clause is the same singular indefinite pronoun. RSV translates: "Why, one will hardly die for a righteous man—though perhaps for a good man one will dare even to die."

**SOMETIME, SOMETIMES, SOME TIME** all refer to a time in the past, as these terms are used in KJ. The three forms, moreover, have the same obsolete meaning, and translate the same Greek adverb. It is somewhat confusing to the modern reader, for whom "sometime" refers to a particular date or period in either the past or the future, "sometimes" means occasionally, and "some time" may denote a period of duration. He may think that when Paul writes "ye who sometimes were far off" (Ephesians 2.13), "ye were sometimes darkness" (Ephesians 5.8), and "we ourselves also were sometimes foolish" (Titus 3.3), he is referring to merely occasional remoteness or darkness or folly. And he will probably think that "In the which ye also walked some time, when ye lived in them" (Colossians 3.7) means "for some time," that is, for a considerable duration. None of these inferences are warranted by the Greek adverb, which in these passages and in the two where KJ has "sometime" (Colossians 1.21; 1 Peter 3.20) simply means "once" or "formerly" and is so translated by RSV.

**SORE,** as adjective and adverb, appears nearly a hundred times in the archaic sense of severe(ly), intense(ly), very great(ly). "The famine *was* sore" means "the famine was severe" (Genesis 43.1), compare 41.56, 57; 47.4, 13; 1 Kings 18.2; Jeremiah 52.6). "Because thou sore longedst after thy father's house" (Genesis 31.30) means "because you longed greatly for your father's house."

Thirty different Hebrew and Greek words are listed in Young's *Con-

*cordance* for "sore" as adjective and adverb. Twenty of these are verbs, with which "sore" is used to intensify their meaning. For example, "wept (weep) sore" occurs 10 times. In 4 of these cases "sore" represents the cognate accusative with the adjective for "great"—a literal translation would be "wept a (very) great weeping" (Judges 21.2; 2 Samuel 13.36; 2 Kings 20.3; Isaiah 38.3). In Ezra 10.1 the cognate accusative appears without the adjective. In 4 cases "sore" represents the Hebrew idiom which expresses intensity of meaning by repetition, using the absolute infinitive as well as the finite verb (1 Samuel 1.10; Jeremiah 13.17; 22.10; Lamentations 1.2; see GENERALLY, SURELY). RSV uses "wept (weep) bitterly" in these 9 cases. The other occurrence of "wept sore" is Acts 20.37, which RSV translates, "And they all wept and embraced Paul and kissed him."

"Sore war" is "hard fighting" (1 Samuel 14.52); "the battle was sore" means "the battle was hard" (Judges 20.34); "there was a very sore battle" means "the battle was very fierce" (2 Samuel 2.17). "Sore wounded" is "badly wounded" (1 Samuel 31.3; 2 Chronicles 35.23). "Sore pained" is better translated "in anguish"; and "he died of sore diseases," by "he died in great agony" (Psalm 55.4; 2 Chronicles 21.19).

In the story of Samson's wedding (Judges 14.17), "lay sore upon him" means "pressed him hard." It stands for the same Hebrew verb which KJ translates, in the case of Delilah, by "pressed him"—Judges 16.16: "she pressed him daily with her words, and urged him, *so* that his soul was vexed unto death." Both versions translate this verb by "constrain" in Job 32.18.

The plaint of the men of Ashdod, "his hand is sore upon us" (1 Samuel 5.7) means "his hand is heavy upon us." "Sore broken" (Psalm 44.19) is simply "broken" in the Hebrew; but "I am feeble and sore broken" (Psalm 38.8) is more accurately translated "I am utterly spent and crushed."

The expression "sore afraid" appears a dozen times, and is rephrased by RSV to express more exactly the meaning of the verb in each particular context. Examples are: "in great fear" (Exodus 14.10); "in great dread" (Numbers 22.3); "feared greatly for our lives" (Joshua 9.24); "much afraid" (1 Samuel 17.24; 21.12); "filled with fear" (1 Samuel 28.20; Luke 2.9); "horribly afraid" (Ezekiel 27.35); "filled with awe" (Matthew 17.6).

"It grieved me sore" (Nehemiah 13.8) means "I was very angry." "We roar all like bears, and mourn sore like doves" (Isaiah 59.11) is better translated:

"We all growl like bears,
we moan and moan like doves."

Psalm 38.2 reads in KJ, "For thine arrows stick fast in me, and thy hand presseth me sore." RSV translates:

"For thy arrows have sunk into me,
and thy hand has come down on me."

RSV does not use "sore" as an adverb. In a half dozen cases, where the meaning is appropriate, it replaces "sore" by "sorely" (Judges 10.9; 1 Samuel 1.6; Psalms 6.3, 10; 118.18; Isaiah 64.12). A verse where KJ needs revision is Genesis 49.23: "The archers have sorely grieved him, and shot *at him,* and hated him." RSV translates it:

"The archers fiercely attacked him,
shot at him, and harassed him sorely."

**SORE,** as noun, appears 11 times in KJ. It is retained by RSV in Isaiah 1.6, Luke 16.20, 21, and Revelation 16.2, 11. For "a boil breaking forth *with* blains" (Exodus 9.9, 10), RSV has "boils breaking out in sores." For Job's "sore boils" it has "loathsome sores" (Job 2.7).

At two points in the Psalms the use of "sore" is misleading. "My lovers and my friends stand aloof from my sore" (Psalm 38.11) is translated by RSV, "My friends and companions stand aloof from my plague." "My sore ran in the night, and ceased not" (Psalm 77.2) is an erroneous rendering for a Hebrew line which RV and ASV translate, "My hand was stretched out in the night, and slacked not." RSV translates the verse:

"In the day of my trouble I seek the Lord;
in the night my hand is stretched out without wearying;
my soul refuses to be comforted."

**SO THAT** occurs three times in a limiting sense which is now rarely used, meaning on condition that, provided that, if only. Examples of this usage, from the fourteenth century to the nineteenth, are cited in OED under "So," paragraph 2b. The occurrences in KJ are in connection with God's promise to David, "There shall not fail thee a man in my sight to sit on the throne of Israel; so that thy children take heed to their way, that they walk before me as thou hast walked before me" (1 Kings 8.25). This is repeated in 2 Chronicles 6.16, with the unwarranted addition of "yet," resulting in the expression "yet so that." In 2 Chronicles 33.8, another promise to David is cited, "Neither will I any more remove the foot of Israel from out of the land which

I have appointed for your fathers; so that they will take heed to do all that I have commanded them." This appears with slightly different wording in 2 Kings 21.8, where "only if" is used rather than "so that." In Deuteronomy 15.4–5 God's blessing is promised, "Only if thou carefully hearken unto the voice of the LORD thy God."

In all five of these cases the Hebrew has the same adverb and conditional conjunction, *raq im,* which mean "only if." The meaning is better expressed in English by "if only," which the revised versions and twentieth-century translations use in these passages.

**SOTTISH.** Until the seventeenth century a "sot" was a foolish or stupid person, "sotie" was folly, and "sottish" was foolish or stupid. Then "sot," "sottish," and "besotted" began to be restricted to drunkards, and the older meanings became obsolete. KJ uses "sottish" once, in translation of the Hebrew word which it everywhere else translates by "fool," "foolish," "foolishly." The passage is Jeremiah 4.22, which reads in KJ: "For my people *is* foolish, they have not known me; they *are* sottish children, and they have none understanding: they *are* wise to do evil, but to do good they have no knowledge." RSV reads:

> "For my people are foolish,
>    they know me not;
> they are stupid children,
>    they have no understanding.
> They are skilled in doing evil,
>    but how to do good they know not."

"Stupid" was a new word in 1611, and does not appear in KJ. Shakespeare used "stupid" once, "sottish" once, and "sot" seven times. When Caliban advises Stephano to seize Prospero's books, "for without them he's but a sot," the meaning is that without their aid Prospero is as stupid or foolish as Caliban himself (*The Tempest,* III, 2, 100).

**SPACE** in KJ usually refers to a period of time rather than to area, lineal extension, or the measureless expanse in which the earth and sun and stars have place. "The space in which we came from Kadesh-barnea, until we were come over the brook Zered, *was* thirty and eight years" (Deuteronomy 2.14) means "the time from our leaving Kadesh-barnea until we crossed the brook Zared was thirty-eight years." "Space to repent" (Revelation 2.21) is "time to repent." "A little space" (Ezra 9.8) is accurately translated "a brief moment." When

Gamaliel "commanded to put the apostles forth a little space" (Acts 5.34) his order was that they "be put outside for a while." "After they had tarried *there* a space" (Acts 15.33) means "after they had spent some time." "About the space of three hours after" means "After an interval of about three hours" (Acts 5.7; compare Luke 22.59). "There was silence in heaven about the space of half an hour" (Revelation 8.1) means "there was silence in heaven for about half an hour." Other examples are Genesis 29.14; Leviticus 25.8, 30; Acts 19.8, 10, 34.

**SPECIAL** appears twice in KJ. In Deuteronomy 7.6 it translates the Hebrew word *segullah,* for which KJ usually has "peculiar." KJ reads, "the LORD thy God hath chosen thee to be a special people unto himself, above all people that *are* upon the face of the earth"; RSV reads, "the LORD your God has chosen you to be a people for his own possession, out of all the peoples that are on the face of the earth." (See PECULIAR)

In Acts 19.11 "special" translates a Greek phrase which means not happening as usual, out of the ordinary run of events. RSV renders the verse: "God did extraordinary miracles by the hand of Paul."

**SPECIALLY** appears five times, always as translation of the Greek adverb which means most of all, above all, especially. RSV uses "especially" in all these cases—Acts 25.26; 1 Timothy 4.10; 5.8; Titus 1.10; Philemon 16.

**SPED** is the past participle of the verb "speed." It occurs once (Judges 5.30), in the Song of Deborah. The mother of Sisera is pictured as reassuring herself, when her son does not return, by the thought that he and his army have won a great victory and are occupied with the division of the spoil. "Have they not sped?" she says; "have they *not* divided the prey?" "Sped" is here used in the oldest sense of the verb "speed," to succeed, to attain one's purpose. "Have they not sped?" means "Have they not won?" There is another complication, however. The Hebrew means to find. RSV translates: "Are they not finding and dividing the spoil?" (See PREY)

**SPEED,** as a noun in Old and Middle English, meant success, prosperity, good fortune; though it could denote the opposite if preceded by such adjectives as "evil" or "ill." The word is used in its primary sense in Genesis 24.12, where Abraham's servant, having arrived at the city where his master's brother lived, prayed, "O LORD God of my master Abraham, I pray thee, send me good speed this day, and shew kindness unto my master Abraham." RSV has, "O LORD, God of my master Abraham, grant me success today, I pray thee, and show steadfast love to my master Abraham."

**SPITEFULLY** is used in the obsolete sense of disgracefully, shamefully, in Matthew 22.6 and Luke 18.32, where KJ has "entreated *them* spitefully" and "be spitefully entreated." The same Greek verb is translated "were shamefully entreated" in 1 Thessalonians 2.2. The revised versions use "shamefully" in all these contexts. The first is the parable of the marriage feast, the second Jesus' prophecy of his death, and the third Paul's reminiscence of his treatment at Philippi. (See ENTREAT)

**SPOIL** as a noun, meaning captured goods, booty, plunder, appears frequently in KJ, and is generally retained by RSV. But "spoil" as a verb meaning to despoil or plunder is archaic and is not retained. "Ye shall spoil the Egyptians" (Exodus 3.22) means "you shall despoil the Egyptians." "All that pass by the way spoil him" (Psalm 89.41) means "All that pass by despoil him." "For the LORD will plead their cause, and spoil the soul of those that spoiled them" (Proverbs 22.23) is an inaccurate and ambiguous rendering; RSV translates, "for the LORD will plead their cause and despoil of life those who despoil them."

"They spoiled all the cities; for there was exceeding much spoil in them" (2 Chronicles 14.14) is reworded by RSV, "They plundered all the cities, for there was much plunder in them." Haman's edict against the Jews, so dramatically reversed by Esther, included the command *"to take* the spoil of them for a prey" (Esther 3.13; 8.11); RSV translates "to plunder their goods." "Because thou hast spoiled many nations, all the remnant of the people shall spoil thee" (Habakkuk 2.8) is reworded, "Because you have plundered many nations, all the remnant of the peoples shall plunder you." In Jesus' saying about the strong man (Matthew 12.29; Mark 3.27) "spoil his goods" and "spoil his house" mean "plunder his goods" and "plunder his house."

In 2 Samuel 23.10 the Hebrew verb rendered "to spoil" means "to strip"; RSV translates "and the men returned after him only to strip the slain." Compare 1 Samuel 31.8 (=1 Chronicles 10.8) where the same Hebrew verb appears and both versions have "to strip the slain." In Nahum 3.16 this verb is used for locusts stripping off the sheaths of their wings; KJ reads, "the cankerworm spoileth, and fleeth away"; RSV reads, "The locust spreads its wings and flies away."

In Isaiah and Jeremiah the word "spoil" is often used for the Hebrew verb which means destroy, devastate, ruin. An example is "the spoiler spoileth" (Isaiah 21.2) where RSV reads "the destroyer destroys." The same verb occurs in Micah 2.4, where KJ has "We be utterly spoiled" and RSV has "We are utterly ruined." So also Jeremiah 4.13, where KJ reads "Woe unto us! for we are spoiled" and RSV reads "woe to us, for we are ruined!"

In Colossians 2.8, "Beware lest any man spoil you . . . ," the Greek verb means to carry off as booty or as a captive. RSV translates the verse, "See to it that no one makes a prey of you by philosophy and empty deceit, according to human tradition, according to the elemental spirits of the universe, and not according to Christ." In 2.15, "having spoiled principalities and powers," the Greek verb means to strip; RSV translates, "He disarmed the principalities and powers and made a public example of them, triumphing over them in him."

The verb "spoil" is appropriate in Song of Solomon 2.15, for the Hebrew verb means to ruin. RSV translates:

> "Catch us the foxes,
> the little foxes,
> that spoil the vineyards,
> for our vineyards are in blossom."

"Spoiled" is better than "marred" in Jeremiah's acted parable of the "girdle" (Jeremiah 13.7, 9) for the Hebrew verb means to be ruined. The entire passage 13.1–11 should be read. In verse 7 RSV has "the waistcloth was spoiled; it was good for nothing."

**SPRING.** In the sixteenth century one spoke as naturally of "the spring of the day" as of "the break of day." Both expressions appear in KJ. 1 Samuel 9.26 has "it came to pass about the spring of the day," and Judges 19.25 has "when the day began to spring." But KJ also has "until the breaking of the day" (Genesis 32.24), "the day breaketh" (Genesis 32.26), "at break of day" (2 Samuel 2.32), "until the day break, and the shadows flee away" (Song of Solomon 2.17; 4.6), "even till break of day" (Acts 20.11). It uses "the dawning of the day" (Joshua 6.15; Judges 19.26; Job 3.9; 7.4) and "the dawning of the morning" (Psalm 119.147). RSV rejects "spring" in this sense, and uses "dawn" and "break." It gives a literal translation of the Hebrew figures of speech in Job 3.9, "the eyelids of the morning"; and in Song of Solomon 2.17; 4.6, "until the day breathes."

Tyndale had an interesting rendering of Jonah 4.7: "The lorde ordeyned a worme agenst the springe of ye morow morninge." Coverdale began the verse with "But upon the nexte morow agaynst the springe of the daye," and this was kept in Matthew's Bible and the Great Bible. The KJ rendering, "when the morning rose the next day," follows the Geneva Bible and the Bishops' Bible.

The verb "spring" is used with vegetation, in the sense of sprout, shoot, grow, be green. For example, Isaiah 44.4 reads in KJ, "they shall spring up *as* among the grass, as willows by the water courses." RSV reads:

"They shall spring up like grass amid waters,
like willows by flowing streams."

"The pastures of the wilderness do spring" (Joel 2.22) means "the pastures of the wilderness are green."

The noun "spring" is used once as a collective term for the fresh green shoots of trees or plants—"it shall wither in all the leaves of her spring" (Ezekiel 17.9). In this rendering KJ stands alone. Coverdale, Matthew, and the Great Bible had "his green branches"; Geneva and the Bishops' Bible "her bud." The revised versions of 1885–1901 have "that all its fresh springing leaves may wither"; RSV has "so that all its fresh sprouting leaves wither."

The word "spring" is not used in KJ as name for the season of the year which begins with the vernal equinox, though the month Nisan (corresponding to part of March and part of April) was regarded as the first month of the year. RSV uses "spring" 15 times where the Hebrew refers to that season. In five of these cases the Hebrew expression means "at the return of the year." It is so translated by KJ in 1 Kings 20.22, 26; but is rendered "after (when) the year was expired" in 2 Samuel 11.1; 1 Chronicles 20.1; 2 Chronicles 36.10. In 2 Kings 13.20 the Hebrew means "at the coming in of the year." In the promises to Sarah and the woman of Shunem the Hebrew means "when the time revives" (Genesis 18.10, 14; 2 Kings 4.16–17). "The latter rain" means "the spring rain," and is so referred to by RSV (Job 29.23; Proverbs 16.15; Jeremiah 3.3; 5.24; Hosea 6.3; Zechariah 10.1). Exceptions are Deuteronomy 11.14 and Joel 2.23, concerning the LORD's gift of "the early rain" and "the later rain."

**STABLISH** appears 18 times and ESTABLISH 121 times as translation for the same group of Hebrew and Greek verbs. There is no apparent distinction in the KJ usage of the terms. RSV does not use "stablish," and replaces it by "establish" in all but 6 cases. Among these are: "Woe to him who builds a town with blood, and founds a city on iniquity!" (Habakkuk 2.12); "who is able to strengthen you" (Romans 16.25); "he will strengthen you" (2 Thessalonians 3.3).

**STAGGER** is used four times in the KJ Old Testament, always with reference to drunkenness, and is retained by RSV (Job 12.25; Psalm 107.27; Isaiah 19.14; 29.9). RSV uses it also, to translate the same Hebrew words, in passages in Isaiah where KJ uses "err" (19.14), "reel to and fro" (24.20), and "out of the way" (28.7).

In Romans 4.20, it is said of Abraham that "he staggered not at the promise of God through unbelief; but was strong in faith, giving glory to God." To stagger at a promise, opinion, or proposal meant to begin to doubt, waver, or hesitate concerning it—an English idiom which is not yet obsolete. The revised versions of 1881–1901 give a literal translation, following the order of the Greek words: "looking unto the promise of God, he wavered not through unbelief, but waxed strong through faith, giving glory to God." RSV puts this into more natural English: "No distrust made him waver concerning the promise of God, but he grew strong in his faith as he gave glory to God."

**STAND UPON** is meaningless in 2 Samuel 1.9, 10: "Stand, I pray thee, upon me, and slay me. . . . So I stood upon him, and slew him." This is not archaic English, but simply a mistranslation of the Hebrew, failing to recognize that "upon" is not the only meaning of the preposition '*al*. In this context "stand over," "stand by," "stand beside," are all sound translations of the Hebrew. The revised versions have taken the last of these. RSV reads: " 'Stand beside me and slay me.' . . . So I stood beside him, and slew him."

**STAY,** as noun and verb, is used 67 times in the Old Testament, and represents 23 different Hebrew words, each with its own meaning. In general, the meanings of "stay," as used in KJ, cluster about the ideas of stop, remain, support, sustain. RSV retains it in many passages, such as: "the moon stayed" (Joshua 10.13), "stay your hand" (2 Samuel 24.16), "stayed until now" (Genesis 32.4), "stayed on the mountain" (Deuteronomy 10.10), "the LORD was my stay" (Psalm 18.18), "stay and staff, the whole stay of bread, and the whole stay of water" (Isaiah 3.1), and the great text from the song of Judah (Isaiah 26.3):

"Thou dost keep him in perfect peace,
whose mind is stayed on thee,
because he trusts in thee."

In many other passages, RSV uses terms closer to the meaning of the Hebrew, such as "waited another seven days" (Genesis 8.10, 12); "refrain from marrying" (Ruth 1.13); "restrain the lightnings" (Job 37.4); "withheld the dew" (Haggai 1.10). Aaron and Hur "held up" Moses' hands at the battle with Amalek (Exodus 17.12); the wounded King Jehoshaphat was "propped up" in his chariot (1 Kings 22.35); the woe to those who "stay on horses" is meant for those who "rely on horses" (Isaiah 31.1). The "stays on each side of the sitting place" of King Solomon's throne were "arm rests" (2 Chronicles 9.18, compare 1 Kings 10.19). "Stay me with flagons" means "Sustain me with raisins" (Song of Solomon 2.5, see FLAGON).

Isaiah 27.8 is a difficult text, because its first word is of uncertain meaning. But the whole verse is misapprehended by the KJ rendering: "In measure, when it shooteth forth, thou wilt debate with it: he stayeth his rough wind in the day of the east wind." RSV reads:

"Measure by measure, by exile thou didst contend with them;

    he removed them with his fierce blast in the day of the east wind."

Another verse that is poorly rendered is Isaiah 29.9: "Stay yourselves, and wonder; cry ye out, and cry: they are drunken, but not with wine; they stagger, but not with strong drink." RSV reads:

"Stupefy yourselves and be in a stupor,

    blind yourselves and be blind!

Be drunk, but not with wine;

    stagger, but not with strong drink!"

**STEAD** is an archaic word for place, which may denote locality, position, situation, or function. Except for its share in such words as "farmstead" and "homestead," it is now used chiefly in phrases referring to one who is in the place of another, whether as successor, substitute, representative, or agent. "Reigned in his stead" is a phrase which appears seven times in the list of the successive kings of Edom, "before there reigned any king over the children of Israel" (Genesis 36.31–39), and it recurs like a refrain throughout the books of Kings and Chronicles. "Dwelt in their stead" is used in Deuteronomy 2.12, 21, 22, 23 to express what the descendants of Esau and Lot did to the older peoples whom they dispossessed. In another context (1 Chronicles 5.22) KJ has "dwelt in their steads," which is an inappropriate rendering because the Hebrew in all these cases has simply a preposition meaning "instead of." For the same Hebrew expression KJ has "dwelt in their rooms" in 1 Chronicles 4.41.

Jacob's impatient reply to Rachel, *"Am* I in God's stead?" (Genesis 30.2) means "Am I in the place of God?" "If your soul were in my soul's stead" (Job 16.4) means simply "if you were in my place." Elihu was a bold and brash young man, but not as brash as the words KJ attributes to him in Job 33.6: "Behold, I *am* according to thy wish in God's stead." RSV translates, "Behold, I am toward God as you are."

"Would God I had died for thee, O Absalom, my son, my son!" is an unfaithful rendering of David's cry of grief (2 Samuel 18.33). The Hebrew contains no appeal to God, and the word translated "for" is the preposition which means "instead of." RSV translates, "Would I had died instead of you, O Absalom, my son, my son!"

"Stead" occurs only twice in the New Testament (2 Corinthians 5.20 and Philemon 13). In both cases it is an awkward rendering for the preposition which means "on behalf of." "We pray you in Christ's stead" means "We beseech you on behalf of Christ"; and in Paul's letter to Philemon "in thy stead" means "on your behalf."

**STILL** in Psalm 84.4—"Blessed *are* they that dwell in thy house: they will be still praising thee"—is used in the old sense of continually, constantly, habitually, always. RSV translates:
"Blessed are those who dwell in thy house,
ever singing thy praise!"
Coverdale translated Isaiah 60.11: "Thy gates shal stonde open still both day and night." KJ has, "thy gates shall be open continually; they shall not be shut day nor night." RSV reads:
"Your gates shall be open continually;
day and night they shall not be shut."
Examples from Shakespeare of this sense of "still" are: "Thou still hast been the father of good news," *Hamlet*, II, 2, 42.
"And then my soul shall wait on thee to heaven,
As it on earth hath been thy servant still."
*King John,* V, 7, 73

**STOMACHER** (Isaiah 3.24) means an ornamental covering for the chest, worn by women under the lacing of a bodice. The term was first used in this sense, and for this text, by Coverdale. It was a modernization derived from sixteenth-century fashions in women's dress. The Hebrew word means a rich robe, and the Greek means a purple robe. RSV reads, "instead of a rich robe, a girding of sackcloth."

**STORE** in the sense of an abundant supply is still current English and is used in modern versions of the Bible as well as in KJ. It no longer applies naturally to persons, however; and the statement that Isaac had "great store of servants" is changed to read "a great household" (Genesis 26.14). Joseph's counsel to Pharaoh, "that food shall be for store to the land," is better translated, "that food shall be a reserve for the land" (Genesis 41.36). "Blessed *shall be* thy basket and thy store" correctly reads, "Blessed shall be your basket and your kneadingtrough" (Deuteronomy 28.5, compare 28.17). The Hebrew word which KJ here renders "store" appears as "kneadingtrough" in Exodus 8.3; 12.34. Nahum 2.9b reads in KJ, *"there is* none end of the store *and* glory out of all the pleasant furniture." RSV reads:

> "There is no end of treasure,
> or wealth of every precious thing."

**STRAIN.** The expression "strain at a gnat" (Matthew 23.24) is not a proper translation of the Greek text, which means "strain out a gnat." This verse was correctly translated by Tyndale and all other sixteenth-century English versions, and has been correctly translated by the revised versions. KJ stands alone in this error.

How did it happen? That is an unsolved mystery. Bishop Lightfoot and Archbishop Trench were convinced that the "at" was a printer's error, and not the fault of the translators. "We have here," wrote Trench, "an unnoticed, and thus uncorrected, error of the press; which yet, having been once allowed to pass, yielded, or seemed to yield, some sort of sense, and thus did not provoke and challenge correction, as one making sheer nonsense would have done." Most Biblical scholars agree with this opinion, on the ground that it is hard to conceive that a group of scholars as competent as the KJ translators could have made so egregious a mistranslation.

On the other hand OED gives evidence, from quotations dated 1583 and 1594, that the translators in 1611 may have adopted a phrase that was already current. Its meaning would be "strain (a liquid) at (the sight of) a gnat." If so, the phrase "strain at a gnat" probably was first used colloquially, in oral speech. It certainly did not come from the Bible translations current from 1580 to 1611—the Bishops' Bible, the Geneva Bible, or the Rheims New Testament.

Whatever its origin, "strain at a gnat" is not a sound translation of Matthew 23.24, and has led to much misunderstanding. As an English idiom "strain at" may mean to balk or scruple at, or it may mean to strive hard for. See OED, under the verb *Strain,* sections 14e, 19, and 21; also Webster's *New International Dictionary.*

**STRAIT, STRAITNESS.** "Strait" as an adjective means tight or narrow, and as a noun means a tight or narrow place. Geographically, the noun is applied to any narrow waterway connecting two large bodies of water. Biographically, it may be applied to any tight place or difficult human predicament. The plural noun is often used in a singular sense, as "the Straits of Gibraltar" or "he was in sore straits." As a waterway, "strait" does not appear in the Bible; the nouns "strait" and "straitness" always refer in KJ to human predicaments.

"Straits" is used by RSV in Judges 2.15; 1 Samuel 13.6; Job 20.22. Elsewhere such changes are made as in Job 36.16: "Even so would he have removed thee out of the strait *into* a broad place, where *there is* no straitness" (RSV "He also allured you out of distress into a broad place where there was no cramping"). Lamentations 1.3, "all her persecutors overtook her between the straits," is more accurately translated "her pursuers have all overtaken her in the midst of her distress." David's reply to the prophet Gad, "I am in a great strait" means "I am in great distress" (2 Samuel 24.14 = 1 Chronicles 21.13). In the Deuteronomic chapter of blessings and curses, the formula "in the siege and in the straitness" (28.53, 55, 57) means "in the siege and in the distress." This language is repeated in Jeremiah 19.9.

"I am in a strait betwixt two" is more literally translated, "I am hard pressed between the two" (Philippians 1.23).

"Enter ye in at the strait gate" (Matthew 7.13) means "Enter by the narrow gate." In Luke 13.24, the most ancient manuscripts have the Greek words which mean "narrow door."

The double superlative in Acts 26.5, "the most straitest sect of our religion," is not called for by anything in the Greek, but is one of Tyndale's vivid touches. RSV reads "the strictest party of our religion." The use of double superlatives was not uncommon in the sixteenth century. Shakespeare's *Julius Caesar* has "With the most boldest and best hearts of Rome" (III, 1, 121). "This was the most unkindest cut of all" (III, 2, 187). In *King Lear* (I, 1, 219) Cordelia is spoken of as

> "she, that even but now was your best object,
> The argument of your praise, balm of your age,
> Most best, most dearest."

The editors of *The Folger Library General Reader's Shakespeare* have revised the last line to read: "The best, the dearest."

**STRAITEN** means to narrow, restrict, hamper, or distress. In Jeremiah 19.9 "shall straiten them" is used for the Hebrew verb which KJ translates "shall distress thee" in Deuteronomy 28.53, 55, 57. In Job 12.23 "straiteneth them *again*" is an erroneous rendering for "leads them away."

The passive participle "straitened" appears eight times, to represent six different Hebrew and Greek verbs. For "The steps of his strength shall be straitened," RSV reads "His strong steps are shortened"; and for "When thou goest, thy steps shall not be straitened," it has "When you walk, your step will not be hampered" (Job 18.7; Proverbs 4.12). In Ezekiel 42.6, instead of *"the building* was straitened," RSV reads "the upper chambers were set back."

The majestic poetry of Job 37.1–13, portraying the acts of God as the Lord of winter, sags with KJ's inept rendering of verses 10 and 11: "By the breath of God frost is given: and the breadth of the waters is straitened. Also by watering he wearieth the thick cloud: he scattereth his bright cloud." RSV translates:

> "By the breath of God ice is given,
> and the broad waters are frozen fast.
> He loads the thick cloud with moisture;
> the clouds scatter his lightning."

In the other contexts, instead of "straitened," RSV translates: "impatient" (Micah 2.7); "constrained" (Luke 12.50); "restricted" (2 Corinthians 6.12).

**STRAITLY** is used in the obsolete sense of tightly in Joshua 6.1, "Jericho was straitly shut up." RSV translates more literally, "Jericho was shut up from within and from without." In 10 other contexts it is used in the archaic sense of strictly, in connection with questions, commands, obligations, or warnings. RSV has: "questioned us carefully" (Genesis 43.7); "solemnly sworn" (Exodus 13.19); "strictly charged" (1 Samuel 14.28; Mark 5.43; Acts 5.28); "sternly charged" (Matthew 9.30; Mark 1.43); "strictly ordered" (Mark 3.12).

**STRANGE, STRANGER** are used in the Old Testament to translate Hebrew words which mean sojourner, foreign, foreigner, alien, an outsider. KJ uses "strange" and "stranger" 301 times; RSV reduces this to 89 times. There is a corresponding increase in RSV's use of "foreign" and "foreigner," 86 times to KJ's 4 times; "alien," 30 times to KJ's 8 times; and "sojourner," 63 times to KJ's 11 times.

Moses' reason for naming his son Gershom, "I have been a stranger in a strange land" (Exodus 2.22), is more accurately translated by the revised versions, "I have been a sojourner (*ger*) in a foreign (*nokri*) land." The sabbath commandment applies to "the sojourner who is within your gates" (Exodus 20.10; Deuteronomy 5.14). "Ye shall have one manner of law, as well for the stranger, as for one of your

own country" means "You shall have one law for the sojourner and
for the native" (Leviticus 24.22; compare Numbers 9.14). "I *am* a
stranger in the earth" (Psalm 119.19) means "I am a sojourner on
earth." The transience of human life is beautifully expressed in Psalm
39.12, where two different Hebrew words for "sojourner" are used:

> "Hear my prayer, O LORD,
>> and give ear to my cry;
>> hold not thy peace at my tears!
> For I am thy passing guest,
>> a sojourner, like all my fathers."

Ruth's reply to Boaz, "Why have I found grace in thine eyes, that
thou shouldest take knowledge of me, seeing I *am* a stranger?" (Ruth
2.10) means "Why have I found favor in your eyes, that you should
take notice of me, when I am a foreigner?" So too David's words to
Ittai and Ittai's reply appear in their full meaning when "foreigner"
is used rather than "stranger" (compare KJ and RSV, 2 Samuel 15.19–
21). The "strange wives" whom Ezra required the men of Judah and
Benjamin to put away were "foreign wives" (Ezra 10).

The Hebrew adjective for "strange" is used in the first line, and that
for "foreign" in the second line, of Proverbs 2.16. Here, and in other
passages in Proverbs where both or one appear, the reference is to
women of loose sexual behavior. RSV translates:

> "You will be saved from the loose woman,
>> from the adventuress with her smooth words."

The other passages are 5.3, 20; 6.24; 7.5; 22.14; 23.27.

"Strange incense" is "unholy incense" (Exodus 30.9), and "strange
fire" is "unholy fire" (Leviticus 10.1; Numbers 3.4; 26.61). "A stranger
shall not eat *thereof*" (Exodus 29.33) means "an outsider shall not eat
of them"—this is part of the law reserving to Aaron and his sons the
rights and duties of the priesthood. So also in Exodus 30.33; Leviticus
22.10, 13. "The stranger that cometh nigh shall be put to death" (Numbers 1.51) is part of the law defining the rights and duties of the Levites;
it means, "if any one else comes near, he shall be put to death." So also
in Numbers 3.10, 38; 18.4, 7. The testimony of the woman before
Solomon, *"there was* no stranger with us in the house" (1 Kings 3.18)
means simply "there was no one else with us in the house."

In two verses of Job 19, the word "strange" occurs as a mistaken
rendering of the Hebrew. In place of "ye are not ashamed *that* ye
make yourselves strange to me" (19.3), RSV translates with a question, "are you not ashamed to wrong me?" In place of "My breath is
strange to my wife, though I intreated for the children's *sake* of mine

own body" (19.17), RSV translates, "I am repulsive to my wife, loathsome to the sons of my own mother." Another mistaken rendering is in Deuteronomy 32.27, "lest their adversaries should behave themselves strangely"; the revised versions have "lest their adversaries should judge amiss."

The comment upon Paul at Athens, "He seemeth to be a setter forth of strange gods" (Acts 17.18) is better translated, "He seems to be a preacher of foreign divinities." In verse 21, "strangers which were there" means "the foreigners who lived there."

**STRANGLED.** The letter sent to the Gentiles by "the apostles and elders, with the whole church," in Jerusalem laid upon them "no greater burden than these necessary things: That ye abstain from meats offered to idols, and from blood, and from things strangled, and from fornication" (Acts 15.29). The same list is stated, in slightly different words, in James' statement of his judgment (15.20) and in the account of Paul's final conference, seven years later, with James and the elders at Jerusalem (21.25). In all three of these statements, Tyndale has the elliptic expression "from strangled," and was followed by the subsequent sixteenth-century versions except Rheims. KJ changed to "from things strangled" in the first two statements, but retained Tyndale's elliptic phrase in 21.25. Rheims had a worse one in this verse, "from the immolated to idols, and bloud, and suffocated, and fornication." RSV reads, "abstain from what has been sacrificed to idols and from blood and from what is strangled and from unchastity."

**STRAWED** is the past tense and past participle of the verb "straw." OED defines "straw" and "strow" as obsolete or archaic verbs which mean the same as "strew." KJ reports that Moses in anger burnt the golden calf which Aaron had made, "and ground it to powder, and strawed it upon the water, and made the children of Israel drink it" (Exodus 32.20). In 2 Chronicles 34.4 it records that Josiah, king of Judah, "brake in pieces" the images his people had been worshiping, "and made dust *of them,* and strowed *it* upon the graves of them that had sacrificed unto them." RSV uses "scattered" in Exodus and "strewed" in 2 Chronicles, the Hebrew verbs being different.

When the multitudes welcomed Jesus to Jerusalem, those who "spread their garments in the way" and those who "cut down branches from the trees and strawed *them* in the way" acted alike—the same Greek verb is used for "spread" and "strawed" (Matthew 21.8 = Mark 11.8).

A quite different Greek verb is used in the parable of the Talents (Matthew 25.24, 26). "An hard man, reaping where thou hast not sown, and gathering where thou hast not strawed" is more accurately translated by RSV: "a hard man, reaping where you did not sow, and gathering where you did not winnow."

Shakespeare does not use the verb "straw" or the participle "strawed." He has "strown" once (*Twelfth Night,* II, 4, 61). "Strew" and "strewed" appear 25 times in his plays.

**STRENGTH** occurs 23 times in KJ Old Testament as translation for the Hebrew noun which means a place or means of safety, protection, refuge; hence, derivatively, a stronghold or fortress. In Psalm 28.8 KJ has, "The LORD *is* their strength, and he *is* the saving strength of his anointed." RSV reads:

> "The LORD is the strength of his people,
>
> he is the saving refuge of his anointed."

RSV uses "refuge" for this noun also in 2 Samuel 22.33; Psalms 31.4; 37.39; 43.2; 52.7; Isaiah 17.10; Nahum 3.11. It substitutes "helmet" for "strength of mine head" (Psalms 60.7; 108.8). It uses "stronghold" in Psalm 27.1; Proverbs 10.29; Isaiah 23.4, 14; 25.4; Ezekiel 24.25; 30.15; Joel 3.16; and "protection" in Isaiah 27.5; 30.2, 3. The verse in Daniel (11.31) which is cited by Jesus in Matthew 24.15 reads in KJ: "And arms shall stand on his part, and they shall pollute the sanctuary of strength, and shall take away the daily *sacrifice,* and they shall place the abomination that maketh desolate." RSV translates it: "Forces from him shall appear and profane the temple and fortress, and shall take away the continual burnt offering. And they shall set up the abomination that makes desolate."

**STUDY.** Except for the Basic Bible, English versions agree that "much study *is* a weariness of the flesh" (Ecclesiastes 12.12). The Basic Bible says it of "much learning"—a change induced by its limited vocabulary. The verb "study" is used twice in Proverbs, where it is replaced in RSV by "ponder" (15.28) and "devise" (24.2). The former of these passages reads:

> "The mind of the righteous ponders how to answer,
>
> but the mouth of the wicked pours out evil things."

In 2 Timothy 2.15 Paul counsels his young friend: "Study to shew thyself approved unto God, a workman that needeth not to be ashamed, rightly dividing the word of truth." RSV translates, "Do your best to present yourself to God as one approved, a workman who has no need to be ashamed, rightly handling the word of truth." "Study" is here used in the archaic sense of endeavor, make it one's aim, set oneself deliberately *to do* something (OED). The Greek verb *spoudazō* is translated "Do your best" in 2 Timothy 4.9, 21 and Titus 3.12; "be zealous" in 2 Peter 1.10; 3.14; "eager" in Galatians 2.10 and Ephesians 4.3; and "strive" in Hebrews 4.11.

The four-verse section, 1 Thessalonians 4.9–12, should be read as a whole in KJ and in RSV. "Study" in verse 11 represents a different Greek verb *philotimeomai,* which means to have as one's ambition, consider it an honor, aspire. RSV translates it "aspire." This verb occurs also in Romans 15.20, "making it my ambition"; and 2 Corinthians 5.9, "make it our aim."

**STUFF** appears in KJ 15 times in the sense of movable property. It is retained by RSV in Joshua 7.11, where Israel is said to have taken some of the things to be devoted to destruction, "and put them among their own stuff." Elsewhere RSV uses "goods" (Genesis 31.37; 45.20; Exodus 22.7; Luke 17.31), "baggage" (1 Samuel 10.22; 25.13; 30.24; Ezekiel 12.3, 4, 7), "household furniture" (Nehemiah 13.8).

"Stuff" appears once in the sense of the material out of which something is or may be made, and is retained by RSV: "the stuff they had was sufficient to do all the work, and more" (Exodus 36.7). In addition, RSV uses the word 36 times for various textile materials, notably those for the making of the tabernacle, as described in Exodus 25–39 and Leviticus 14. "Thou shalt not wear a garment of divers sorts, *as* of woolen and linen together" reads in RSV: "You shall not wear a mingled stuff, wool and linen together" (Deuteronomy 22.11, compare Leviticus 19.19).

**SUBURBS.** Because the suburbs of modern cities tend to become desirable centers of residence, the word "suburbs" does not convey the meaning of the Hebrew *migrash,* for which it is used more than 100 times in KJ. The RSV substitutes "pasture lands" or "common land," except in Ezekiel, where the word is used for the open country about the holy city and the open space which was to be left around the sanctuary.

"Suburbs" is used once (2 Kings 23.11) to represent another Hebrew word, *parwar,* the exact meaning of which is uncertain. But "suburbs" is clearly wrong; the chamber of Nathan-melech could not be at the entrance to the house of the LORD and in the suburbs at the same time. The revised versions use "precincts"; this chamber was in the precincts of the house of the LORD.

**SUCCOUR** is derived through French from the Latin verb *succurro,* "run to the aid of," and means help, aid, assist. It is used in 2 Samuel in military contexts, and RSV replaces it with "help" (8.5), "send us help" (18.3), "came to his aid" (21.17). It is used in the sense of moral and spiritual help in Hebrews 2.18 (RSV "because he himself has suffered and been tempted, he is able to help those who are tempted") and in 2 Corinthians 6.2 (RSV "helped you on the day of salvation"). The latter clause is a quotation from Isaiah 49.8, which KJ blurs somewhat by using "succoured" where it used "helped" in Isaiah.

Romans 16.1–2 reads in KJ: "I commend unto you Phebe our sister, which is a servant of the church which is at Cenchrea: that ye receive her in the Lord, as becometh saints, and that ye assist her in whatsoever business she hath need of you: for she hath been a succourer of many, and of myself also." RSV has: "I commend to you our sister Phoebe, a deaconess of the church at Cenchreae, that you may receive her in the Lord as befits the saints, and help her in whatever she may require from you, for she has been a helper of many and of myself as well." In this passage "servant" is the wrong word (Tyndale and the Great Bible had "minister") and "a succourer" is an obsolete and awkward noun which no other of the English versions uses.

We know nothing about Phoebe except what these verses imply. She must have been a person of some wealth and position, a resident of the eastern seaport of Corinth, where she could afford aid and hospitality to Paul and others as they made the journey by sea between Corinth and Ephesus. The Geneva Bible, indeed, translates the last clause, "for she hath gyuen hospitalitie unto many, and to me also." Tyndale had "she hath suckered many," and this was retained in the Great Bible and the Bishops' Bible. The KJ translators followed the Greek more closely, which states that "she has been a *prostatis* of many and of myself." The word is the feminine form of *prostatēs,* which means leader, protector, guardian, patron, even ruler or administrator. Arndt and Gingrich translate, "she has been of great assistance to many, including myself."

**SUCH A ONE** appears 3 times and "such an one" 10 times in KJ. Except for the inconsistent use of "a" and "an," the phrase causes no trouble when it refers to a person or thing just mentioned or when it is defined by a subsequent clause. Yet RSV retains the phrase only in Job 14.3 and 1 Corinthians 5.11. For "thou thoughtest that I was altogether *such an one* as thyself," RSV has "you thought that I was one like yourself" (Psalm 50.21). For "Let such an one think this, that, such as we are in word by letters when we are absent, such *will we be* also in deed when we are present," RSV has "Let such people understand that what we say by letter when absent, we do when present" (2 Corinthians 10.11). Compare also the KJ and RSV translations of Philemon 8–14.

The phrase "such a one" may be used without qualification, as an archaic equivalent of "so-and-so," to designate someone whose name is not mentioned. It is so used by RSV in Matthew 26.18. It is not an appropriate form of direct address, however. Boaz did not call to his fellow kinsman of Ruth, "Ho, such a one! turn aside, sit down here." There is no word for "Ho" in the Hebrew, which has two words to express the fact that Boaz definitely indicated whom he was addressing, but did not use his name. It was a friendly greeting, not a challenge. RSV translates what he said, "Turn aside, friend; sit down here" (Ruth 4.1).

**SUCHLIKE,** printed as one word, is recognized as old but still living English by OED and Webster. OED quotes its use in the 11th edition of the *Encyclopaedia Britannica,* and Webster its use by Henry James. In the Bible it is printed as two words. The word of the LORD by the prophet Ezekiel assures freedom from a father's iniquity to a son "that seeth all his father's sins which he hath done, and considereth, and doeth not such like" (Ezekiel 18.14). RSV has "does not do likewise."

The second half of Mark 7.8 is not in the ancient manuscripts; but the last clause of 7.13 reads in KJ, "and many such like things do ye," which RSV rewords, "And many such things you do." In Galatians 5.21, for "and such like" RSV has "and the like."

**SUDDENLY.** "Lay hands suddenly on no man" (1 Timothy 5.22) seems to warn against attacking or arresting another person without warning. But the laying on of hands here referred to was the gesture of ordination (see 1 Timothy 4.14; 2 Timothy 1.6), and "suddenly" is used in the obsolete sense of hastily. RSV translates: "Do not be hasty in the laying on of hands."

**SUFFER** is used by KJ in two quite distinct senses. It is used, of course, to translate the Hebrew and Greek verbs which mean to endure hardship, pain, affliction, insult, penalty, and the like—there are 69 cases of its use in this, which is the primary sense of the word. But it is also used 60 times to translate Hebrew and Greek verbs which mean to let, allow, or permit.

The RSV eliminates the use of the word "suffer" in the sense of let or permit, and retains it only when it is used in the sense of undergo or endure. It thus removes an ambiguity for which there is no warrant in the original languages.

A little girl asked her mother, "Why does Jesus want little children to suffer?" The mother replied, "He doesn't. What makes you think so?" The child said, "That is what they taught us in Sunday school today."

In the year 1952 two magazines of wide national circulation carried poignant accounts of the sufferings of children in Korea, with the headline "Suffer, little children."

In the order for the baptism of infants contained in the Manual published in 1936 by one of our Protestant denominations the text of Matthew 19.14 is printed as follows:

> And Jesus said, Suffer little children,
> And forbid them not to come unto me;
> For of such is the kingdom of heaven.

By printing this verse in three lines as though it were poetry, and by omitting the comma which KJ has after "forbid them not," the expression "Suffer little children" is made to stand by itself as though it were an injunction to endure or tolerate little children. But the meaning in the Greek is unmistakably, "Let the children come to me, and do not hinder them."

It is to the credit of the Book of Worship for the use of the Methodist Church that it adopted an unambiguous rendering of this verse even before the publication of the RSV New Testament. The word "suffer" is rejected by all modern translations of this verse which I have consulted —Twentieth Century, Weymouth, Moffatt, Ballantine, Goodspeed, Williams, Verkuyl, Confraternity, Torrey, Phillips, Rieu.

**SUPPLE** appears once (Ezekiel 16.4): "in the day thou wast born thy navel was not cut, neither wast thou washed in water to supple *thee*. . . ." KJ stands alone in this rendering. All but one of the sixteenth-century English versions had "to make thee clean." The Geneva Bible had "to soften thee," which KJ changed to "supple." The meaning of the Hebrew word is uncertain, and so is its authenticity. There is nothing corresponding to it in the Vaticanus codex of the Septuagint, or in the Syriac. It may be an explanatory gloss that got into the text. In any case the German translations from Luther down, and modern translations in general, agree that the idea is "for cleansing" or "to cleanse you." If "soften" or "supple" had any foundations more substantial than conjecture, they have not been passed on to subsequent translators.

**SURELY** appears 266 times in the Old Testament, and in 140 of these cases there is no corresponding Hebrew word. The KJ translators commonly used "surely" to express the emphasis or intensity of meaning that is expressed in the Hebrew by repetition, which in the case of verbs consists of the absolute infinitive plus a finite form. (See GENERALLY.) RSV usually omits the "surely" in these cases, as tending in English to weaken rather than to strengthen the statement. Thus it has "you shall die" (Genesis 2.17); "You will not die" (Genesis 3.4); "Abraham shall become a great and mighty nation" (Genesis 18.18); "shall be put to death" (Exodus 21.12, 15, 16, 17). On the other hand, "surely" is retained in some contexts, as in Joseph's reception of his brothers, "surely you are spies" (Genesis 42.16), and in the LORD's answer to David, "you shall surely overtake and shall surely rescue" (1 Samuel 30.8).

In the injunction to give to the poor, RSV replaces "surely" by "freely"—"You shall give to him freely" (Deuteronomy 15.10). David's answer to Nathan's parable of the rich man who caught and killed the poor man's one ewe lamb was "*As* the LORD lives, the man who has done this *thing* shall surely die," which RSV translates ". . . deserves to die" (2 Samuel 12.5); the Hebrew idiom is the same as in 1 Samuel 26.16, which KJ translates "ye *are* worthy to die" and RSV "you deserve to die." Job 13.3 begins with a strong adversative "But" rather than "Surely." Numbers 14.20–23 is too long to quote here, but the two versions should be compared.

Instead of "those things which are most surely believed among us," RSV translates the Greek, in accordance with evidence in the papyri, "the things which have been accomplished among us" (Luke 1.1).

**SURFEITING.** A surfeit of anything is too much of it. In the sixteenth century the word was much used as an intransitive verb meaning to overindulge in something. The opening lines of Shakespeare's *Twelfth Night* are:

"If music be the food of love, play on;
Give me excess of it, that, surfeiting,
The appetite may sicken, and so die."

The Archbishop of York, in *King Henry IV, Part II*, IV, 1, 55, says:
"we are all diseased,
And with our surfeiting and wanton hours
Have brought ourselves into a burning fever."
The word was applied particularly to excessive eating or drinking, to the consequent sickness or nausea, and to the resulting disgust or loathing. As such, it was a natural translation for the Greek *kraipalē*, which stands for carousing, intoxication, and the subsequent headache and hangover. It appears in Luke 21.34: "Take heed to yourselves lest at any time your hearts be overcharged with surfeiting, and drunkenness, and cares of this life. . . ." Because "surfeiting" is now obsolete in this sense, RSV reads: "Take heed to yourselves lest your hearts be weighed down with dissipation and drunkenness and cares of this life. . . ." The word "gluttony," which some translators have used, was rejected because its primary reference is to eating, whereas the primary reference of *kraipalē* is to excessive drinking and its effects.

**SWELL, SWELLING,** in reference to bodily ills, are retained by RSV. But "a breach ready to fall, swelling out in a high wall" (Isaiah 30.13) is reworded, "a break in a high wall, bulging out, and about to collapse."

"The swelling of Jordan" (Jeremiah 12.5; 49.19; 50.44) represents a Hebrew phrase which KJ elsewhere translates "the pride of Jordan" (Zechariah 11.3). It does not refer to a swelling flood of water in the Jordan river, but to the lush, rank vegetation on its banks. As the cited texts indicate, this was the covert of lions. It is now known as the jungle of the Jordan, and RSV uses this term. Jeremiah 12.5 reads in KJ: "If thou hast run with the footmen, and they have wearied thee, then how canst thou contend with horses? and *if* in the land of peace, *wherein* thou trustedst, *they wearied thee,* then how wilt thou do in the swelling of Jordan?" In RSV it reads:
"If you have raced with men on foot, and they have wearied you,
how will you compete with horses?
And if in a safe land you fall down,
how will you do in the jungle of the Jordan?"
For 2 Peter 2.18, "when they speak great swelling *words* of vanity," RSV translates the Greek more literally: "uttering loud boasts of folly." In Jude 16 "and their mouth speaketh great swelling *words*" is a clause which interrupts the syntax of the sentence. It was for this reason placed within parentheses by the revised versions of 1881–1901. RSV rewords it to fit the syntax, translating the verse: "These are grumblers,

malcontents, following their own passions, loud-mouthed boasters, flattering people to gain advantage."

In 2 Corinthians 12.20 appears a list of faults which Paul frankly says that he fears he may find in the church at Corinth. Most of the words in this list are used in an archaic sense. KJ has "debates, envyings, wraths, strifes, backbitings, whisperings, swellings, tumults"; RSV has "quarreling, jealousy, anger, selfishness, slander, gossip, conceit, and disorder."

**TABERING** occurs once (Nahum 2.6–7), which reads: "The gates of the rivers shall be opened, and the palace shall be dissolved. And Huzzab shall be led away captive, she shall be brought up, and her maids shall lead *her* as with the voice of doves, tabering upon their breasts." RSV translates:

> "The river gates are opened,
>     the palace is in dismay;
> its mistress is stripped, she is carried off,
>     her maidens lamenting,
> moaning like doves,
>     and beating their breasts."

There is uncertainty at some points in this passage, but the last line is not one of them. "Taber" was the old name for a drum, and the verb "taber" means to beat as upon a drum. The lamenting maidens, beating their breasts, are a natural part of the picture.

**TABLE** is retained by the revised versions of the Bible, not only for an article of furniture, but where it refers to the two tables of stone on which were inscribed the words of the LORD (Exodus 24, 31, 32, 34; Deuteronomy 4, 5, 9, 10; 1 Kings 8.9; 2 Chronicles 5.10; Hebrews 9.4). But it is also used by KJ to refer to a portable tablet, of whatever material, upon which to write. Zechariah, unable to speak, asked for "a writing tablet" rather than "a writing table" (Luke 1.63). The word to Habakkuk is: "Write the vision; make it plain upon tablets, so he may run who reads it" (2.2). The injunction concerning the commandments and teachings of Proverbs is to "write them on the tablet of your heart" (3.3; 7.3). The sin of Judah, says Jeremiah, "is engraved on the tablet of their heart" (17.1). Paul, in 2 Corinthians 3.2–3, tells the Corinthians that he needs no recommendation to them: "You yourselves are our letter of recommendation, written on your hearts, to be known and read by all men; and you show that you are a letter from Christ delivered by us, written not with ink but with the Spirit of the living God, not on tablets of stone but on tablets of human hearts."

**TABRET** is the diminutive of "taber," thus a small drum, timbrel, or tambourine. KJ uses "tabret" 8 times and "timbrel" 9 times, as translations of the Hebrew *toph;* RSV uses "tambourine" 5 times and "timbrel" 12 times. The word "tabret" is probably wrong in Ezekiel 28.13 and is certainly an error in Job 17.6. (See AFORETIME, where this error is explained.)

**TACHE.** An obsolete word for a means of fastening two parts together, such as a clasp, a buckle, a hook and eye. The word "tack" originally had the same meaning, and both are related to "attach" and "detach." "Tache" is used in Exodus for the clasps of gold that fitted into loops on the curtains of the tabernacle to couple them together, and for the clasps of bronze that coupled together the curtains of its tent. The arrangement is described in chapters 26 and 36.

**TACKLING.** An obsolete term for the rigging or tackle of a ship. It appears in Luke's account of Paul's shipwreck (Acts 27.18–19), where RSV reads: "As we were violently storm-tossed, they began next day to throw the cargo overboard; and the third day they cast out with their own hands the tackle of the ship." A more obscure passage is Isaiah 33.23, which reads in RSV:
> "Your tackle hangs loose;
>> it cannot hold the mast firm in its place,
>> or keep the sail spread out."

**TAKEN WITH THE MANNER.** The "law of jealousies" recorded in Numbers 5.11–31 begins with the hypothetical case of a wife's infidelity, if *"there be* no witness against her, neither she be taken *with the manner."* The phrase "taken with the manner" goes back to Tyndale, and was passed on through the other sixteenth-century translations to KJ. It means "taken in the act."

The word here is "mainour," an Anglo-French term which as early as Tyndale's day had begun to be spelled "maner" or "manner." The phrase "taken with the mainour" meant, in the case of a thief, taken with the stolen property in his possession; and in the case of others, taken in the act of doing something unlawful.

In Shakespeare's *King Henry IV, Part I,* II, 4, 347, Prince Hal says to Bardolph: "O villain, thou stolest a cup of sack eighteen years ago, and wert taken with the manner." In *Love's Labour's Lost* (I, 1, 205), Costard admits his approach to Jaquenetta: "The matter of it is, I was taken with the manner . . . I was seen with her in the manor-house, sitting with her upon the form, and taken following her into the park."

"Mainour" is related to "manoeuvre," and the question whether it originally meant a stolen thing or an unlawful act is still open. There is an interesting discussion, with ample illustrative material, in OED. Both there and in Webster, the reader should look up "mainour" rather than "manner."

**TALE,** in the numerical sense, means the complete number or amount.

It has this meaning in two notable occurrences: "the tale of bricks" which Pharaoh daily required the people of Israel to make (Exodus 5.8, 18); the 200 Philistine foreskins which David presented "in full tale" to King Saul, that he might marry the king's daughter (1 Samuel 18.27). KJ says that certain of the Levites "had the charge of the ministering vessels" of the house of God, "that they should bring them in and out by tale" (1 Chronicles 9.28). RSV translates: "Some of them had charge of the utensils of service, for they were required to count them when they were brought in and taken out."

In the sense of a story or narrative, "tale" appears in KJ only as part of the word "talebearer." This is retained by RSV in Proverbs 11.13, but replaced by "whisperer" (Proverbs 18.8; 26.20, 22), "gossiping" (Proverbs 20.19), and "slanderer" (Leviticus 19.16).

Coverdale's rendering of Psalm 90.9b is retained in the Book of Common Prayer: "we bring our years to an end, as it were a tale that is told." KJ has "we spend our years as a tale *that is told.*" Just what Coverdale meant by the last five words is uncertain; he may have meant a sum that is counted, or a story that is told. The Hebrew gives no clear basis for either of these interpretations. It means "we bring our years to an end like a sigh."

The Greek Septuagint and Latin Vulgate have the equivalent of "our years are spent like a cobweb." Martin Luther's rendering was *wir bringen unsere Jahre zu wie ein Geschwätz*—"we bring our years to an end like empty talk." It may be that Coverdale got from Luther the idea for "a tale that is told."

Most twentieth-century versions have "as a sigh" or "like a sigh"— RV note, ASV, Moffatt, Zurich, Leslie, Confraternity, RSV, and

Riessler and Storr. The New Latin Translation of the Psalms approved by Pope Pius XII and published in 1945, renders the verse:

> *Nam omnes dies nostri transierunt in ira tua;*
> *finivimus annos nostros ut suspirium.*

Knox, however, has "swift as a breath our lives pass away"; and J. M. P. Smith, "our years are like a cobweb wiped away."

**TARGET** is defined by OED, historically, as a light shield or buckler.
"King Solomon made two hundred targets of beaten gold: six hundred *shekels* of gold went to one target" (1 Kings 10.16 = 2 Chronicles 9.15); "Asa had an army *of men* that bare targets and spears" (2 Chronicles 14.8). The Hebrew word is *tsinnah*. In view of differing contexts, RSV uses "shields" for Solomon's display and "bucklers" for the men of Asa's army. (See BUCKLER)

KJ uses "target" once as translation for the Hebrew word *kidon*. It says that Goliath had "a target of brass between his shoulders" (1 Samuel 17.6). This is simply a mistake, for *kidon* means a javelin, and is so translated by the revised versions.

The target of concentric circles for shooting and the figurative use of the word are fairly recent developments in English, not common before the nineteenth century. Robin Hood's men shot at a "butt," and we still use this term in referring to a person who is a target for ridicule. Where Job says "he hath . . . set me up for his mark" (16.12), RSV has "He set me up as his target."

**TEACH.** "He speaketh with his feet, he teacheth with his fingers" is part of the quaint description of "a naughty person" in Proverbs 6.13. The second of these verbs means to throw, shoot, direct, point out, show, and hence teach; while the word here represented by "naughty" means "worthless." The KJ rendering of the description is: "A naughty person, a wicked man, walketh with a froward mouth. He winketh with his eyes, he speaketh with his feet, he teacheth with his fingers; Frowardness *is* in his heart, he deviseth mischief continually; he soweth discord." The RSV rendering is quite as faithful, and in some respects more faithful, to the Hebrew:

> "A worthless person, a wicked man,
> goes about with crooked speech,
> winks with his eyes, scrapes with his feet,
> points with his finger,
> with perverted heart devises evil,
> continually sowing discord."

**TEACH, TEACHER, TEACHING.** The verb *didaskō* appears 97 times in the Greek New Testament and is always translated "teach." It is used more often than any other verb to describe what Jesus did throughout his ministry—more often than even the word for "heal."

As Jesus lived and worked among men, he chose the role of teacher (*didaskalos*). The four Gospels agree in so portraying him. People spoke of him as such, and they addressed him as "Teacher." Unfortunately KJ tends to hide this fact from the English reader. It represents the Gospels as applying the word "teacher" to Jesus only once. But that is only because it used the English word "master" as a translation for the Greek word for "teacher" in 41 other cases where this word is applied to Jesus. This overwhelming preference of KJ for the word "master" simply reflects the usage in schools in Britain, where teachers are called "masters." (See MASTER)

The word "doctor" originally meant teacher, and it is so used three times in KJ. When Jesus' parents "found him in the temple, sitting in the midst of the doctors" (Luke 2.46), he was "sitting among the teachers." The expression "doctor of the law" (Luke 5.17; Acts 5.34) stands for the Greek word *nomodidaskalos,* which means "teacher of the law." In 1 Timothy 1.7 KJ itself translates the plural of *nomodidaskalos* as "teachers of the law."

In 1611, the word "doctrine" denoted the act of teaching as well as the content of teaching. "He said unto them in his doctrine" means "in his teaching he said to them" (Mark 4.2; 12.38). This sense of the word is now obsolete, and the revised versions use "teaching" more often than "doctrine." Where KJ translated *didachē* and *didaskalia* as "learning" once, "teaching" once, and "doctrine" 48 times, RSV has "teaching" 33 times, "doctrine" 14 times, "instruction" twice, and "lesson" once.

**TELL** occurs eight times in the archaic sense of number or count. In the word of the LORD to Abram, "Look now toward heaven, and tell the stars, if thou be able to number them," the same Hebrew verb is translated "tell" and "number"; and in both cases it means "count" (Genesis 15.5). "They told the money" (2 Kings 12.10) means "they counted the money." "I may tell all my bones" (Psalm 22.17) means "I can count all my bones." "Walk about Zion, and go round about her: tell the towers thereof" (Psalm 48.12) means ". . . number her towers." Other occurrences are in 2 Chronicles 2.2; Psalms 56.8; 147.4; Jeremiah 33.13. An example of Shakespeare's use of "tell" for count is in *Hamlet,* I, 2, 238, where Hamlet asks concerning the ghost, "Stay'd it long?" and Horatio answers "While one with moderate haste might tell a hundred."

In Milton's *L'Allegro,* the picture of dawn and early morning in the country includes:

> "While the ploughman, near at hand,
> Whistles o'er the furrowed land,
> And the milkmaid singeth blithe,
> And the mower whets his scythe,
> And every shepherd tells his tale
> Under the hawthorn in the dale."

The last lines do not mean that the shepherd is an idle storyteller, but that he is counting his sheep as they come from the fold.

**TELL** occurs 9 times in the expression "cannot tell," meaning "do not know." The KJ New Testament translates the Greek verb *oida* by the English verb "know" 280 times. But in 9 cases it translates *oida,* used with a negative, by "cannot tell."

Three of these passages are Matthew 21.27 = Mark 11.33 = Luke 20.7, the answer of the Pharisees to Jesus' question concerning the baptism of John. Three are in the Gospel of John: 3.8, addressed to Nicodemus; 8.14, addressed to the Pharisees; 16.18, the puzzled comment of the disciples, "We cannot tell what he saith." Three are in 2 Corinthians 12.2–3, Paul's statement concerning his visions and revelations.

These 9 cases of "cannot tell" come from the translation by William Tyndale, and appear also in Coverdale, Thomas Matthew, the Great Bible, the Geneva Bible, and the Bishops' Bible. They are examples of Tyndale's lively and occasionally wayward style. He uses the expression elsewhere—3 times in the account of the man born blind (John 9.21, 25), who answers: "Whether he be a sinner or no, I cannot tell; one thing I am sure of, that I was blind, and now I see." Tyndale's version of Mary Magdalene's excited words to Peter and John is (John 20.2): "They have taken away the Lord out of the tomb, and we cannot tell where they have laid him." In 1 John 2.11 Tyndale had "cannot tell whither he goeth."

Thus out of 14 cases where Tyndale and the other sixteenth-century translators from the Greek used "cannot tell" for "do not know," the KJ translators kept 9 and rejected 5.

Modern translators, beginning with the English Revised Version of 1881, have rejected "cannot tell" in all these cases (except that J. B. Phillips uses "I couldn't tell" in John 9.25). The reason is not so much that the expression is wrong, as that it is inaccurate and ambiguous. "Do not know" is a clear and accurate translation.

**TEMPER** occurs as a verb four times but in no modern sense. "Cakes unleavened tempered with oil" (Exodus 29.2) means "unleavened cakes mixed with oil." "The third part of a hin of oil, to temper with the fine flour" (Ezekiel 46.14) means "one third of a hin of oil to moisten the flour." In the instructions given to Moses for making the incense to be used in the worship of the LORD (Exodus 30.34–38) the expression "tempered together" is an erroneous rendering of the Hebrew participle which means "seasoned with salt." This error seems inexplicable, for KJ translates the verb properly in Leviticus 2.13, "every oblation of thy meat offering shalt thou season with salt."

"God hath tempered the body together, having given more abundant honour to that *part* which lacked: That there should be no schism in the body" (1 Corinthians 12.24–25) is reworded by RSV: "God has so adjusted the body, giving the greater honor to the inferior part, that there may be no discord in the body." The entire passage concerning the body and its members, 12.14–26, should be read in the two versions.

**TEMPERANCE** in the Bible means self-control. It was one of the four cardinal virtues of Greek philosophy—wisdom, courage, temperance, and justice. Paul spoke before Felix of justice and self-control and judgment to come (Acts 24.25). Self-control is part of "the fruit of the Spirit" described in Galatians 5.22–23. It is central among the means through which the followers of our Lord may escape from corruption and passion and become partakers of the divine nature (2 Peter 1.3–8).

"Every man that striveth for the mastery is temperate in all things" (1 Corinthians 9.25) represents Greek which RSV translates, "Every athlete exercises self-control in all things." "A bishop," says Titus 1.7–8, must be "hospitable, a lover of goodness, master of himself, upright, holy, and self-controlled."

**TEMPT, TEMPTATION.** "Tempt" is sometimes used in the sense of test, make trial of, put to the proof, without the present implication of seeking to allure, entice, and lead into evil. Examples are: "And it came to pass after these things, that God did tempt Abraham" (Genesis 22.1); RSV "After these things God tested Abraham." "Why tempt ye me, *ye* hypocrites?" (Matthew 22.18); RSV "Why put me to the test, you hypocrites?" "Then one of them, *which was* a lawyer, asked *him a question,* tempting him" (Matthew 22.35); RSV "And one of them, a lawyer, asked him a question, to test him."

"Temptations" is used in the sense of trials in Deuteronomy 4.34; 7.19; 29.3, where the word is linked with signs and wonders in a recurring formula of reminder. RSV translates the first of these verses: "Or has any god ever attempted to go and take a nation for himself from the midst of another nation, by trials, by signs, by wonders, and by war, by a mighty hand and an outstretched arm, and by great terrors, according to all that the LORD your God did for you in Egypt before your eyes?" The entire paragraph, 4.32–40, should be read, followed by 7.17–19 and 29.2–4.

**TENDER EYED.** Jacob's preference for Rachel over Leah is explained simply: "Leah *was* tender eyed; but Rachel was beautiful and well favoured" (Genesis 29.17). Many a reader has given Leah credit for melting, doelike eyes. The expression comes from Tyndale, and was adopted by Coverdale and succeeding versions. It is not a literal translation, for both the Hebrew and the Greek Septuagint say directly, "The eyes of Leah were weak."

**THANK,** as a noun in the singular number, was still used in the sixteenth century in the sense of a grateful thought, a feeling of gratitude. It had begun to be replaced, however, by the plural form "thanks." The plural is used in KJ, except for one passage, Luke 6.32–34. Instead of "what thank have ye," RSV here translates the Greek, "what credit is that to you?"

**THANKWORTHY** means worthy of thanks, deserving gratitude or credit, meritorious, creditable. The adjective is more often applied to action and the results of action, than to the person who acts. It appears once, in a passage addressed to servants (1 Peter 2.18–25). Verses 19–20 read: "For this *is* thankworthy, if a man for conscience toward God endure grief, suffering wrongfully. For what glory *is it,* if, when ye be buffeted for your faults, ye shall take it patiently? but if, when ye do well, and suffer *for it,* ye take it patiently, this *is* acceptable with God." In this translation "conscience" and "grief" are used in obsolete senses, and the same Greek word is rendered by "thankworthy" in the beginning and by "acceptable" at the end. RSV translates: "For one is approved if, mindful of God, he endures pain while suffering unjustly. For what credit is it, if when you do wrong and are beaten for it you take it patiently? But if when you do right and suffer for it you take it patiently, you have God's approval." Other modern translations agree, with minor differences of wording, that it is the approval of God that is meant at both points (Twentieth Century, Weymouth, Moffatt, Goodspeed, Williams). For this reason "thankworthy" has been replaced. While not in common speech, like "blameworthy" and "praiseworthy," it is still living English.

**THAT,** by ellipsis, may sometimes stand alone in the sense of that (thing) that, or that (person) that. OED records the usage as applied to things to have been common down to the sixteenth century. Examples in KJ are: "beat out that she had gleaned" (Ruth 2.17); RSV "beat out what she had gleaned." "I uttered that I understood not" (Job 42.3); RSV "I have uttered what I did not understand." "Take *that* thine *is,* and go thy way" (Matthew 20.14); RSV "Take what belongs to you, and go."

The convenient word "what" is not available when this elliptic construction is applied to persons, as in Proverbs 11.24: "There is that scattereth, and yet increaseth; and *there is* that withholdeth more than is meet, but *it tendeth* to poverty." RSV translates this:
"One man gives freely, yet grows all the richer;
        another withholds what he should give, and only suffers want."
The supreme example of this terse idiom is the name of God: "I AM THAT I AM" (Exodus 3.14). RSV translates: "I AM WHO I AM," and gives alternative renderings in a footnote.

**THEREUNTO** is an archaic adverb which KJ uses nine times in the sense of "to it" or "for it." ". . . sacrificed thereunto" is "sacrificed to it" (Exodus 32.8); "made thereunto" is "made for it" (Exodus 36.36); and the word is simply in the way in Exodus 37.11, 12. ". . . unto all *the places* nigh thereunto" is more accurately translated "to all their neighbors" (Deuteronomy 1.7). The New Testament passages are Ephesians 6.18; 1 Thessalonians 3.3; Hebrews 10.1; 1 Peter 3.9.

**THITHERWARD** means toward that place, in that direction. RSV replaces it by "thither" (Judges 18.15) and "there" (Romans 15.24). "They shall ask the way to Zion with their faces thitherward" is reworded, "They shall ask the way to Zion, with faces turned toward it" (Jeremiah 50.5).

**THOUGHT** occurs 13 times in the sense of anxiety. In each case it appears in the expression "take thought," which means to be anxious. "Take no thought for the morrow" means "Do not be anxious about tomorrow" (Matthew 6.34). "Take no thought how or what ye shall speak" means "Do not be anxious how you are to speak or what you are to say" (Matthew 10.19). Other occurrences in the Gospels are Matthew 6.25, 27, 28, 31; Mark 13.11; Luke 12.11, 22, 25, 26. The same Greek verb, which means "be anxious," is used in all these cases.

This use of "take thought" occurs once in the Old Testament (1 Samuel 9.5) where the young Saul, failing to find his father's asses, says to his servant, "Come, let us go back, lest my father cease to care about the asses and become anxious about (take thought for) us." In 1 Samuel 10.2, Samuel informs Saul that the asses are found, "and now your father has ceased to care about the asses and is anxious about you (sorroweth for you)." The same Hebrew verb is translated "take thought" and "sorroweth."

As an illustration of this now obsolete use of the word "thought" in the sense of anxiety or trouble OED cites a sentence from Samuel Purchas' *Pilgrimage* (1613) which informs the reader that "Soto died of thought in Florida." Instances in Shakespeare's *Hamlet* are:

> "Thus conscience does make cowards of us all,
> And thus the native hue of resolution
> Is sicklied o'er with the pale cast of thought."
> (III, 1, 83–85)
> "and there is pansies, that's for thoughts."
> (IV, 5, 177)

**TIRE,** as used in KJ, has nothing to do with fatigue or with the rims of wheels. It is a shortened form of "attire." As a noun, it means a headdress or an ornament; as a verb it means adorn. "Bind the tire of thine head upon thee" (Ezekiel 24.17) means "Bind on your turban." So also in Ezekiel 24.23. The Hebrew noun represented here by "tire" is translated "bonnet" in Isaiah 3.20 and Ezekiel 44.18, "beauty" in Isaiah 61.3, and "ornaments" in Isaiah 61.10. When Jezebel "painted her face, and tired her head, and looked out at a window" (2 Kings 9.30), the Hebrew verb for "tired" has the general meaning "adorned."

The "round tires like the moon" (Isaiah 3.18) were crescent-shaped ornaments, here included in a list of feminine finery. The Hebrew word is simply translated "ornaments" in Judges 8.21, 26. That they were items of luxury, probably of gold, may be inferred from the fact that they were worn by the kings of Midian and were hung on the necks of their camels. The revised versions use "crescents" both in Isaiah and in Judges.

**TITLE** has the obsolete sense of an inscribed monument or tomb in 2 Kings 23.17. King Josiah's question, "What title *is* that that I see?" means "What is yonder monument that I see?" The account of the man of God, whose monument it was, appears in 1 Kings 13.

The inscription over the head of Jesus upon the cross is described with general agreement, but different wording, in the four Gospels. Matthew 27.37 reads in RSV: "And over his head they put the charge against him, which read, 'This is Jesus the King of the Jews.' " Mark 15.26 has: "And the inscription of the charge against him read, 'The King of the Jews.' " Luke 23.38 says, "There was also an inscription over him, 'This is the King of the Jews.' " John 19.19–22 has the fullest account: "Pilate also wrote a title and put it on the cross; it read, 'Jesus of Nazareth, the King of the Jews.' Many of the Jews read this title, for the place where Jesus was crucified was near the city; and it was written in Hebrew, in Latin, and in Greek. The chief priests of the Jews then said to Pilate, 'Do not write, "The King of the Jews," but, "This man said, I am King of the Jews." ' Pilate answered, 'What I have written I have written.' "

John's is the only Gospel which used the customary term for such an inscription. In Greek, it was *titlos;* in Latin, *titulus.* From Wyclif on to KJ, all the early versions used "title" here, and the revised versions have kept it. There is no better way to record the fact that Pilate, in contemptuous sarcasm, publicly attributed to Jesus the title "King of the Jews."

**TITTLE** was used by Tyndale to translate the Greek *keraia* in Matthew 5.18 and Luke 16.17. Meaning "horn," this word, like the Latin *apex,* was applied to any projection, extremity, hook, or serif of a written letter, then to vowel-points, accents, dots, diacritical marks —in short, to any small stroke or point in writing. In Jesus' use of the term, it stands for the smallest possible part of the written law; RSV therefore translates it by "dot." Luke 16.17 reads: "But it is easier for heaven and earth to pass away, than for one dot of the law to become void." (See JOT)

**TO.** An uncommon use of the preposition "to" occurs in Judges 17.13, "I have a Levite to *my* priest," and in Matthew 3.9 (=Luke 3.8), "We have Abraham to *our* father." RSV translates "I have a Levite as priest," and "We have Abraham as our father." OED describes this use of "to" as obsolete or archaic, meaning "for, as, by way of, in the capacity of" (*To*, A, 11b).

The Latin Vulgate translated the Greek of John the Baptist's words simply and exactly, *Patrem habemus Abraham*. The Anglo-Saxon Gospels, about A.D. 1000, complicated this by inserting a double dative, "us" and "to faeder," reading "We habbao us to faeder abraham." Wyclif read in Matthew "we han abraham to fadir," and in Luke "we han a fadir abraham." Tyndale translated "we have Abraham to oure father," which was accepted by the other sixteenth-century versions and by KJ.

Examples of this idiom are: "So forward on his way (with God to frend) He passed forth" (Spenser, *The Faerie Queene*, I, 1, 28). "I have a king here to my flatterer" (Shakespeare, *King Richard II*, IV, 1, 308).

**TOUCHING,** the present participle of the verb "touch," is used as a preposition, described by OED as now somewhat archaic. It is so used 30 times in KJ, in half of which it appears in the form "as touching." RSV replaces "touching" with "concerning" (Isaiah 5.1; Jeremiah 22.11; Colossians 4.10; 1 Thessalonians 4.9) or "about" (Matthew 18.19; 2 Corinthians 9.1; 2 Thessalonians 3.4); and replaces "as touching" with "as for" (1 Samuel 20.23; Matthew 22.31; Mark 12.26; Acts 21.25; 1 Corinthians 16.12).

In other passages it replaces these archaic terms with "regarding the words" (2 Kings 22.18); "upon any one" (Ezra 7.24); "to the king" (Psalm 45.1); "for all their wickedness" (Jeremiah 1.16); "with respect to the resurrection" (Acts 24.21). "Behold, thy brother Esau, as touching thee, doth comfort himself, *purposing* to kill thee" (Genesis 27.42) is unnecessarily cumbrous English for "Behold, your brother Esau comforts himself by planning to kill you." "*Touching* the Almighty, we cannot find him out" (Job 37.23) is an ambiguous statement created by the KJ insertion of the word "touching."

The ambiguous "as touching things offered unto idols" (1 Corinthians 8.1) represents the Greek preposition *peri,* which appears also in 1 Corinthians 12.1 and is there properly translated, "concerning spiritual *gifts.*" In Philippians 3.5–6 the Greek preposition *kata,* in three parallel clauses, is translated in three different ways: "as touching the law, a Pharisee; Concerning zeal, persecuting the church; touching the righteousness which is in the law, blameless." RSV maintains the parallelism: "as to the law a Pharisee, as to zeal a persecutor of the church, as to righteousness under the law blameless."

**TRANSLATE, TRANSLATION.** "By faith Enoch was translated that he should not see death; and was not found, because God had translated him: for before his translation he had this testimony, that he pleased God" (Hebrews 11.5). To a schoolboy studying Latin this seems to put Enoch in the category of Caesar, Cicero, and Virgil. But it makes better sense if he remembers that "transferre" is the infinitive and "translatus" the participle. Instead of "translate the kingdom" (2 Samuel 3.10), RSV has "transfer the kingdom." Instead of "translated *us* into the kingdom of his dear Son" (Colossians 1.13), RSV has "transferred us to the kingdom of his beloved Son." In Hebrews 11.5 RSV has: "By faith Enoch was taken up so that he should not see death; and he was not found, because God had taken him. Now before he was taken he was attested as having pleased God." The Greek noun here used, *metathesis,* has passed directly into the English language and is fairly common in English grammar and in chemistry, for the transposition of letters or atoms.

**TREATISE** now means a book or essay which deals with the principles of a subject. The term was formerly applied also to a story or narrative. When Luke refers to his Gospel as "the former treatise" (Acts 1.1) the word is used in this obsolete sense. RSV translates "the first book."

**TRIBUTE** means the tax paid by a subject state or vassal in token of submission or as the price of peace and security. The Bible does not use the word in the derived sense of compliment or praise. Almost half the occurrences of the word "tribute," however, are due to KJ's use of it for the Hebrew *mas,* which means "forced labor." The revisers in the 1870's were aware of this slip, and made an attempt to correct it, but chose the term "taskwork," which is too weak for the grim reality. For "a servant unto tribute" (Genesis 49.15) RSV has "a slave at forced labor"; for "put the Canaanites to tribute" (Joshua 17.13; Judges 1.28) RSV has "put the Canaanites to forced labor." "Adoram *was* over the tribute" means "Adoram was in charge of the forced labor" (2 Samuel 20.24; compare 1 Kings 4.6).

"This *is* the reason of the levy which king Solomon raised" means "this is the account of the forced labor which King Solomon levied." The passage which begins with these words, 1 Kings 9.15–22, is a summary list of Solomon's vast building operations and of the human material he employed. It should be read in RSV, because the KJ translators were not aware that verses 16 and 17a are an explanatory parenthesis, and because "upon those did Solomon levy a tribute of bondservice unto this day" (vs. 21) is a faded way of saying "these Solomon made a forced levy of slaves, and so they are to this day." There are a dozen other "forced labor" passages, which can be located under "forced" in *Nelson's Concordance to RSV*.

**TROW** is an archaic word for think, believe, be of the opinion that.
It appears in Luke 17.9, "Doth he thank that servant because he did the things that were commanded him? I trow not." But the last three words are not a part of what Jesus said. They do not appear in the most ancient Greek manuscripts. The *ou dokō,* "I do not think," which they represent, were probably a marginal comment or gloss by some copyist who felt it incumbent upon him to answer the Lord's rhetorical question.

**TRUE** in Genesis 42.11, 19, 31, 33, 34 means "honest," a sense which OED notes as archaic. It survives perhaps in the phrase for a jury, "twelve good men and true." Genesis 42.11 reads in RSV: "We are all sons of one man, we are honest men, your servants are not spies."

John 19.35 has the awkward archaism "saith true," as well as an obsolete use of "record" and misleading punctuation. It reads in KJ: "And he that saw *it* bare record, and his record is true: and he knoweth that he saith true, that ye might believe." RSV has: "He who saw it has borne witness—his testimony is true, and he knows that he tells the truth—that you also may believe." (See RECORD)

**TURTLE** is used 5 times and TURTLEDOVE 10 times for the Hebrew and Greek terms which mean turtledove. The revised versions use "turtledove" throughout, except that RV retains "turtle" in Song of Solomon 2.12 and Jeremiah 8.7, and RSV uses "dove" in

Psalm 74.19. "The voice of the turtle is heard in our land" is a text that has gotten into general literature; and OED cites more examples of "turtle" as a term of endearment than it does for "turtledove," and as many as for "dove." The latest of these is from E. W. Benson (1865): "I am a solitary Turtle (Dove, not Reptile) just now, my wife being at Rugby."

**TUTOR** means "guardian" in the one place where the word occurs in the English Bible (Galatians 4.1–2): "the heir, as long as he is a child, differeth nothing from a servant, though he be lord of all; but is under tutors and governors until the time appointed of the father." In Roman law, the Latin word *tutor* was used for the guardian, and administrator of the estate, of a youth not yet of legal age to manage his own affairs. The word "tutor" passed into English with the same meaning. This meaning is now obsolete except in the language of law. The Greek word here is *epitropos,* which is translated "steward" in its other two occurrences (Matthew 20.8; Luke 8.3). "Tutor" was a correct translation in this passage, both in Latin and in English, but it has now become misleading. RSV translates: "the heir, as long as he is a child, is no better than a slave, though he is the owner of all the estate; but he is under guardians and trustees until the date set by the father."

**TWAIN** is an old word for two. OED says that "its use in the Bible of 1611 and in the Marriage Service, and its value as a rime-word, have contributed to its retention as an archaic and poetic synonym of two." It appears 15 times in KJ, but is not used in RSV. "Wherefore Saul said to David, Thou shalt this day be my son in law in *the one of* the twain" (1 Samuel 18.21) is better translated, "Therefore Saul said to David a second time, 'You shall now be my son-in-law.'" For "shut the door upon them twain" RSV has "shut the door upon the two of them" (2 Kings 4.33).

"They twain shall be one flesh" means "the two shall become one" (Matthew 19.5–6; Mark 10.8). "Whether of the twain will ye that I release unto you?" means "Which of the two do you want me to release for you?" (Matthew 27.21).

In Ephesians 2.15 "for to make in himself of twain one new man" means "that he might create in himself one new man in place of the two." The entire passage (Ephesians 2.13–18) should be read and the two versions compared.

**UNAWARES** appears three times in the phrase "at unawares," in which the word "at" adds nothing to the meaning. The first of these appearances is Numbers 35.11: "Then ye shall appoint you cities to be cities of refuge for you; that the slayer may flee thither, which killeth any person at unawares." This leaves some doubt as to who was unaware. RSV translates ". . . who kills any person without intent." There is a similar passage in Joshua 20.9. In Psalm 35.8 RSV simply omits the "at" and reads "Let ruin come upon them unawares!"

In the account of Jacob's fleeing from Laban, the expression "stole away unawares to" appears twice (Genesis 31.20, 26). The Hebrew literally means "stole the mind of." RSV translates it "outwitted Laban" (vs. 20) and "cheated me" (vs. 26).

When the two sons of Jacob took revenge upon Shechem (Genesis 34.25), according to KJ, they "came upon the city boldly, and slew all the males." The revised versions have a sounder translation of the Hebrew, that they "came upon the city unawares. . . ."

In Luke 21.34 "come upon you unawares" is more accurately translated "come upon you suddenly"; in 1 Thessalonians 5.3, the only other occurrence of this Greek word in the Bible, both versions have "sudden destruction."

"False brethren unawares brought in" (Galatians 2.4) is corrected by RSV to "false brethren secretly brought in." So too in Jude 4: "For there are certain men crept in unawares . . ." is revised to read, "For admission has been secretly gained by some. . . ."

**UNCOMELY**, as an adjective, is used in 1 Corinthians 12.23 in the archaic sense of unseemly, improper, not in accord with propriety. It refers to the *aschēmona,* the unpresentable, indecent parts of the body, which it contrasts with the *euschēmona,* the presentable, decent parts. "Comely" and "uncomely" well expressed the contrast in 1611, when these words still had a moral meaning; but now that they have practically become synonyms of "pretty" and "ugly," they are no longer proper translations of the Greek terms. RSV chooses "presentable" and "unpresentable."

**UNCOMELY**, as an adverb, is an obsolete word for unbecomingly, unsuitably, improperly. It occurs in 1 Corinthians 7.36: "But if any man think that he behaveth himself uncomely toward his virgin . . ." RSV reads: "If any one thinks that he is not behaving properly toward his betrothed . . ." The KJ rendering of 7.36–38 assumes that the man is a father and the virgin his daughter, and that the man's problem is whether or not to give her in marriage to someone else who is not mentioned. The RSV assumes that Paul is here discussing the problem of a couple who are betrothed, but are in doubt whether their Christian faith requires them to remain unmarried. The whole of chapter 7 should be read in RSV. *The Times Literary Supplement,* London, 24 May 1947, commented on this chapter thus: "The passages in the Epistles which deal with sexual morality are especially striking: by a judicious use of current terms, and by rendering such injunctions as 'defraud ye not one the other' by 'do not refuse one another,' the translators have managed to make 1 Corinthians 7 read like a chapter of sound common sense instead of the cento of out-of-date maxims which so many Christians are apt to think it, largely because our existing versions have done St. Paul far less than justice." There is a good discussion of verses 36–38 in *The Interpreter's Bible,* vol. 10, pp. 87–88.

**UNCORRUPTNESS** occurs once, as translation of a Greek word which means incorruptibility, soundness, integrity. Titus 2.7–8 is awkwardly rendered as an incomplete sentence, because the KJ translators substituted "shewing thyself" for the imperative "shew thyself" which had been used by Tyndale and his sixteenth-century successors. KJ reads: "In all things shewing thyself a pattern of good works: in doctrine *shewing* uncorruptness, gravity, sincerity, Sound speech, that cannot be condemned; that he that is of the contrary part may be ashamed, having no evil thing to say of you." RSV returns to the construction of Tyndale: "Show yourself in all respects a model of good deeds, and in your teaching show integrity, gravity, and sound speech that cannot be censured, so that an opponent may be put to shame, having nothing evil to say of us."

**UNCTION.** The Greek word *chrisma* is used only in the second chapter of 1 John. In verse 20 it is translated "unction" and in verse 27 "anointing." The revised versions, and modern translations generally, agree in the use of "anointing" or "anointed" in both verses. The first reads in KJ, "But ye have an unction from the Holy One, and ye know all things." Relying on the more ancient manuscripts for the last clause, RSV reads, "But you have been anointed by the Holy One, and you all know." The text refers to the gift of the Holy

Spirit (compare 3.24; 4.2, 13; 5.7, 8). An explanation of its meaning is in *The Interpreter's Bible,* vol. 12, pp. 245–246.

**UNDERTAKE.** Isaiah 38.9–20 is a psalm of thanksgiving which bears the title, "A writing of Hezekiah king of Judah, after he had been sick and had recovered from his sickness" (RSV). In verse 14 appears the line: "O LORD, I am oppressed; undertake for me." "Undertake" is here used in the sense of become surety or security for, assume responsibility for, which is the meaning of the Hebrew verb which it translates. The revised versions of 1885–1901 have "be thou my surety"; RSV "be thou my security!"

**UNICORN.** A mythical, legendary animal often depicted in heraldry, with the head and body of a horse, the legs of a deer, the tail of a lion, and one long horn projecting straight from the center of its forehead. The word appears nine times in KJ, to represent the Hebrew *re'em,* which the revised versions translate by "wild ox" (Numbers 23.22; 24.8; Job 39.9, 10; Psalms 22.21; 29.6; 92.10; Isaiah 34.7). In Deuteronomy 33.17 it is clear that a *re'em* has more than one horn, but KJ evades this by resorting to the plural, "the horns of unicorns."

The mistaken rendering began with the Greek Septuagint, which used *monokerōs,* and the Latin Vulgate, which used *unicornis* or *rhinoceros.* But the animal referred to was probably *bos primigenius,* which the Old Germans called *Auerochs.* Caesar mentioned it in his *Gallic Wars,* and it is pictured on Assyrian monuments as one of the animals hunted by the kings. The *Auerochs* was noted for its size and strength and for the prodigious length of its horns.

**UNJUST** is sometimes used by KJ in a broad sense which includes all sorts of wrongdoing. RSV retains the word where it implies injustice or unfair dealing, and in statements like "he . . . sends rain on the just and the unjust" (Matthew 5.45). But elsewhere it substitutes more specific terms. The "unjust *men*" of Proverbs 11.7 are "the godless," and "unjust gain" (Proverbs 28.8) is simply "increase." The "unjust steward" was "dishonest" (Luke 16.8, 10). The "unjust judge" was "unrighteous" (Luke 18.6). No one would ever "go to law before the unjust," and the RSV rendering of 1 Corinthians 6.1 is more realistic: "When one of you has a grievance against a brother, does he dare to go to law before the unrighteous instead of the saints?" "He that is unjust, let him be unjust still" is more accurately rendered "Let the evildoer still do evil" (Revelation 22.11).

**UNLEARNED** occurs six times, and represents four distinct Greek words. When Peter and John are termed "unlearned and ignorant" (Acts 4.13), the first of these adjectives means illiterate, uneducated. RSV reads, "that they were uneducated, common men." In 2 Peter 3.16 Paul is said to have written "some things . . . hard to understand, which the ignorant and unstable twist to their own destruction, as they do the other scriptures" (RSV). Here the Greek word for "unlearned" means "ignorant." "Foolish and unlearned questions avoid" (2 Timothy 2.23) is reworded by RSV, "Have nothing to do with stupid, senseless controversies."

In 1 Corinthians 14.16, 23, 24 "unlearned" represents the Greek noun *idiōtēs*—which, it should at once be said, does *not* mean what the English word "idiot" has come to mean. The Greek *idiōtēs* was the ordinary, common man, as contrasted with the man of rank or official position, or with the expert or specialist of any sort. He was the unskilled man, the uninitiated, the outsider, the one who does not belong to the social or professional group which at the moment occupies the stage. RSV uses "outsider" as translation for *idiōtēs* in this chapter.

**UNPERFECT** occurs once (Psalm 139.16): "Thine eyes did see my substance, yet being unperfect." These nine words stand for three Hebrew words, one meaning "thine eyes," one meaning "saw," and one meaning "my embryo." ASV and RSV read "my unformed substance."

"Unperfect" is an old word, now rarely used, which has the same general meanings as "imperfect." Other old words beginning with "un," which RSV has replaced by later equivalents, are "unmoveable" and "unsatiable." RSV has "immovable" (Acts 27.41; 1 Corinthians 15.58) and "insatiable" (Ezekiel 16.28).

**UNSAVOURY.** "Thou will shew thyself unsavoury" (2 Samuel 22.27) is an incredibly strange item in a song of praise to God. The Baals, Ashtoreth, Chemosh, and Molech were unsavoury. But who could think of applying that adjective to the Most High God, the Holy One of Israel? Its presence here results from the dropping out of a consonant from the Hebrew text, which thus became the word for "unsavoury" instead of the word for "perverse." Fortunately 2 Samuel 22 and Psalm 18 are almost identical. Except for this slip, the Hebrew

text of verse 27 is identical with that of Psalm 18.26, and a comparison shows that the error should be corrected. The verse reads in RSV:
"with the pure thou dost show thyself pure;
        and with the crooked thou dost show thyself perverse."

**UNSPEAKABLE** tends to be applied now to bad or objectionable things rather than to good. RSV therefore has "Thanks be to God for his inexpressible gift!" (2 Corinthians 9.15). "He . . . heard unspeakable words, which it is not lawful for a man to utter" (2 Corinthians 12.4) means "he heard things that cannot be told, which man may not utter."

**UNTO** is related to "to" as "until" is related to "till." Fowler, *Dictionary of English Usage,* says that *"until* has very little of the archaic effect as compared with *till* that distinguishes *unto* from *to.* . . . Nevertheless, *till* is now the usual form, and *until* gives a certain leisurely or deliberate or pompous air."

There can be no doubt concerning the archaic effect of "unto." OED records that since the end of the seventeenth century "unto" has been "employed chiefly in poetry, or in formal, dignified, or archaic style, or after Biblical use." Samuel Johnson's *Dictionary,* in the eighteenth century, noted it as "now obsolete." Noah Webster omitted it entirely from his revision of the English Bible, published in 1833, entitled *The Holy Bible, containing the Old and New Testaments, in the Common Version, with Amendments of the language.* In the introductory notes he wrote concerning it: *"To* is used for *unto.* The first syllable *un* adds nothing to the signification or force of *to;* but by increasing the number of unimportant syllables, rather impairs the strength of the whole clause or sentence in which it occurs. It has been rejected by almost every writer, for more than a century."

An unpublished study by P. Marion Simms, Jr., shows that "unto" appears 1,468 times in the KJ New Testament, and that Webster substituted "to" 1,447 times, "before" once (Luke 12.11), "in" once (Matthew 26.3), and omitted "unto" 19 times. RSV New Testament substitutes "to" 1,130 times, omits "unto" 258 times, and substitutes other prepositions 76 times. It retains "unto" in 4 cases, each involving the phrase "unto death" (John 11.4; Philippians 2.8; Revelation 2.10; 12.11).

In KJ "unto" stands for 14 different Hebrew or Greek prepositions. Examples of RSV translations from the Old Testament are: "into one place" (Genesis 1.9); "for Adam and for his wife" (Genesis

3.21); "I have sworn to the LORD" (Genesis 14.22); "until the morning" (Exodus 29.34); "until the second year" (Ezra 4.24); "up to a hundred talents of silver" (Ezra 7.22); "her house sinks down to death" (Proverbs 2.18). From Matthew: "no one puts a piece of unshrunk cloth on an old garment" (9.16); "Come to me, all who labor and are heavy laden" (11.28); "the kingdom of God has come upon you" (12.28); "Let the children come to me, and do not hinder them" (19.14); "the chief priests and the Pharisees gathered before Pilate" (27.62). From Acts: "as far as Paphos" (13.6); "Up to this word they listened to him" (22.22). From the epistles: "through being hitherto accustomed to idols" (1 Corinthians 8.7); "you were called to freedom" (Galatians 5.13); "created in Christ Jesus for good works" (Ephesians 2.10); "you have not yet resisted to the point of shedding your blood" (Hebrews 12.4). In Romans 9.29 and Hebrews 2.17 "like unto" means simply "like." In Hebrews 8.5 "serve unto" means "serve." In 1 John 5.16–17 for "sin unto death" RSV has "mortal sin."

The word "unto" is redundant in the expression "shall be forgiven unto men" (Matthew 12.31), as is shown by the next verse in KJ, which has "it shall be forgiven him." The Lord's Prayer does not read "forgive unto us our debts" (Matthew 6.12). Jesus did not say, "Man, thy sins are forgiven unto thee" (Luke 5.20). The grammatical structure of the Greek is the same in all these cases, and the word "unto" is simply an intruder. It is similarly redundant in Mark 3.28, and "to" is redundant in 2 Corinthians 2.10.

**UNTOWARD,** applied to persons or animals, means difficult to manage, restrain, or control; intractable, unruly, perverse. OED, from which this definition is taken, states that the word was in frequent use, in this sense, from about 1580 to about 1700. The Greek adjective *skolios,* for which it stands in Acts 2.40, means crooked, unscrupulous, dishonest. It is the first of the two adjectives in the phrase which KJ translates, "in the midst of a crooked and perverse generation" (Philippians 2.15). RSV translates Peter's exhortation on the day of Pentecost, "Save yourselves from this crooked generation" (Acts 2.40).

**UPHOLDEN** is the old past participle of "uphold." RSV replaces it by "upheld" in Job 4.4 and Proverbs 20.28. The first of these passages reads:

> "Your words have upheld him who was stumbling,
> and you have made firm the feeble knees."

**USURY** in KJ means the practice of lending money or goods at interest; the word is also used to denote the interest which is charged and paid. It is not employed in the modern sense of excessive or illegal interest. Consequently, the word "usury" does not appear in RSV. It is replaced by "interest," a word which does not appear in KJ.

The Jewish law with respect to lending is thus stated in RSV: "If you lend money to any of my people with you who is poor, you shall not be to him as a creditor, and you shall not exact interest from him" (Exodus 22.25). "You shall not lend upon interest to your brother, interest on money, interest on victuals, interest on anything that is lent for interest. To a foreigner you may lend upon interest, but to your brother you shall not lend upon interest; that the LORD your God may bless you in all that you undertake in the land which you are entering to take possession of it" (Deuteronomy 23.19–20).

Nehemiah's condemnation of the "usury" that was practiced among the remnant of the Jews at Jerusalem (5.1–13) was based upon the principle that interest should not be exacted of a brother Jew. When Psalm 15 praises the man that "putteth not out his money to usury" it is to be understood in the light of this same principle.

The New Testament reflects the commercial practices of the Roman Empire, and assumes the legitimacy of banking, credit, and interest: "Thou oughtest therefore to have put my money to the exchangers, and *then* at my coming I should have received mine own with usury" (Matthew 25.27) means "Then you ought to have invested my money with the bankers, and at my coming I should have received what was my own with interest."

**UTTER,** as a verb, was frequently used in the sixteenth century in the sense of disclose or reveal something, or make known the character or identity of a person. It has this meaning in Joshua 2.14, 20, where the spies enjoin upon Rahab not to "utter" their business. RSV translates: "The men said to her, 'Our life for yours! If you do not tell this business of ours, then we will deal kindly and faithfully with you when the LORD gives us the land. . . . But if you tell this business of ours, then we shall be guiltless with respect to your oath which you have made us swear.' " In Leviticus 5.1 it is declared to be a sin if one is a witness and does not "utter" what he knows. The Hebrew verb is *nagad,* which has a similar meaning in Proverbs 29.24 (KJ "bewray"; RSV "disclose") and Jeremiah 20.10 (KJ "report"; RSV "denounce"). The one thing that is certain about the difficult first line of Job 17.5 is that the KJ rendering, "He that speaketh flattery to *his* friends," is wrong. The revised versions and other modern translations, such as Smith, Zurich, Menge, and the Basic Bible, agree in the interpretation which is expressed by RSV, "He who informs against his friends to get a share of their property."

Tyndale's translation of Mark 3.12 was, "And he straygtly charged them that they should not utter him." In Genesis 45.1 Tyndale had, "Joseph commaunded . . . that there shuld be no man with him, whyle he uttred him selfe unto his brethern."

Examples of Shakespeare's use of "utter" in this sense are:

"My duty pricks me on to utter that
Which else no worldly good should draw from me."
*Two Gentlemen from Verona*, III, 1, 8–9

"I will, like a true drunkard, utter all to thee."
*Much Ado about Nothing*, III, 3, 112

"I am glad to be constrain'd to utter that
Which torments me to conceal."
*Cymbeline*, V, 5, 141

**VAIN.** For "vanity" the meaning undue self-esteem is as old as the fourteenth century, but the adjective "vain" was not used in this sense until 1692. In the Bible "vain" always has its original meaning of empty, worthless, futile, foolish. It is used in KJ 100 times, and is retained by RSV in 53 of these cases, 37 of which have the phrase "in vain."

"Vain" is used by KJ as translation of a dozen Hebrew words, each of which has its distinct meaning. "Thy vain thoughts" (Jeremiah 4.14) are "your evil thoughts." "Vain knowledge" (Job 15.2) is "windy knowledge," and "vain words" (Job 16.3) are "windy words." "For vain man would be wise, though man be born *like* a wild ass's colt" (Job 11.12) has no word for "like" in the Hebrew, and is better trans-lated: "But a stupid man will get understanding, when a wild ass's colt is born a man." The Hebrew word for which KJ has "vain" and RSV has "stupid" means literally "hollow" or "empty-headed." In Isaiah 45.18, 19 KJ has "in vain" for the Hebrew word which means "chaos"; in Jeremiah 3.23 and 8.8 it has "in vain" for the word which means "a delusion," "false," "a lie."

The KJ rendering of Lamentations 2.14 is obscure and misleading at several points. It reads: "Thy prophets have seen vain and foolish things for thee: and they have not discovered thine iniquity, to turn away thy captivity; but have seen for thee false burdens and causes of banish-ment." RSV translates:

"Your prophets have seen for you
    false and deceptive visions;
they have not exposed your iniquity
    to restore your fortunes,
but have seen for you oracles
    false and misleading."

Zechariah 10.2 is another obscure rendering in KJ: "For the idols have spoken vanity, and the diviners have seen a lie, and have told false dreams; they comfort in vain: therefore they went their way as a flock, they were troubled, because *there was* no shepherd." In RSV this verse reads:

"For the teraphim utter nonsense,
    and the diviners see lies;
the dreamers tell false dreams,
    and give empty consolation.
Therefore the people wander like sheep;
    they are afflicted for want of a shepherd."

In the New Testament, the meaning represented by "vain" is more clearly put by RSV in "empty words" (Ephesians 5.6); "empty deceit" (Colossians 2.8); "foolish fellow" (James 2.20); and "futile" (1 Corinthians 3.20; 15.17; Titus 3.9; 1 Peter 1.18). "Profane *and* vain babblings" is better translated "godless chatter" (1 Timothy 6.20; 2 Timothy 2.16).

**VAINGLORY** is an old word for empty conceit or idle boasting. It appears as one word in Philippians 2.3, *"Let* nothing *be done* through strife or vainglory," and as two words in Galatians 5.26, "Let us not be desirous of vain glory." The Greek has the noun *kenodoxia* in Philippians and the adjective *kenodoxos* in Galatians. RSV translates: "Do nothing from selfishness or conceit"; "Let us have no self-conceit."

**VANITY** occurs 98 times in KJ, but never in the sense of conceit or undue self-esteem. It means emptiness, worthlessness, futility, or is applied to things that are empty, worthless, or futile. The word appears 37 times in the Book of Ecclesiastes, and is there retained by RSV. The keynote of the book is set in the opening verses:

"Vanity of vanities, says the Preacher,
    vanity of vanities! All is vanity.
What does man gain by all the toil
    at which he toils under the sun?"

The Preacher's refrain, "all *is* vanity and vexation of spirit," is better translated "all is vanity and a striving after wind" (1.14, etc.).

Outside the book of Ecclesiastes, RSV generally uses English terms that are closer to the primary meaning of the several Hebrew and Greek words for which KJ uses "vanity." "Man is like to vanity" (Psalm 144.4) means "Man is like a breath." "Vanity shall take *them*" (Isaiah 57.13) means "a breath will take them away." "They *are* altogether *lighter* than vanity" (Psalm 62.9) means "they are together lighter than a breath." "Therefore their days did he consume in vanity" (Psalm 78.33) means "So he made their days vanish like a breath."

For "vanity" RSV also uses "empty" and "emptiness" (Job 7.3; 15.31; 35.13; Psalm 41.6; Isaiah 40.17; 59.4); "worthless" and "worthlessness" (Jeremiah 2.5; 10.15; 16.19; 51.18); "false," "false-hood," "lies," "delusions," "delusive visions" (Job 31.5; Psalms 12.2; 24.4; 144.8; Isaiah 5.18; Ezekiel 13.6, 8, 9, 23; 21.29; 22.28). Agur's prayer is translated (Proverbs 30.8):

"Remove far from me falsehood and lying;
give me neither poverty nor riches;
feed me with the food that is needful for me."

The word "vanity" is used in KJ for idolatry and idols. "Are there *any* among the vanities of the Gentiles that can cause rain?" (Jeremiah 14.22) means "Are there any among the false gods of the nations that can bring rain?" "Strange vanities" (Jeremiah 8.19) are "foreign idols." "Lying vanities" (Psalm 31.6; Jonah 2.8) are "vain idols." "They have provoked me to anger with their vanities" (Deuteronomy 32.21) means "they have provoked me with their idols"; so also 1 Kings 16.13, 26. "The stock *is* a doctrine of vanities" (Jeremiah 10.8) is a cryptic rendering of Hebrew which means "the instruction of idols is but wood!"

KJ uses "vanity" occasionally for one of the Hebrew words which mean iniquity. "They conceive mischief, and bring forth vanity" (Job 15.35) means "they conceive mischief and bring forth evil." "Under his tongue *is* mischief and vanity" (Psalm 10.7) is better translated "under his tongue are mischief and iniquity." "He that soweth iniquity shall reap vanity" (Proverbs 22.8) is more accurately rendered "He who sows injustice will reap calamity."

In the New Testament RSV replaces "vanity" with "futility" (Romans 8.20; Ephesians 4.17) and "folly" (2 Peter 2.18).

**VESSEL.** The Hebrew word *keli* may stand for any material thing or object, any tool, implement, or weapon, any vessel or receptacle that can be handled and carried. KJ translates it 146 times by "vessel," and 136 times by other terms including "armour," "artillery," "bag," "carriage," "furniture," "instrument," "jewel," "pot," "sack," "stuff," "thing," "wares," "weapon." RSV rejects "artillery," "carriage," and "stuff," in favor of "weapons," "baggage," or "goods"; and uses the term "utensils" rather than "vessels" where the context indicates it. The only passage which needs to be cited here is Hosea 13.15, where "he shall spoil the treasure of all pleasant vessels" is opaque and misleading. RSV has: "it shall strip his treasury of every precious thing." To get the context clearly, the whole of chapter 13 should be read, and the two versions compared.

The Greek word *skeuos* likewise stands for any thing or object which may be used for any purpose. "And would not suffer that any man should carry *any* vessel through the temple" (Mark 11.16) unduly limits Jesus' prohibition, which RSV translates, "he would not allow any one to carry anything through the temple." "Something" is a better translation than "a certain vessel" in the case of Peter's vision (Acts 10.11, 16; 11.5). The plural of *skeuos* is rendered "his stuff" in Luke 17.31, but should be translated "his goods" as in Matthew 12.29 and Mark 3.27—the Greek is the same. The word is used for a ship's "gear" in Acts 27.17, and for "the vessels used in worship" in Hebrews 9.21.

RSV has retained the word "vessel" in the notable passages Romans 9.20–24 and 2 Timothy 2.20–21, where the term is applied to persons. Key verses to Paul's thought are Acts 9.15, which RSV translates "he is a chosen instrument of mine," and 2 Corinthians 4.7, "we have this treasure in earthen vessels." The relevance of the term *skeuos* is not so much that the body is a vessel containing the mind, as that the body is the instrument of the person, and the person an instrument of God's will.

The expression "the weaker vessel" (1 Peter 3.7) shares with "filthy lucre" the doubtful distinction of descent from Biblical associations to jocular slang. This verse reads in RSV: "Likewise you husbands, live considerately with your wives, bestowing honor on the woman as the weaker sex, since you are joint heirs of the grace of life, in order that your prayers may not be hindered."

In 1 Thessalonians 4.4 ". . . know how to possess his vessel . . ." is an expression about which there has been much debate. Does "vessel" here mean "body"—one's own body, or does it mean "wife"—one's own wife? Chrysostom, Tertullian, and Calvin are the most notable of those who have taken it to mean "body." Augustine, Thomas Aquinas, and

Zwingli took it to mean "wife," as do most modern scholars and modern translations. The Greek verb translated "possess" means to gain possession of, take, acquire. The Greek possessive pronoun is not a simple "his" but the word which means "his own." Such a rendering as "know how to acquire his own body" would be mystifying. But the noun *skeuos* is applied to the wife in 1 Peter 3.7; and this not only accords with Hebrew usage, but fits better into the context of the whole passage, 1 Thessalonians 4.3–8. RSV translates verse 4: "that each one of you know how to take a wife for himself in holiness and honor." (See POSSESS)

**VEX** appears 37 times in KJ as translation for 23 different Hebrew or Greek verbs, which modern translations render more literally. RSV retains "vex" in only two cases: where Delilah pressed and urged Samson day after day, until "his soul was vexed to death" (Judges 16.16); and where Lot "was vexed in his righteous soul day after day" by the wickedness of Sodom (2 Peter 2.8).

"Vex" was a popular Elizabethan word which had far more strength than it has today. It stood for physical aggression or affliction as well as for irritating behavior. In KJ "vex" usually means to hurt, harass, oppress, afflict, torment, distress. In only one fourth of the cases is the emphasis upon the feeling of the victims of such aggression or affliction.

To "vex a stranger" means to "wrong a stranger" (Exodus 22.21; Leviticus 19.33). "Vex the Midianites" is "harass the Midianites" (Numbers 25.17, 18; compare Isaiah 11.13). "The Egyptians vexed us, and our fathers" (Numbers 20.15) means ". . . dealt harshly with us and our fathers." "Vex" is used for the Hebrew verb which means "crush" (Judges 10.8) and for Hebrew verbs which mean "terrify" (Psalm 2.5; Isaiah 7.6). Elisha's word to his servant concerning the Shunammite woman, "Let her alone; for her soul *is* vexed within her," is properly translated, "Let her alone, for she is in bitter distress" (2 Kings 4.27). The same Hebrew verb occurs in Job 27.2, where "the Almighty, *who* hath vexed my soul" means "the Almighty, who has made my soul bitter." The reluctance of David's servants to tell him that Bathsheba's child had died is understated by KJ, "how will he then vex himself?" RSV correctly translates, "He may do himself some harm" (2 Samuel 12.18).

A woman of Canaan cried out to Jesus that her daughter was "grievously vexed with a devil" (Matthew 15.22); RSV translates, "severely possessed by a demon." The son who was a "lunatick, and sore vexed" was "an epileptic" who "suffers terribly" (Matthew

17.15). The "vexed with unclean spirits" (Acts 5.16) were "afflicted with unclean spirits." The verbs which replace "vexed" in these three cases are exact translations of the Greek verbs.

RSV uses "vexed" in 1 Kings 21.4, 5 as translation of the Hebrew adjective applied to Ahab after Naboth's refusal to sell his vineyard. KJ had used "heavy" in verse 4 and "sad" in verse 5 for this same adjective.

**VEXATION** stands in KJ for more than annoyance or irritation. Like "vex" it was a strong term in the sixteenth and seventeenth centuries. (See VEX.) Even with the stronger connotation that it had in 1611, "vexation" was too weak a translation in Isaiah 28.19, "it shall be a vexation only *to* understand the report." The revised versions of 1885–1901 have, "it shall be naught but terror to understand the message"; RSV, "it will be sheer terror. . . ." In Isaiah 9.1 KJ reads, "Nevertheless the dimness *shall* not *be* such as *was* in her vexation"; following the revised versions, RSV has "But there will be no gloom for her that was in anguish." The entire verse should be compared in KJ and RSV, for KJ misconstrues it.

Again, "ye . . . shall howl for vexation of spirit" (Isaiah 65.14) means "you . . . shall wail for anguish of spirit." In Ecclesiastes the often repeated "vexation of spirit" (1.14, etc.) is a mistaken rendering of a different Hebrew phrase which means "a striving after wind." (See VANITY)

**VILE.** Like the Latin *vilis,* "vile" has meant cheap, paltry, or worthless. But it also means despicable or disgusting, whether morally or physically, and this is modern usage. The KJ translators were overfond of the word "vile," using it 18 times to translate 9 different Hebrew words, each of which had a distinct meaning—despised, worthless, a fool, disgusting, stupid, trifling, dishonored, defiled, whipped —and 3 times to translate 3 quite distinct Greek words. RSV retains "vile" in 4 cases (Judges 19.24; Psalm 12.8; Jeremiah 29.17; Nahum 1.14).

In Isaiah 32.5 "vile person" represents the Hebrew word for "fool." "I am vile" means "I am of small account" (Job 40.4) and "I am despised" (Lamentations 1.11). Bildad's question, "Wherefore are we reputed vile in your sight?" is more accurately translated "Why are we stupid in your sight?" (Job 18.3). "They were viler than the earth" (Job 30.8) is an erroneous translation for the Hebrew text which means "they have been whipped out of the land."

In the New Testament "vile body" means "lowly body" (Philippians

3.21). The study in recent years of Greek papyri has made it clear that the "vile raiment" of James 2.2 is "shabby clothing." "Vile affections" is not as exact a translation, either for the adjective or for the noun, as "dishonorable passions" (Romans 1.26).

**VIRTUE** may be misleading in two contexts of the New Testament. It does not refer to moral character in the statement made by Jesus when a woman touched him in the hope of being healed: "Somebody hath touched me: for I perceive that virtue is gone out of me" (Luke 8.46; compare Mark 5.30). "Virtue" here, and in Luke 6.19, means nothing more than "power," and "power" is the proper translation of *dynamis,* the Greek term which is used in these passages.

**VISAGE** means face, and in the story of Nebuchadnezzar's anger against Shadrach, Meshach, and Abednego "the form of his visage was changed" means "the expression of his face was changed" (Daniel 3.19). In Isaiah 52.14, however, the word "visage" is used in the more general sense of appearance. "His appearance was so marred" is a more faithful rendering of the Hebrew than "his visage was so marred." The passage is difficult, with various uncertainties, but this is not one of them. Isaiah 52.13–15 should be read together, as the first of the five strophes in the great prophecy concerning the Suffering Servant of the LORD, which ends with 53.12.

**VOLUME.** Literally, something rolled up. The English word is an adaptation of the Latin *volumen,* from *volvere,* which means "to roll." It originally meant a roll of manuscript, such as constituted a book or part of a book in ancient times. The expression "the volume of the book," which appears twice in KJ, means "the roll of the book," and is so rendered by the revised versions. KJ translated the Hebrew word *megillah* 21 times as "roll," and once as "volume" (Psalm 40.7). In Hebrews 10.7 this verse from the Psalms is quoted, and "volume" appears as a translation for the Greek word which the Septuagint had used for *megillah.*

**WAIT ON** or **UPON,** according to OED, means "in Bible phrase, to place one's hope in (God)." OED goes on to say that the expression is very common in the Bible of 1611, rendering several Hebrew verbs of identical meaning. RSV usually replaces it by "wait for" (Psalms 25.3, 5, 21; 27.14; 37.9, 34; 62.1, 5; Proverbs 20.22; Isaiah 8.17; 40.31; 51.5; Hosea 12.6; Zephaniah 3.8), but in some contexts expresses more clearly the implied attitude of hope: "We set our hope on thee" (Jeremiah 14.22); "Let not those who hope in thee be put to shame through me" (Psalm 69.6).

In Psalms 104.27 and 145.15 "look to" is the appropriate expression. The second of these verses reads in RSV:

> "The eyes of all look to thee,
> and thou givest them their food in due season."

Psalm 123.2 reads:

> "Behold, as the eyes of servants
> look to the hand of their master,
> as the eyes of a maid
> to the hand of her mistress,
> so our eyes look to the LORD our God,
> till he have mercy upon us."

"Wait on" is sometimes used by KJ in the sense of attend or serve. "They waited on their office" (1 Chronicles 6.32) means "they performed their service"; and "to wait on the sons of Aaron" (1 Chronicles 23.28) means "to assist the sons of Aaron." "The priests waited on their offices" (2 Chronicles 7.6) means "The priests stood at their posts." "These waited on the king" (2 Chronicles 17.19) means "These were in the service of the king." To "wait at the altar" (1 Corinthians 9.13) is to "serve at the altar."

**WAKE.** While most people know that a "wake" is a watch over the dead, the verb in this sense has gone out of standard speech. It originally meant to remain awake and, hence, to watch over something. Psalm 127.1 is a much quoted verse, but the second half of it is frequently omitted: "Except the LORD build the house, they labour in vain that build it; except the LORD keep the city, the watchman waketh *but* in vain." RSV has "the watchman stays awake in vain."

> "Watch thou and wake when others be asleep."
>
> *King Henry VI, Part II*, I, 1, 249

"Thus must we do though, that wake for the public good; and thus hath the wise magistrate done in all ages."

> Ben Jonson, *Bartholomew Fair*, II, 1

**WANT.** "And when they wanted wine, the mother of Jesus saith unto him, They have no wine"—so reads KJ in its account of the marriage at Cana in Galilee (John 2.1–11). To the modern reader this means that when some of the guests grew thirsty and desired wine, the mother of Jesus realized that there was none and turned to him for help.

But that is not what the Greek text of John 2.3 means. Its first clause was translated by Tyndale: "And when the wine failed." Tyndale's rendering is correct, and was used in the successive versions of Coverdale, Thomas Matthew, the Great Bible, the Geneva Bible, and the first edition of the Bishops' Bible. The Greek text implies that the bridegroom had supplied wine, according to Jewish custom, but that he had miscalculated and did not supply enough. Tyndale's translation of the clause has been reinstated by the revised versions. Other modern translators say that the wine "ran short" (Moffatt, Weymouth, Twentieth Century, Ballantine, Rieu) or "gave out" (Goodspeed, Phillips, Verkuyl).

The wording of KJ, "when they wanted wine," is an ambiguous rendering for which a reviser of the Bishops' Bible is responsible. It first appeared in the second edition of the Bishops' Bible, and was taken from it by the KJ translators. These two versions stand alone in this translation.

In 1611 no ambiguity was apparent, for "want" is always used by KJ in the older sense of "lack," and not in the sense of "desire." The seventeenth-century reader understood the clause to mean "when they lacked wine" just as naturally as the reader of today understands it to mean "when they desired wine."

The RSV uses "want" in the older sense 27 times, retaining such renderings as "The LORD is my shepherd, I shall not want" (Psalm 23.1); "those who fear him have no want!" (Psalm 34.9); "he began to be in want" (Luke 15.14); "Not that I complain of want" (Philippians 4.11). "When I was present with you, and wanted" (2 Corinthians 11.9) is changed to "when I was with you and was in want."

In 31 passages RSV replaces "want" with another word, usually "lack." Examples are: "him that wanteth understanding" (Proverbs 9.4); RSV "him who is without sense." "Fools die for want of wisdom" (Proverbs 10.21); RSV "fools die for lack of sense." "A prince that wanteth understanding" (Proverbs 28.16); RSV "a ruler who lacks understanding." "He wanteth nothing for his soul of all that he desireth" (Ecclesiastes 6.2); RSV "he lacks nothing of all that he desires." A familiar verse is Psalm 34.10, which reads in KJ: "The young lions do lack, and suffer hunger: but they that seek the LORD shall not want any good *thing*." RSV translates:

> "The young lions suffer want and hunger;
>> but those who seek the LORD lack no good thing."

An obscure passage where KJ misses the meaning is Proverbs 13.23, "Much food *is in* the tillage of the poor: but there is *that is* destroyed for want of judgment." RSV translates:

> "The fallow ground of the poor yields much food,
> but it is swept away through injustice."

The verb "want" did not begin to be used in the sense of "desire" until almost a hundred years after the publication of KJ. This is now, however, its more common meaning. RSV uses "want" 61 times in the New Testament as translation of Greek verbs which mean to wish, desire, or will. These verbs are usually represented in KJ by "would," "will," or "wilt," which may easily be mistaken for auxiliary verbs denoting a future tense. Examples are: "What wilt thou?" (Matthew 20.21); RSV "What do you want?" "He would not reject her" (Mark 6.26); RSV "he did not want to break his word to her." "Wilt thou be made whole?" (John 5.6); RSV "Do you want to be healed?" "Wherefore would ye hear *it* again? will ye also be his disciples?" (John 9.27); RSV "Why do you want to hear it again? Do you too want to become his disciples?" "Wilt thou kill me . . . ?" (Acts 7.28); RSV "Do you want to kill me . . . ?" "Would pervert the gospel of Christ" (Galatians 1.7); RSV "want to pervert the gospel of Christ." The outstanding example is Romans 7.15–21, Paul's account of his sinful plight. In these verses "I would" constantly serves as translation of the present tense of the Greek verb *thelō*, which means wish, desire, want.

**WARD,** as noun, occurs 23 times in KJ and is not used in RSV. It stands for custody, a place of custody, a body of guards or watchmen or the duties of such men. RSV uses "custody" in the story of Joseph's imprisonment (Genesis 40.3, 4, 7; 41.10) and in two incidents leading to the death penalty while the people of Israel were in the wilderness (Leviticus 24.12; Numbers 15.34). It uses "prison" consistently in Genesis 42.16, 17, 19. When David returned to Jerusalem after the collapse of Absalom's rebellion, and put his ten concubines "in ward," the meaning is that he "put them in a house under guard, and provided for them, but did not go in to them" (2 Samuel 20.3). The word "cage" is the right translation in the lamentation over the puppet kings of Judah who were ensnared like young lions (Ezekiel 19.1–9).

In 1 Chronicles 9.23; 25.8; 26.12, 16 and Nehemiah 12.24, 25, 45; 13.30 the term "ward" refers to guards and their duties. The statement concerning the tribe of Benjamin, that "hitherto the greatest part of them had kept the ward of the house of Saul" (1 Chronicles 12.29) means that "the majority had hitherto kept their allegiance to the house of Saul." "In my ward" (Isaiah 21.8) means "at my post." "A captain of the ward" (Jeremiah 37.13) is "a sentry." "The first and the second ward" of the prison in which Peter was confined means "the first and the second guard" (Acts 12.10).

**-WARD.** The suffix "-ward" means in the direction of; it appears in such words as upward, downward, inward, outward, earthward, heavenward, skyward, etc. In the sixteenth century it was still a matter of taste or mood whether to write "toward you" or "to you-ward," "toward us" or "to us-ward," and the like. KJ uses "toward" 320 times, but has 11 instances of the archaic usage. Numbered for subsequent reference, these are:

(1) "Be thou for the people to God-ward" (Exodus 18.19)
(2) "And such trust have we . . . to God-ward" (2 Corinthians 3.4)
(3) "your faith to God-ward" (1 Thessalonians 1.8)
(4) "to the mercy seatward" (Exodus 37.9)
(5) "his words *have been* to thee-ward very good" (1 Samuel 19.4)
(6) "thy thoughts *which are* to us-ward" (Psalm 40.5)
(7) "his power to us-ward who believe" (Ephesians 1.19)
(8) "is longsuffering to us-ward" (2 Peter 3.9)
(9) "more abundantly to you-ward" (2 Corinthians 1.12)
(10) "which to you-ward is not weak" (2 Corinthians 13.3)
(11) "the grace of God which is given me to you-ward" (Ephesians 3.2)

Of these instances, the archaic expressions were derived: (6) from the second edition of the Bishops' Bible; (3), (4), (5), (10) from the first edition of the Bishops' Bible; and (1), (2), (7), (8), (9), (11) from Tyndale. In the lack of an adequate concordance for Tyndale, we cannot be sure that the count is complete, but we have found eight other cases. Tyndale uses "to Godwarde" (Acts 22.3; 1 John 3.21); "to me warde" (2 Corinthians 7.7); "to manwarde" (Titus 3.4); "to us warde" (Ephesians 2.7; 1 John 4.9); "to Jewrye warde" (2 Corinthians 1.16); and "to his buryinge warde" (Mark 14.8). All but the last of these appear also in the Geneva Bible; but they were rejected by KJ.

The most astonishing fact in this connection is that the revisers in 1881 and 1901 inserted the archaic expression in four passages where KJ did not use it: "to us-ward" (Romans 8.18); and "to you-ward" (Galatians 5.10; Colossians 1.25; 1 Thessalonians 5.18).

**WARE** as an adjective is now obsolete, with "aware" and "wary" the present words. When an attempt was made at Iconium to organize a gang to stone Paul and Barnabas, "they were ware of *it*, and fled unto Lystra and Derbe" (Acts 14.6). RV and ASV have "they became aware of it"; RSV "they learned of it." Paul did not forget Alexander the coppersmith, saying that he "did me much evil" and adding the injunction to Timothy, "Of whom be thou ware also" (2 Timothy 4.14, 15). RSV translates "Beware of him yourself."

**WASTENESS** occurs just once, Zephaniah 1.15, "a day of wasteness and desolation." The Hebrew has "a day of *sho'ah* and *mesho'ah*." The interchangeability of these Hebrew words is attested by the fact that in KJ *sho'ah* is usually translated by "desolation," and *mesho'ah* by "waste." Zephaniah 1.15 RSV reads "a day of ruin and devastation." OED calls this sense of the word "chiefly Biblical" and marks it as obsolete.

**WASTER.** "He also that is slothful in his work is brother to him that is a great waster" (Proverbs 18.9) seems to link the man who wastes time with the man who wastes money. But the Hebrew word here rendered "waster" does not mean a spendthrift, but one who lays waste, ravages, destroys. RSV translates, "He who is slack in his work is a brother to him who destroys." The only other occurrence of "waster" is in Isaiah 54.16, where KJ reads "I have created the waster to destroy" and RSV reads "I have also created the ravager to destroy."

**WAX** is a common verb in KJ meaning to grow, but it is no longer in common use except for the phases of the moon and in the idiom "wax and wane." Otherwise, as OED remarks, the word is obsolete or literary "with a somewhat archaic flavor." It is retained by RSV in only one verse (Deuteronomy 32.15):
"But Jeshurun waxed fat, and kicked;
     you waxed fat, you grew thick, you became sleek."
The second line of that verse, in the Hebrew, consists of only three words. If put as tersely into English, it would read: "you fattened, you thickened, you sleekened." "Waxed," "grew," and "became" have a merely auxiliary status here, equivalent to the suffix "-en"; moreover, these three auxiliary verbs are synonyms.
This status is characteristic of the verb "wax" as used in KJ. It

carries no connotation of increase in magnitude or strength; it is equivalent to "grow" only in the sense that both "wax" and "grow" are equivalent to "become." See OED, *Grow*, 12; *Wax*, 9(b).

"Wax old" means "grow old" (2 Chronicles 24.15; Job 14.8; Hebrews 8.13). "Is the LORD's hand waxed short?" means "Is the LORD's hand shortened?" (Numbers 11.23).

In the parable of the Grain of Mustard Seed "it grew, and waxed a great tree" is misleading (Luke 13.19), for "great" is not supported by the ancient Greek manuscripts, and the Greek word here represented by "waxed" means simply "became." So also in Hebrews 11.34, "waxed valiant" represents Greek words which mean "became mighty." In Luke's statements concerning the child John (1.80) and the child Jesus (2.40) "waxed strong" means "became strong."

**WEALTH** was used in the sixteenth century not only to denote riches, but also in the sense of weal, well-being, or welfare. Unless we remember this, Paul's counsel in 1 Corinthians 10.24 looks like encouragement to theft: "Let no man seek his own, but every man another's *wealth.*" RSV translates, "Let no one seek his own good, but the good of his neighbor."

In KJ Old Testament, the word "wealth" is used three times as a translation for the Hebrew *tob,* which means "good," either as an adjective or as a noun. The passages are Ezra's recital (Ezra 9.12) of the commandment not to intermarry with the people of the land, "nor seek their peace or their wealth"; the praise of Mordecai (Esther 10.3) as "seeking the wealth of his people"; and Job's description of the prosperity of the wicked who "spend their days in wealth" (Job 21.13). RSV uses "prosperity" in the passages from Ezra and Job, and "welfare" in the passage concerning Mordecai—"he sought the welfare of his people."

Both KJ and RSV use "welfare" as the translation for *tob* in Nehemiah 2.10, which tells how Sanballat and Tobiah were greatly displeased that Nehemiah had come "to seek the welfare of the children of Israel."

**WENT FOR** appears in 1 Samuel 17.12, "Jesse . . . had eight sons; and the man went among men *for* an old man in the days of Saul." That seems to imply that he was regarded as an old man, though he was not really such. Tyndale and Coverdale had "was an old man." Geneva said "was taken for an old man," and was followed by the Bishops' Bible. KJ was the first to use "went for an old man."

But these qualifications are not called for by the Hebrew, and the revised versions have returned to the direct statement, "was an old man."

**WHAT** is used in the sense of "why" in 2 Kings 6.33, "what should I wait for the Lord any longer?" and in Luke 22.71, "What need we any further witness?" In the first of these passages RSV uses "why," and clears up the context by identifying the speaker. It recasts the second in closer touch with the Greek text, "What further testimony do we need?" In *Paradise Lost,* II, 329 Milton wrote "What sit we then projecting peace and war?"

"What time" is used for "when" in Numbers 26.10, "what time the fire devoured two hundred and fifty men." Psalm 56.3, "What time I am afraid, I will trust in thee," is reworded by RSV, "When I am afraid, I put my trust in thee." Job 6.17 reads in KJ, "What time they wax warm, they vanish: when it is hot, they are consumed out of their place." RSV translates:

> "In time of heat they disappear;
> when it is hot, they vanish from their place."

**WHEN AS** is an archaism for "when," which is found just once in the English Bible (Matthew 1.18): "When as his mother Mary was espoused to Joseph. . . ." It appears in KJ only, for the prior English translations have "When his mother . . ." and no subsequent translation has followed KJ's wording at this point. OED assigns to 1593 a quotation from Shakespeare's *King Henry VI, Part III* (V, 7, 34):

> "So Judas kiss'd his master,
> And cried 'all hail!' when as he meant all harm."

And it assigns to 1610 a quotation from Shakespeare's *The Tempest* (II, 1, 139):

> "you rub the sore,
> When you should bring the plaster."

Shakespeare's choice of "when as" in the one line and "when" in the other was probably determined by his sense of cadence.

The most famous use of "when as" in English poetry is Robert Herrick's lyric, "Upon Julia's Clothes," beginning, "When as in silks my Julia goes . . ."

**WHEREABOUT** does not refer to place, but interest and concern, in 1 Samuel 21.2. "The business whereabout I send thee" means "the matter about which I send you."

**WHEREBY** appears 38 times in KJ, and is not used in RSV. In Acts 4.12 ("by which we must be saved") and 11.14 ("by which you will be saved"), and in 10 other passages, RSV has "by which." "Whereby" asks a question, and means "how?" in Genesis 15.8 (Abraham) and Luke 1.18 (Zechariah, father of John the Baptist). Ten times "whereby" is unnecessary; for example, in Jeremiah 33.8, which reads in KJ: "I will cleanse them from all their iniquity, whereby they have sinned against me; and I will pardon all their iniquities, whereby they have sinned, and whereby they have transgressed against me." RSV reads: "I will cleanse them from all the guilt of their sin against me, and I will forgive all the guilt of their sin and rebellion against me." In the 14 other cases, the meaning of the Hebrew or Greek is better expressed in other words. Examples are Romans 8.15, where RSV has "When we cry, 'Abba! Father!' " and Ephesians 4.30: "Do not grieve the Holy Spirit of God, in whom you were sealed for the day of redemption."

**WHEREFORE** is an adverb which may introduce a relative clause, "for which reason . . . ," or ask a question, "for what reason . . . ?" THEREFORE has demonstrative force, "for that reason . . . ," or the more general sense of "consequently." KJ uses "wherefore" 337 times; RSV only 7 times. KJ uses "therefore" 1,228 times; RSV 801 times. Both words were overdone in KJ, being often used where not called for by a corresponding Hebrew or Greek expression. RSV often substitutes "therefore" for "wherefore"—for example, in 1 Corinthians 8.13: "Therefore, if food is a cause of my brother's falling, I will never eat meat, lest I cause my brother to fall." In asking a question, it uses "why"—Isaiah 55.2: "Why do you spend your money for that which is not bread?" In the most notable of the seven passages where RSV uses "wherefore" KJ has "whereupon"— Acts 26.19: "Wherefore, O King Agrippa, I was not disobedient to the heavenly vision."

**WHEREIN** is a formal adverb meaning "in which" or "where." It may be used interrogatively, meaning "in what?" or "how?" It occurs 162 times in KJ, and is retained by RSV only in the case of Samson ("wherein his great strength lies," Judges 16.5, 6, 15) and Job ("Let the day perish wherein I was born," Job 3.3). In 1 Kings 18.9 RSV substitutes "Wherein have I sinned?" for KJ "What have I sinned?" Examples of the other 158 occurrences are: "all flesh, wherein *is* the breath of life" (Genesis 6.17); RSV "in which." "The roll wherein thou hast read in the ears of the people" (Jeremiah 36.14); RSV "the scroll that you read in the hearing of the people." "Wherein have we despised thy name?" (Malachi 1.6); RSV "How have we despised thy name?" "The bed wherein the sick of the palsy lay" (Mark 2.4); RSV "the pallet on which the paralytic lay." "This grace wherein we stand" (Romans 5.2); RSV "this grace in which we stand." "For what is it wherein ye were inferior to other churches?" (2 Corinthians 12.13); RSV "For in what were you less favored than the rest of the churches?" "Wherein I suffer trouble, as an evil doer, *even* unto bonds" (2 Timothy 2.9); RSV "the gospel for which I am suffering and wearing fetters, like a criminal."

**WHEREINSOEVER** occurs once (2 Corinthians 11.21): "Howbeit, whereinsoever any is bold, (I speak foolishly,) I am bold also." The rendering comes from Tyndale. In RSV this reads, "But whatever any one dares to boast of—I am speaking as a fool—I also dare to boast of that."

**WHEREINTO** occurs three times. "Every earthen vessel, whereinto *any* of them falleth, whatsoever *is* in it shall be unclean" (Leviticus 11.33) is reworded by RSV: "If any of them falls into any earthen vessel, all that is in it shall be unclean." The other passages are Numbers 14.24 (RSV "into which") and John 6.22, where the clause containing "whereinto" is a gloss which does not appear in the text of the more ancient manuscripts.

**WHEREOF** is a formal or archaic word for "of which." It appears 69 times in KJ; never in RSV. "Whereof I Paul am made a minister" (Colossians 1.23) reads in RSV, "of which I, Paul, became a minister." A particularly clumsy rendering is 2 Corinthians 9.5: "Therefore I thought it necessary to exhort the brethren, that they would go before unto you, and make up beforehand your bounty, whereof ye had notice before, that the same might be ready, as *a matter of* bounty, and not as *of* covetousness." The KJ translators might have done much better than this, if they had paid enough attention to Tyndale and the other sixteenth-century translations. RSV has: "So I thought it necessary to urge the brethren to go on to you before me, and arrange in advance for this gift you have promised, so that it may be ready not as an exaction but as a willing gift."

**WHEREON** means "on which." It appears 24 times in KJ and once in RSV, in the poetic line "whereon hang a thousand buck-lers" (Song of Solomon 4.4). The word is used interrogatively in 2 Chronicles 32.10: "Whereon do ye trust, that ye abide in the siege in Jerusalem?" This means, "On what are you relying, that you stand siege in Jerusalem?"

**WHEREUNTO** is an archaic adverb which may be used to ask a ques-tion or to introduce a relative clause. It appears 26 times in KJ, and nowhere in RSV. "Unto what is the kingdom of God like? and whereunto shall I resemble it?" (Luke 13.18) is more clearly expressed, "What is the kingdom of God like? And to what shall I compare it?" Other questions are Matthew 11.16; Mark 4.30; Luke 7.31; 13.20; Acts 5.24.

Introducing a relative clause, "whereunto" means "to which" (Num-bers 36.4; 2 Chronicles 8.11; Esther 10.2; Jeremiah 22.27; Ezekiel 20.29; Acts 13.2; 1 Timothy 6.12). Some passages are clarified by making the relative clause a new sentence, beginning "For this" (Colossians 1.29; 1 Timothy 2.7; 2 Timothy 1.11) or "To this" (2 Thes-salonians 2.14). Compare KJ and RSV also in 2 Peter 1.19.

Strangely jumbled English appears in Ezekiel 5.9: "I will do in thee that which I have not done, and whereunto I will not do any more the like, because of all thine abominations." RSV reads: "Because of all your abominations I will do with you what I have never yet done, and the like of which I will never do again." Another jumble is 1 Peter 3.21: "The like figure whereunto *even* baptism doth also now save us (not the putting away of the filth of the flesh, but the answer of a good con-science toward God,) by the resurrection of Jesus Christ." RSV has: "Baptism, which corresponds to this, now saves you, not as a removal of dirt from the body but as an appeal to God for a clear conscience, through the resurrection of Jesus Christ." "Whereunto thou hast at-tained" is a mistaken translation of the Greek which means "which you have followed" (1 Timothy 4.6).

**WHEREUPON** is an adverb of place, meaning "on which"; or of time, "immediately after which"; or of reason, "in consequence of which." It appears 17 times in KJ, and is not used by RSV. "Whereupon" is a heavy translation for the simple Hebrew word meaning "and," "so," or "then," which introduces 1 Kings 12.28 and 2 Chronicles 12.6. "The glory of the God of Israel was gone from the cherub, whereupon he was" (Ezekiel 9.3) is better translated "the glory of the God of Israel had gone up from the cherubim on which it rested." ". . . that whereupon they set their minds" means ". . . their heart's desire" (Ezekiel 24.25). RSV uses "so that" (Matthew 14.7); "thus" (Acts 26.12); and "hence" (Hebrews 9.18).

**WHEREWITH** appears 106 times in KJ, and is retained by RSV only in the language of the blessing which King Solomon invoked upon the assembly of Israel at the dedication of the house of the LORD (1 Kings 8.59). The following are examples of the other cases: "Esau hated Jacob because of the blessing wherewith his father blessed him" (Genesis 27.41); RSV "with which his father had blessed him." Gideon asks, "wherewith shall I save Israel?" (Judges 6.15); RSV "how can I deliver Israel?" Jeroboam's apostasy is referred to as "his sin wherewith (RSV "which") he made Israel to sin" (1 Kings 15.34). The LORD's question in Micaiah's vision, "Wherewith?" is now phrased, "By what means?" (1 Kings 22.22). ". . . against the house wherewith I have war" means "against the house with which I am at war" (2 Chronicles 35.21). "Wherewith (RSV "With what") shall I come before the LORD?" (Micah 6.6). "Make ready wherewith I may sup" (Luke 17.8); RSV "Prepare supper for me." ". . . for all the joy wherewith we joy for your sakes" (1 Thessalonians 3.9); RSV "for all the joy which we feel for your sake."

**WHEREWITHAL** appears once, in the Sermon on the Mount. "Wherewithal shall we be clothed" is more simply translated in RSV, "What shall we wear?" (Matthew 6.31).

**WHETHER** is used nine times as an interrogative pronoun, meaning which of the two. "Whether is easier, to say, *Thy* sins be forgiven thee; or to say, Arise, and walk?" (Matthew 9.5) means "Which is easier, to say, 'Your sins are forgiven,' or to say, 'Rise and walk'?" This appears also in Luke 5.23, and in a more complicated form at Mark 2.9. "Whether is greater" means "Which is greater?" (Matthew 23.17, 19; Luke 22.27). "Whether of them twain" (Matthew 21.31) and "Whether of the twain" (Matthew 27.21) mean "Which of the two?" The prayer of the apostles, "Thou, Lord, which knowest the hearts of all *men,* shew whether of these two thou hast chosen," did not ask whether the Lord had chosen one of them, but "which one of these two thou hast chosen" (Acts 1.24).

**WHICH,** as relative pronoun, is used by KJ for persons as well as for things. "Lot also, which went with Abram" (Genesis 13.5) and "a new king over Egypt, which knew not Joseph" (Exodus 1.8) are renderings derived from Tyndale. So too is the wording of 1 Corinthians 15.57: "Thanks *be* to God, which giveth us the victory through our Lord Jesus Christ." A count shows that in Genesis (KJ) "which" occurs 177 times and refers to persons in 37 of these instances, while "who" and "whom" as relative pronouns occur 32 times. In Galatians (KJ) "which" refers to persons in 11 out of 37 occurrences, while "who" and "whom" occur 20 times. The practice of using "which" in the sense of "who" or "whom," referring to persons, has been discontinued by ASV and RSV.

The chief point at which this practice continues, even among some who read the Scriptures in ASV or RSV, is in the Lord's Prayer. One man argued that we should always say "Our Father which art in heaven" because the word "which" removes God from the company of men and sets him apart as unique and transcendent. The KJ translators would have laughed at such a statement; for them, in such a context, "which" and "who" had the same meaning.

Professor Lane Cooper defends "which" in the address to God on the ground that "who art" involves hiatus (*Certain Rhythms in the English Bible,* p. 3); and he devotes a page to labored portrayal of the "yawn" induced by the attempt to enunciate "who" and "art" without an intervening consonant. But on his own principles, the hiatus is "technical, not real," and is "easily excused, because both of the words involved are short, while one of them lacks any accent, and the other carries a stress." These quoted words, with which he defends four immediate successions of vowels which have been called to his attention in Genesis and Exodus, are applicable to "who art." Following his method of indicating accent and cadence, the first line of the Lord's Prayer in RSV contains an iamb, an anapaest, and an iamb:

$$\text{Our Fa} \mid \text{ther who art} \mid \text{in heaven}$$

Or may be scanned as a bacchius and two iambs:

$$\text{Our Father} \mid \text{who art} \mid \text{in heaven}$$

It should be added that the KJ translators, whose sense of euphony he praises in extravagant terms, did not hesitate to use "who art," "who are," "who am," "who answered," "who inhabited," "who is." A look at the concordance shows that in Genesis, Joshua, and 1 Samuel these expressions occur in KJ 22 times.

**WHILE AS** is an obsolete idiom for "while." It appears in Hebrews 9.8. Shakespeare, like KJ, uses it just once:
"While as the silly owner of the goods
Weeps over them and wrings his hapless hands."
*King Henry VI, Part II*, I, 1, 225

**WHILES, WHILST** are obsolete forms of the conjunction "while." The KJ translators used "whiles" 10 times and "whilst" 9 times, but "while" over 200 times. There is no difference in meaning of the three terms. In Shakespeare's plays, "while" appears 34 times, "whiles" 13 times, and "whilst" 10 times.

**WHISPER, WHISPERING, WHISPERER** are used in KJ in senses still current and readily understood (2 Samuel 12.19; Psalm 41.7; Isaiah 29.4). RSV adds Psalm 31.13, Jeremiah 20.10, and two passages in Job:
"Now a word was brought to me stealthily,
my ear received the whisper of it." (Job 4.12)
"Lo, these are but the outskirts of his ways;
and how small a whisper do we hear of him!
But the thunder of his power who can understand?"
(Job 26.14)
The Hebrew word *nirgan* is consistently translated "whisperer" by RSV in Proverbs: "a whisperer separates close friends" (16.28); "where there is no whisperer, quarreling ceases" (26.20);
"The words of a whisperer are like delicious morsels;
they go down into the inner parts of the body." (18.8; 26.22)
In the New Testament, "whisperings" and "whisperers" translate the plural of Greek words which sound like whispers, *psithurismos* and *psithuristēs* (2 Corinthians 12.20; Romans 1.29). These words are immediately linked in these verses with the Greek words for "slander" and "slanderers." RSV uses "gossip" but might well have retained "whisperings" and "whisperers." In classical mythology, *psithuristēs* was an epithet of Hermes (Mercury) and Eros (Cupid), and in its feminine form was an epithet of Aphrodite (Venus).

**WHO** is used in several ways that seem odd to the modern reader but were common speech around 1600. "Who steals my purse steals trash," wrote Shakespeare in *Othello*, III, 3, 157. Matthew 13.9, 43 have the same construction, "Who hath ears to hear, let him hear." This was an innovation of KJ, for Tyndale and his successors had "Whosoever hath . . ." and Rheims had "He that hath . . ." Moreover, KJ it-self, for the same Greek wording of the sentence, had "He that hath ears to hear, let him hear" in Matthew 11.15 and Luke 8.8; 14.35. RSV uses "He that hath . . ." in all of these passages.

Acts 21.37 has an archaic usage. Paul "said unto the chief captain, May I speak unto thee? Who said, Canst thou speak Greek?" RSV translates the Greek literally: "Paul said to the tribune, 'May I say something to you?' And he said, 'Do you know Greek?' "

The cry of the unclean spirit, "I know thee who thou art, the Holy One of God," is a mechanically literal translation of the Greek (Mark 1.24; Luke 4.34). As an English sentence, it may be compared to Cordelia's farewell to her sisters:

> "I know you what you are;
> And, like a sister, am most loath to call
> Your faults as they are named."
>
> *King Lear*, I, 1, 272

**WHOLE** has two basic meanings: (a) sound, unimpaired, in good con-dition; (b) complete, entire, undivided. KJ uses "whole" in the second of these meanings 81 times, and "wholly" 16 times. It uses "whole" in the first of these meanings 34 times, in 33 of which it is applied to persons, in the sense of healthy, well, healed or made well. OED regards this usage as archaic or "Biblical." Out of these 33 cases RSV retains "whole" twice: when Jesus told the man with the withered hand to stretch it out, "it was restored, whole like the other" (Matthew 12.13); and later, when he healed those who were brought to him in the hills by the Sea of Galilee, "the throng wondered, when they saw the dumb speaking, the maimed whole, the lame walking, and the blind seeing, and they glorified the God of Israel" (Matthew 15.31).

Elsewhere RSV uses heal, well, or make well, depending upon the Hebrew or Greek word. "When the circumcision of all the nation was done, they remained in their places in the camp till they were healed" (Joshua 5.8). "Those who are well have no need of a physician, but those who are sick" (Matthew 9.12). "Daughter, your faith has made you well; go in peace, and be healed of your disease" (Mark 5.34). An interesting case is John 7.23, where KJ reads: "If a man on the sabbath day receive circumcision, that the law of Moses should not be broken; are ye angry at me, because I have made a man every whit whole on the sabbath day?" The expression "every whit whole" goes back to Tyn-dale, but is a mistranslation. The Greek word represented by "every whit" is not an adverb modifying the adjective represented by "whole," but is itself an adjective which modifies the word for "man." The Greek is literally translated, "I have made a whole man well." The Latin Vulgate has *totum hominem sanum feci;* Wyclif translated this "I made al a man hool." Martin Luther's translation was *ich den ganzen Menschen habe gesund gemacht.* RSV has, "If on the sabbath a man receives circumcision, so that the law of Moses may not be broken, are you angry with me because on the sabbath I made a man's whole body well?"

**WHOLESOME** occurs twice in the sense of healing or health-giving. "A wholesome tongue" translates Hebrew which means literally "the healing of the tongue" (Proverbs 15.4); ASV and RSV have "A gentle tongue is a tree of life." In the Pastoral Epistles the participle of the Greek verb which means to be healthy or sound is applied to Christian teaching. "Wholesome words" (1 Timothy 6.3) are "sound words" in 2 Timothy 1.13. The other passages have "sound doctrine" (1 Timothy 1.10; 2 Timothy 4.3; Titus 1.9; 2.1); "sound speech" (Titus 2.8); "sound in the faith" (Titus 1.13); "sound in faith, in charity, in patience" (Titus 2.2); RSV "sound in faith, in love, and in steadfastness."

**WHOSESOEVER** is an archaic genitive of "whosoever." It appears in one verse, John 20.23: "Whosesoever sins ye remit, they are remitted unto them; *and* whosesoever *sins* ye retain, they are retained." The remoteness of this form from present English is indicated by the fact that many present editions of KJ print it as though it were two words, "whose soever sins," which may awaken curiosity as to what a "soever sin" is. RSV translates: "If you forgive the sins of any, they are forgiven; if you retain the sins of any, they are retained."

**WHOSO** is an archaic form of WHOSOEVER, which is itself on the way toward becoming archaic. "Whoso" appears 51 times in KJ, 25 of which are in the Book of Proverbs. "Whosoever" appears 169 times, 81 of which are in the Gospels. "Whomsoever" appears 20 times. None of these words appear in RSV, which uses "whoever" and "whomever," neither of which is to be found in KJ.

"Whoso sheddeth man's blood, by man shall his blood be shed" (Genesis 9.6) is worded in RSV, "Whoever sheds the blood of man, by man shall his blood be shed." "Whoso looketh into the perfect law of liberty" (James 1.25) is in RSV, "he who looks into the perfect law, the law of liberty."

"Whosoever" is replaced in RSV by "whoever," "he who," "every one who," "if any one." A simple test of the variety of usage is to examine the verses in the Sermon on the Mount which have "whosoever" in KJ. "Whoever" replaces it in Matthew 5.19, 21, 22, 31, 32; "he who" in 5.19; "every one who" in 5.22, 28, 32; 7.24; "if any one" in 5.39, 41.

**WILL,** as a verb, is often used by KJ in the obsolete sense of desire, wish for, want, without implying definite determination or responsibility for decision and action. Caleb's question to his daughter Achsah is translated as "What wouldest thou" in Joshua 15.18, and "What wilt thou?" in Judges 1.14. The Hebrew is identical in the two passages, and is better translated "What do you wish?" Salome's answer to Herod—"I will that thou give me by and by in a charger the head of John the Baptist"—means "I want you to give me at once the head of John the Baptist on a platter" (Mark 6.25). Peter's suggestion to Jesus on the Mount of Transfiguration was not "If thou wilt . . ." but "If you wish, I will make three booths here, one for you and one for Moses and one for Elijah" (Matthew 17.4). Festus' question to Paul was not "Wilt thou go up to Jerusalem?" but "Do you wish to go up to Jerusalem?" (Acts 25.9).

". . . to whomsoever the Son will reveal *him*" is more accurately translated ". . . to whom the Son chooses to reveal him" (Matthew 11.27). "Herod will kill thee" is "Herod wants to kill you" (Luke 13.31). "Ye will not come to me" is "you refuse to come to me" (John 5.40). In these and other cases the KJ "will" may seem to be an auxiliary verb denoting futurity, but in the Greek it stands for the main verb of the clause, which is followed by an infinitive. In 1 Timothy 5.11 KJ reads, "But the younger widows refuse: for when they have begun to wax wanton against Christ, they will marry." This is not a prediction of the future; it is the statement of a present general condition. RSV translates, "But refuse to enrol younger widows; for when they grow wanton against Christ they desire to marry."

"If any man will do his will" is an undue compacting and easing of the clause which reads, "if any man's will is to do his will" (John 7.17)—the reference is to the will of God, as the whole sentence, verses 16–17, makes clear. The outstanding example of the use of the verb "will" in the sense of desire is in Paul's great chapter on sin, Romans 7.19, "For the good that I would I do not; but the evil which I would not, that I do." RSV reads, "For I do not do the good I want, but the evil I do not want is what I do."

**WILL-WORSHIP** is defined by OED as "Worship according to one's own will or fancy, or imposed by human will, without divine authority." The word is a literal reproduction in English of a Greek compound word *ethelothrēskeia*, which occurs in Colossians 2.23. Paul is here warning against the misdirected zeal and practices of ascetics. KJ translates: "Which things have indeed a shew of wisdom in will worship, and humility, and neglecting of the body; not in any honour to the satisfying of the flesh." RSV translates: "These have indeed an appearance of wisdom in promoting rigor of devotion and self-abasement and severity to the body, but they are of no value in checking the indulgence of the flesh."

While the point of the entire passage is that these ascetic practices are not in accord with Christ, Paul grants in verse 23 that they have "an appearance of wisdom." Among these appearances is rigor of devotion, which is the better translation of *ethelothrēskeia* in the one verse where it appears.

**WINEBIBBER.** From the Latin verb *bibere*, to drink, are derived the English verb "bib," to drink or tipple, and the nouns "bibation" and "bibber." "Winebibber" occurs three times in KJ. It is retained by RSV in Proverbs 23.20–21:
"Be not among winebibbers,
or among gluttonous eaters of meat;
for the drunkard and the glutton will come to poverty,
and drowsiness will clothe a man with rags."
Here "winebibbers" represents a Hebrew phrase which means "drinkers of wine," and "drunkard" stands for the Hebrew word which appears also in Deuteronomy 21.20.

"Winebibber" is not retained by RSV in the comment which Jesus quoted concerning himself: "Behold, a glutton and a drunkard, a friend of tax collectors and sinners" (Matthew 11.19 — Luke 7.34).

**WINEFAT.** (See Fat)

**WISE** is an old noun which means way, manner, fashion. "On this wise" was a common phrase which meant in this way. Since the sixteenth century the use of "wise" in this sense has tended to disappear; it survives chiefly as a suffix in such words as crosswise, lengthwise, likewise, otherwise, sidewise. OED quotes from a publication of 1677: "Let us try once more to argue Cardinalwise." And from one of

1916: "We trod the pilgrim road in pilgrim wise." The comment, "He spoke Coolidge-wise," refers to the laconic speech of Calvin Coolidge, President of the United States, 1923–1929.

The noun "wise" appears in KJ 31 times, in the phrases "on this wise," "in any wise," "in no wise," "in like wise." In the place of "on this wise" RSV has "in this way" (Matthew 1.18; John 21.1; Acts 13.34; Hebrews 4.4) and "to this effect" (Acts 7.6). "In no wise" is replaced by "not fully" (Luke 13.11) and "not at all" (Romans 3.9). "Speaketh on this wise" is replaced by "says" (Romans 10.6).

These 8 passages are the only ones in which the Greek text contains an adverb or clause to justify the use of a "wise" clause in English. In the other 23 passages there is no corresponding Hebrew or Greek term. The "wise" clauses are either periphrastic, like the word "manner," or an attempt to reproduce an emphasis which in Hebrew is conveyed by repetition of the verb, and in Greek by a double negative. (See MANNER, GENERALLY, SURELY)

In Leviticus 19.17, "Thou shalt in any wise rebuke thy neighbour, and not suffer sin upon him," the clause "in any wise" represents the Hebrew absolute infinitive. A literal translation would be "To rebuke thou shalt rebuke thy neighbour. . . ." The revised versions of 1881–1901 had "Thou shalt surely rebuke thy neighbour. . . ." RSV corrects the translation of the verb, changing "rebuke" to "reason with," and secures the necessary emphasis by expressing the logical correction of the two parts of the verse, which reads as a whole: "You shall not hate your brother in your heart, but you shall reason with your neighbor, lest you bear sin because of him." Other examples are Deuteronomy 17.15; 21.23; 22.7. In 1 Samuel 6.3 RSV uses "by all means," and in 1 Kings 3.26, 27 "by no means."

"He shall in no wise lose his reward" represents Greek which is more directly translated, "he shall not lose his reward" (Matthew 10.42). ". . . shall in no wise enter therein" means simply "shall not enter it" (Luke 18.17). Peter's word to Jesus, "If I should die with thee, I will not deny thee in any wise," is stronger when translated literally, "If I must die with you, I will not deny you" (Mark 14.31). See also Matthew 5.18; John 6.37; Acts 13.41; Revelation 21.27. In Matthew 21.24, "I in like wise will tell you" stands for Greek which means "I also will tell you."

**WISH,** as verb, is used only eight times in KJ, partly because its meaning is often assigned to "will" and "would" (see WILL). It stands for feelings of desire in Psalms 40.14 and 73.7 but represents the

Hebrew verb which means "ask" in Job 31.30 and Jonah 4.8. Jonah not only "wished in himself to die," but prayed for death; the Hebrew is identical with the statement concerning Elijah, 1 Kings 19.4, which KJ translates, "he requested for himself that he might die." In three New Testament passages KJ uses "wish" for the Greek verb which also means "pray." Instead of "they wished for the day," RSV has "they prayed for day to come" (Acts 27.29); and instead of "I wish above all things that thou mayest prosper," it has "I pray that all may go well with you" (3 John 2). In 2 Corinthians 13.7 both versions translate this Greek verb by "pray," but in verse 9 of this chapter KJ renders it by "wish." RSV has "What we pray for is your improvement."

The one occurrence of "wish" as a noun is in Job 33.6, where KJ has a notorious mistranslation, "Behold, I *am* according to thy wish in God's stead." RSV translates the verse:

"Behold, I am toward God as you are;
I too was formed from a piece of clay."

**WIT,** as a noun, is used only once in KJ, in the vivid description of the sailors' plight in a storm at sea (Psalm 107.27): "They reel to and fro, and stagger like a drunken man, and are at their wit's end."

The adjective "witty" appears in Proverbs 8.12, "I wisdom dwell with prudence, and find out knowledge of witty inventions." But the "witty inventions" were an invention of the KJ translators, to represent a Hebrew word for which the earlier versions had "counsel" or "understanding," and the present revised versions have "discretion."

The author of the Wisdom of Solomon, one of the books of the Apocrypha, says of himself, as translated by Coverdale and the Bishops' Bible, "I was a lad of ripe wit" (8.19). The Geneva Bible said, "I was a witty child," and KJ adopted this. But the Greek adjective refers to good natural gifts, both of body and mind. RV puts it, "I was a child of parts"; and RSV has "As a child I was by nature well-endowed."

**WIT, WIST, WOT.** The Old English verb "wit" means to know or to find out. Without inflection, it appears 20 times in KJ; its present tense, "wot," 11 times; and its past tense, "wist," 13 times.

While Rebekah drew water for his camels, Abraham's servant "wondering at her held his peace, to wit whether the LORD had made his journey prosperous or not" (Genesis 24.21). RSV translates: "The man gazed at her in silence to learn whether the LORD had prospered his journey or not." When the baby Moses was put in a basket of bulrushes and left by the river's brink, "his sister stood afar off, to wit what would be done to him" (Exodus 2.4). RSV reads, "his sister stood at a distance, to know what would be done to him."

The most familiar example of the use of the past tense "wist" is the answer of the twelve-year-old Jesus to his mother's reproach: "Wist ye not that I must be about my Father's business?" The revised versions translate this: "Did you not know that I must be in my Father's house?" (Luke 2.49).

"Do you to wit" is an idiom which means "cause you to know." It was in common use in the thirteenth to the seventeenth centuries, but is now obsolete. Tyndale used it at 1 Corinthians 15.1 and 2 Corinthians 8.1, and KJ retained it in the latter passage.

The expression "to wit," meaning "that is" or "namely," is used 17 times in KJ, and in all but one case has been inserted by the translators in the interest of clarity, without any corresponding Hebrew or Greek term. The one which has a corresponding Greek word is 2 Corinthians 5.18–19, "All this is from God, who through Christ reconciled us to himself and gave us the ministry of reconciliation; that is, God was in Christ reconciling the world to himself" (RSV).

Because most concordances do not list the passages where *"to wit"* has been inserted, the list is given here: Joshua 17.1; 1 Kings 2.32; 7.50; 13.23; 2 Kings 10.29; 1 Chronicles 7.2; 27.1; 2 Chronicles 4.12; 25.7, 10; 31.3; Esther 2.12; Jeremiah 25.18; 34.9; Ezekiel 13.16; Romans 8.23.

**WITCH** appears twice in KJ. "Thou shalt not suffer a witch to live" (Exodus 22.18). "There shall not be found among you . . . an enchanter, or a witch" (Deuteronomy 18.10). The Hebrew word denotes a woman in the first of these passages, and a man in the second; but the English does not bring out this distinction. Yet KJ itself translates the masculine plural of this word by "sorcerers" in Exodus 7.11, Daniel 2.2, and Malachi 3.5. While it is true that the word "witch" was formerly applied to men as well as to women, the revised versions use "sorcerers" in Exodus 22.18, and "sorcerer" in Deuteronomy 18.10.

**WITHAL** as a preposition is an archaic form of "with," which was used at the end of a relative clause or a question. The prize exhibit of its use and meaning is Rosalind's speech in Shakespeare's *As You Like It,* III, 2, 328–329: "I'll tell you who Time ambles withal, who Time trots withal, who Time gallops withal and who he stands still withal." The word occurs in KJ 24 times as a preposition, but is not retained by RSV.

A typical passage is Job 2.8, "he took him a potsherd to scrape himself withal," where RSV reads "he took a potsherd with which to scrape himself." RSV uses "with which" in place of "withal" in Exodus 30.4; 37.27; Leviticus 5.3; 11.21; Isaiah 30.14, 23; Mark 10.39. The "with which" construction provides smoother English in all of these cases except Job 2.8, where a more natural expression would be "he took a potsherd to scrape himself with."

The KJ rendering of Exodus 25.29 is erroneous, "thou shalt make the dishes thereof, and spoons thereof, and covers thereof, and bowls thereof, to cover withal"; RSV translates, "you shall make its plates and dishes for incense, and its flagons and bowls with which to pour libations." So also Exodus 37.16. ". . . to wash *withal*" means "for washing" (Exodus 30.18; 40.30), and "to overlay the walls of the houses *withal*" (1 Chronicles 29.4) means "for overlaying the walls of the house." In Leviticus 6.30 "to reconcile *withal*" means "to make atonement"; and in Judges 7.20, 2 Chronicles 26.15, and Esther 6.9 RSV simply drops the "withal" which the KJ translators had inserted. Exodus 36.3 and 2 Chronicles 24.14 are more complicated, and should be compared in the two versions.

"Withal" as an adverb means with everything else, in addition, also. It occurs eight times, and is not retained by RSV. "Now he *was* ruddy, *and* withal of a beautiful countenance" (1 Samuel 16.12) represents Hebrew which means "Now he was ruddy, with beautiful eyes." In Psalm 141.10 "withal" represents the Hebrew adverb which means "together," and which belongs to the first line of the verse rather than to the second; RSV translates:

> "Let the wicked together fall into their own nets,
> while I escape."

Instead of "they shall withal be fitted in thy lips" (Proverbs 22.18), RSV has "if all of them are ready on your lips"; verses 17 and 18 go together as one sentence, the whole of which should be compared in the two versions.

"Withal" is omitted by RSV in 1 Kings 19.1 and Acts 25.27 as unnecessary to the translation and confusing to the English reader. It is reduced to "and" in Colossians 4.3. The statement about the younger widows, "withal they learn *to be* idle" (1 Timothy 5.13), reads in RSV "Besides that, they learn to be idlers." The closing request of Paul's letter to Philemon, "But withal prepare me also a lodging," is literally translated by RSV, "At the same time, prepare a guest room for me."

**WITHHOLDEN** is the old past participle of "withhold." RSV replaces it by "withheld" in Job 22.7; 38.15, Psalm 21.2, Jeremiah 3.3, Joel 1.13, and Amos 4.7. "The LORD hath withholden thee from coming to *shed* blood" means "the LORD has restrained you from bloodguilt" (1 Samuel 25.26). Job's answer to the LORD, "I know . . . *that* no thought can be withholden from thee" is inaccurately translated; the Hebrew means "I know that no purpose of thine can be thwarted" (Job 42.2). Again, "hath not withholden the pledge" (Ezekiel 18.16) is a mistranslation for "exacts no pledge."

**WITHOUT,** as adverb or preposition, is frequently used in KJ in the sense of "outside," and in these cases is usually replaced by "outside" in RSV. Examples are: "wherefore standest thou without?" (Genesis 24.31); RSV "why do you stand outside?" "Thou shalt set the table without the veil" (Exodus 26.35); RSV "you shall set the table outside the veil." "Peter sat without in the palace" (Matthew 26.69); RSV "Peter was sitting outside in the courtyard." "But them that are without God judgeth" (1 Corinthians 5.13); RSV "God judges those outside."

In 2 Corinthians 10.13, 15 "without" is used in the archaic sense of "beyond"—"we will not boast of things without *our* measure" means "we will not boast beyond limit." RSV translates 11.28 of the same letter of Paul: "And, apart from other things, there is the daily pressure upon me of my anxiety for all the churches."

**WITHS.** The "seven green withs" used by Delilah to bind Samson (Judges 16.7–9) were "seven fresh bowstrings." The Hebrew word clearly refers to a bowstring in Psalm 11.2, "For, lo, the wicked bend *their* bow, they make ready their arrow upon the string" (RSV "for lo, the wicked bend the bow, they have fitted their arrow to the string"). In Job 30.11, both versions have "loosed my cord." RSV reads:

"Because God has loosed my cord and humbled me,
they have cast off restraint in my presence."

The first line of this verse is probably to be understood as the opposite of the second line of 29.20, which reads in RSV:

"my glory fresh with me,
and my bow ever new in my hand."

**WOE WORTH** is an archaic lamentation or curse occurring only once in the Bible (Ezekiel 30.2): "Son of man, prophesy

and say, Thus saith the Lord GOD; Howl ye, Woe worth the day!"
RSV translates: "Son of man, prophesy, and say, Thus says the Lord
GOD: Wail, 'Alas for the day!' " "Worth" is here an archaic verb mean-
ing come to be, become, happen. "Woe betide the day!" is a somewhat
less archaic expression which has the same meaning. Scott's *Lady of the
Lake* (1, 9) has a couplet with two appearances of this idiom:

> "Woe worth the chase, woe worth the day,
> That costs thy life, my gallant grey."

**WORSHIP,** down to the seventeenth century, meant to show due honor
and respect, to human beings as well as to God. "Then
shalt thou have worship in the presence of them that sit at meat with
thee" (Luke 14.10) means simply "you will be honored. . . ." The
servant who "fell down and worshipped" his lord, who had commanded
that he be sold, simply "fell on his knees, imploring him" to have
patience (Matthew 18.26). To the church in Philadelphia the promise is
given that "those of the synagogue of Satan . . . will come and bow
down before your feet" (Revelation 3.9 RSV). Wyclif translated John
12.26, "If ony man serue me, my fadir schal worschip hym"; Tyndale
changed the last clause to "him will my father honoure," and this is the
wording of the subsequent versions.

The problem of translation in the Old Testament is complicated by
the fact that the Hebrew verb *shaḥah* may mean bow down, make
obeisance, or worship. Coverdale rendered 1 Kings 2.19, "The kynge
stode up, and wente to mete her, and worshipped her." KJ has, "The
king rose up to meet her, and bowed himself unto her." An Aramaic
verb of similar range appears in Daniel 2.46, where KJ says that "the
king Nebuchadnezzar fell upon his face, and worshipped Daniel" and
RSV has ". . . and did homage to Daniel."

In the New Testament the Greek verb *proskuneō* means to kneel or
prostrate oneself in honor or supplication of a human being, or to do
this in worship of God. The problem of the translator is to find the right
English word in the light of the context. For example, Cornelius fell
down at Peter's feet and worshiped him as a messenger of God, but Peter
lifted him up, saying, "Stand up; I too am a man" (Acts 10.25). Where
homage is paid to Jesus Christ, RSV translates *proskuneō* by "worship" in Matthew 2.2, 8, 11 (the visit of the wise men); Matthew 4.9,
10 and Luke 4.7, 8 (the temptation by the devil); Matthew 14.33,
Mark 5.6, John 9.38 (explicit recognition that he is the Son of God
and the Son of man); Matthew 28.9, 17 (meetings with his disciples
after his resurrection). In cases of personal requests made of Jesus, it

translates *proskuneō* by "kneel before" (Matthew 8.2; 9.18; 15.25; 20.20). In the account of his mockery by Pilate's soldiers, "homage" fits the scene better than "worship" (Mark 15.19).

The older meaning of worship lingers in the title "your worship" or "his worship" applied to magistrates or mayors, and in the honorific adjective "worshipful" which appears in various rituals and lists of protocol. It is chiefly in these forms that the word appears in Shakespeare. An example of the older meaning is:

> "he shall render every glory up,
> Yea, even the slightest worship of his time."
> *King Henry IV, Part I*, III, 2, 150–151

**WORTHY** is an adjective which implies worth, excellence, merit. But it is also used in KJ in cases of fault or wrongdoing, deserving blame or punishment. "If the wicked man *be* worthy to be beaten" (Deuteronomy 25.2) means "if the guilty man deserves to be beaten." "Did commit things worthy of stripes" (Luke 12.48) means "did what deserved a beating."

"A sin worthy of death" (Deuteronomy 21.22) is "a crime punishable by death." Solomon's judgment upon Abiathar, "thou *art* worthy of death" (1 Kings 2.26) means "you deserve death." Pilate's statement concerning Jesus, "nothing worthy of death is done unto him" (Luke 23.15) is more accurately translated by RSV, "nothing deserving death has been done by him"—the "unto him" of KJ is an old error in translation that goes back to Wyclif and Tyndale, who failed to recognize that the word for "him" was in the dative case, denoting the agent, after a verb in the passive voice and perfect tense. Again, the "worthy of death" idiom appears four times with respect to Paul, Acts 23.29; 25.11, 25; 26.31.

The KJ rendering of Hebrews 10.29 is: "Of how much sorer punishment, suppose ye, shall he be thought worthy, who hath trodden under foot the Son of God, and hath counted the blood of the covenant, wherewith he was sanctified, an unholy thing, and hath done despite unto the Spirit of grace?" RSV has: "How much worse punishment do you think will be deserved by the man who has spurned the Son of God, and profaned the blood of the covenant by which he was sanctified, and outraged the Spirit of grace?" In Revelation 16.6 the concluding clause may easily be misunderstood—"for they are worthy." RSV translates "It is their due!" This agrees with Knox; Goodspeed and Moffatt have "as they deserve"; Phillips "They have what they deserve."

"Unto Hannah he gave a worthy portion" (1 Samuel 1.5) is based upon a corrupt Hebrew text. Most modern translations follow the Greek and Latin versions, as did Martin Luther in his German translation. RSV translates the verse: "although he loved Hannah, he would give Hannah only one portion, because the LORD had closed her womb."

**WOULD GOD** is an obsolete or archaic expression of earnest desire or longing. The little captive maid from Israel said to her mistress, Naaman's wife, "Would God my lord *were* with the prophet that *is* in Samaria! for he would recover him of his leprosy" (2 Kings 5.3). RSV has: "Would that my lord were with the prophet who is in Samaria! He would cure him of his leprosy." The expression "would God" appears also in Numbers 11.29; 14.2; 20.3; Deuteronomy 28.67 (twice); 2 Samuel 18.33. In the form "would to God" it appears in Exodus 16.3; Joshua 7.7; Judges 9.29; 2 Corinthians 11.1. In the form "I would to God" it appears in Acts 26.29 and 1 Corinthians 4.8. In 12 of these 13 cases the Hebrew or Greek contains no reference to God, and this is dropped by twentieth-century translations. The one exception is Paul's response to Agrippa's sneer, "In a short time you think to make me a Christian!" Paul said, "Whether short or long, I would to God that not only you but also all who hear me this day might become such as I am—except for these chains" (Acts 26.29).

In its simplest form, "would God" is an English idiom that had little currency later than the sixteenth century and its use in KJ. Of 6 occurrences in Shakespeare, 5 are in the longest form, "I would to God"; the one "would God" is in *King Richard II,* IV, 1, 117. A free translation of the Latin hymn *Beata urbs Hirusalem,* made about 1600, has as the last of its twenty-six stanzas:

> "Hierusalem! my happie home!
> Would God I were in thee!
> Would God my woes were at an end,
> Thy joyes that I might see!"

**WREST,** as verb, is to twist, deflect, misapply, pervert. The prohibition, "Thou shalt not wrest judgment," means "You shall not pervert justice" (Deuteronomy 16.19; compare Exodus 23.2, 6). "Every day they wrest my words" is better translated by RSV, "All day long they seek to injure my cause" (Psalm 56.5). Writing concerning Paul's letters, Peter said, "There are some things in them hard to understand, which the ignorant and unstable twist to their own destruction, as they do the other scriptures" (2 Peter 3.16).

**YESTERNIGHT.** This old form appears in Genesis 19.34 and 31.29, 42, and is rendered "last night" by RSV and other twentieth-century translations. We retain "yesterday" but have dropped yestermorn, yestereve, yesternoon, yesterweek. D. G. Rossetti is credited with coining yester-year for last year. There is even a record of "yesterdayness," which would be a good name for a widespread affliction.

**YET** occurs 699 times in KJ, and in 332 of these cases Strong's *Concordance* records no corresponding Hebrew or Greek word. In these cases the translators inserted "yet" for stylistic reasons—for clarification, emphasis, elaboration, perhaps even for euphony. RSV does the same in a few cases, but sticks closer to the Hebrew or Greek text. It uses "yet" 460 times.

In Judges 9.5, "notwithstanding yet Jotham the youngest son of Jerubbaal was left," the Hebrew text calls for a simple "but" in place of "notwithstanding yet." In 1 Samuel 8.9, "howbeit yet protest solemnly unto them," the "yet" is redundant, and is dropped by the revised versions. So also in 2 Chronicles 32.15, "neither yet believe him," where RV and ASV have "neither" and RSV has "and do not believe him."

"Yet" is often used to intensify a "nor." The most familiar example is Matthew 6.25, "nor yet for your body." Others are Luke 14.35, "nor yet for the dunghill"; John 4.21, "nor yet at Jerusalem"; Acts 25.8, "nor yet against Caesar." RSV drops "yet" in all these cases.

When Noah "stayed yet other seven days" (Genesis 8.10, 12), he "waited another seven days." "Esther spake yet again before the king" (Esther 8.3) means "Esther spoke again to the king." "*Yet* a little sleep, a little slumber" (Proverbs 6.10) has no word for "yet" in the Hebrew, and the English translation is better without it.

**YOURSELVES** is used in the nominative case, as subject of a verb, without the implied "ye" or "you," in 1 Thessalonians 2.1; 3.3; 5.2 and 2 Thessalonians 3.7. In each of these verses KJ has "yourselves know," which in the 1611 edition was written as three words "your selues know." But in each of these cases Tyndale and his sixteenth-century successors had "ye youre selves knowe." The KJ translators took their rendering from the Rheims New Testament. Just why they accepted the Rheims rendering at these four passages remains a mystery; they did not accept the same idiom at other points where Rheims had it: Luke 11.46; John 3.28; Acts 20.34; 1 Thessalonians 4.9.

The use of a reflexive pronoun as the subject of a verb is not uncommon in Shakespeare. The 1608 edition of *King Lear* had: "If you doe loue old men . . . if your selues are old" (II, 4, 194). Later editions printed "yourselves" as one word. The *Pocket Library* edition (1957) reads ". . . if you yourselves are old." Examples of this use of other reflexive pronouns are:

"Myself hath often heard them say."

*Titus Andronicus,* IV, 4, 74

"Thyself thyself misusest."

*King Richard III,* IV, 4, 376

"Ourselves will hear
The accuser and the accused freely speak."

*King Richard II,* I, 1, 16

"O could their master come and go as lightly,
Himself would lodge where senseless they are lying!"

*Two Gentlemen of Verona,* III, 1, 143

# INDEX

Key words and phrases, printed in CAPITAL AND SMALL CAPITAL letters in this Index, are discussed in alphabetical order in the text.

393

marred 319, 364
MASTER 156, 157, 218–219, 340
   (*see* TEACHER)
MAUL 219
maxims 286
MEAN 219–220
means 382
measure 223
MEAT 220–221
meat market 302
meat offering 221, 302
meddle 192
meditate 183, 228, 271
medium (*n.*) 130
meet 267
melt 128
memorable sayings 286
MEMORIAL 221
memory 221
menstruation 137
MERCHANTMEN 63, 221–222 (*see*
   CHAPMEN)
MERCIES 222–223
MERCIFUL 222–223
MERCY 68, 211, 222–223 (*see*
   LOVINGKINDNESS)
merry 312
merrymakers 312
MESS 223
mete 281
METEYARD 223–224
might 163
mighty 156, 370
mind 285
MINISH 224
minister 331
mirror 150–151
misfortune 238
MITE 224
mixed 342
moan 315
moaning 170
MOCK 224–225
mocking 225
model 131
MODERATION 225

moisten 342
molest 101
moment 316
mónument 346
MORE 226
mortal 356
MORTIFY 226
most 226
MOTIONS 226
mottled 159
mouldy 90
mound 227
mourning 169
MOUNT 226–227
move 66, 274, 286, 288
mow down 105
MUCH 227, 314
multitude 227
MUNITION 227–228
MUSE 228
mutilate 78
myrrh 165
myth 127, 242


nail 249
name 25, 221
namely 123, 384
narrow 325
native (*n.*) 37
nature 383
NAUGHT 228
NAUGHT, SET AT 235, 284
NAUGHTINESS 213, 228–229
NAUGHTY 228–229, 339
near 31, 163
near to 15
necessary 229
NECESSITY 229
necklace 174
needed 290
needful 84
NEEDS 229–230
NEESING 230
NEITHER 230–231, 390
neophyte 236